From the Great Game

to the Great War

India and the British Empire.

"In a time of chaos, it is the micro-manager who ascends"

Niall Ferguson, The Square and the Tower

Contents

5

Introduction

The British Empire: The Empire on which the sun never sets, and one which the sun has not yet set. After more than 400 years.

A group of rainy islands off the coast of Europe has managed to create the largest Empire in history. At its height, immediately after the First World War, Britain was at the head of more than a quarter of the world's population, dominated all the oceans, extended over all the continents and covered an area corresponding to a quarter of the earth's surface. The main questions in this book are two: Whether the Empire was a good thing or a bad thing and whether the Empire's involvement in World War I harmed the Empire itself and Britain's role as a global power.

I will try to show how the nature of the British Empire has been, and still is, good and positive. By this I don't mean to justify or deny any act or atrocity committed under the Union Jack, but instead I will try to show how the positive aspects outweigh the negative aspects in large numbers.

The other important aspect in the book is the role of the Empire in the First World War. Every country that has taken sides in the conflict has changed in one-way or another. What I have tried to understand is whether the changes that have taken place in the United Kingdom during and after the conflict have triggered a tragic chain of events that have then caused the end of the Empire as it was intended until the eve of the war. To do this I took as a "case" the largest and most famous part of the Empire: India.

There would be no Empire without India, and perhaps there would be no India without the Empire. India was an empire within the Empire, a world of its own and a reality quite different from any other colony. My research covers a period from the formation of a first embryonic form of Empire under the reign of Elizabeth I to the months immediately after the end of the First World War.

Within this period we have all the imperial vicissitudes, the creation of the Empire, the various enemies that England and the later Britain had to fight, problems and insecurities related to the Great Game and the administration of the Raj until the conflict. The work is divided into six parts each dealing with a character. I have tried to reconstruct the historical environment through the biographies and vicissitudes of these six individuals who have maintained a *double* relationship with both Great Britain and India. The first is Kim, the character from the pen of Rudyard Kipling, the prophet of the British Empire. Following the novel, I tried to explain what is meant by Great Game and why education was so important for the creation of the imperial ruling class.

The second character is the young Winston Churchill, he stayed in India for two years and there included his main dowry, not the Army but politics.

The third part is dedicated to Lord Curzon, the most famous Viceroy of the Raj, who left the heaviest mark on the subcontinent. Its history is intertwined with the economy and imperial expansion not only in Asia.

The fourth character is the explorer Francis Younghusband, the last great *player*. His mission to Lhasa was the last great imperial adventure before the great conflict.

The fifth individual I have dealt with is Lord Kitchener the nation hero. I tried to reconstruct his complex figure especially in his role as head of the Indian Army, Army reformed and reorganised by him in his years in India.

The last character was Khudadad Khan, the first non-British soldier to be awarded the *Victoria Cross*. Through his figure I was able to illustrate the role of the Indian soldier in the conflict and the plots for the destruction of the Raj by Germany and Turkey.

To carry out this work I filled my hands with suggestions and tools in the works of Peter Hopkirk for the part about the Great Game and Niall Ferguson for the parts about the economy and the Great War. I used the works of many historians but these two represented a very valid and professional starting point, not only for the experience and bibliography but also for the narrative spirit, especially Hopkirk, and the theses on conflict, developed by Ferguson. The work would never have come about without all the material consulted in the libraries of the Imperial War Museum, the India Office and the British Library. The pleasure and emotion of having been able to see with my own eyes and touch with my own hands letters, dispatches and newspapers of the time allowed me to feel all the weight of the story told here. Weight that I still feel as I deliver the fruit of that research to you.

Breno Duarte

York, February 2019

Part One

GREAT GAME

Preamble

"Why should we not form a secret society with but one object, the furtherance of the British Empire and the bringing of the whole world under British rule, for the recovery of the United States, for making the Anglo-Saxon race but one Empire? What a dream, but yet it is probable; it is possible."

Cecil Rhodes

Chapter One

Goods, God & Glory

1. An imperial problem.

The route to India goes through Derbyshire. There, north of London, in an idyllic Palladian house, was born the one who left his mark, more than others, in the *jewel of the crown*: Lord Curzon[1]. The man who more than anyone else left his imperial footprint in India. Even with his house, that has been used as a model for the Viceroy Palace in New Delhi, City that he built and transformed into the Capital of the Raj.

The Curzons were not a prestigious family. They did not belong to the high nobility, so they did not sit in the *House of Lords,* but they were in politics practically since always. They loved to make their origin descend from the Norman conquest. The family probably comes from the small village of Notre-Dame-de-Courson in Lower Normandy. The most famous member of the family was undoubtedly the first Marquis of Kedleston.

---

[1] Earl Of Ronaldshay, *The Life of Lord Curzon: Being the Authorized Biography of George Nathaniel Marquess Curzon of Kedleston,* Kessinger Publishing, London 2010; L. Mosley, *The glorious fault: the life of Lord Curzon,* Harcourt, Brace & Co, London 1960; D. Gilmour, *Curzon*, John Murray Publishers Ltd, London, 1994.

Kedleston Hall[2] is located just a few kilometres from Derby, in the centre of England. The palace was built by Sir Nathaniel Curzon, who later became the first Baron of Scarsdale, and was designed by a couple of architects, James Paine and Matthew Brettingham, who based their projects on the drawings of Andrea Palladio, the Venetian architect had in fact prepared some sketches for Villa Mocenigo, but this was never build. Work on the construction of Kedleston began in the spring of 1759. A young Robert Adam, the future famous landscape architect, was busy designing the park of the residence. His work was so innovative and elegant that Curzon was so impressed by his drawings that he decided to put him in charge of the work not only of the park but of the entire estate. Curzon's main intention was to overshadow the residence of his political rival, the Whig parliamentarian George Augustus Cavendish, Duke of Devonshire, owner of Chatsworth House[3]. Landscapist William Emes was given the task of replacing the artificial lakes and fountains previously built with natural ponds, forests and streams. All apparently spontaneous but studied in detail. John Linnell, a successful cabinetmaker, contributed to the magnificence of the residence. George Nathaniel Curzon was born in the family residence on the 11th of January 1859. Considered *unbearable* by his contemporaries, he reached the top of the Raj in a very short time, but for every position he conquered he certainly did not have an easy life. Like any aristocratic scion, he had a ruler who was probably

---

[2] The National Trust, Kedleston Hall, The National Trust Press, London 1999; R. Adams, *Tiaras and Tantrums: Twenty-five Years in Service at Kedleston Hall.* DB Publishing, London 2010.

[3] D. Devonshire, S. Upton, *Chatsworth: The House*, Frances Lincoln; 1st Frances Lincoln Ed edition, London 2002; D. Devonshire, G. Rogers, *The Garden at Chatsworth*, Frances Lincoln; New Ed edition, London 2001.

mentally unstable. She forced him to cross the village in the middle of winter, with a hat on his head with the words: "*liar, sneak* and *coward*" She will say later: "*I suppose, he later mused, 'no children well-born and well-placed ever cried so much or so justly.* "[4]

In Eton "*bent on being first in what I undertook and ... I meant to do it in my way and not theirs* The time spent in Oxford was basically compulsory. The university, for those like him, was "*that brief interval which must intervene between Eton and the Cabinet.*"[5]

Curzon made a good impression, one of the few, on the wife of the one who would later become Prime Minister: Margot Asquith. In fact, she was impressed by his intelligence and self-confidence.

It is said that some people are born for a specific role. Others are self-convincing that they should. Some fail miserably, others do not. This was the case with Curzon. In 1898, Robert Arthur Talbot Gascoyne-Cecil, third marquis of Salisbury, at the head of the Tory Government, appointed him Viceroy of India.

At the age of 39, he was placed at the head of the complex system that managed the most important part of the Empire. Curzon felt predestined for that role. "*The dream*

———————————————

[4] *The Tablet,* 5 May 1928, Tablet Publishing Company, London. p. 12.

[5] N. Fraser, *The Importance of being Eton. Inside the world's most important school,* Short Book Ltd, London 2006, p. 150.

of my childhood, the fulfilled ambition of my manhood, and my highest conception of duty to the State. "[6]

The Empire for Curzon was a mosaic of hierarchical structures, idyllic relations between the occupied and the occupying and festive commemorations. He really believed that everything was *under Providence.* In Curzon there was the unbridled belief that "*There has never been anything so great in the world's history as the British Empire, so great an instrument for the good of humanity.*"[7] He devoted himself body and soul to achieving this goal, but only partially succeeded.

"Recollect that your opponent or your victim very often cannot answer you; and that he is often just as good a man, perhaps even a better and wiser than yourself. Never descend to personalities; avoid that which is scurrilous and vulgar and low. There is always a stratum of society of depraved and prurient tastes. Do not write down to its level, but draw it up to your own. Perhaps, have been told that the press ought to be no respecter of persons. Yes, but that is a very different thing from respecting nobody. First learn to respect others, and you will find before long that you have learnt to respect yourself. Do not sharpen your pen-point, and think that mere sharpness is wit. Remember the saying of Disraeli in the House of Commons that petulance is not sarcasm, and insolence is not invective. Above all, never forget that the press has a mission: and that that mission is not to inflame the passions, or to

---

[6] G. N. Curzon, *Lord Curzon's farewell to India. Being speeches delivered as viceroy & Governor-general of India. During Sept.-Nouv. 1905,* Thacker and Co, Bombay 1907. p. 12.

[7] G. N. Curzon, *Lord Curzon in India: Being a Selection from his Speeches as Viceroy & Governor-General of India 1898-1905*, Adamant Media Corporation, London 2002. p. 347.

cater to the lower instincts of your fellow men, but to elevate the national character, to educate the national mind, and to purify the national taste.

And now to all of you together let me address these concluding words. The spirit of nationality in the world, and it is an increasing force in the lives and ideals of men. Founded upon race, and often cemented by language and religion, it makes small nations great, and great nations greater. It teaches men how to live, and, in emergencies, it teaches them how to die. But, for its full realization, a spirit of unity, and not of disintegration, is required. There must be a sacrifice of the smaller to the larger interest, and a subordination of the unit to the system. In India it should not be a question of India for the Hindus, or India for the Musulmans, or, descending to minor fractions, of Bengal for the Bengalis, or the Deccan for the Mahratta Brahmans. That would be a retrograde and a dissolvent process.

Neither can it be India for the Indians alone. The last two centuries during which the British have been in this country cannot be wiped out. They have profoundly affected the whole structure of national thought and existence. They have quickened the atrophied veins of the East with the life-blood of the West. They have modified old ideals and have created new ones. And not by eastern windows only.

When daylight comes, comes in the light; In front the sun climbs slow, how slowly, but westward, look, the land is bright!

Out of this intermingling of the East and the West, a new patriotism, and a more refined and cosmopolitan sense of nationality are emerging. It is one in which the Englishman may share with the Indian, for he has helped to create it, and in which the Indian may share with the Englishman, since it is their common glory. When an Englishman says that he is proud of India, it is not of battlefields and sieges, nor of exploits in the Council Chamber or at the desk that he is principally thinking. He sees the rising standards of intelligence, of moral conduct, of comfort and prosperity, among the native peoples, and he rejoices in their advancement Similarly, when an Indian says that he is proud of India, it would be absurd for him to banish from his

21

mind all that has been, and is being, done for the resuscitation of his country by the alien race to whom have been committed its destinies. Both are tillers in the same field, and both are concerned in the harvest from their joint labours it is that this new and composite patriotism is springing into life. It is Asian, for its roots are embedded in the traditions and the aspirations of an Eastern people; and it is European, because it is aglow with the illumination of the West. In it are summed up all the best hopes for the future of this country, both for your race and for mine. We are ordained to walk here in the same track together for many a long day to come. You cannot do without us. We should be impotent without you. Let the Englishman and the Indian accept the consecration of a union that is so mysterious as to have in it something of the divine, and let our common ideal be a united country and a happier people. "[8]

Lord Curzon spent his Viceroy years as in a sort of Honeymoon with the Empire. His years of Government were the quietest, with few exception as we will see later on. The whole Raj came from the exhausting season of the Great Game and was about to end up straight in the mud of the trenches.

In addition to this we should ask: why England decided to conquer India? Did it really decide that? Was that the best choice? Was the British Empire really a *good* Empire or just one of many oppressive and racist Empires?

Curzon represented both the dominant mentality of the imperialist with good intentions and the limits of the British Imperialism. Limits that appeared immediately and never changed.

India was the most precious jewel of the Empire and every jewel had to be protected. But the Raj was in the worst of the coffers: Asia.

---

[8] G. N. Curzon, *Lord Curzon's Farewell...*, pp. 487-489.

Throughout the British domination, London and Calcutta's worst concern was to defend their territories from foreign invasions and above all to keep the natives under control. The beating heart of the Empire was not London but India and was conquered not with a precise and calculated plan but with mistakes, attempts, failures and unexpected successes. In short, British imperialism looked more like a scientist in search of medical rather care than a soldier or an explorer. But if conquering happened almost by chance, defending and expanding became a precise discipline. Keeping out the enemies but above all keeping subjects under control. The British Government was not used to ruling over such a large population. Most of the Empire's possessions were made up of islands, little inhabited, or moreover by territories where the population was mainly concentrated on the coasts. India, as well as not being an island was huge, inhabited everywhere and above all had a much more complex problem. The white population was in fact 0.05%[9]. So how to govern 400 million inhabitants? In countries such as Canada, New Zealand or Australia the indigenous population was reduced to an insignificant minority but in India, the British had to understand with blood that the use of Indians in the administration was crucial. The rulers sent from London saw in a collaboration the only way to keep the subcontinent at bay but the English, the few who lived in India did not agree. Make them do it occasionally but never use them in a regulated system. This was an imperial problem. Maybe the biggest. A sword of Damocles that with the time would decapitate not only India but the whole Empire.

------

[9] In 1805 there were 31,000 British in India, 22,000 soldiers, 2,000 in the *Civil Service* and 7,000 in private industry. In 1881 the number was 89,778 and in 1931 it reached the highest figure of 168,000 British citizens living there, 60,000 soldiers, 4,000 in the *Civil Service* and 60,000 private employees.

2. An Empire almost by accident?

In 1883 John Robert Seeley published a work that gave history the definition of Empire that most struck and impressed the English mentality: *We seem, as it were, to have conquered and peopled half the world in a fit of absence of mind.*[10]

The greatest Empire in history built in a *moment of distraction*? As we shall see, there was a precise plan for expansion and conquest and England implemented a meticulous project of imitation: London behaved like a thieving magpie stealing, piece by piece from every Empire everything necessary: territories, techniques, models and systems.

Although England came first in the race for industrialisation, in matters of Empire it was the last one on the scene. When the British appeared on the scene, in search of a territory they could take over the globe was firmly in Iberian hands. Spain and Portugal dominated unquestionably. In 1493 Pope Borgia granted Spain, his homeland, the right to trade with the Americas whilst Portugal had the same right but for Asia. Together they divided the American continent, the African coasts, a piece of India and many territories in Asia. From Madrid to Malina, passing through the Andes and the Mexican deserts, Spanish and Portuguese became the main languages, imposed, of course, with the sword and the crucifix. From the Escorial palace the Habsburgs led the largest Catholic Empire. And the Portuguese themselves were no less[11]. This is how Catholicism lived its golden age: expansion

---

[10] J. R. Seeley, *The Expansion of England*, Macmillan and Co, London 1883, p. 10.

[11] The most complete volume on the diatribe between the British and Spanish crowns is undoubtedly the text by J. Elliott, *Empire of the Atlantic world. British and Spanish in America, 1492-1830,* Yale University Press, New Haven 2007. See also

and money. An island nation on the edge of Europe took care of it and put the stick in the wheels of them all.

England wanted its goose with golden eggs. They tried several times, exploiting, above all, their maritime skills, to find their El Dorado. As did the Spaniards, whose ships loaded with precious metals crossed the Atlantic every year and ended up directly in the King's coffers. Soon, however, the British had to surrender to the facts and reinvent themselves. From scouts to pirates. It was easier to plunder enemy ships than to look for a place where they could find their own precious metal.

The impulse to British imperialism was mainly given by the Reform of the Church. With the split of the Christian world into two factions it was necessary to demonstrate that the new Protestant faction had nothing to envy to the Catholic world. As well as religious, the two factions also had a clear difference: the political administration. On the Catholic front the Spanish King was an absolute Monarch who aimed for personal glory and absolute wealth, in comparison the English Sovereign was a poor man without power, forced to disentangle himself between two branches of Parliament and the rich nobility. This, however, rather than a handicap was a long-term advantage. Since taxes could not be levied, for real will but only with parliamentary approval, made the investments more secure the wealthy landowners in fact, did not fear the confiscation by the King of their property and could thus risk some investment. This was a situation that never occurred in Spain. Spain's central control over its Empire could only survive if the rich loot from the

---

M, Donattini, *Dal Nuovo Mondo all 'America. Scoperte geografiche e colonialismo (secoli XV-XVI)* Carocci, Rome 2004, F. Morelli, *Il mondo atlantico. Una storia senza confini (secoli XV-XIX)* Carocci, Rome 2013, C. Mann, *1493,* Mondadori, Milan 2013, J. Elliott, *La Spagna Imperiale 1469-1716,* Il Mulino, Bologna 2012.

Americas had survived. In the absence of money, the whole system creaked with the risk of collapse.

Britain conquered the most important part of its Empire, not through colonial wars but through a commercial company. All this constituted a rather unusual phenomenon for the public opinion of the time, but above all for the direct participants of the enterprise.

But where to build the Protestant Empire?

In the west there was the Spanish gold and on the east spices, silk and fabrics. There was pressure at court to persuade the King to grant licences for explorations in Mexico and Peru as the pirate vessels, often with the permission of the Crown, went up the Thames full of Spanish booty. In the light of this, the conviction spread throughout the country that everywhere in the New World there were mines and treasures. The Geographer Richard Hakluyt even went so far as to say, *"There is no doubt that we shall make subject to England all the golden mines in Peru and all the coast and tract of that firm of America upon the Sea of Sur"*. Slowly, London managed to carve out its own small space in America. Defeating Catholicism also included taking away land, but as time went by the merchants of Bristol became more interested in Newfoundland cod than in the gold of Peru. A handful of Caribbean islands and a few plantations in North America now formed the first non-European nucleus of English territories. The economic, political and naval power was far from the Victorian period but was already moving its steps in the global chessboard. The danger of destruction, however, was always behind the corner and although they were excellent sailors, the British were clearly inferior to the Spanish fleet and it was only because of its destruction that the gates of the world were opened to diplomats, soldiers and especially to English merchants. After the victory over the *Spanish Armada,*[12] the gates were also opened towards the east. The news immediately made the tour of Europe. The Protestants celebrated and saw in the Spanish defeat a positive message to their cause whilst the desperate Catholics sought through masses and commemorations forgiveness for the sins that caused the defeat.

"According to Spanish writers, there were only thirty-two war woods lost there, as well as cargo wood, and about ten thousand soldiers. The loss of the Spaniards to 20 thousand men and eighty ships was ascended from the enemies. What is certain, inexplicable was the damage of the Spaniards, and in that good fortune of the sea, every hope of rekindling the pride of the English Queen, and of welding the folds of the Flemish peoples, was wrecked.[13]

Muratori points out very well that, although there were uncertainties about the real material damage, the symbolic impact of the English victory on the mammoth

---

[12] N. Hanson, *The Confident Hope Of A Miracle: The True History Of The Spanish Armada: The Real History of the Spanish Armada,* Doubleday, New York City 2003: A. Martelli, *La disfatta dell'Invincibile Armada,* Il Mulino, Bologna 2008.

[13] L. Muratori, *Annali d'Italia. From the beginning of the vulgar era until the year 1749.* Vol. XV. Society of Italian Classics. Milan 1820. p. 78. *"Secondo gli scrittori spnoli, vi perirono solamente trentadue legni da guerra, oltre a quei da carico, e circa dieci mila soldati. Da i nemici si fece ascendere la perdita d'essi spnoli a venti mila uomini e ad ottanta navi. Quel che è certo, inesplicabile fu il danno degli spnuoli, e in quella fortuna di mare naufragò ogni speranza di rintuzzar l'orgoglio della regina inglese, e di saldar le pieghe de' popoli fiamminghi"*

Spanish Empire was immense and not only marked a new era but gave a vibrant blow to the *Siglo de oro*.

The British immediately took advantage of the miraculous victory and the London merchants began to put pressure on the court to guarantee trade with Asia. The first English trade expedition to the East Indies began on the 10th of April 1591. Departing from Torbay, they arrived in India and then in Malaysia, and returned home in 1594. Two years later, three more ships left for the Indies but sank. In 1598 a confederation of merchants with limited capital tried to find a trading company and in order to do this they required the royal consent. The attempt failed but the London merchants did not stop and two years later they presented the request to the Queen, strong with their own fleet and 68.373 thousand pounds they were able to receive the royal licence, lasting 15 years for trade with Asia. It was the 31st of December 1600.

The first Indies Company[14] or as it was known at the time, *Governor and Company of Merchants of London trading with the East Indies,* was composed of 216 people: Sir George, Count of Cumberland and 215 sailors, accountants and officials. The paper gave them permission to trade with all nations east of the Strait of Good Hope and west of the Strait of Magellan. King James I, given the initial profits, granted several companies a royal licence but in 1609 the first card was renewed and the EIC was granted a monopoly without expiry date. However, the contract provided for a termination clause if profits had been low for three years in a row. For the first 20 years England imported mainly black pepper from the island of Java.

---

[14] M. Jasanoff, *Edge of Empire: Conquest and Collecting on the Eastern Frontiers of the British Empire, 1750-1850,* Vintage, London 2006; H. V. Bowen, *400 years of the East India Company* in *History Today* Vol: L, Andy Patterson, London 2000. pp. 47-53.

After a victory over the Portuguese, the King entrusted the Company with a mission to Emperor Moghul in 1612. India was not a unitary nation but a mosaic of states and Kingdoms. Some as large as European nations, others no larger than two or three villages. Above all there was the Islamic Moghul Empire, whose dynasty was of Turkish-Mongolian origin and began their rule in India in 1526. In a short time, they were able to put the rich Hindu communities under their control, thanks to skilful alliances. In this way, the Muslim Emperor was able to rule over a territory from Afghanistan to Bengal. Sitting on the Peacock Throne, inside the Red Fort of Delhi, the Emperor first had every merchant prostrate and then granted the licence for trade. At that time no European nation was so powerful as to overpower the military power of the Mughals so it was necessary to come to terms with them, in order to carry out their trade.

The Emperor welcomed the English missionaries very kindly and, above all, accepted all their requests in exchange for precious goods from Europe, which were poor quality in the eyes of the Europeans, but the Emperor certainly could not have known this. The Company was thus given permission to build factories and emporiums in Surat and other parts of the country. In a letter sent to James I the Emperor congratulated and hoped for a long and fruitful business and friendship relationship, but ignoring that this was in practice the first blow to his already weak Empire:

"When your Majesty shall open this letter let your royal heart be as fresh as a sweet garden. Let all people make reverence at your gate; let your throne be advanced higher; amongst the greatness of the Kings of the prophet Jesus, let your Majesty be the greatest, and all Monarchies derive their counsel and wisdom from your breast as from a fountain, that the law of the majesty of Jesus may revive and flourish under your protection.

The letter of love and friendship which you sent and the presents, tokens of your good affections toward me, I have received by the hands of your ambassador, Sir

Thomas Roe (who well deserves to be your trusted servant), delivered to me in an acceptable and happy hour; upon which mine eyes were so fixed that I could not easily remove them to any other object, and have accepted them with great joy and delight.

Upon which assurance of your royal love I have given my general command to all the Kingdoms and ports of my dominions to receive all the merchants of the English nation as the subjects of my friend; that in what place soever they choose to live, they may have free liberty without any restraint; and at what port soever they shall arrive, that neither Portugal nor any other shall dare to molest their quiet; and in what city soever they shall have residence, I have commanded all my Governors and captains to give them freedom answerable to their own desires; to sell, buy, and to transport into their country at their pleasure.

For confirmation of our love and friendship, I desire your Majesty to command your merchants to bring in their ships of all sorts of rarities and rich goods fit for my palace; and that you be pleased to send me your royal letters by every opportunity, that I may rejoice in your health and prosperous affairs; that our friendship may be interchanged and eternal.

Your Majesty is learnt and quick-sighted as a prophet, and can conceive so much by few words that I need write no more.

The God of heaven gives you and us increase of honor"[15]

---

[15] J. Harvey Robinson, *Reading in European History, Vol II from the opening of the Protestant Revolt to the Present Day,* Ginn and Co, Boston 1904-1906, pp. 333-335

In Asia, the main English competitor was not the Spanish but the Dutch. Trade in the east was mostly controlled by the *Vereenigde Oostindische Compagnie*[16], the Dutch East-India Company. Founded two years later, the English one, immediately conquered the Asian market, especially because at that time, the Flemish had managed to build a tax and banking system much more advanced if compared to the medieval and slow English system. They created a system of public debt that allowed the Government to borrow large amounts of money at low interest rates and had an indirect tax system. Thanks to scientific progress, they were able to acquire maritime information from the Portuguese and improve it. The Dutch managed to make up for the shortage of timber through trade with the Baltic Sea by ship. They set in motion a mix that recalls both the contemporary Ikea and the assembly line designed years later by Henry Ford The ships were built in standard sections and assembled in series. The *Fluyt* was the most widely used sailing ship. Economical, easy to manoeuvre and with considerable cargo capacity. It became so famous that amongst the Dutch it became a sort of *status symbol,* so much so that even small traders invested in ships rather than in shares of the *VOC.* This system allowed the Netherlands to send a large fleet to the Indian Ocean. It was five times older than the Portuguese and two times older than the English. Compared to the Portuguese company, here the state did not participate financially but only granted the monopoly. However, the Dutch had a commercial exclusivity reduced to spices alone. Monopoly control remained in place only during the journey. Goods were auctioned off at home. The company could not set prices, which at first also happened in England, but obviously in case of market saturation the company could store the goods and sell them at a more profitable time. Compared to the British,

---

[16] C. Rei, *Careers and wages in the Dutch East India Company*, In *Cliometrica*, Vol VIII, Springer Berlin Heidelberg, Berlin 2014. pp. 27-48.

however, the Dutch rewarded officials based on gross income and not on net profits. This led them to expand their base of merchants to do business with. The *VOC* was more interested in Indonesia than in India from the outset. The situation was dictated by the fact that with the Indians they traded mainly in fabrics, a product not covered by the monopoly, whilst in Indonesia were the spices that dominated the market. The Dutch preferred to bind Indian textile merchants not by physical occupation but by tax and banking methods whilst it was easier to subdue the weak Indonesian rulers.

The English, thanks to the marriage of King Charles II to Catherine of Braganza, obtained the city of Bombay as a dowry, and thus managed to first put the Portuguese under control and then concentrate their forces against the Dutch. With the Treaty of Munster of 1648, the *Company* suffered a severe blow because Holland, no longer having to be under the control of Spain, began a fierce competition. The first two Anglo-Dutch wars dealt a severe blow to the London Government. The Dutch even managed to climb the Thames as far as Rochester. Whilst the Netherlands was able to absorb the costs of war more easily, the London Government found itself on the brink of bankruptcy, even though it was winning on paper. This only widened the gap between the City bankers and the Court. England was going through a period of great change. Whilst on the continent the Dutch were putting themselves in serious trouble on the other side of the English Channel a civil war culminated with a King without a crown and above all without a head on which to rest it. This period oscillated between the parliamentary republic and the dictatorship.

Oliver Cromwell renewed the *Company*'s monopoly charter and in 1651, in order to counter the *VOC*, promulgated an act of navigation in which every ship not flying the British flag was prevented from entering and transporting goods to ports under British control. This effectively excluded the Flemish from trade and severely hampered their economy, as the largest income for the Dutch krona came from trade with England. To solve this crisis, the best thing to do was to copy. In 1688, tired of the Catholicism of James II, a group of nobles and merchants from the City decided to get rid of him and put William of Orange on the throne of England. A Dutch. With the arrival of William, England implemented a series of structural reforms that allowed the nation to get rid of those institutions anchored in the Middle Ages and aim for a modern state structure. Six years after the *Glorious Revolution[17]*, on the model of the *Wisselbank*, the *Bank of England* was founded. The main task was to manage the loans made by the Government and to administer the national currency. The system of public debt managed by a stock exchange that could buy or sell bonds was also copied. The reforms had such a positive impact on society and Government that a few years later Daniel Defoe came to say:

"Credit makes war, and makes peace; raises armies, fits out navies, fights battles, besieges towns; and, in a word, it is more justly called the sinews of war than the money itself, because it can do all these things without money nay, it will bring in money to be subservient, though it be independent. Credit makes the soldier fight without pay, the armies march without provisions, and it makes tradesmen keep open shop without stock. The force of credit is not to be described by words; it is an

---

[17]J. Beckett, *Glorious Revolution, Parliament, and the making of the first industrial nation* in *Parliament History Parliament, Politics and Policy in Britain and Ireland, c. 1680-1832 Vol XXXIII,* Clive Jones and James Kelly, Oxford 2014. pp. 36-57; U. Niggemann, *Some Remarks on the Origins of the Term 'Glorious Revolution'* in *The Seventeenth Century,* Manchester University Press, Manchester 2013, pp. 477-487; N. Zahedieh, *Regulation, rent-seeking, and the Glorious Revolution in the English Atlantic economy* in *Economic Historic Review* 63, 4, Steve Hindle, Steven Broadberry, Hoboken 2010. P 865-890; G. Cox, *War, Moral Hazard, and Ministerial Responsibility: England after the Glorious Revolution* in *The Journal of Economic History* Vol VXXI, The Economic History Association, Tucson 2011. pp. 133-161.

impregnable fortification, either for a nation, or for a single man in business; and he that has credit is invulnerable, whether he has money or no; nay, it will make money, and, which is yet more, it will make money without an intrinsic, without the materia medica (as the doctors have it); it adds a value, and supports whatever value it adds, to the meanest substance; it makes paper pass for money, and fills the Exchequer and the banks with as many millions as it pleases, upon demand. As I said in last chapter, it increases commerce; so, I may add, it makes trade, and makes the whole Kingdom trade for many millions more than the national specie can amount to."[18]

After the *merger,* the Dutch and the British shared out trade in Asia. The Flemish maintained control over Indonesia[19] and spices, the Mughal Empire in India was at its height and the Indonesian rulers were much easier to control, whilst the English concentrated on India. At first, they had a lot of problems. In India, besides pepper, there were no spices, and, above all, the Indians were not interested in English goods, which is why the *Company* was forced to pay everything in money. The British had to adapt to the Indian situation and began to ask for trade permits not only from the Emperor but also from the small local rulers. The initial Dutch advantage was soon eroded by English business skills. In a short time, they were able to create a trading area for Indian goods in Europe. Fabrics such as Chintz, Mussola and Calicò, Indigo and especially Saltpetre, used for the production of gunpowder, whilst the Dutch depended on the demands of cinnamon, pepper, nutmeg, cloves and mace. The

---

[18] D. Defoe, *The Complete English Tradesman,* Dodo Press, London 2007. p. 206.

[19] B. Luttikhus, A. D. Moses, *Mass violence and the end of the Dutch colonial Empire* in *Indonesia, Journal of Genocide Research*, Vol XIV Routledge, Sidney 2012, pp. 257–276.

market was quickly saturated at the expense of fabrics. In the space of 30 years, between 1670 and the early 1700s, the *Company*'s imports rose from a turnover of 360,000 pounds to over 2 million, whilst the Dutch saw their profits fall more and more, eroded by the bureaucracy of the *VOC*. In a way, tea is missing from the list of goods of this period. The *English* drink par excellence became popular only at the beginning of the eighteenth century when prices fell. Legend has it that tea was introduced to England by Queen Catherine Di Braganza, wife of Charles II[20]. The King had grown up in Holland where the first load of tea had arrived in 1606 from the island of Java[21] whilst the Queen had grown up in a Portugal under Spanish rule where the tradition of tea was already well rooted amongst the nobles. The first tea request was sent by Richard Wickham, a *Company* agent on the Japanese island of Hirado, to his peer in Macao. The letter dates 27th of June 1615. The first publicity in England dates to 1658. In 1703, 65,000 pounds of tea leaves arrived in Kent, the equivalent of the annual consumption of previous years.

A total of four wars were fought against the Dutch. Between 1652 and 1784. With the time in the conflict also involved France, first in favour of England then in favour

---

[20] L. C. Martin, *Tea: the drink that changed the world*, Tuttle Publishing, London 2007, pp. 120–123; A. McCants, *Poor consumers as global consumers: the diffusion of tea and coffee drinking in the eighteenth century,* in *The Economic History Review*, Vol VXI, Wiley-Blackwell, London 2008. pp. 172-200.

[21] C. R. Boxer, *The Dutch India Company and the China trade, in History Today*, Vol 29. London 1979; L. Yong, *The Dutch East India Company's Tea Trade with China*, 1757–1781. *In History of the Asian-European Interaction* Vol VI. Leiden, Brill, 2008; K. H. Kian, *How Strangers Became Kings, Javanese-Dutch relations in Java1600–1800, in Indonesia and the Malay World*, Vol XXXVI, Taylor & Francis, London 2008. pp. 293-307.

of the Dutch, and Spain that supported his former rule. London came out on top and obtained for itself not only territories in India but also in Africa and North America. Although not destroyed, the *VOC* never recovered, the cost of coping with the many indigenous rebellions and misgovernment brought the company to the brink of bankruptcy several times.

The British could now focus their attention on the French.

Since 1617, when Emperor Jahangir granted James I's ambassador, Sir Thomas Roe, permission to establish *factories* in certain ports, the British built warehouses for storing goods. But permission was denied to fortify them. Surat was initially the *Company*'s main base, but after the defeat of the Dutch, the British shifted their attention to the east coast. Madras, which rose around Fort St George and Calcutta, grew up around the *Company*'s port traffic. Bombay was already an advanced city when, thanks to the royal wedding, it came under English control. Traders and merchants who left followed the English from Surat to Bombay. By this time, realities had formed around the factories that depended entirely on European officials. The intermediaries created a credit line and advance between traders and textile manufacturers. The taxes that the Europeans paid to the Emperor kept alive the Moghul cavalry alone. The Empire thus focused on agriculture and was happy to give others control over trade. If precious metals and sumptuous goods arrived in the imperial coffers from the coastal emporiums, there was no reason to break off relations. The *Company,* however, went a step too far and between 1688 and 1691, tried to create its own private Army sending the Aurangzeb Empire on a rampage. In a short time, he beat down the English, inflicting a humiliating defeat on London. The *Company*'s directorate ran for cover imploring imperial forgiveness to re-establish relations prior to the war.

The *Compagnie française des Indes orientales*[22] was the last European trading company to be founded. Created in 1664, its main purpose was to hinder British and Dutch companies. Conceived by Jean-Baptiste Colbert and officially established by King Louis XIV, it was not in fact a new creation, but rather the result of the merger of three smaller companies that traded with different parts of Asia. Unlike the English and Dutch companies, the shares were not in the hands of merchants but of the nobles who populated the court of the Sun King. The shares were bought more out of a desire to please the King than out of a real economic interest

In the beginning, India was not to be the main commercial basin, so much so that the King had granted perpetual possession of the island of Madagascar, but after poor results they decided to move to the subcontinent. The headquarters was in Pondicherry, south of Madras, where the English base was already located.

Unlike the Dutch, the English did not fear the French because of their company but because of their politics. At the beginning of the eighteenth century, the French economy was practically twice as large as the British one[23]. The times of Elizabeth I were long gone, when the English, with shyness and few resources, tried to build an Empire. Under the control of London passed Gibraltar and Menorca, opening control of the Mediterranean to the British. The French, on the other hand, were the masters on the continent. Their non-European Empire ran from Quebec to India and included Louisiana and the rich Caribbean islands of Martinique and Guadeloupe. It

---

[22] P. Kaeppelin, *La Compagnie Des Indes Orientales and Francois Martin: Study on The History Of Trade And French Establishments In India Under Louis XIV*, Nabu Press, Paris 2014.

[23] From 1707 with the Act of Union between England and Scotland, Great Britain was created.

was not just the future of the *Company* that was at stake, but the future of the whole nascent Empire. The Critical Review in 1756 came to write:

"Every Briton ought to be acquainted with the ambitious views of France, her eternal thirst after universal dominion, and her continual encroachments on the properties of her neighbours [...] Our trade, our liberties, our country, nay all the rest of Europe, are in a continual danger of falling prey to the common Enemy, the universal Cormorant, that would, if possible, swallow up the whole globe itself."

In 1746, after having relocated the *Compagnie des Indes* and saved it from yet another bankruptcy, the French Governor Joseph François Dupleix decided to hit the British in India.

From the diary of Ananda Pillai, the Indian *dubash* of Dupleix, we have a primary testimony of the situation in Pondicherry during the preparation for the siege.

"Public opinion now says that the tide of victory will henceforth turn in favour of the French ... The people ... assert that the Goddess of Fortune has departed from Madras to take up her residence at Pondicherry. The English Company is bound to die out. It has long been in an impecunious condition, and what it had to its credit has been lent to the King, whose overthrow is certain. The loss of the capital is therefore inevitable, and this must lead to collapse. Mark my words. The truth of them will be brought home to you when you, ere long, find that my prophecy has been realised"

The siege began on the 26th of February 1747.

"hurled themselves against Madras [...] as a lion rushes into a herd of elephants [...] surrounded the fort, and in one day astonished and bewildered the Governor ... and all the people who were there [...] They captured the fort, planted their flag on the ramparts, took possession of the whole city, and shone in Madras like the sun, which spreads its beams over the whole world"

In a report to the directors of London, the *Company's* officials wrote alarmedly about the intentions of the French: "*at nothing less than to exclude us from the trade of this coast and by degrees from that of India*". The blindfolded goddess, however, had not yet abandoned the English.

Another conflict was coming and was about to rewrite maps and destroy Empires. The *Seven Years War* had an indescribable impact on the society and psyche of the time. It was the first European conflict to be fought outside Europe as well. From Canada to Madras, from Guadeloupe to Manila, wherever Europeans, African slaves and American Indians fought each other. Imagine a game of poker. Two players: France and Great Britain where the chips are the colonies and the world is at stake. At the beginning of the game, France had an ace in its hand.

William Pitt led the game from the British side, whose family was linked by a double thread to India. His uncle Thomas Pitt joined the company in 1673. He was the son of a cleric and everyone expected him to behave honestly but when he arrived in India, despite the monopoly of the company, he started doing business on his own. The *Company* ordered him to return home, but he did not listen and was later forced to face a trial and the payment of a fine to the company. Small in comparison to the fortune he had built himself. Thomas Pitt was just one of many, who used the *Company* to make his own personal fortune. The *EIC* itself did not respect London's orders. At the time, travelling between England and India meant being at sea for six months. Orders arrived late or when they arrived on time they were interpreted at will.

In fact, the *Company* never really opposed people like Pitt because when the monopoly began to crumble these *interlopers*[24] allowed the company to survive[25]. Wanting to maintain the monopoly at all costs is what has put an end to the Dutch, Portuguese and French East-India Companies. Pitt was later summoned and made Governor of the Fort George of Madras and as soon as he arrived, he had to face a crisis against an imperial measure. Emperor Aurangzeb had banned trade with Europeans, ordered the arrest of Westerners and the confiscation of property. Pitt had to face a siege to protect the *Company*'s warehouses. He was therefore more than motivated to destroy France and protect British interests. Whilst the English's allies were keeping the French at bay and allies on land, the British used their best weapon to defeat the French at sea: the fleet.

Pitt increased it and implemented a shameless policy with the intention of cutting off connections between the colonies and France. And he did it well.

In India the conflict was very heated. Especially in Bengal.

From the early eighteenth century onwards, Bengal had quickly become the *Company*'s main trading region. In 1750, 75% of the revenue came from purchases and sales in the Calcutta area and along the Ganges valley.

---

[24] P.J, *Stern, Soldier and Citizen in the Seventeenth-Century English East India Company*, in *Journal of Early Modern History* Vol XV, Brill, York 2011. p. 83-104.

[25] O. Jokic, *Commanding Correspondence: Letters and the "Evidence of Experience in the Letter book of John Bruce, the East India Company Historiographer*, in *The Eighteenth Century*, Volume LII, University of Pennsylvania Press, Baltimore 2011 p. 109-136.

Dean Mahomet, an employee of the *Company* describes the city of Dhaka, today in Bangladesh:

"Having completed the most pleasant voyage imaginable, we, at length, arrived at Dacca, one of the most extensive cities in the province of Bengal, which lies in twenty-four degrees north latitude, on an eastern branch of the Ganges. It is near five miles in length, but very narrow, and winding with the river.

Dacca is considered the first manufactory in India, and produces the richest embroideries in gold, silver, and silk. It also receives considerable advantages from its cottons, of which the finest striped and worked muslins, callicoes, and dimities, are made, much superior to those finished in other parts of the country. The best kind manufactured for the immediate use of the Great Mogul, and his Zannanahs, are of exquisite workmanship, and greater value than any permitted to be sold either to the natives or foreigners.

The filligrane, in particular, is admirable, the workmanship being costlier than the metal itself. It is not perforated, as with us, but cut in shreds, and joined with such inimitable art, that the nicest eye cannot perceive the juncture. The embroidery and needle-work, for elegance, surpass all description, and greatly exceed anything of the kind done in Europe: but it is remarkable that there are no female embroiderers or seamstresses here; the men do all the work in these branches, and their patience is astonishing, as their slowness is singular. Provisions of all sorts are exceeding cheap and plentiful in Dacca: the fertility of its soil, and the advantages of its situation have, long since, made it the centre of an extensive commerce; it has still the remains of a very strong fortress, in which, a few years back, was planted a cannon of such extraordinary weight and dimensions, that it fell into the river, with the entire bank on which it rested; the length of the tube was fourteen feet, ten and a half inches, and the diameter of the bore one foot, three and one-eighth inches: it contained two hundred and thirty-four thousand four hundred and thirteen cubic inches of wrought iron, weighed sixty-four thousand four hundred and eighteen

41

pounds avoirdupois, and carried a shot of four hundred and sixty-five pounds weight.

Here is also the residence of a grand Nabob, who, at his accession to the throne, conformable to a custom, something similar to that of the Doge of Venice on the Adriatic, enjoys a day's pleasure on the river, in one of the most curious barges in the world, called a samsundar. It is sheathed with silver, and in the centre is a grand eminence of the same, on which his crown is placed on the day of coronation: nearer the stern is a brilliant seat encompassed with silver rails, and covered with a rich canopy embroidered with gold, under which he reclines in easy majesty. This boat and another of considerable value, that conveys his attendants, are estimated at a lack of rupees. He is accompanied by several the most distinguished personages, and there are no bounds to the lavish waste of money expended on this occasion, in order to aggrandize the pomp of this ancient ceremony. Travellers of every description, who pass this way, are led by a prevailing curiosity to see these elegant boats."[26]

Tales like this only increased, in European minds, the mystical and stereotypical image of India as a land where gold and wealth never end.

The Mughal Empire was exhaling its last breaths and the richest Kingdoms were now behaving like autonomous states. The capital Delhi had already been plundered several times and almost total independence was now in force in Bengal. Murshid Quili Khan, after his conversion to Islam, had climbed to the top of his military

---

[26] D. Mahomet, *The Travels of Dean Mahomet, A Native of Patna in Bengal, Through Several Parts of India, While in the Service of The Honourable The East India Company Written by Himself, In a Series of Letters to a Friend,* University of California Press, Berkeley 1997. Letter XXXV.

career and became King of Bengal. In order to prevent the British from taking possession of his country, he implemented a series of tax and administrative reforms. He centralised state control and ensured that land taxes were levied on money and not on property. From 1717 the English no longer had to pay duties to the Emperor and enjoyed the freedom of minting in Bengal. *Company* officials preferred not to use this benefit because they realised how much more useful it was to have Murshid Quili Khan as a friend than the other way around. His banker, Fatehcand called *Jagat Sheth,* a title not at all redundant *world merchant,* was the true master of the region. He decided the rates and prices in silver and controlled every movement of the *Company* within the mint. In the meantime, the British moved most of their traffic from the port of Surat to that of Madras and Calcutta. The centre of gravity of British trade now revolved around the coasts of eastern India. Many local merchants moved with them, preferring physical and economic security to connection with the territory, especially as the British had long since replaced the indigenous intermediaries with their own officials. This had taken away a group of people who had rapidly enriched themselves at the expense of the merchants for whom they were dealing, the real lobbyists of fabrics.

It will be a Frenchman, however, who will introduce into the region the element that will give an unexpected turn to the colonisation of the subcontinent. Joseph François Dupleix began training Indian mercenary soldiers using European military techniques. This would have made it easier to control and deal with the imperial troops. The English, in a very short time, copied the idea and began in turn to enlist indigenous soldiers. After a series of victories against the English, Dupleix disagreed with his Parisian superiors and not only was he forced to give back the territories and factories he had taken, but he also had to return to France, where he died in misery.

With the outbreak of conflict in Europe, *Company* officials decided to fortify their settlements throughout the region. The defeats at the hands of the French were still alive in memory and they wanted to avoid others. The Bengal *nawab*[27] did not welcome this decision. Siraj-ud-daula had recently ascended the throne and in no way wanted to appear weak. So, he decided to punish the English in an exemplary manner. He marched on Calcutta and had all the English garrison and civilians present imprisoned.

What went down in history as *The Black Hole of Calcutta*[28] was a fact that deeply marked the British imperial psyche. According to the testimony of the only witness, John Zephaniah Holwell, the *nawab* had 146 men and children locked up in a cell without windows, four metres by five in size. The next morning, only 23 of them survived. Leaving aside the reasoning on the real ability to bring so many people into such a narrow space and especially on the faults of Siraj-ud-daula, the episode became emblematic and was used for years to come as proof of the cruelty of the natives. Some people were probably imprisoned, but not because of the cruelty of Siraj-ud-daula, but almost certainly because of the stupidity of some zealous officer. The fact is that 146 or even just 1, the British certainly could not suffer such an affront passively. They wanted an excuse and the *nawab* had served it on a rich serving dish. Colonel Robert Clive was called to lead the punitive mission. Already distinguished in some battles against the French in the south of the country, Clive saw India as the best way to make money, and he was not the only one. Enriched in his previous trip he had wasted all his assets in an election campaign won with a result later declared null and void. Lacking a penny, he shifted his gaze back to India and the appointment of lieutenant colonel came at the best time.

---

[27] A role that could be translated as a Viceroy or Governor.

[28] The most precise report is by Noel Barber, *The black hole of Calcutta*, Colimns, London 1968.

Returning to India in 1757, he gathered an Army and left Madras to reconquer Calcutta. He managed to conquer the French factories in Chandernagar, but after the victory he disobeyed the orders given to him by the directorate of the *Company*.

Clive did not want to give up the advantage he had over the *nawab in* any way. Allied secretly with the commander of the troops of Siraj-ud-daula, a certain Mir Jaffar, he marched at the head of his reduced Army towards Plassey. During the battle Mir Jaffar kept his word and left the *nawab* to take sides with Clive. It was the 23rd of June 1757. After the victory the traitor became the new *nawab* of Bengal. Robert Clive now had a puppet in his hand. He was rewarded with a fief and about 28 million rupees, almost 3 million pounds. With this move the English had taken back all the silver poured the previous years into the coffers of *Jagat Sheth*.

Robert Clive's ambition did not stop there anyway. In an unprecedented move, he was appointed Governor of Bengal by his company's officers. The Emperor welcomed the news without disappointment. Siraj-ud-daula had in fact rebelled against Delhi's power and his defeat could only cheer up the court of the Red Fort. Moreover, it had been the Emperor himself, years before, who had granted the *Company* the right to mint money. After a change of puppet in power, the British had fought a battle against the "puppet King" Mir Kasim and some allies. On the 23rd of October 1764 in Buxar, the British victory effectively delivered all eastern India to the East-India Company. The following year, thanks to a rich tribute to the Emperor, the British secured a fundamental privilege: the *Diwani,* or civil administration. The puppet *nawab* was left with only the *nizamat,* i.e. justice. The *Company* had become the legitimate imperial delegate for tax collection throughout the region of Bengal. Siraj-ud-daula had opposed the British throughout his life because he wanted to avoid at all costs that the *EIC* became a state within the state. Now the *Company*, in effect, the only real state.

However, Clive wanted the Crown and not the *EIC to* take power in Bengal[29]. From London, William Pitt was of a different opinion, however. One of the basic principles of English society was in fact, the inviolability of private property. The *EIC* never became public therefore it had to be protected and respected. The astute Prime Minister also wanted to prevent George III's power from being extended to include the very rich region. At that time, the Parliament was not yet authorised to legislate for India, so the King could only bypass parliamentary controls by putting his hand in the treasures of Bengal. It was preferable for that fortune to end up in the pockets of private citizens rather than in the King's private coffers. He acted as a true capitalist. However, the state could legislate on the relationship between Great Britain and the *Company.*

In the meantime, the clash between the French and the English had continued far and wide across the globe and after seven years of conflict, battles in three continents and eight countries at war with each other: Prussia, Austria, Portugal, Spain, Saxony, Hanover, Russia and Sweden, the war ended. Britain ended up with a poker game of aces.

The treaty that ended the first *global* conflict was discussed at a conference held in Paris in February 1763. The British negotiator, sent to France, was the low, arrogant Duke of Bedford. He had never been in any of the places that the European nations were spreading and in fact, he had struggled a lot to get to Paris because sick of gout. After the Treaty of Paris, the French renounced all interest in India. Apart from Pondicherry, who remained French until 1950, everything else soon came under British control. For the Duchess and the Duke, the stay in Paris was anything but

---

[29] In a letter of 1759, he personally explained his point of view to William Pitt.

unhappy. The Duchess returned home with a porcelain service consisting of 800 pieces, given to her by the King of France, whilst the Duke obtained India[30].

In short, from that distant 31st of December 1600, in less than two hundred years, after robbing the Spaniards, deceiving the Portuguese, copying the Dutch, defeating the French and in fact plundering the Indians, Britain found itself dominating the world. The Empire was not born in a moment of distraction but since Shakespeare's contemporaries the intent had always been very precise: to take away the Empire from others.

In those years, and more precisely in 1740, the most famous of the popular and imperial songs was composed:

"Rule, Britannia! Rule the waves:

"Britons never will be slaves"

Rules that became fundamental and thus came into force on more than 1\4 of the world.

Obviously, the conflict did not only have negative consequences for France and its allies. British public debt had doubled by the end of the war and the only way to replenish the state's coffers was to milk colonial cows. Since India was not yet fully under the political control of London, which in fact did not want it, the Government could not tax the Indians but only collect part of the *Company*'s revenue. It was therefore necessary to look elsewhere to find subjects and goods to be taxed.

On the other side of the Atlantic, in the meantime, the 13 colonies were flourishing. In order to rebalance the accounts, the parliament decided to increase taxes on newspapers, glass, lead, sugar, paint and, of course, tea. A few years after getting

---

[30] J. Paxman, *Empire,* Penguin, London 2012. p. 40.

India, Britain lost America. The French were able to take revenge, allying themselves with the settlers, but despite this, American independence did not inflict such a heavy blow on the Empire. The rulers of London were now beginning to get used to the fact that they had become a power in Asia.

Now under the London Government there was the richest province in the Indian subcontinent. The British needed two more things to complete everything: an imperial discipline and the remaining part of India.

A famine in 1770 in Bengal and the risk of bankruptcy for the London Government in 1772 were a useful pretext for renegotiating the role of the state in India.

The *Company* was forced to bear the costs and risks of administering a region. There was basically a total *revolution[31]* in his duties. The state could not let the fattest cow in the Empire die now. Government and nobility now depended on the performance of the shares of the *EIC* and the directorate was always against this form of control. The more time passed, the more they were forced to finance a larger Army. An Army they did not want. The first advantages of direct tax control soon became apparent. In short, the company stopped paying for the goods it was exporting with gold bars and was able to finance all purchases from the tax revenues of the province alone.

In 1773 the *Regulation Act* was passed which in practice sanctioned the authority of the Government over the *East-India Company*. Furthermore, the office of Governor-General was instituted, which enjoyed administrative control over all three presidencies and was an absolute novelty and had its seat not in Leadenhall Street but in Calcutta. In theory, the Governor was chosen by the board of directors, but in practice, he had to have the Government's pass. The tasks were so separated. The

---

[31] P. Lawson, *The East India Company: A History,* Longman, London 1993. p. 103.

new *Commissioners for the affairs of India* had political and military power, whilst the directorate was left with commercial power.

The first Governor-General was Warren Hastings. He was assigned the task of putting order in Indian chaos. Now officials could no longer fill their pockets, corrupt and conquer, ignoring all moral constraints. From this period derives in fact the term *nabob*, that is an Englishman enriched in India who acts as a local lord.

Hastings' mandate was marked by this two-headed hybrid monster called the British Empire. For years he had been working for the *Company,* struggling to take on a partial role and was in constant conflict with London.

A very intelligent man, he was an admirer of Indian culture. He spoke perfectly both Hindi and Persian, promoted out of his own pocket English translations of Islamic texts, founded an institute that had the task of studying and linking English and Muslim law and encouraged the study of geography and botany. Hastings believed that everything that could highlight the advantages of British rule and the gains that the Indians would make from it, should be highlighted and disclosed.

"Every instance which brings [the Indians'] real character home to observation will impress us with a more generous sense of feeling for their natural rights, and teach us to estimate them by the measure of our own. But such instances can only be obtained by their writings; and these will survive, when the British dominion of India shall have long ceased to exist, and when the sources which it once yielded of wealth and power are lost to remembrance."[32]

From the very beginning, the British in India began to mingle with the natives. Soldiers married local women, scholars immersed themselves in culture and customs

---

[32] B. Cohn, *Colonialism and its forms of Knowledge* Oxford University Press, Oxford 1997. p. 122.

and the Empire grew without the original sin of racism. Although, as we will see, it was not always so easy.

Hastings was a lover of culture, but the *Company* was not the *Royal Society*. Their task was to make money and under the first Governor began the flow of capital transfer that served to grease the gears of the whole Empire.

William Pitt, rich thanks to his uncle, who had made his fortune in India, probably did not believe any of the words he uttered in the House of Commons in January 1770:

"The riches of Asia have been poured in upon us, and brought with them not only Asiatic luxury, but, I fear, Asiatic principles of Government ... The importers of foreign gold have forced their way into Parliament, by such a torrent of private corruption, as no private hereditary fortune could resist."[33]

Hastings himself will be very rich during his years as Governor. It was difficult to say no and for the mentality of the *Company*'s men, it was right that everyone should first take care of themselves and only then of the company.

The major problems arising from the *Regulation Act were* dictated by the fact that in India it was not intended as a law to be respected but more as a canvas adaptable to situations. Hastings believed that India should be governed by Indian law. He therefore worked to *purify* Indian legislative codes from misinterpretation and posthumous additions, and at the same time did not interfere with the main laws of Hindu and Muslim law. The British, unlike the Portuguese Inquisition and the French missionaries, immediately renounced the idea of Christianising India. They were convinced, in fact, that *civilisation* could be introduced even without touching religion. A great step forward for a nation that had begun its imperialist work

---

[33] William Pitt, *The state of the Nation,* 1770.

precisely with the intention of creating a Protestant Empire in contrast to the Spanish Catholic Empire.

Hastings moved in the wake left by Clive and refused to entrust inexperienced and foreign officials with the most important task: the collection of taxes. He left it to the employees who were already working for the moguls to carry out this delicate task. Their stay in those places depended on the taxes they collected. Without conquests and spoils of war, however, the *Company*'s shares began to fall and, despite hard work under the mandate of Hastings, the Company's debt reached an exorbitant 8.4 million pounds. In London, they used this pretext to get him out of the way. When he returned home, he was tried. The accusations, almost all of which were unfounded, did, however, produce the required result. He was not a great speaker and found himself debating the famous Edmund Burke. The trial was almost like a play and despite the acquittal, he had been publicly humiliated.

In 1784 the *Regulation Act* was changed, and the *India Act was* approved in its place. The Governor was no longer chosen from within the company and Calcutta took on a role of superiority over the other two presidencies of Madras and Bombay. The Governor also acquired the right of veto over his council and the other two presidencies.

Horace Walpole described that time as follows

"Peaceable, quiet set of tradesfolks had become the heir-apparent to the Romans."[34]

---

[34] N. Ferguson, *Empire. The Rise and Demise of the British World Order*, Penguin, London 2003. p. 29.

3. Divide and conquer

After the surrender of Yorktown in 1781, the war of independence of the 13 American colonies ended. Lord Cornwallis made returned to England and in 1786 took the place of Warren Hastings in India as Governor-General.

The state of the company on its arrival was not to its liking, even though the administration of Hastings had increased earnings and raised the price of shares, which surprised especially the management. The task of collecting taxes had to be regulated so that losses could be avoided. Under the Governorate of Hastings, the whole system was run by the winner of an auction, but the first problems arose after the great famine that struck Bengal in 1770, killing a quarter of the population. The current Governor was unable to solve the problem but an idea for reform was studied by his rival, Philip Francis. He was convinced that the only state claim could be that on land tax so the monopoly on trade had to be abolished and the *Company* should no longer export precious metals. For Francis, the Government should not use the region as an area from which to draw money, but the rules of good governance should create a stable society and consequently, an honest tax collection system. The quotas for taxation had to be fixed rigidly and the property on which it weighed had to become inalienable and heritable. Hastings completely ignored Francis' proposal, who later left India and returned to England. The Governor was more interested in the legal system than the tax system. A solution had to be found by the successor to Hastings.

In 1793 Lord Cornwallis passed a tax reform that revolutionised the system then in force. The new Governor adopted some of Francis' ideas. The alienability of the land and the inheritance were fixed by law and the tax rate was regulated. The principle behind English society since the Middle Ages, namely private ownership, was also implanted in India. However, it was not the farmers who became the owners as much as the *zamindar,* the actual owners of the land who, until then, had simply been tax collectors. In India, in fact, the peasants had no fixed abode but were nomads and moved in search of work. The *zamindars* used to exploit their work and in addition to collecting taxes they also secured their own percentage. During the Moghul period and the Hastings administration, revenue had never been secure because owners often lied about the actual number of farmers or declared that they had escaped before paying the due fee and that therefore the tax was not actually calculated on the land but on who was above it at the time it was collected. With the Cornwallis *permanent settlement,* if the established quota had not been paid, the property would have been auctioned off.

Once the fiscal problem had been solved, which would have produced its first fruits with the passing of time, an internal problem of the company was dealt with: corruption. Since its creation, the wages of officials reached the threshold of misery and this allowed the formation of a vast network of corruptors and corrupted. Often, as already mentioned, officials created their own micro-company with which to round up revenues. Cornwallis decided to raise salaries and completely cancel the intermediaries between the producer and the *Company*, cutting the problem of internal competition at its roots. In this way, new, well-paid jobs were created that were able to attract the best and not the waste of society as had been the case until now. Now that it was carrying out a political task rather than a commercial one, the management of the company could not afford any failure. Hastings had limited himself to hiring the same Mughal Empire officials in the company, trusting that they were more experienced in Indian affairs, but Cornwallis did not trust the natives and therefore fired all the tax officials and replaced them with English employees. In practice, the system that would govern the entire Raj was born at that time: the incorruptible and inaccessible *Indian Civil Service*[35]. With time it was regulated both in India and at home. Before leaving, all officials had to attend a two-year course in Haileybury[36] and Calcutta, and Lord Wellesley later established Fort William College[37] where officials leaving Haileybury learnt the languages and rules of local Government.

Richard Wellesley's main intent, The New Governor, was to establish an Empire in India to replace the lost colonies in America. A great friend of William Pitt, he immediately dedicated himself to the destruction of the last French forces in the subcontinent. After a couple of inexperienced and weak Governors, he proved to be the ideal person to hold the office.

When he arrived in India in April 1798, he discovered that Fateh Ali Tipu, sultan of Mysore, had allied himself with the new-born *République française* to wage war against the English. The Kingdom of Mysore was a southern state confined to the British possessions of Madras. Tipu has always been a sworn enemy of the *Company*. His father had already fought two wars against the British and he pursued the road. After the *third Anglo-Mysore war* he was forced to sign a humiliating treaty

---

[35] C. Dewey, *Anglo-Indian Attitudes: Mind of the Indian Civil Service,* Continnuum-3PL, London 1993; A. Kirk-Green, *On Crown Service: a History of HM Colonial and Overseas Civil Services 1837-1997*, I.B. Tauris, London 1999; L. S. S. O' Malley, The Indian Civil Service, Murray, London 1931.

[36] L. S. Milford, *Haileybury College, Past and Present*, BiblioBazaar, Charleston 2009.

[37] T. Roebuck, *The Annals of the College of Fort William: From the Period of its Foundation to the Present Time*, Cambridge University Press, Cambridge 2013.

and decided to reorganise the state and take revenge on what he believed to be infidels and invaders.

A young Napoleon, at the time of the events, had recently invaded Egypt and in his plans, there was a march along Persia to India. Bonaparte wanted to take resources away from Great Britain and Tipu was not only his ally, but also driven by feelings of hatred and revenge. Wellesley did not want to give him the time he needed to get well organised and immediately put together an Army of English and Indians. With the battle of the Nile, Horatio Nelson had managed to block the French in Egypt forcing Napoleon to postpone the Indian invasion. And the British preferred to take away an ally of the French.

Three armies were sent to besiege the capital of Mysore, two British and one from Bombay. The siege of Srirangapatnam became one of the most well-known facts in the *Company*'s memorials. The feat was celebrated with ballads, books and paintings. On the 44th of May 1799, the British entered the city and fought against the last forces in the pay of Tipu. It must be said that the sultan never escaped in the face of danger, on the contrary, he tried in every way to block the entry into the city of enemy troops. It was Governor Wellesley himself who ensured that the Sultan's body was lifeless. He took his wrist and then asked a captured servant to recognise his body. Captain Benjamin Sydenham described the scene like this:

"Wounded a little above the right ear, and the ball lodged in the left cheek, he had also three wounds in the body, he was in stature about 5 ft 8 in and not very fair, he was rather corpulent, had a short neck and high shoulders, but his wrists and ankles were small and delicate. He had large full eyes, with small arched eyebrows and very small whiskers. His appearance denoted him to be above the Common Stamp and his countenance expressed a mixture of haughtiness and resolution. He was dressed in a fine white linen jacket, chintz drawers, a crimson cloth round his waist

with a red silk belt and pouch across his body and head. He had lastly his turband and there were no weapons of defence about him. "[38]

The fourth and last war against the Kingdom of Mysore ended with a clear British victory and with the annexation of the Kingdom to the possessions of the company that rose in the neighbouring area of Madras.

Lord Wellesley's military adviser and commander of one of the armies was his younger brother, Arthur. It went down in history not for having defeated a rebel sultan in southern India but because 16 years later, on a June afternoon, he defeated in Belgium, at Waterloo, the young general, now Emperor, who had invaded Egypt.

The Duke of Wellington, together with his brother, was responsible for the expansion of the territories directly controlled by the company of the Indians. After Tipu's death, he first became Governor of Srirangapatnam and Mysore, then responsible for the Deccan, the vast plain in the centre of India. Here he fought against the Marathon population by defeating them and adding another slice of India to the British booty. In 1805 the three brothers, since the third, Henry, was the personal secretary to the Governor, returned home where they had to defend themselves against accusations of imperialism. One of the *Company*'s great counter-senses was to be born to create an English Empire that could compete with the Spanish Empire but that became a useful tool of Government. The directorate never welcomed the idea that trade should be neglected at the expense of the expansive aims of the Governors appointed by the Parliament. Now the orbit of power of the *Company* reached the gates of Delhi and it was not the company that did a job for the Emperor Moghul but the Emperor who did a job for the company. He had become so much of a puppet.

---

[38] Report written to George Macartney in Srirangapatnam on the 25th of May 1799.

With time, the costs of maintaining the entire administrative apparatus were no longer covered by the income from trade, the company no longer only did a job of collecting taxes but governed directly and this led to the emergence of forced loans and taxes.

The Napoleonic Wars, however, had created serious problems for trade with India. The domestic market greatly reduced the demand for Indian products and the export of English fabrics to India dropped dramatically. At that time British supremacy at sea was put in jeopardy and the protection of commercial convoys became increasingly risky. Napoleon put in place a real embargo, and the British mobilised with all their might to enlarge the mesh of Bonaparte's network. Textile exports fell from £1400,000 in 1800 to £900,000 in 1809, whilst goods of British origin rose from £6 million to £18 million in the same period[39], thanks to the courage of sailors. This change of direction led in 1813 to the abolition of the monopoly on trade from India. The *Charter Act* reversed the old mercantile system: India no longer sold its goods but bought from Great Britain.

With the Industrial Revolution, British manufacturers were able to produce good quality goods at low prices and in a short time the Parliament began to pass a series of laws in defence of domestic goods, this put Indian trade in crisis and in a few years English goods invaded Indian markets. Local producers, already tried by the *Company*'s treatments, ended up disappearing almost completely. We have already seen how in principle the company used intermediaries to deal with producers. The *Company was* anticipating sums that the brokers were passing on to the Indian weavers. In most cases the amount paid to Indian merchants was not the same as the amount paid to producers. In this system, it was always the EIC, the intermediaries, but never the producers, that earned the money. They were the last ones in the queue,

---

[39] H. Kulke, D, Rothermund, *Storia dell'India*, Garzanti, Milan 1991, p. 272.

they had a high technical quality but not a cunning in business. From 1753 intermediaries were eliminated and company officials began to deal directly with Indian weavers. A few years later, with the conquest of Bengal, this system proved to be very useful. The weavers practically became slaves to the company. Their names were written down in special registers where the dates of delivery of the raw material, of the finished product were recorded and, in the event of delay, the producers were forced to pay up to 35% more of the price as a fine; often the company used real henchmen, called *peon*, who had the task of following and terrorising the producers. In case the producers tried to sell the products freely in a bazaar, where they could increase the price up to almost 45 percent, considering that the company demanded bargain prices, they were punishable by law. Once they started trading with the British, they could no longer back down or trade with anyone else. Very often local producers were forced to leave the profession and often also the region. There were rumours of weavers mutilating their thumbs themselves so that they would no longer have to work for the company:

"The story is current in Bengal that in order to avoid being forced to weave for the Company many weavers used to cut off their own thumbs"[40]

These voices, often used by Indian historians, are not fully documented, but reading some testimonies we can see how much they do not deviate from the legends. William Bolts describes some of these techniques in his work *Considerations on Indian Affairs,* published in London in 1767. Whilst the report of the parliamentary committee that supervised the trafficking of the EIC, published in 1813, describes some minutes and testimonies that are not far from the metropolitan legends that arose in that period. So much so that it was also these practices that prompted a part

---

[40] R. C. Majumdar, H.C. Raychaudhuri e K. Datta, *An advanced History of India,* Macmillan, London 1956. p. 808.

of public opinion to press for the abolition of the monopoly. Reading the *Minutes of evidence taken before the Honourable House of Commons, in a committee of the whole House, to whom it was referred to consider of the affairs of the East-India Company* allows us to understand how these practices were seen and judged by an English audience. Indian historians often used this argument as the basis for their anti-imperialist work. Some even went so far as to say that it was the British themselves who maimed the weavers in order to make their products more sought-after as last examples:

"Instances of thumbs of workers being cut off to prevent them from winding raw silk or weaving fine cloth were not unknown"[41]

Cornwallis had done everything to put an end to the corruption and disorganisation of company officials and the separation between administrative and commercial affairs premixes at the EIC to treat weavers' producers in a more humane manner. This calm did not last long because when the Indian textile trade began to get used to the new system and grow, the first trade from Great Britain began.

It was not the old, small producers and traders who disappeared, i.e. those who produced low-value but low-priced material, who survived because they had managed to create a small business within the self-sufficiency systems of the villages. Often those who traded in household utensils were the same ones who also sold those for working the land; it was in this way that they survived even periods of crisis thanks to the traffic with ordinary people. The changes and treatments were suffered by the craftsmen of a high-income bracket, that is, those who traded in large cities. There the competition and the vastness of the bazaars made the diffusion of

---

[41] T. Chand, *History of the Freedom Movement in India* Publications Divisions, Ministry of Information and Broadcasting, Delhi, 1961. Vol I. p. 391.

local products decidedly complicated. In the pre-company period, saying city meant referring to a local or imperial court, but with the appearance of a foreign central power, the local craftsmen experienced a first phase of glory with British interest in Indian customs but later fell into oblivion. The disappearance of the courts or their impoverishment also led to a change in the richer classes that traditionally were based on the choices made by the court and with the appearance of the English were the first to want to imitate European customs and traditions looking at and spending on goods from Britain.

Competition from English products on the British, American and European markets led to a sharp contraction in exports. In 1798-99 the value of Indian cotton goods in these three areas amounted to 3,215,745 pounds, with the new century the figure fell more and more until almost disappear. Until 1806, it remained at around 2,000,000 up to the ridiculous figure of £100,000 in 1833[42]. In 1840, British historian and traveller R. Montgomery Martin deposed before the parliamentary committee appointed by the House of Commons the year before. The purpose of the commission was to investigate the possibility of abolishing duties on Indian textile products. He said:

"In 1815 the cotton goods exported from India were of the value of £1,300,000. In 1832 they were less than £st. 100,000. In 1815 the cotton goods imported into India

---

[42] C. J. Hamilton, *The Trade relations between England and India 1600-. 1896,* Thacker, Spinker and Co, Calcutta 1919. p. 258, Tabel II.

from England were of the value of £st. 26,300. In 1832 they were upwards of £st. 40.000"[43]

In that same deposition he also denounced what he himself had seen, namely:

"The decay and destruction of Surat, of Dacca, of Murshidabad and other places where native manufactures have been carried on"[44]

At the same time, British products rose sharply. From 1740, the year in which they began to sell in Europe not only Indian products but also English ones, the figures would always rise. In 1766 the annual value was around 220,000 pounds but in 1788 the figure was already 1,252,240 pounds, in 1798 it was 3,602,488, in 1808 it was 12,503,918 and in 1818 it reached the exorbitant figure of 21,292,354.[45]

A few years before the abolition of the monopoly, the products of the Lancashire industries appeared in the Indian bazaars, but the *Company* preferred to maintain the old market relations, creating in fact an obstacle to British goods. It should not be forgotten that the company always remained a commercial organisation whose first purpose was to please and enrich the shareholders in London, so it is not surprising the manoeuvres that often collided with the interests of British or British merchants. With the abolition of the monopoly in 1813, the British producers had carte blanche.

---

[43] *Parliamentary Papers*, Westminster Parliament press, London 1840. Vol VIII. p. 275.

[44] Ibidem.

[45] C. J. Hamilton, *The Trade Relations...*, p. 260. VII. Statistics.

In one year, they exported 680,234 yards of calicoes; in 15 years the figure had grown by 5,000 percent and finally reached 34,162,876 yards in 1828.[46]

In a short time, not only was the textile industry supplanted by British goods, but products from Europe also became part of every aspect of Indian life. Goldsmiths, metals and carpets managed to maintain their own market despite everything; the production of glass, paper and dyeing instead, almost disappeared. It was the latter that suffered the greatest blow. The new chemical products synthesised in England because they had a low cost, put in serious difficulty the Indian producers who instead still relied on recipes handed down from father to son, and that often required more expensive natural materials and difficult to find.

The British also, and above all, became involved in sectors in which, in addition to processing, capital and more articulated forms of association were needed. In a short time, the iron foundries of Mysore and the saltpetre industry of Chota Nagpur, territories conquered by Governor Wellesley as seen above, were completely excluded from the world market. Iron was extracted in Great Britain, whilst thanks to the discoveries in Chile, around 1860, of larger and purer deposits, the Indian saltpetre was practically abandoned. The English, in fact, preferred to exploit the mines in Latin America because they were closer to the sea and therefore easier to transport. India already had a developed shipbuilding industry in the Mughal period. Calcutta and Bombay were able to produce excellent merchant and war ships, above all thanks to the use of the investments made but, with the advent of the steam ships also the shipyards had to surrender in front of the Victorian economic power. Local investment was no longer able to outstrip British investment and the shipyards were

---

[46] *Report of the Select Committee on East India Affair,* London 1833. Vol II, P. II, p. 311.

unable to modernise. It took several years for the shipbuilding industry in India to flourish again.[47]

In addition to the parliamentary sources we also have an extensive personal bibliography. Travellers at that time documented almost everything they saw, especially when they were passing through regions that had remained unknown to Europeans until recently. This is the case of the Bishop of Calcutta, Reginald Heber, who in 1824 described in his diary the English goods he found in the bazaars of Dhaka[48] whilst the Catholic abbot J. A. Dubois, the following year, testified to the poor condition of the Indians who once belonged to the caste of weavers, accusing European industrial machines of starving the workers of India[49]. The most famous testimony, however, remains that of Governor-General Lord Bentinck. In 1834, in a letter to the directorate of the company, he said:

"The misery hardly finds a parallel in the history of commerce. The bones of the cotton weavers are bleaching the plains of India"

---

[47] A. Guha, *Parsi Seth as Entrepreneurs P.I.* in *Economic and Political Weekly, Bombay 29 August 1970.*

[48] R. Heber, *Narrative of a journey through the Upper provinces of India,* Carey, Lee & Carey, Philadelphia 1829. p.208 Vol II.

[49] J. A. Dubois, *Vice, Institutions and Ceremonies of the Peoples of India,* Chez J. S. Merlin, Paris 1825. pp. 118-119 Vol I.

The phrase became one of the favourite quotes for Indian nationalists and for those who wanted to criticise the British power over India. Marx in primis but also Nehru[50].

The British brought the Indian economy from a consumer society to an exchange society. Not only did industry undergo a drastic change, but also and above all, agriculture. Since the end of the eighteenth century, taxes had been fixed and were no longer based on crops and arable land, so they became an asset on which to make cash or debt. These two aspects, together with the now widespread use of coins and the appearance of English artefacts in markets, led the farmers to a crossroads. Those who lived in the areas near the ports or the emporiums resold part of their stocks to make capital and pay taxes, but then bought back at higher prices the same goods, those who lived in the hinterland, however, were practically forced to get into debt by renting, selling or mortgaging the land.

In the villages at first the advent of British industry did not affect the small artisans because there were ancient rules, called *jajmani*[51]system. this system ensured a barter between the craftsman and the farmer: the first made the products of his art and was later repaid with the products of the earth from the second. With the passing of time and with the massive intervention of the British also in the cultivation and breeding, even small handicrafts began to disappear. The raw materials useful to the craftsman such as sugar, leather or cotton were now intercepted by the European merchant because they were requested by the foreign market. The craftsmen were

---

[50] K. Marx, Das Kapital, Libro I, Sex IV, Cap XIII, Par 5, J. Nehru, *The Discovery of India,* Oxford University Press, Oxford 1994. p. 299.

[51] T. O. Beidelman, *A comparitive Analysis of the Jajmani system,* Monographs of the Association for Asian Studies, VIII, New York 1959.

thus forced to go to the markets and compete with the exporters for the purchase of the necessary material; to do this they were forced to sell the finished product since they could no longer in fact barter with the farmers of their own village, who had been forced in turn to buy the artisan products in the bazaars. A chain of events that not only cut out local craftsmanship but forced artisans and peasants to relate to English markets in order to survive.

Before British rule, India did not know about industrial cultivation. The Mughal Empire was never interested in the creation of an articulated and organised system of plantations useful for the production of commercial goods. The plantations were for private use and the percentage put up for sale was very small in itself. The British introduced vast plantations for export. Tobacco, cotton, indigo, sugar and opium had been cultivated for centuries, even before the arrival of Europeans, but they had all been destined for internal trade. The subsistence economy could no longer survive from an imperial point of view.

Cotton, produced almost everywhere, was absorbed by local artisans and only a small percentage of the cotton produced in the north was sold in Asia. There was no regulated system and most of the time it was bought by caravan merchants and then taken across the border through mountain passes or more often by sea. The company tried in every way to block the English cotton because it competed with the one it exported from India. Indian cotton never found an easy life in Europe for almost the entire nineteenth century, whilst the cotton of the Americas, better in strength, especially that of the area of Bombay, had a fibre not suitable for mechanical looms. Manchester producers tried to convince the company to graft American varieties into India, but every attempt failed miserably. However, exports rose sharply as a result of the war of American succession and the abolition of slavery. Before the war most

Indian cotton was sold in China[52]. In 1830, the company began the production and export of jute that was used instead of the more expensive hemp, especially when with the outbreak of the Crimean War the exports of Russian hemp ceased.

Sugar, on the other hand, was produced mainly for the courts and for the richer castes. Only a small percentage was refined and reduced to powder. Most of the cane *juice was* processed rudimentarily in the villages and consumed raw; it was not considered real sugar but rather a syrup called *Gur.* Around 1790, sugar plantations were introduced in Bengal. These had a moment of glory during the Napoleonic wars but with the French defeat the Indian product lost market in favour of sugar from the West Indies.

Tobacco was introduced to India by the Portuguese in the late sixteenth century. It was cultivated in Gujarat and although its use was not prohibited, with the spread of cultivation also spread its consumption, not only within the wealthier classes.[53]

A different speech should be made for indigo and opium.

The company already exported indigo to Europe in the 1600s, but with increasing profits on fabrics it stopped concentrating on this commodity. Before the American War of Independence, the British Parliament protected products and goods from the West Indies because they were better processed and of superior quality than Indian products. With the loss of the colonies in North America and the industrial revolution, a reversal of the march was necessary so that Indian products became

---

[52] V. A. Gutha, *The Comprador role of Parsi Seths 1750-1850*, P. II, in *Economic and Political Weekly* Bombay, 28th of November 1970. Tab 3.

[53] For agriculture in the pre-colonial period: I. Habid, *The Agrarian System of Mughal India,* New York 1963. pp.1-60.

fundamental for British industries. The merchants pushed for the company to increase the export of products that were useful to British industries but not in competition with them. John Prinsep, an English merchant, took advantage of the wars in America to create the first plantations in Bengal, copying the American production model[54]; with the continuation of the war others imitated him, realising that the lack of American colonies would open up the market in India. However, this system, managed by British people who demanded high profits and not by Indians, did not bring much profit to the *Company*, which in fact suspended the purchase for the next three years. With the abolition of slavery in the French colonies of the Antilles and the revolt of the blacks in Haiti, the remaining western indigo market disappeared and the EIC had to return to business with the British producers of indigo in Bengal. After the renewal of the company's commercial licence in 1793, the EIC was forced to reserve 3000 tonnes of its fleet for private trade. The monopoly began to creak, so much so that 20 years later it was lifted. Between 1814 and 1827, exports rose from 724,934 to 1,917,160, reaching around £3 million in the second half of the nineteenth century.[55] Indigo was the case with the agricultural and human exploitation caused by the British. Farmers were not used to market fluctuations and price rises and falls, they were very reluctant to devote themselves to unknown crops and were in practice forced by the British. The demand for indigo from Great Britain and Indian factories was constantly increasing and at one-point, the company began to directly administer some plantations in Bengal and the Bihar region. Workers were hired whose condition ranged from wages to slavery. The working conditions

---

[54] H. Furber, *Henry Dundas, First Viscount Melville, 1724-1811,* Humphrey Milford, London 1931.

[55] H. Murray, *Historical and Descriptive Account of British India,* 3 Vol, J & J Harper, Edinburgh 1843.

were terrible, the Company tied the farmers to itself through contracts and advances and in exchange it demanded an increasing production. There were so many revolts that in 1859 the English Parliament had to appoint a commission to investigate the revolt of the peasants of the Nuddea region who worked for the Bengal Indigo Company. 77 farmers were questioned and listened to. The commission found that the farmers secured the farmers with five-year contracts, which in fact became devoid of deadlines because the signature was placed on a document whose date was left blank. Also promised were advances and loans that hardly ever arrived. After the first signature, the farmer stopped being essentially a free man. Many intimidation techniques were used, ranging from the destruction of livestock and houses to murder.

Indigo is tied by a double thread to the credit argument. In the Mughal Empire there was a rudimentary system of loans, although it was quite developed for the time. After the Emperor Akbar introduced the payment of taxes in money and no longer in goods, systems called *Shroff* were created, i.e. archaic banking forms. They exchanged foreign coins for local ones, weighed the content of precious metals, issued and collected exchange letters, kept precious deposits, issued loans and even managed an insurance system. Until 1813, i.e. for the entire period of the monopoly, the company maintained this system, but with the end of the monopoly more articulated, more practical and above all more British systems were needed. At first it was the same factories for the production of indigo that acted as a bank but their capital, being very limited, was not entirely safe. The system needed indigo factories to survive because during a period of crisis they could not have been sold without the collapse of the system.

In 1833 the London Parliament decided that the company should cease to be a commercial organisation. Its goods were to be catalogued and sold, including the indigo factories. At the same time, the first banks began to appear in the territories controlled by the British. They had much higher capital and were able to enjoy the protection of their subsidiaries at home. With the dismantling of the Company, several avenues were opened for local investors. One of the most famous cases was that of Dwarkanath Tagore. He was a local entrepreneur who, together with a British businessman, decided to found Carr, Tagore & Co. Tagore put the capital and Carr's knowledge into the British administration. Since his properties surrounded the indigo and silk factories, he forced the Company to sell them for less than their value, mortgaged his indigo and mulberry tree plantations for silkworm breeding, and took over the production of indigo and silk. His company quickly became a management company. Whenever a fruitful opportunity presented itself to him, he created a new company and placed Carr, Tagore & Co. in charge of the business. In this way he was able to control indigo, silk but also steam ship companies and coal mines. He could thus ask for a price higher than the market prices because, managing product and offer, the companies underlying his were forced to rely on him for any type of supply needed. He created a bank in Calcutta: the Union Bank. It had to be a bank independent of any company or company and had to perform the classic tasks of a bank, respecting international rules. For several years he succeeded, becoming also one of the most famous credit institutions in the country. With the banking crisis of 1846 and 1847, both the Union Bank and the Carr, Tagore & Co. No other Indian entrepreneur will be able to create such a vast Empire later. In 1847 the railway era began, and the British capital no longer ended up in agriculture but in companies that produced locomotives and rails or in the purchase of land that was in the tracks for future railway lines. In this way, they could be sold at an increased price to builders or to those who wanted to build in the vicinity of the railway. So, the Indians no longer invested in works but in people. Those with rich amounts of money specialised in interest-bearing loans. British and Indian investments separated and diversified sharply.

The goods that most of all filled the coffers of the company and the coffers of the state were not indigo, which still did its part, but opium.

Opium was grown almost everywhere in India, especially in the Malwa and Bihar regions. It was mainly used in medicine as a painkiller and calming, especially on

69

exaggerated children. The use for which we know it today was virtually unknown to the Indians. In fact, they preferred tobacco smoke to opium because it was easier to grow, smoke and sell.

4. War for drugs

The *India Act* of 1813 had abolished the monopoly with the Indian subcontinent but not with China, which remained in force for another 20 years. In these two decades the company moved all its commercial interests to the Celestial Empire. Before opium, the most purchased product was tea. The ever-increasing interest in this drink led the company almost to focus exclusively on it. The Indian climate, however, was not very suitable for the cultivation of tea, in fact, the plantations were located mainly in the Himalayas. However, the duties were very high and often exceeded 100%. Until 1784 the company managed to export to Europe only about 100 thousand piculs[56]. Larger quantities came from English, Dutch and Spanish smuggling. In 1784, Pitt increased the duties to 12.5 percent and in a short time imports rose sharply. By 1786 they had risen to 157,291,000 piculs, by 1796 to 213,624. There was a decline in the period of the Napoleonic wars where in 1806 the picul fell to 187,373 thousand but immediately after the French defeat, they rose to 277,091; in 1816 and 1826 the figure was around 329,522 thousand piculs per year. The British also managed to exclude other European nations from trade in China and the only rivals were the Americans, even if they were very far apart.

The main problem for the British in China was not the Europeans but the Chinese. The closure imposed by the Emperor made trade very difficult. The ports enjoyed some autonomy, but the British could not find a market for their products. The almost

---

[56] One picul: 133, 33 lbs, 49.752 kg.

tropical climate of southern China, especially in the Canton region, was certainly not suitable for the market for wool produced in Scotland or for skins from the Americas. The British then began to bring Indian products to China. The European watches and the small objects could not balance the scale, they served other goods.

Until the end of the eighteenth century the Company had bought the goods in Canton with silver, from the nineteenth century onwards they began to buy cotton from Bombay, wood from the south, pepper and spices from the north and above all opium from Bengal.[57] The system used was divided into three parts: the private merchants invested the gains in bonds issued by the Company payable in London and the EIC later used this money for its own purchases on the spot. The major problem for British trade with China was, however, dictated by imperial political choices. The Chinese company was virtually closed to all external contacts. In 1757 the Chinese Emperor Ch'ien-lung had concentrated in the port of Canton all trade with the Western *barbarians*. The duties were very high, and the merchants had to move within an elaborate and complex system. The British wanted to buy silk in Ningbo, closer to the production sites but with the new rules it was made practically impossible to trade something outside the Kwangtung region. The port of Guangzhou was managed by the *Hong,* companies authorised by the imperial Government to handle and administer the ports traffics. By 1720 they had joined the Co-Hong, an organisation to which the Emperor had given responsibility and granted a monopoly on trade with the West. Each incoming ship had to put itself under the

---

[57] V. A. Gutha, *The Comprador Role....,* I, In *Economic and Political Weekly* Bombay, 29th of August 1970.

protection of one of the *Hong,* pay a commission to it, use its interpreters, stay in[58] its establishments and submit to its every request under penalty of exclusion from the negotiations. The main purpose of *Hong* officials was to fill the coffers of the state and satisfy its protectors at court, on average they were in office for three years and in such a short time it was difficult to devote themselves also to the interests of Western merchants.

The *Company* adapted to this system for a long time because the volumes of trade with China were much lower than those of India. Trade with China was a kind of appendix to that with the Indians but with the seizure of power in India and with the English market increasingly hungry for Chinese goods, the situation became almost unmanageable. With the lowering of duties on tea, the British wanted to provide themselves with a port closer to the production areas. Canton's transport costs and duties made the port unsuitable, and private merchants, who did most of the EIC's work, grew in number and demanded that Lancashire goods find a market in China.

The Company found itself squeezed between strict Chinese rules and British demands. His greatest fear was in fact that they could to lose that little of autonomy

---

[58] The rules were first introduced by the local authorities through decrees between 1700 and 1750. In 1755, they were removed by Hoppo, the imperial officer in charge of taxes. In 1760 the rules were codified in an imperial edict. The text in Lo-Shu Fu, *A documentary chronicle of Sino Western Relations 1644-1820,* 2 Vol, Association for Asian Studies, Tucson 1966. Vol, I p. 224 and H. B. Morse, *The East India Company trading to China,* 5 vol., Oxford University Press, Oxford 1926-29. Vol V. p. 94. In 1809 they were completed and partially modified.

they gained[59]. In the past, other countries had tried to plead their case before the imperial court, simply causing an increase in duties on their ships. The Company was, however, a private company and wanted at all costs to avoid relying on politics for it traffics. This situation was reversed in 1784 with the *India Act* of Pitt. After the conquests in Bengal, the parliament became a controlling body over the company, and this led politics to take an interest in relations with China. The chairman of the *Board of Control*, Henry Dundas, proposed that Pitt send an ambassador to the imperial court to try to obtain more favourable conditions for British trade. An EIC officer, Charles Cathcart, was chosen to lead the mission, not to mention. He was ambassador to the St. Petersburg court from 1768 to 1771[60]. His mission failed before he even got to China. He left London in 1787 but died in June of the following year in Sumatra. However, Dundas was intent on his plan and a few years later, when he became Home Secretary, he set up a new expedition. This time to lead the group was called the former Governor of madras Lord George

---

[59] The Anglo-Chinese trade before the Opium wars was in a continuous search for balance. H. B. Morse, *East India Company trading to China,* 5 Vol. Oxford University Press, Oxford 1926; J. K. Fairbank, *Trade and Diplomacy on the China coast,* Cambridge University Press, Cambridge 1953; H. Pritchard, *Anglo-Chinese relations during the Seventeenth and Eighteenth centuries,* University of Illinois Press, Urbana 1930; H. Pritchard, *The crucial years of Anglo Chinese relations 1750-1800* in *Research Studies of the State College of Washington,* Vol IV. N. 3-4, Washington 1936; M. Greenberg, *British trade and the opening of China1800-42,* Cambridge University Press, Cambridge 1951.

[60] The first proposal to send an ambassador to Beijing was made by Frederick Pigou in 1754, in a letter to the Court of Directors of the Company. In 1783 the proposal was presented directly to Dundas by a free merchant.

MaCartney. Leaving England in September 1792, he led an expedition of 95 people, three ships, one of which was a warship, 50 soldiers and 600 cases of gifts for the Emperor. They had the main tasks: negotiating new trade treaties for the benefit of British merchants, obtaining a licensed island, possibly close to areas of silk and tea production, THE largest number of English products for sale, less restrictions in Canton, a port in the North and above all, an English ambassador in Beijing. Dundas also entrusted a *secret* mission to MaCartney to spy on Chinese territories and record any information useful to an invasion.

MaCartney arrived in Beijing and after three weeks of negotiations was received by the Emperor on the 14th of September 1793. A few months after the beheading of the King of France, whilst Europe was entering the period of the Napoleonic wars, an English merchant was on the other side of the world talking to the Emperor of the Chinese. The Emperor was very friendly with the ambassador but refused any request. Lord MaCartney was sent home with gifts and many greetings to the English King. Another attempt was attempted in 1816 but the ambassador, Lord Amherst, was not even received by the Emperor because he had refused to do the *kotow*.[61] The company lost its monopoly in India and found itself in serious difficulties. Private merchants wanted more autonomy and shareholders more income. Relations with China were increasingly complicated, and officials tried to maintain the *status quo* whilst English merchants evaded the monopoly in China, trading under foreign flags within real companies based in Guangzhou.[62]

---

[61] An act of homage to the throne. In practice, the foreigner had to kneel three times and prostrate himself nine times by touching the floor with his forehead.

[62] J. K. Fairbank, *Trade and Diplomacy...,* pp. 62-3.

In all this context, opium found a place of honour. At the beginning it was only one of the many products imported from India, to balance the balance of purchases, but with the weakening of the Chinese imperial power and the Company's grip on trade, the Canton companies began to import huge quantities first as a complement to raw cotton and then as a drug. The EIC managed to return to the scene because even though it did not directly control sales in China, it remained the main producer in India. The best quality was Bengal. The farmers received, as usual, an advance for production, the product was then bought at low prices, processed and sold under a monopoly by the company to merchants who exported it first to Malaysia and then to China. In the Rajputana region, an independent Kingdom, a lower quality was produced than in Bengal, but in order to avoid competition, every year the Company bought all the production and sold it again.

The difficult and rigid relations between Europeans and Chinese were part of China's tax system. The Co-Hongs were used to manage and incorporate the port's revenue into a tax system. With the disappearance or rather weakening of these officials and the appearance of private companies run by individual merchants, the fragile balance was at risk. The smuggling of opium was necessary because its consumption was banned throughout the country. The merchants tried to bring drugs into the areas north of Canton and this broke another strict rule of relations with Europeans: any traffic had to take place only in the port of Canton and in periods decided by Chinese officials. The abolition of the monopoly led to a rapid increase in trade. From 20,220,027 pounds in 1831-32, it went to 34,435,622 pounds in 1836-37 in the opium trade alone. The *Hong* were no longer able to control such a vast and disjointed system, they found themselves pressed into a deadly vice, on the one hand they were squeezed by court officials who demanded their side, on the other hand English merchants over the years had lent huge sums to the Chinese and the latter often found themselves in situations of insolvency. The Canton system was not made to withstand the British capitalist *invasion*. If that square remained marginal for London interests it could have worked but now that Asia was no longer seen as a market in which to buy but sell, China had to adapt to the new structure. India had been forced to reverse course and English goods had invaded the bazaars of the whole subcontinent in a British perspective. Wing China would be touched the same fate. Lancashire fabrics were only present with 818,208 yards in 1814, but by 1835 the yards had grown to 51,777,277. The biggest damage to the EIC was not so much the lack of monopoly when the reversal of course. The lack of a European market for Indian goods took away liquidity from the trade he made with China. All traffic in the Canton was handled with income from Indian goods. As the import of Indian products into Great Britain almost completely disappeared, the system in Canton went into crisis. The triangulation Europe - India - China was like a engine where if you blocked a wheel the whole system would go into tilt. It was necessary to find a way of selling Indian products in China, bypassing European intermediation.

The Chinese trusted the London Government more than the Company. Merchants, in fact, were seen more as pirates than as sellers. When the news of the end of the monopoly reached China, the head of Canton, called by the European viceroys, a nobleman named Lu wrote in London through the merchants *Hong* that in case the monopoly ended they would require a representative responsible for the merchants, a *Taepan*. The Prime Minister of the time, Palmerston, took advantage of the opportunity and saw in that request an excellent opportunity to resume the speeches interrupted after the three failed missions.

Lord Napier in December 1833, a few months after the end of the monopoly, was sent to Canton with the title of Chief Superintendent of Trade with China. Napier had been a Nelson officer, a skilled strategist and soldier but completely ignorant in matters concerning China, trade and diplomacy. Not the most suitable man. Palmerston did not want to ruin this golden opportunity and ordered that Napier should behave in an exemplary manner, without offending or insulting the Chinese Government. He was to try to expand the trade in British goods to other ports and to promote and protect the interests of the British in China. A Canton was established on a ship, a *Court of Judicature* that had jurisdiction over all British citizens present

76

in the port. The British Government had completely misunderstood Lu's request. He had simply asked for a merchant who could control the others, a vigilante but the British had mistakenly understood the request to send a chief who had authority and jurisdiction over all the British, merchants and not. Palmerston imposed on Napier the respect for traditions but never bothered to entrust him with the necessary credentials to carry out the diplomatic task with which he had been invested. Napier arrived in Macao on the 15th of July 1834. As soon as he arrived, he wrote to the Viceroy of Canton And this one immediately asked for orders in Beijing and ordered Napier to remain in Macao until further notice. When Lu's envoys arrived, he had already left, not respecting a rule of the agreements that required anyone moving to the Canton to receive permission first. Napier had also addressed Lu directly without using a *Hong* as an intermediary and above all had written a letter and not a petition. The letter, in fact, was a form of communication between equals whilst in the eyes of the Chinese Napier was a lower form of communication because trade was understood within the tax system. For the Chinese Emperor, the English ruler was nothing more than a vassal. The letter was not even opened, and Lu ordered the *Hong* to send Napier back. Napier refused to move, getting angry with the *Hong* because it was in his interests the only trade with the Chinese, but this was hindered by the Chinese Government that refused to justify itself.

Lu forced the *Hong* to cease all relations with British merchants, forbade the Chinese to act as interpreters and to offer board and lodging to Europeans. The British superintendent tried to force the hand, sending two frigates into the port and having the factories protected by armed soldiers. After a period of tension, he decided to return to Macao where he died of tropical evil. His two successors tried to re-establish relations, the *Hong* started again with their traffics whilst Lu sang victory with Beijing.

Palmerston replaced the third superintendent, Robinson, with Elliot who acted like Napier, addressing letters to the viceroy and above all beginning to request back all the money lent to the *Hong*.

The first opium war is part in this situation, which was a territorial clash limited to the Kwangtung region. Or so the Chinese understood it. As for the British, they meant the opposite.

The British ignored bans on the sale of opium. The Chinese authorities were easily corrupted, and any prohibition had only value on paper. In 1729 and 1796 the Emperor had issued edicts to prohibit all use of drugs and in 1800 his import was also banned. This was a huge blow to British finances. Governing India was expensive and trading with China was the ideal solution to keep the budget stable and shareholders' pockets full.

The Company no longer directly imported opium but sold it to private merchants who then took care of illegally entering the country and reselling it in the various smokehouses. They used smugglers who picked it up in Whampoa or Macao, in front of Canton but not yet inside the port. The port authorities were corrupted by smugglers and they could unload the goods without any problem. After a series of clashes between corrupt officials and corruptors, the central authority of Canton had to intervene because it could no longer ignore the traffics that took place under the scorching sun of the South China Sea. The merchants decided to move everything to the island of Lintin, not far from Canton. Here the smugglers and the British had to work their way up. Ships were anchored and used as warehouses. In this way, merchants from India no longer had to unload their goods directly onto smugglers' ships but were able to use floating warehouses as an interchange point. That way they washed their hands of it. After carefully bribing Chinese officials on the north-east coast, the British decided to go back to doing business in Canton, completely ignoring the increasingly strict rules of the viceroy.

Opium was no longer just a physical problem for China. In addition to turning the Chinese into drug addicts, he also drained the state's silver. With the lack of precious metal, the imperial Government had to raise the price. In 1830 for the first-time the Chinese trade balance was in deficit. The nation bought more products than it sold.

In India it was a phenomenon that was repeated, followed the fluctuations of the market, but in China the market was a voice of the tax system and a contraction of trade influenced negatively or positively, depending on the case, the coffers of the Celestial Empire. China was based on a bi-metallic system. Silver and copper were the current coins for every deal. The ratio was one ounce of silver for every thousand copper coins but with the shortage of the first the percentage rose to nearly 1:2000. This doubling of the price influenced above all the citizens, they traded their goods with copper coins, but the taxes were calculated in silver. As the price of silver increased, more copper coins were needed to pay taxes. The cantonal authorities highlighted two ways to solve the problem. Increase controls and eradicate or legalise the opium black market. In Canton, in fact, almost all were in favour of legalisation. In 1836, the Emperor received a letter from the cantonal authorities explicitly requesting legalisation.

"Since it would not be a solution to close our ports to any trade and since, on the other hand, the laws against opium imports are completely ineffective, the only thing to do is to return to the old system, allowing barbaric merchants to import opium by taxing it at customs as a medicine and stipulating that it can only be sold through Hong merchants and in exchange for arta goods, with the exclusion of any cash payment [...] allowing the import of opium in exchange for other goods would prevent the leakage from the Middle Kingdom of more than 10 million tails[63] per year. Which side would the advantage be, and which would the loss be?"[64]

---

[63] Ounce.

[64] H. F. Mac Nair, *Modern Chinese History Selected of the Nemesis,* Commercial Press, Shanghai 1923. p. 93.

All Kwangtung authorities supported legalisation. A region that depended on trade could not do otherwise. The problem, however, was the authorities in Beijing. The imperial court had very little contact with foreigners and the Emperor himself had lost a son to opium. They did not have the *mindset* of the coastal merchants who dealt with the *barbarians* every day.

The answer did not take that much to arrive:

"I humbly allow myself to observe that wherever evil exists it must be promptly eradicated; that laws must not be allowed to fall into disuse. The harmful and increasingly widespread influence of opium is of little importance when looking at material interests, but it must arouse anxious concern for its harmful effects on the people, since the people are the foundation of the Empire. I believe it is my duty to ask that Your Majesty's orders be issued to the Governors and vice-Governors of the provinces to instruct all officials to redouble their efforts and that the current prohibition of opium be respected; and that it be made absolutely clear that all those who have been contaminated must be redeemed; and that if anyone continues along the same path, deaf to repentance and unable to amend himself, that he be subjected in full to the penalties provided for by law without indulgence".[65]

This change of position made the situation more difficult for the British. They interpreted the positions of the cantonal authorities as imperial choices and were even less concerned about the anti-smuggling rules. The Chinese tightened the rules by expelling merchants and adopting even stricter regulations. They were requirements laden with opium and even led to the beheading of a smokehouse owner. The event, which took place in front of some English merchants, triggered a small uprising.

---

[65] H. F. Mac Nair, *Modern Chinese...*, pp. 98-102.

A new commissioner, Lin Tse-Hsu, was sent to the port and forced the barbaric merchants to stop all opium trafficking. The drug was requisitioned, and some Europeans were even seized. Eliot headed to Canton and came to terms with Lin. The Europeans were freed, and he tried, timidly, to enforce the rules against smuggling. After a jurisdictional problem, a Chinese citizen had been killed in a brawl and the Chinese wanted the British to deliver the culprit or someone to blame, but the British refused, cut off supplies to Macao, forcing British merchants to settle on the island of Hong Kong. On the 4th of September 1839, the Chinese moved to the island and the British decided to open fire.

In fact, the war was never a real war. Towards May 1840 Captain George Eliot, cousin of the commissioner, conquered the fort in defence of Canton and arrived only up to the walls of the city and then retire later. A treaty was signed but immediately defeated by each Government. For the Chinese it was too humiliating and for the English there were too few concessions. Palmerston replaced Elliot and got the war back on track. This time the British did not just want to push the Chinese to reason but to defeat them definitively. The British soldiers almost arrived in Beijing and the Emperor, fearing that they would occupy the city, decided to send ambassadors to discuss a treaty.

The delegates met in Nanking. According to the treaty, the island of Hong Kong passed under perpetual British control, the five ports of Canton, Shanghai, Ning Po, Amoy and the Pagoda island became *treaty ports* where the English, and later the Europeans, enjoyed the rights of extraterritoriality and could only be judged by a consular court present at the port area. Opium had been so important to the war that it was not even mentioned in the treaty. Narcotics was not the only commodity that the British wanted to sell in China despite becoming the best-known and most harmful.

It was also thanks to this war that the Government of London decided to keep the company of the Indies still standing, despite the abolition of the monopoly. His apparatus had been a very useful means of transferring the tributes paid by the Indians to their homeland. Since the shipment of cash coins by sea or by land would have entailed an enormous risk as well as a high cost, different forms of international financial transactions were adopted. The monopoly on trade with China remained in force until 1833 and from 1813 the revenues from the taxes of Bengal and other territories were transferred to the Celestial Empire where they were used for the purchase of direct tea at home; the Indian producers who traded cotton paid the revenues in the offices of Canton and were able to withdraw a receipt of credit to be collected in Calcutta or London. All transactions were not exempt from interest rates and in this way not only the taxes of an Indian Bengal farmer could arrive directly at the coffers of the state in London, having passed between India, China and England produced other profits. The balance for India's economy needed China but what made China important for London's balance was the money from the opium trade. The export of Indian opium to China was of fundamental importance to the Company. The EIC had accumulated a gigantic debt over the years and from 1814 to 1856, the interest on the huge debt and the opium inputs were almost equal.[66]

In the period of maximum expansion of opium traffic, revenues, about £10 million[67], represented 1/6 of all revenues of the British Treasury.

For the British, exporting Indian opium was like printing banknotes. It became the most widely traded single merchandise in the world for much of the nineteenth century. Opium was not part of Chinese culture, he was known but not used to be smoked. The Chinese took very little to get used to tobacco and then opium. Not

---

[66] N. Ferguson, *Empire. How Britain made the modern world*, Mondadori, Milan 2009. p. 145.

[67] £800 million today.

82

even Europe was able to exceed the number of Chinese opiates in number. There were more opium smokers in China at the time than there were today. Even the moralistic Victorian society never went so far as to condemn the use of opium. Just think of the biography of Thomas de Quincey, *Confessions of an English opium-eater,* published in 1821 and revised in 1856. The author in the work, despite describing his addiction to drugs, never goes so far as to condemn it and on the contrary affirms that thanks to it, he always reached a certain personal freedom that was impossible to find elsewhere. Just as the British managed to naturalise sugar by moving it from an expensive niche product to a staple food in every diet, the Chinese introduced a drug into their society. For a society that had chosen to close in on itself dramatically ironic the risk that runs because of a foreign product. In short, for London to become rich, and for the Company to pay its debts, the Chinese would have to smoke. Great contradiction for an Empire that in the same period had used the fleet both to dismantle the slave trade in the Atlantic, both to spread the use of a drug on the other side of the world.

The British and the Chinese would clash again over opium a few years later, but before that Queen Victoria's subjects had other problems to deal with, not in the country that consumed opium but in the country that produced it.

5. The *Great Mutiny*

The last years of the *Company*'s life were very troubled. The moral brake and respect for Indian traditions waned and in recent years the British not only legislated against local religious rules, but also opened the doors of the country to Anglican missionaries. India was no longer to be just a huge market, the Indians had to be educated morally, religiously and socially.

Turning Indians into English was not just a matter of style or feeling of superiority, or worse still racism, it was an essential technical matter. If the British simply bought

Indian goods and products for resale in Europe, local beliefs had no practical interest in the British, apart from the academic one. Now that the Indians had to buy English goods, the producers needed a pool of *civilised* consumers.

The first topic to review was justice. Hastings had already dealt with the problem by establishing 18 Courts of Justice. Civil justice in the Islamic system had as its summit the *diwan* but Hastings wanted to delegate to the judge of the Supreme Court of Calcutta, Sir Eliah Impey had all responsibility. All the bureaucracy of a trial was completely unknown to the previous Islamic system and establishing it was not easy. Impey was greatly criticised for the fact that the court of Calcutta was an entity independent of the Company and accepting the post in Bengal, he found himself serving two masters. However, his task was carried out properly as the Indians soon got used to the new system and preferred the new English courts at the expense of the old rudimentary previous systems.

Impey's successor, Sir William Jones, decided to deal with the codification of previous laws. He had the various codes and treaties translated into English and dismantled the work of the *Brahmins* who mediated between the rules and situations that arose from time to time. With a certain codification, every magistrate, even inexperienced, could consult and deliberate with ease.

The criminal aspect of Islamic law was under the jurisdiction of the *nawab*, which as mentioned above, maintained its independence from British control. He was bound to respect the Koranic law in a rigid manner and this often-implied mutilations. The English hated these punishments because they considered them barbaric and outdated. When they managed to take control of this branch of the law too, despite having to listen to the Islamic officials in charge, they often found a way of changing the sentence. It may seem paradoxical, but under the British, death sentences increased. They were not in fact against Islamic mutilations because they were wrong but simply because they were macabre. Overlooked on this aspect,

Indian thieves were treated like English thieves at home. At that time in England, all crimes against private property were treated with a little rope and a little knot.

In both criminal and civil cases, all the apparatus and procedures of the trials were missing. Crimes were only punished if the perpetrator was directly accused by the injured party and the witnesses did not exist. The British turned the system into an excellent working machine and many criminals ended up before a judge.

Most of the successive Governors preferred to focus on conquests rather than religions. Once it had established a power large enough to satisfy even the most ravenous of the conquerors, the local administration could no longer ignore the gulf between the British and Indian legal and religious traditions. The British came to a point where they could no longer mediate between practices, customs and norms considered archaic and the advanced Anglo-Saxon legal system. In order to regulate justice, it was necessary to regulate religion, or rather religions.

It was under the mandate of Lord Bentinck that the British began to legislate against practices widespread in various religions. First, infanticide was prohibited[68]. In India, as in China, children were killed to control the number of family members. Especially the female daughters were killed or abandoned, in Bengal there was also the ritual infanticide in the name of the Goddess Ganges.

Another practice hated by Europeans and banned was sati[69]. This was a technique widespread since the Middle Ages and consisted in burning the widow, alive, on her husband's funeral pyre. The woman was considered a useless object and when her husband died, suicide was practically the only way to go. On the 4th of December 1829, it was forbidden for young widows or widowers expecting a child, and later

---

[68] R. C. Majumdar, *An Advanced History of India,* Macmillan, London 1956, p. 822.

[69] Regulation XVII

the ban was extended to all widows. The custom became a crime and for those who forced, threatened or mistreated widows who refused to kill themselves, there was the death penalty. The Orthodox Hindus appealed to the Supreme Court but got nothing. Ram Mohan Roy, the famous philosopher, was against the norm despite having tried several times to convince his fellow countrymen of the absurdity of the norm. He was convinced that it was a practice unrelated to the sacred texts of Hinduism but banning it by law was a violation of religious freedom. The Rajputana was the region where it was most difficult to eradicate this rule, it was so widespread that until 1846 the British were unable to do anything to abolish it. Between 1831 and 1837 the Thug, a sect devoted to Kali and practising human sacrifice, was exterminated. A few years later slavery was abolished, even though in India it was never used for economic or domestic purposes.

From 1848 to 1856 James Ramsey, Marquis of Dalhousie, was chosen as Governor. He had a very specific plan for India. A mix of legislative and territorial unification in favour of the development of communications and means of transport. As soon as he arrived in India, he found himself with a war to win. North of Indian territory was the Sikhs' Empire. The various Sovereigns had always maintained an ambiguous relationship with the EIC. On the one hand they granted territories and benefits to the British and on the other they strengthened the Army in case of war. The situation remained peaceful until 1839 when Ranjit Singh died. The Kingdom went into chaos and the British piled up troops on the border of Punjab. This caused the first Anglo-Sikh war from which the Empire came out defeated but still alive. The English imposed the transfer of a series of territories and their own representative who would in fact dictate the policy of the Empire. As time passed, the situation became more and more difficult. A second war began and ended with the destruction of the Empire and the annexation of the whole Punjab to the Raj. Now the British controlled territories up to the Khyber Pass, which linked India to Afghanistan. In 1852 the Governor moved real east to conquer Lower Burma. Dalhousie was more than convinced that the Company should take every opportunity to unify as many territories as possible and remove all forms of archaic state. He was the creator of the doctrine of *lapse*[70]. It was this that allowed the British crown to add miles and miles of territory to its Empire without fighting wars. Dalhousie claimed for the Company all those Kingdoms that remained without heirs. In India it was commonplace because of the heated rivalry between the children of the various rulers and the wars they fought. The Company had won the right of pre-eminence over the various states and thus regulated the successions. In the beginning, only Kingdoms with extinct dynasties entered the Raj, but later the right to equate adopted children with legitimate children was abolished and many dynasties were forced to extinction. There was no longer any British intention of concealing the aims of conquest. The titles of *nawab* of the Carnatic, Surat and Raja of Tanjore were declared extinct and not transferable. The adoptive heir of the last *peshwa* of the Marats, Nana Sahib, was denied the right to the throne and the pension that the Company paid to his father. The most sensational gesture, however, was to notify the same Mughal Emperor, Bahadur Shah II, that he would be the last Emperor. The title would have fallen on his death and his family would have to leave Delhi. For many years now, the Emperor only had power within the Red Fort. Only an opposition prevented him from letting the Great Moghul leave his home. In seven years, the Company obtained seven Kingdoms. The new territories were divided between central India, Bengal, Rajasthan and Punjab. The important Kingdoms of Nagpur, Satara and Jhansi ceased to exist as independent nations.

However, the most drastic reforms took place in family law and matrimonial law. In 1850 Lord Dalhousie, despite a series of protests and petitions, signed a law that changed a strict rule of Hindu customary law that if you change religion you lose the

---

[70] *Falling.*

right to inherit. In 1856 the marriage of the Hindu widows became valid and all property rights were included.[71] The greatest work of change, however, was done not by the Governor on duty but by the dozens and dozens of English magistrates who tried in every way to interpret the Hindu and Muslim laws according to a British standard. Equality before the law was a completely unknown concept in a caste society. The magistrates who came from Great Britain had the task not only of enforcing the laws but also of interpreting them and making them understood.

Lord Dalhousie was not a despotic conqueror but had a much more moral interest. For him it was wrong to conquer economically and let the population live according to rules considered erroneous and ancient. With time, bad Government also became a reason for *lapse*. This was the case, for example, of the Kingdom of Oudh where, despite the existence of a dynasty, the Kingdom became part of the Raj.

He was also interested in public works, from an economic and commercial point of view. Westernising India also meant bringing the new inventions that were having great success in Europe. The train, telegraph, post office and steamboat were to not only unite and connect India inside, but also the colony with the motherland. These four inventions made the British Empire the true master of the world. The ability that the English had to exploit them to the maximum allowed to bring all competition and enemy to their knees. Before coming to India, Dalhousie had worked with Gladstone, the future Prime Minister, at the London Ministry of Commerce and had learnt a lot from the railway boom between 1840 and 1850. The first British railway network was born in 1826 and from the beginning the state intervened very little, whilst in the colonies, although they were open to individuals, the state assured the earnings and in case, would also be willing to absorb debts. The project was entirely financed by English capital. Several companies from all over the world put their

---

[71] Act XV, 1856.

money on Indian rails. The EIC and then the Crown guaranteed everyone 4.5% to 5%. It was the first case of transfer of capital from England to India because until then every investment was made with the income from taxes collected. The trains shortened the distances and reduced the transport costs of the goods and above all made the transport of the troops decidedly more agile and faster. With the expansion of the British domains, no longer confined to Bengal and the eastern coast, transport and connection lines were needed. Dalhousie followed the work personally. The projects approved included two lines, one from Bombay and one from Calcutta. From Calcutta to Punjab it took 24 days to travel but not even three days by train. All the materials used came from Great Britain, rails, trains, locomotives, wood and of course coal. The main links were the big cities and ports, but over time, and with other investments, smaller lines spread almost everywhere. The first line to be inaugurated was the Calcutta - Thane. About 30 kilometres by rail. It was 1853 and in little more than 50 years the kilometres became 38,000. The costs were reasonable and in principle effective rail networks were built. The Indians immediately fell in love with the new means of transport and began to use it to visit relatives and sacred places throughout the country. The war purpose of the railway was not masked but rather exalted. Just think of Lucknow station, more like a fortress than a train station. In addition to the railways, the Governor also worked on road communications and waterways for irrigation. Under his rule, 800 kilometres of the Ganges Canal were completed and were used for both transport and irrigation of crops. The telegraph was one of those inventions almost ignored at first but then became essential. In 1816 Francis Ronald's, the inventor, offered his discovery to the admiralty but was rejected. Thanks to the private sector, the invention was improved and put on the market. In the beginning, the railway infrastructure was used, but over time its use grew so much that it needed its own structure. Dalhousie's intuition was essential especially in the period of the revolt, a condemned man from the gallows came to define the telegraph:

"The accursed string that strangles me"

The Empire, once it understood the usefulness of the telegraph, decided to invest immediately. His invention together with the money produced the submarine cables. The main problem was the permeability, but everything was solved thanks to the gutta-percha, a rubber of Malay production. As was often the case, some of the innovations were first tested in India and then imported into Great Britain. The same telegraph was no less important; the first submarine cable in the world was laid at the bottom of the Hooghly River in Calcutta in 1839. In 1851 there was the first case of cable deposited in the Channel whilst 15 years later the first transatlantic cable. On July 27, 1866, the *Great Eastern* of Isambard Kingdom Brunel reached the American coast after unwinding the longest cable in the world on the seabed. The ship was designed precisely with the intention of demonstrating the superiority of steam over sail. Six times larger than the largest ship of the time, it was 211 metres long and weighed 20,000 tonnes. Its double steel hull was so well designed and built that it only took two years to dismantle it. Inside it was even found the body of a worker forgotten inside, during the construction.

Only the British national network was state owned, all other plants in the colonies were born thanks to private investment. In 1880, the figure of 150,000 kilometres of submarine cables was reached. India, Canada, Australia and Africa were now connected to the mother country. In India Dalhousie installed more than 7000 kilometres of telegraph cables from north to south. In addition to political and military use, private use spread, in fact, a message sent from Bombay could be read in London within a day, all at only four shillings per word. Before the Suez Canal, the same letter took almost two years to reach its destination. Charles Bright described the telegraph as:

"The world's system of electrical nerves"

The Indian postal system is also part of the communication expansion projects. Created in 1854, it established the same *post penny* that had been created years before in Great Britain. Standard rates allowed anyone to send letters to every corner of the Raj. This facilitated the creation of publishing houses and newspapers as well as the sending of information and personal communications. Often those who knew how to write offered free help in writing letters and correspondence. The shipbuilding industry also has its place in this development perspective. Indian ships had lost their position to the detriment of vessels produced in Europe but with the advent of steam, an innovation in the shipyards, allowed Indian shipowners to regain positions. The Imperial Navy was initially convinced that steam technology would vibrate the death blow to British supremacy, but it did not take long for them to understand how wrong they were. The first battleship, the *Warrior,* launched in 1860, became the symbol of the power of steel and coal. In her whole life no one dared to challenge her and today she rests intact in the port of Portsmouth. Although the British tried to improve the conditions of Indian subjects, this sudden acceleration, understood by many as an intrusion, mixed with the discontent of many princes deprived of their inheritance, of farmers, artisans and producers, fed the phenomenon that exploded near Calcutta on the 23rd of January 1857 and that spread throughout northern India, at the risk of wiping out all traces of British rule.

Mutiny or Great Uprising of 1857, as historians called it. It all began in Dumdum on the outskirts of Calcutta when the Company's indigenous troops refused to obey English officers. The beginning was due to a trail of false information, a pretext or a lie. Word began to spread that the gunpowder cartridges of the new rifles were lubricated with pig or cow grease, and for the conformations of these weapons it was necessary to use the mouth to tear off the casing. The Hindus and Muslims were forbidden to touch the two animals, and all this was seen as a way to force the soldiers to become impure and convince them to convert to Christianity. The British did not understand the gravity of the revolt and from Dumdum the mutiny struck the garrisons at Barrackpore, Meerut, Berhampur and Lucknow. In May of the same year it was no longer a matter of mutiny scattered here and there but of a real revolt. In Meerut prisoners were released and English officers killed. The rebel soldiers then marched on Delhi. When they arrived in the city, they decided to massacre every

Englishman, the British properties were plundered and with the taking of Fort Red they proclaimed the restoration of the Mughal Empire. The Emperor welcomed the mutinies and willingly accepted the commission. At the beginning of the summer, the whole north was on fire. The British survivors had retreated to Lucknow, Agra and Kanpur.

The British had the disorganisation of the revolt from theirs. Nothing had been studied previously and it was even difficult to identify the various leaders of the revolt. British expeditions departed from Punjab and Bengal to regain control of India. Delhi was resumed in September 1857 by troops stationed in Punjab. The rebels had also restored the Marathon Empire, proclaiming Nana Sahib Emperor. The two Empires were always fighting each other and the intention to restore them both demonstrated the fragility and disorganisation of the whole revolt.

The English, taking advantage of the arrival of troops destined for China and diverted to India, collected a series of victories in the winter of 1857. The general who led the British attack, Colin Campbell, regained the entire Doab region by re-establishing the lines of communication between Allahabad and Delhi. In 1858 the revolt shifted its centre of gravity in the middle of the subcontinent, the Oudh, the Gwalior, the Sansor, the Indore and the Jhansi, where they became places of confrontation and reprisals. Right in Sangor during a battle, Queen Ranu of Jhansi died. She was struck by *lapse* in 1853 and lost her right to her father's throne.

On the 5th of January 1859, a communication arrived in London announcing its arrival:

"The utmost tranquility prevails throughout Oudh"[72]

The uprising had been calmed down but the price in life and money had been very high. Now the British had to identify the cause and avoid and thus prevent a flashback.

Sayyid Ahmad Khan, an Indian official in the service of the British, wrote what he thought were the main causes of the revolt:

"I believe that the revolt has only had one main cause, the others being secondary and consequential. This opinion is not based on fantasies or conjectures, but on the theories of wise men of the past: and all the writers who have expressed themselves on the subject the foundations of the state agree with it [...] it is well-known that the participation of subjects in the Government under which they live is indispensable for its efficiency, prosperity and permanence. Moreover, the natives of India, practically all without exception, accuse the Government of depriving them of their position and dignity and of keeping them in a state of subjugation [...] the pride and arrogance perhaps induced to consider the natives of India as second-class human beings? Didn't the Government know that the natives of the upper classes trembled in front of its officials, fearing at all times that they would have to suffer the worst insults[73] and outrages at their hands?

---

[72] Letter from Montgomery to Canning, 7th of January 1859. *Canning Papers* present in T. R. Metcalf, *The Aftermath of Revolt, India 1857-1870,* Princeton University Press, Princeton. 1964. p. 54.

[73] S. A. Khan, *The causes of the Indian Revolt,* Oxford University Press, Oxford 1873. p. 124.

93

The British Government immediately tried to justify the revolt by considering it only as a military event, but the words of Khan were shared by many. Especially at home. Disraeli himself[74], in a heated speech in parliament, had identified the guilt of everything in the reckless policy of reforms. The British had taken power in India and had dominated it without much trouble precisely because they had moved with lead feet. The revolt could not succeed from the beginning because everyone fought for a personal matter. The Emperor wanted his Kingdom back, the Marathons his own, the regent of Oudh his own independence, the princes his own inheritance, the peasants the land. At times, no leader had emerged, but the movement was never unified. Some took advantage of the chaos to plunder their neighbours, whilst others allied themselves with the British to take revenge. Thanks to the enmity between Punjab and Bengal, the Sikhs remained faithful to the Company and helped it defeat the Bengali Sepoys; Madras' troops did not want to lose the economic power of the city, which is why the revolt never reached the south.

The British in the Army were decidedly inferior but keeping all the power, the local soldiers were virtually impossible to make a career and the last military campaigns had made the troops aware of their importance also, the British recruited from the highest castes, Brahmins and especially Rajput. India, amongst other things, had also been the barracks of the British Empire and very often if there was a need for some expedition, Indian soldiers had been sent and this meant for some of them losing their caste rights. Perhaps only for the garrisons involved it was a military affair but for all the other realities involved there were also religious, political and economic aspects.

---

[74] Hansard, M., *Parliamentary Debates*, 3d series vol. 147, H. C. 27th of July 1857, p. 440 ff.

The Emperor Moghul paid the highest price. His sons were shot, and he was exiled to Burma. Jhansi had died in battle and the leaders of the revolt in Oudh stopped after yet another defeat.

The last Emperor became the symbol of the revolt. Historians do not really agree on his real faults in the uprising. Maybe he did not play an active role in the design, also because perhaps there was no design, but he got involved later, when the rebels took Delhi.

Just as there was not only a military intent is wrong the consideration of some Indian historians, who see in the revolt a kind of first Indian war of independence. India never had the idea of national unity, which should be the basis of an idea of independence, after all, the Mughal Empire was nothing more than an authority above other Kingdoms, each with its own religion, its own politics and its own economy.

The uprising marked the psyche of the British in India and at home. From that moment on, there was almost always the idea of a certain bestial nature inherent in the Indians. The stories of the massacres perpetrated against the British became a *leitmotiv* in Anglo-Indian literature and the idea of the risk of the white woman amongst Indian men[75], born after the massacre of Cawnpore, stained the last century of British domination with the virus of racism. In racism, as in everything else, the English were different from the others because if from the motherland there was an interest in cancelling all the causes of the revolt for the British in India there was an interest in separating the two *races* there was never the idea of an apartheid, but the

---

[75] The best-known case is certainly Forster's masterpiece novel, a *Passage to India* where the whole story revolves around an alleged rape perpetrated by an Indian doctor to an English woman.

burden of the white man could not be shared with the natives. According to them, Anglo-Saxon superiority did not derive from the colour of the skin but from culture, a culture that could only be passed on to a certain extent. The idea of westernising subjects disappeared.

With the end of *Mutiny,* the existence of the Company also ended. That hybrid form of Government was no longer acceptable and on 2nd of August 1858 the parliament approved a new *India Act* which transferred all the powers of the EIC to the Crown. The Governor became viceroy and Indian affairs ended up under the Secretary of State for India. The viceroy was joined by an executive council no longer formed only by British. The revolt allowed the imperial power to run for cover and correct things everywhere. Random politicians like Lord Dalhousie could no longer find fertile land. There was a kind of slow and gradual progress. The councils, commissions and organs were open to the indigenous people or as desired by London.

The last Sovereign Moghul died in November 1862 and was buried without much compliment in the prison of Rangoon.

Captain H. Nelson Davies, the company commissioner in charge of maintaining relations with the Mughal court, wrote these words to his bosses in London after the funeral:

Have since visited the remaining State Prisoners - the very scum of the reduced Asiatic harem; found all correct. None of the family appear much affected by the death of the bed-ridden old man. His death was evidently due to pure decrepitude and paralysis in the region of the throat. He expired at 5 o'clock on the morning of the funeral. The death of the ex-King may be said to have had no effect on the Mahomedan part of the populace of Rangoon, except perhaps for a few fanatics who watch and pray for the final triumph of Islam. A bamboo fence surrounds the grave for some considerable distance, and by the time the fence is worn out, the grass will again have properly covered the spot, and no vestige will remain to distinguish where the last of the Great Moghuls rests

He has not been Emperor since 1858. He never had the spirit of a politician, he was more interested in poetry and songs. With his death, the Emperor's post remained vacant, but not for long. In 1877, at Disraeli's request, the parliament conferred on Queen Victoria the title of *Empress of India.*

Exactly 277 years after the first royal licence, signed by Elizabeth I, England had built a Protestant Empire, the largest Empire in history. Spain was just a pale reminder of the past. Portugal was now a small state on the edge of Europe, France had surrendered to any idea of supremacy and Holland no longer had an Empire.

India was the jewel and now the enemies no longer came from Europe but surrounded the Raj.

I

"India was awake, and Kim was in the middle of it, more awake and more excited than anyone, chewing on a twig that he would presently use as a toothbrush; for he borrowed right- and left-handedly from all the customs of the country he knew and loved."

Rudyard Kipling, Kim

KIM

1881 – 1900

Chapter Two

From Russia with love, death, blood and money

1. James Bond in turban.

The jewel of the Crown had always been a greedy spoil for all the enemies of Great Britain but only one managed to put in difficulty, several times, the subjects of Victoria: Russia. Or so the English were convinced, because the facts show a different *truth*.

Ian Fleming has never written a novel about them, Q has never designed any useful gadgets for their missions but SPECTRE, in a way existed, the Russians were the enemies and the Empire was in danger

Great Game for the British, *Bol'šaja Igra* for the Russians. Great Game the largest, most articulated and dangerous game of chess in history. The pawns were agents, soldiers, missionaries, spies and travellers and the players were the Tsar of all Russia on the one hand, and the Sovereign of Great Britain on the other. The chessboard? One of the most inhospitable territories in the world: Central Asia.

What was the Great Game, the secret mission, the giant game of chess? Theoretically, keeping an eye on your imperial neighbour.

At the beginning of the nineteenth century, there were three thousand kilometres between the Russian and British borders in India, whilst at the end of the century, the distance was reduced to a few hundred, and just 30 thousand metres in the Pamir area. In four centuries the Tsarist Empire had conquered an average of one hundred and 50 kilometres of territory a day, 50 thousand kilometres a year. The Asian territories for the rulers of St. Petersburg were nothing more than goods to conquer

103

and the greatest fear for the ministers of London and Calcutta was that the Cossacks would aim to water the horses in the Indus and Ganges. As we shall see, however, between the beliefs of the British in London and the interests of the Russians in St Petersburg, there was a much wider gap than the distance between their borders.

2. A suspicious will

Every will creates problems, big or small. If the testament in question is that of a Sovereign who bequeaths to the whole people a war to be fought over the centuries, over time the problems become enormous and if we also consider that the aforementioned testament is a fake, the complications outweigh all measures.

Peter the Great[76] was a man of ambitions and bold plans. He had managed to transform Russia from a semi-medieval nation to a powerful modern war machine. He had replaced the domination of the Nordic Monarchies with a European state

---

[76] Much of the academic literature on Peter the Great is produced in Russian and translations into European languages are not available. I have consulted some works in English and in my opinion the following are the most complete P. Bushkovitch, *Peter the Great: The Struggle for Power, 1671–1725*, Cambridge University Press, Cambridge 2001; J. Cracraft. *The Revolution of Peter the Great*, Harvard University Press, Cambridge 2003; L. Hughes. *Russia in the Age of Peter the Great*, Yale University Press, New Haven 1998; L. Hughes, *Peter the Great and the West: New Perspectives* Palgrave Macmillan, Basingstoke 2001; · L. Hughes. *Peter the Great: A Biography*, Yale University Press, New Haven 2002; M. R. Massie, *Peter the Great: His Life and World,* Ballantine Books, New York City 1981; H. Troyat, *Peter the Great*, E.P. Dutton, New York 1987.

apparatus. His *famous* will[77] made his intentions and plans known to all. The primary aim was to dominate all the neighbouring territories and consequently the world.

Actually, that will is a well-articulated fake document. The text was already known at the time of Tsarina Elisabeth, a first copy arrived in France thanks to the famous spy Chevalier d'Eon, who accomplished his mission in Russia disguised as a woman. Later we have news of a copy read by Platon Zubov, the last *favourite* of Catherine the Great, and it is probably thanks to him that the version we know, has reached France. He was a compatriot, friend and colleague of the Polish general Michał Sokolnicki who served in the Polish Legion within the French Army. In 1797 it was presented to the Directorate of France and Napoleon wanted to use it to increase *Russophobia*[78], which had soon taken hold in French, English and European public

---

[77] D. V. Lehvich, *The Testament of Peter the Great, American Slavic and East European Review,, Association for Slavic*, East European, and Eurasian Studies, *Pittsburgh* April 1948, Vol. 7, No. 2, pp. 111-124.

[78] Russophobia appeared overwhelmingly in Great Britain in the Napoleonic period. With the alliance between the French Emperor and the Tsar, the press and public opinion began to build on the Russians the myth of the conquering, crude and bloodthirsty people. The news of Napoleon moving the Army to conquer Russia in 1812 sent the British Government into panic. They had not even considered the idea that it could fail, on the other hand it had been marching and conquering territories throughout Europe for years and the British knew of the disorganisation of the Tsarist Army, when news arrived of a burning Moscow and of the Russians in route towards Asia all of Europe interpreted it as yet another Napoleonic conquest. A frightening scenario for London because it gave free access to India to the French Army. The defences in India were not and never were numerous and a Napoleonic

advance had high chances of success. Over time, however, the news began to change and what seemed to be the greatest French conquest turned out to be its defeat. The Army was retreating all over the front, Moscow was on fire, but because of the Russians and their tactics of the scorched earth, and the Tsar chased and massacred foreign troops arriving in Paris. In London they quickly forgot about the fear of the Russians and filled them with praise, in the end they were allies against the French and a Russian victory was also a British victory. The Cossacks became the symbol of Russian courage and simplicity. Stories, partly real and partly imaginary, filled books and newspapers. In one of these, a commander who had led a failed expedition against India fourteen years earlier, was even awarded an *honorary* degree at Oxford and filled with gifts. The peace lasted very little, however, because despite everything a weak France left free manoeuvre to a Russia at the height of its moment of glory. Tsar Alexander had declared expansionist aims and if in Europe the Congress of Vienna succeeded in blocking it in Asia no one could do anything about it. Following the French defeat at Waterloo, the fear of the Tsarist Empire did not diminish, but rather grew more and more. The Anglo-Afghan wars and the Crimean War were the culmination of this phenomenon. The British created the Empire's number one enemy from this issue. Russia was a danger to India and to all British economic and military interests in Asia and the world. Political figures such as Lord Robert Thomas Wilson fanned the flame of fear and scaremongering in public opinion. He has always been interested in Russian affairs. An informant of him was present at Tilsit when in 1807 Napoleon and Alexander met and referred to him the phrase of the Tsar, from the Tsar to the Emperor: *"Sir, I hate the English as much as you do."* In the beginning he was an admirer of the Russians and a friend of the Tsar, but after witnessing the fire in Moscow and the retreat of the French Army, he made a commitment at home to dismantle the good-looking mask created by the press and opinion. Bonaparte's intention was to demonstrate how Europe appeared to the St. Petersburg court as a spoil of war[79]. In 1812 Charles-Louis Lesur published what is

---

public opinion on the Russians. He accused them of massacres and unjust punishments against French prisoners, of not respecting the rules of war and above all having let Napoleon escape. His attack on the Russians, allies of the British and in fact the saviours of Europe, was not well received even though no one could contest it because he was a respected person and told what he had seen. In 1817 he was elected parliamentarian and had a pamphlet published. *A Sketch of the Military and Political Power of Russia* was released anonymously but everyone knew who the author was. Wilson raised the question of Peter the Great's will and brought light on the growth of the Tsarist Army and unlimited expansion to support his theses. In the volume there was a map that marked in green the ancient border of Russia and in red the current one after the more than five hundred thousand kilometres conquered in the 16 years of Alexander's reign. It was a clever theatre coup because it allowed everyone to understand how close they were to the European capitals and to the domains in India. Tsar Alexander was presented as an even more dangerous threat than the Napoleonic one. The vastness of the Empire also meant a practically unlimited basin of soldiers. The debate around the book went on for almost a century. Despite much criticism, Russophobia had also taken hold in England. As time went by, others followed in Wilson's footsteps and published texts that alerted the Russian advance. Kinneir, De Lacy Evans and Mc Neill are just a few. When Wilson's predictions began to come true, such as the crisis in Constantinople with Russian troops a few kilometres from the city walls or with the disaster of the first Anglo-Afghan War, even the most critical of him began to change their minds.

[79] P. Blackstock, *Agents of Deceit,* Quadrangle Books, Chicago 1966; S. Blanc, *Histoire D'une Phobie: Le Testament de Pierre le Grand,* Cahiers du Monde Russe

probably the most *Russian-phobic* text ever printed: *Des progrès de la puissance russe*. The volume that came out at the expense of the Ministry of Foreign Affairs contained within it the full text of the will. The document deals with various topics ranging from war to economy, from state finances to the Army. It mentions the most important nations of the time of Peter and especially Napoleon.

The parts we are interested in are number 7 and 9. The ones that describe relations with England and India.

7. *"We must be careful to keep up our commercial alliances with England, for she is the power which has the most needs for our products for her navy, and at the same time may be of the greatest service to us in the development of our own. We must export wood and other articles in exchange for her gold and establish permanent connections between her seamen and our own".*

9. *"We must progress as much as possible in the direction of Constantinople and India. He who can once get the possession of these points is the real ruler of the world. With this in view we must prevail constant quarrels at the one time with Turkey, at another with Persia. We must establish wharves and docks in the Euxine and by degrees make ourselves master of that sea, as well as the Baltic, which is a doubly important element in the success of our plan. We must hasten the downfall of Persia, push on to the Persian Gulf, if possible, re-establish the ancient*

---

et Soviétique 9, Paris 1968. p. 265-293; S. A. Mezin, *Zaveshchanie Petra Pervogo: Evropeiskie Mify i Rossiiskaia Realnost,* Rossiiskaia Istoriia 5, Moscow 2010. p. 18-27; H. Ragsdale, *Détente in the Napoleonic Era: Bonaparte and the Russians,* The Regents Press of Kansas. Lawrence 1980; A. Reis, *Russophobia and the Testament of Peter the Great,* Slavic Review 44 (4), Urbana 1985. pp. 681-693.

commerciality with the Levant through Syria, and force our way into the Indies, which are the storehouses of the world. Once there, we can dispense with English gold."

According to the so-called will, the Russians should have used Great Britain as a market in which they would have procured gold to finance the various campaigns of conquest, including the one for the domination of India because it was intended as a very rich country, where they could buy up any precious good. The document does not specify whether India was already a British territory or not. It is certain that in Peter's time it was not yet, but when the document was circulated by Napoleon it was. We can only understand, then, that England's usefulness had a very specific purpose that could have been lost once it got its hands-on Indian gold. Unlike other false historians such as the Donation of Constantine, here we are faced with a text, which in its falsity, is accurate in the historical reconstruction, within it.

The document, however false it may have been, in a certain sense shaped and created the *mindset* of Peter's successors. All the Romanovs have reigned with the intent to dominate the world. The de facto will rewritten Russian foreign policy for the following centuries. But if the expansionist aims on the European side were and always were clear, can we really be so sure and clear about Russian interest in India? Was there a plan designed for the domination of the Indian subcontinent, or did most of the British efforts to defend the Raj come from an excess of fear or rather a militarised Russian phobia? Did what we call *the Great Game* really have two players or was it a solo game? Did the *Shadow Tournament* really serve to protect domains, or was it a useful propaganda tool?

Before going into the meanders of India's conquest plans, the terror of the English for the Russians and the complex British machinations to defend the Empire, we must dwell on two aspects not entirely taken for granted, first, what is meant by Great Game and why do we talk about it in this context? And secondly, what was the use made of it in imperial propaganda?

3. Great Game: 101 ways to call a problem.

The term *Great Game* has multiple meanings, in a broad sense, we can say that it means everything and the opposite of everything. The term is used everywhere: politics,[80] geopolitics[81], reconstruction in Britain[82], control of South Africa[83],

---

[80] E. Law, Lord Ellenborough, *A Political Diary, "If we play the Great Game, striking at the mass, we must succeed"*, Cambridge Scholars Publishing, Cambridge 1881. p. II, 60 (30 June 1829); H. Drummond, *The Great Game,* St Paul, London 1918; F. R. Kent, *The Great Game of Politics,* Ayer Company Publishers, Manchester 1923. p. 29; Sir E. Clarke, *The Story of my life, "the Great Game of Politics"* John Murray, London 1923, p. 213.

[81] P. F. Thomas, *Can the Great Game really be deconstructed? A Geopolitical challenge for philosophers and warriors,* Kashtan Press, Kingston 1996.

[82] J. Buchan, *A Prince of Captivity,* House of Stratus, Looe 1996, p. 116.

[83] R. Hyam, *Britain's Imperial Century, 1815-1914, "The great game between ourselves and the Transvaal for the mastery of South Africa"* Palgrave Macmillan, Basingstoke 1976. Quoted by Lord Milner 1899/1900.

business[84], high finance[85] card games, chess[86], reform of the Ottoman Empire[87], football,[88] the struggle for Arab independence[89] horse racing[90],, cooking[91], polo[92],

---

[84] T. G. Frederick, *The Great Game of Business*, D. Appleton and company, New York 1920. p. V, IX, 7, 8, 96.

[85] H.C. Bailey, *The Great Game,* Sun Dial Press, New York 1940. pp. 156, 189, 219, 262, 279. A. W. Dragon, *Intellectual Whist: Conversations, Discussions and Anecdotes on the Great Game,* George Routledge & Sons Limited, London 1899.

[86] L. Carroll, *Through the Looking Glass, "It's a great game of chess that's being played all over the world..."* Macmillan and Co., London 1872. p.25.

[87] H. Temperley, *England and the Near East: the Crimea, "The great game of improvement is altogether up for the present"*, Green Longmans, London 1936. p. 242. In a letter of Stratford de Recliffe to Palmerston on the 5th of April 1851.

[88] S. Horler, *The Great Game,* John Crowther, Huddersfield 1935.

[89] T. E. Lawrence, *Secret Despatches from Arabia,* "The dice of the great game between us and the rest, for Arab suffrage after the war..." Bellew Publishing, London 1918.

[90] E. Spencer, *The Great Game: and how it is played,* Grant Richards, London 1900. p. 2, 6, 10, 13, 30, 226.

[91] R. J. Courtine, *Le Gran Jeu de la Cuisine, Larousse*, Paris 1980.

[92] C. Falls, *Rudyard Kipling,* M. Kennerley, New York 1915. p. 140.

war[93], poaching[94], the American Union[95], board games,[96] diplomacy[97] and the order of the Ungulate quadrupeds[98].

Its most widespread use is certainly the political one. Even today, any balance of power between two or more powers with a minor state in between still gets the label of *New Great Game* and it is not difficult to understand why. If we took some newspapers from the late nineteenth century and read the titles about Afghanistan or the Middle East, we will find it hard to understand whether if they refer to the present

---

[93] W. Tecumseh Sherman, "This great game of war" citato in Shelby Foote, *The Civil War*, 3 vol, Random House, New York 1991. P 781; E. B. Osborn, *The Muse in Arms*, "the greatest of all great games", John Murray, London 1917. p.VI-VII.

[94] H. Wyman, *The Great Game: The Life and Times of a Welsh Poacher*, Fieldfare Publications, Cambridge 1993.

[95] S. Foote, *The Civil War*, 3 vol, *"The fitting if not indispensable adjunct to the consummation of the great game we are playing"*. Random House, New York 1991. P 749. Quoting President Lincoln in a speech from the 1st of February 1865.

[96] W. Pett, *Rules and Regulations of the Great Game of Jetball*, Exeter, Exeter 1914; Anonym, *Tri-Tactics: The Great Game of Tactics on Land, Sea and in the Air*, messo in vendita nel 1933; *The Great Game: The Dover Patrol or Naval Tactics*, del 1929. (All the copies of this game were destroyed during the Second World War).

[97] A. Sinclair, *The Other Victoria: The Princess Royal and the Great Game of Europe*, Littlehampton Book Services Ltd, Faraday Close 1981. p. 2.

[98] The quotations are numerous, the oldest one I found dates back to 1892.

day or to those of the past. The Great Game is nothing more than the proof of the circular motion of history.

Two meanings can be given to the term[99]:

1) The alleged activity of espionage through Russian and British secret agents in Central Asia, with the intention of creating alliances and spreading the influence of their own nation.

2) The military rivalry between Britain and Russia, and the alleged danger of invasion of India from the northwest.

At that time, this use of the term was virtually unknown to public opinion and only spread to the general public after World War II.

The origin of the academic use of the term has a very precise date: 10 November 1926, the day on which Professor Henry William Carliss Davis gave a lecture at the British Academy entitled *The Great Game in Asia (1800-1844).*[100] The conference focused on the events that led to the First Anglo-Afghan War and the years immediately following. Davis had developed his career, until the eve of the First World War, as a medieval historian, he was not known but not even completely unknown; from 1914 onwards, thanks also to his contribution to the war effort as a revisionist of secret despatches, at the *War Trade Intelligence Department,* he shifted

---

[99] M. Yapp, *The Legend of the Great Game,* in *Proceedings of British Academy,* The British Academy, London 2001, Vol. III p. 180.

[100] J. R. H. Feaver and Austin Lane-Poole, *H. W. C. Davis, A Memoir and Selection of his Historical Papers,* Constable and company, ltd, London 1933. p. 164-202.

his interest to the contemporary era. Despite everything, and especially about the Great Game, he remained an amateur of the subject although he influenced more than anyone else, the academic work on this subject. His definition of Great Game: *"A bid for political ascendancy in Western Asia"[101]* is the one who has been able to put the age-old issue in a nutshell.

Davis had found the term in a letter from July 1840. It was written by a *player,* a spy in Asia. Colonel Arthur Conolly.

"You've a great game, a noble game before you, and I have strong hope that you will be able to steer through all jealousy, and caprice, and sluggishness, till the Afghans unite with your own countrymen in appreciating your labours for a fine nation's regeneration and advancement"[102]

In the letter, written to Major Henry Rawlinson, the new British agent in Qandahar, Conolly firmly believes that the Major, his friend, had to exploit his position to start the civilisation of Afghanistan. Conolly was more interested in the human side than in the possible Russian expansionist aims. He felt more like a missionary because, when he moved to India to seek his fortune, on the way he met the Reverend of Calcutta, Reginald Heber, who instructed him and rekindled in him, the evangelising fervour. That experience deeply marked him and led him to enlist later.

In fact, Conolly had already used the term, albeit slightly different, in a previous letter to Rawlinson.

---

[101] J.R.H. Feaver and Austin Lane-Poole, p. 165.

[102] J.W. Kaye, *Lives of Indian Officers,* W. H. Allen & Co, London 1867. 2 vol p. 101.

"if the British Government would only play the grand game – help Russia Cordially to all that she has a right to expect – shake hands with Persia – get her all possible amends from Oosbegs – force the Bokhara Amir to be just to us, the Afghans, and other Oosbegs sate, and his own Kingdom – but why go on; you know my, at any rate in one sense, enlarged, views. Inshallah! The expediency, nay the necessity of them will be seen, and we shall play the noble part that the first Christian nation of the world ought to fill"[103]

Once again, the subject, and the intent, were not espionage or international rivalry between the two Empires but altruism and the need for Christians to help others. It is not present in Conolly, father of the concept of Great Game, no mention of that war of spies that instead, will distinguish him.

Conolly himself will find death in an all-English context. After a brilliant career in the Indian Army, which began in 1823, the year in which he enlisted in the 104*6th Bengal Native Light Cavalry,* he reached the rank of captain in a few years. In 1830 he crossed the whole of Asia and became known thanks to his account *Journey to the North of India through Russia, Persia and Afghanistan,* published in 1834. In the book he enthusiastically and almost fanatically describes the usefulness of British control in those still independent areas. The Crown could have abolished slavery, protected the local cities from the Russians, civilised the natives and above all, opened the region to trade with British merchants. His journey in fact, had been under several points a failure. The path he wanted to take had changed several times along the way, he had risked his life more than once, both because of illness and

---

[103] J.W. Kaye, *Lives*, p. 104.

[104] H. W. C. Davis, *The Great Game in Asia (1800 – 1844).* Proceedings of the British Academy, Vol. 12, London 1926. p. 243.

because of the bandits' hands. His crossing, nevertheless, in addition to motivating him internally, had borne fruit, the information collected in fact, became his currency of exchange with the military, in India. On his journey he had been escorted by the Russians to the Karakum desert, when he left in fact, in 1829, the Russians were still allies of the British and officially he was returning to India after the end of his licence at home. He arrived in India from the Quetta pass, the southern twin of the Khyber Pass, exhausted but alive and despite the chaos of the journey he was ready for a new adventure. His idea was to leave for Kabul and gather information *"for the sake of adding to the information possessed by the Government about those countries"* but whilst he was waiting for the waters to calm down another British agent stole his scene. In 1838 Charles Stoddart was captured and imprisoned whilst carrying out a diplomatic mission in Bokhara. The local Emir, Nasrullah Khan, was a person known for his violence and boldness. According to him, Stoddart, on his arrival in the city, had disrespected him by greeting him without dismounting from his horse. Stoddart was not aware that this could be cause for contempt, because he was accustomed to the customs of the British forces. Conolly decided to leave to try to free his colleague and shortly before crossing Asia he wrote the two aforementioned letters to Rawlinson. Along the way many tried to persuade him, but he, moved by a Christian rather than *political-diplomatic* feeling, continued his way. A few weeks after his arrival, he was imprisoned as a spy and thrown into the *Siah Cha,* the black hole, a six-metre deep pit accessible only by a rope, invaded by mice and cockroaches. It is so likely that is things went differently. The two managed to write letters and receive visits during imprisonment, hardly they would have been able to do so in a hole in the ground. It is much more likely that they were confined to the city prison, the *Zindan.* Stoddart himself, in a letter of March 1839, to his sister, speaks of it. In this story is inserted an important piece for our analysis of the Great Game, Colonel Buteneff. He was a Russian soldier who tried in every way to convince the Emir to let Stoddart go. He had managed to relieve the English agent's imprisonment by making sure that he resided in the private residence of the Russian mission. In my opinion, it would have been difficult for a Government, in a climate of declared conflict, to attempt to free foreign prisoners, especially in highly *disputed* territories. It is true that Great Britain and Russia were allies but it is also true that for the theologians of the Great Game, the plot of spies went on undisturbed, ignoring the agreements made in Europe. Buteneff could do nothing for the salvation of the two agents; when he left the city, they were alive but still prisoners.

On the 10th of December 1841, Prime Minister Palmerston sent a despatch to Bokhara for Stoddart. London still did not know that Conolly had also been captured. The Emir was very offended because, according to him, the Queen had not written to him personally, seizing the cause of his two subjects. The fate of the two soldiers changed for the worse after the death of Alexander Burnes[105] on the 2nd of

---

[105] Burnes was born in Montrose, Scotland in 1805. Very intelligent and expert in the traditions and languages of Asia, he had distinguished himself in the eyes of his superiors for his cleverly designed mission on the Indus. The British wanted to find out if the Indus was navigable and if it was possible to transport goods from the territories of the Company to the Silk Road bazaars beyond the mountain passes. Lord Ellenborough took a golden opportunity, an exchange of gifts between the King of England and the lord of Punjab, to control the river without arousing suspicion among the local lords. Ranjit Singh was a horse lover and it was decided to send 5 horses. Due to the unfavourable climate and the distance, one thousand kilometres, between the mouth of the river and Lahore, capital of Punjab, permission was requested to transport animals on barges. The mission was led by Burnes at the time 25 years old. Short in stature and not at all beautiful, however, he had the adventure in his blood. She was a perfect polyglot because he knew Arabic, Hindu and Persian and a myriad of dialects, dressed in oriental style and knew how to adapt to any situation. Before the mission he was transferred from his regiment, the 1st Bombay

117

November 1841, in Kabul. The news in the city came almost simultaneously with the letter from London. After the British defeat in Afghanistan, culminating in the massacre of more than 16.500 British soldiers and civilians[106], in retreat from the

---

Light Infantry, to the office of the Indian protectorate in Calcutta. Five months of navigation, several charts drawn, and several notebooks filled afterwards, the group arrived in Lahore. Ranjit Singh greeted them in a royal way. The horses, the carriage and the English gifts struck him and the court. Burnes had the task of finding out about the health of his interlocutor and the political moods in case of death. The stop in Lahore lasted about two months, the Marjah reviewed the troops together with Burnes, fired cannonballs in honour of King William IV and treated the British as his peers. The group left Lahore in August 1831 for Ludhiana, the northernmost outpost of the Company. There Burnes meet the person to whom his destiny was destined to bind. The exiled Afghan Sovereign Shah Shujah. The Sovereign had been dethroned in 1826 by the violent Dost Mohammed and Burnes could very well understand why. He was melancholic, weak and without charisma, he did not consider him worthy nor able to sit on the throne of Kabul. Burnes later reached Shimla, the summer capital of the British Raj, where he reported the results of his mission to Governor Lord William Bentick. He received the compliments and above all the trust from the Governor. The opening of the trade was possible and another well-known player, Henry Pottinger, was sent to deal with the emirs of the Sind with the consent of Ranjit Singh. Burnes did not want to stand by and using all his influence on the Governor he proposed a new mission: to explore all the roads leading to India.

[106] If India was the jewel of the Crown, Afghanistan was its thorn in the side. The British never managed to bite the population, they always took the matter lightly and paid with the blood of many the mistakes and wrong choices of a few officials.

118

Afghanistan was in the perspective of the Great Game, the wake-up call for the call to arms. In case of Russian military presence in those territories the British would have been in serious trouble and with them all of India. The Empire never had the same interest in the country as it did in India, and this never allowed the administration of Calcutta and London to fully understand the traditions, customs and above all the needs of the region. While several players studied languages and customs, trying to integrate as much as possible, on the other hand the leaders were more concerned with the colour of the flag that waved over Bala Hisar, the fort of Kabul. With a continuously expanding Russian Empire and the Indian administration in the hands of the Company, the British wanted to avoid in any way a direct confrontation that would lead to crises in trade and debt. Afghanistan was therefore to become a buffer state between the two Empires. London could not risk expanding the Raj as far as Herat and in the same way could not leave free ground to the Russians. Afghanistan needed to be controlled but not colonised. Every secret mission was disguised as a commercial expedition. Officially the British went to Afghan territory to spread English goods in those regions but in reality, their main purpose was to spy and if necessary, discuss with the court of Kabul.

Afghanistan was, and is, a poor little state. Poor because of the fragility of its economy, whose most profitable income comes from opium, small because of the low demographic percentage. The very identity of a unitary state had developed very late, thanks to the weakening of the Safavid dynasty in Persia in 1747. The English themselves contributed to the birth of the land of the Afghans, their expansionist aims in India had put the Moghul Empire in crisis, distracting the court of Delhi from the continuous wars with the populations beyond the borders of Punjab. After a rapid territorial expansion, the Afghan Empire reached the boarders of the Indian Empire, but in a short time everything was reduced. The state was politically very weak

119

because its multi-ethnic structure was varied and often in conflict with each other. Uzbechi, Turkmeni, Tagiki, Hazara and Beluci, with all of Iran's Pashtun Sunnis above them, made up the colourful people under Kabul's control. But before the people, the main obstacle was the geography of the place. Wedged between the Iranian plateau to the west, the Amu Darya River flowing north, the Baluchistan Desert to the south and the Punjab to the east.

Given the delicate nature of the mission was chosen a veteran of the Great Game: Alexander Burnes. He wanted to continue and improve the work of Arthur Conolly done the previous year. By mistake of Burnes in Kabul Conolly would have lost his life, and his head, in Khiva. Burnes' idea was to go to Kabul to try to establish friendly relations with the local usurper Dost Mohammed and in the meantime control his military forces and the defense of the city, then cross the Hindu Kush and the Oxus river, arrive in Bukhara and do similar tasks there and then return to India via the Caspian and Persian. He expected criticism and opposition but in reality, the approval from the Governor arrived in December 1831. As he later learnt, the Whig Government in London was taking the same positions as the Tory Governments, namely extreme Russian-phobia. His expedition was a success. In every city he was very well received and could find out about the situation of the Kingdoms and his power relations in the area. He reached Bokhara where he did not meet the emir who, a few years later, would have two English beheaded. The trip earned him the title of Burnes of Bokhara and the accounts of his trip became very popular. Back in India, he carried out some missions for the Government and then in 1837 he went to Kabul at the short of Dost Mohammed. Burnes was convinced that he was a King worthy of his title because he managed to rule such a turbulent territory. He was convinced that it was useful for English interests to keep him on the throne, but the Governor General, Lord Auckland, was of discordant opinion, and he thought it right to put

Shujah Shah back on the throne of Kabul, even by force if necessary. Meanwhile a Russian captain, Jan Vitkevič, had arrived in the city. The Governor had asked for his removal, but Dost Mohammed had refused and received him at the palace. From Shimla, the Governor had issued a manifesto that disowned Dost Mohammed as Sovereign and in response he had named himself Emir of Afghanistan. After a rapid series of victories, the British took over several cities and succeeded in putting their candidate on the throne. Most of the Army returned to India while Burnes stayed in the city with Sir William MaCnaghten, the representative of the British Government, and a small contingent of men commanded by General William Elphinstone. In the autumn of 1841, a series of factors precipitated the situation, the country was going through an economic crisis and the British presence was perceived as a real invasion. Moreover, according to many, the British paid too much attention to Afghan women. On the 2nd of November, the house of Burnes was attacked by the rebels. He and his brother and his servant were torn apart. The British reprisal only increased the tension. The fort inside the city was poorly defended and fell on the 9th of November. The leader of the revolt was his Dost Mohammed son Akbar Khan. MaCnaghten had understood that the English position was difficult because in deficiencies of a strong military force able to resist the revolt. The various tribes always kept out of state affairs but the British supported Khan. Secret negotiations began. The British envoy wanted to ensure the protection of British interests and the lives of his men. On the 23rd of December they met to negotiate peace but as soon as Akbar Khan arrived, he had them killed and Lord MaCnaghten body was hung in the city market. The last British representative still alive Elphinstone decided for a return to India with all the military and civilians stationed in the country. On the 6th of January 1846, 16,500 men, women and children left the city in the direction of the Khyber Pass. What Elphinstone could not have known was that in reality Khan had no intention of letting

country, Nasrullah Khan no longer felt worried about a British reprisal. On 17th of June 1842 the two prisoners were taken to the main square and beheaded. Some historians report that the two were forced to convert to Islam and even, previously, for saving their lives, Stoddart had to abjure Christianity. The sources, however, question the last point because, in two letters of 14th and 17th March 1839, he not only denied the question of the *black hole,* claiming to be in the city prison, healthy and well fed, but does not mention the religious question at all. Stoddart speaks of freedom if he had chosen to stay and serve the emir and this does not suggest the obligation of abjuration and conversion.

Conolly, despite his contribution paid with his life, was not the first to use the term in a political-diplomatic context. Already in his research Davis had identified, also thanks to the works of J. W. Kaye, some extracts of communications between British

them to reach India alive. Along the way the British had to fight against the Afghan winter, the pitfalls of mountain pass and ambushes, the number of victims increased. The last survivors were massacred in Gandamak a few miles from the English fort of Jalalabad. The only survivor was Doctor William Brydon, who arrived in Jalalabad almost dead. A famous painting by Lady Butler portrays him exhausted on horseback as he reaches the entrance to the fort. The massacre was a shock to the whole Empire. Only overcome in negative by the great mutiny of 1857. The British immediately acted to avenge all the dead, but the answers did not prove to be up to the task, due to a change in leadership of the *Company.* Lord Auckland had had a stroke and the new Governor Sir Ellenborough was determined to end the conflict as soon as possible. After a series of reprisals including the fire in the Kabul Bazaar, the British withdrew from the country and immediately after Dost Mohammed was freed and resumed his place on the throne.

politicians and soldiers in India, on the subject. In the context of the First Anglo-Afghan War, the only testimony is that of Conolly, although in a letter from the most important British agent in Afghanistan, Sir William Hay MaCnaghten, we find a similar sentence. In the summer of 1840, arguing the need to annex Herat to the country, he said: *"We have a beautiful game on our hands"[107]*. This is a statement that can be placed within a geographical context, in case we want to give the Great Game a geographical meaning, but it lacks the idea of an intricate and cumbersome secret service. MaCnaghten seems more interested in having soldiers, weapons and money for his exploits not at all secret.

If we move back in time, we find the term in a despatch by Arthur Wellesley. In 1804, referring to the possibility of military action against the Maratha leader, Holkar, he wrote to Colonel Murray: *"You have now a great game on your hands"[108]*. The term here seems to have a mere symbolic meaning and once again, it cannot be assigned to any of the meanings listed above but is similar, if not identical, to the meaning attributed by MaCnaghten.

These quotations, as well as the many uses of the term made by Kaye in his works, make us understand two fundamental things: the term is much older than the use that Conolly makes of it and every use of it is always linked to an idea of risk. The research I did, including the largest British archives, did not produce a result that

---

[107] J. W. Kaye, *History of the War in Afghanistan*, W. H. Allen & Co, London 1857. p. 56.

[108] Arthur Wellesley al Colonel Murray, 2 May 1804, J. Gurwood, *The Dispatches of field Marshal the Duke of Wellington,* Oxford University Press, Oxford 1837. Vol III pp. 297-298.

included its use before Wellesley. Its oldest French equivalent dates to 1585[109], in the form of *Gros Jeu* whilst *Le grand Jeu* is a term related to tarot and fortune[110]. In German *Grosspiel* is a word used in the Skat card game. In Russian *Igrat po bolshoi* means to play a game with high goals.

We cannot know for sure, but given the many uses in card games[111], and the use linked to an idea of risk, perhaps Conolly has taken the term from this context, to apply it to his idea of mission.

4. *"Little Friend of all the World"*

One of the most interesting aspects of the Great Game is not so much the intricate network of spies and conspiracies, especially considering the real events and not those told, but the use made for propaganda. Imperialist writers have often used historical facts in a fictional way to bring the good version of the Empire to the general public. Before the Second World War, the term was practically unknown to public opinion. Except for some academic texts like those of Davis and Kaye, and

---

[109] N. du Fail, Contes et discours d'Eutrapel, Librairie des Bibliophiles, Paris 1875. p. 252. Vol I. p. 252; A. Renè Lesage, *Gil Blax de Santillane,* Pierre Ribou, Paris 1715. VII, Pe X. Here the term is related to the meaning of high risk.

[110] H. Balzac, *Le Cousin Pons,* Calmann-Lévy, Paris 1847. p. 127, 629.

[111] C. Perry Hargrave, *A History of Playing Cards*, Literary Licensing, LLC, New York 1966.

some stories like those of Maud Diver[112] and John Buchan,[113] the use was rare and often with a completely different meaning. Only one author managed to make the great game the central plot of his novel, and moreover his most famous novel. He was able to create around the theme that exotic and *Victorian* frame that over time have obscured the historical aspect, leaving behind only a fictional idea of a *spy story*, amongst the deserts of Asia.

Rudyard Kipling was for India what Charles Dickens was for London. The narrating voice, the soul and its most famous face.

Kim is his best-known novel. Appearing in 1901 somehow represents his only true novel. Unlike other books and stories, *Kim* can also be appreciated by an adult audience and indeed, the novel does not fit easily into children's literature.

The book was written during his convalescence from pneumonia. He had not lived in India for 12 years, but his fame in the world was at its peak.

Kipling belonged to India. He was born there, grew up there and in many ways his childhood was more like that of Kim than that of David Copperfield.

He was a son of the Empire as well as a son of India, and his two natures meet in his pen. Like every Brit, he was fascinated by the Raj and as an Indian he knew well the nature of his country and the aspects that could produce fascination for a British audience. The culture of the subcontinent exerted a huge influence on British culture. Every great English writer or thinker has written something about Raj. From William

---

[112] M. Diver, *The Great Amulet,* John Lane Company, New York 1908. p. 366; *The Hero of Herat,* Constable & Company, London 1912. p. 162; The *Judgement of the Sword,* G. P. Putnam's sons, New York 1913. p. 530.

[113] J. Buchan, *Greenmantle,* G. H. Doran Company, New York 1916. p. 13.

Jones to Edmund Burke, passing through William Makepeace Thackeray, Jeremy Bentham, John Stuart Mill, James Mill, Lord Macaulay, Harriet Martineau and of course Kipling.

The idea of India as a world suspended in time, full of mystery, charm, riches and peculiarities comes largely from Kipling. He did not tell India how he saw it but how every English man would have liked to see it. Any particularity can be inserted within the Western parameters. To use the words of one of his biographers, Charles Allen:

"What made Kipling so hugely popular in the 1890s was his seemingly unerring instinct for saying, not exactly what the public wanted to hear but what most needed to be said, and for saying it directly and in a way that was instantly quotable, if not singable"[114]

The most obvious example is *Kim*.

The plot of the novel is normal and has nothing *exceptional*. A young Anglo-Indian, the son of an Irish soldier and a local woman, lives his life in the bazaars of Lahore. One day a Buddhist lama from Tibet arrives in the city. The holy man immediately creates a bond with Kim and the two become inseparable friends and travel companions. Kim decides to follow the Tibetan in his search for the sacred river, which flowed from the arrow shot by Buddha. Kim himself is looking for something: his father told him that one day a red bull on a green background will save him. The two cross India far and wide until Kim finally discovers the meaning of her father's words. The Red Bull on a green background was nothing more than the coat of arms of a division of the Anglo-Irish Army. Kim is recognised as a *Sahib*, a white man,

---

[114] C. Allen, *Kipling Sahib. India and the Making of Rudyard Kipling,* Abacus, London 2007. p. 5.

and is taken and sent to St. Xavier, a school for *Sahib*'s children. It is Lama himself who provides for the tuition of the school because he understands the importance of the education and talents of the young man. In the summer Kim is free and once he finishes his studies, he returns to the river with his Buddhist friend. The book ends with the Lama finding the river and purifying himself of his sins.

Apparently, nothing particularly exciting. One of the many novels about India and its many characters, but what makes Kim special is the subplot or the relationship between him and the Game. Kim has been a player since he remembers and as much as he feels free to go around the country, on foot or by train, he acts like a puppet in the hands of the central Government.

Kim has always known Mahbub Ali, an Afghan horse dealer who uses the business as a cover for his job as a spy, paid by the British. Once he discovers his origins, Kim meets Colonel Creighton, the head of the British intelligence service in India. The two of them decide to invest in Kim because they consider it an excellent spy for the imperial cause.

So begins a new search for Kim. He must investigate and discover Russian plans for an imminent uprising in the north and a subsequent invasion.

A novel about the great game written by a writer born in India, during the war of spies, would be a historical source that every scholar of that period would like to have, but unfortunately Kim is not that source because the great game of Kipling is a pure invention, something that never existed.

The great game in *Kim,* on the other hand, is almost a religion. Somehow Kipling builds a new caste that as such has its own rules, habits, traditions and customs: the caste of spies

At the time the novel was set[115], Great Britain did not have an *intelligence service* or even an ethnography department[116]. At the time, in fact, there was only a small Government department that responded to the name of *Survey of India,* responsible for mapping the entire territory of the Raj and more than for espionage, it served to appease the anxiety, all-English, of control. Kipling must have taken the term from Conolly or some work derived from the dead agent's letter to Bokhara. In fact, the protagonist of the novel and the unfortunate missionary have more than one thing in common: they are both Irish, linked to India and have a deep relationship with a spiritual guide. He almost looks like a sacrificial victim on the altar of the defence of the Raj. For Kim, the great game is a ground that grows at the same age as his age: first Lahore, then the north and then the whole country.

Kipling was aware of his creation, he knew that his novel was creating something false and non-existent, but his work was an important piece in the construction of the canon of what he called *The White Man's Burden*. He had a very specific political intent and *Kim* was to be a sort of manifesto of the Empire. Being born in India, he knew very well the problems of the country and the risks that the Empire was running. The English had built an Empire based on trade and not on conquests, if on one hand it could be a boast on the other it was their Achilles' heel. Kipling always put his fame at the service of the *imperial cause*, British public opinion was always very active and interested and the best way to defend certain positions was either to shift attention through literature better than with heated speeches in Parliament, regularly repeated in the *Times*. Often it was writers who dictated the agenda to

---

[115] We do not have the exact dates, but we know from clues in the text that it is set between the Second and Third Anglo-Afghan War and presumably in the last years of the 800.

[116] The department in the novel is the cover for espionage activities.

politicians and not vice versa. Just think of the debates that arose after the publication of the books by Dickens or Thackeray.

After the two Afghan wars the risk of a Russian invasion was very felt, as a man of the Empire and institutions Rudyard Kipling was not immune to the disease of the colonialist: the fear of losing everything. Fear that for the British in India, as well as at home, now had a very specific name: Russia. From the very beginning, he showed resentment towards the Russians. When he was a young student at the United Services College in Westward Ho! he had proposed a petition against Russia but was hindered by the headmaster of the school. A war correspondent during the conflict against the Boers, which we will see later, he realised how difficult it was for English troops to fight in unknown territories and without a reliable system of Intelligence. He was convinced that the only way to keep the Empire's possessions safe was to carry out continuous and targeted border military operations, especially in India.

The reasons that led Kipling to use the Great Game as a backdrop for his novel are many. The first one was certainly the political one, because being interested in the control of Central Asia was an easy call for the integrity of the Empire itself. In a pessimistic scenario, in fact, a Russian invasion would not only have deprived the Crown of the subcontinent but would have shaken all relations with China and Asian countries, cut off communications with Australia and the oceanic colonies, put the colonies in Africa in difficulty and taken millions and millions of pounds out of the state budget and hundreds and hundreds of soldiers out of the Army.[117] But there

---

[117] The question of the defence of the Empire was always one of the problems at the top of the list of the various Prime Ministers in office. For a long time now, the British Army was composed of a very limited number of men, apart from the two world wars there was never the compulsory conscription. Rather than an Army of

129

land, the British have given more importance to the navy. The European territories were defended by the Royal Navy stationed in the territorial waters and in the Mediterranean. After the 1857 revolt for security reasons the number of Indian soldiers had been reduced and that of the British increased by about a third but the number of soldiers that the British could afford to keep in India was limited. In 1863 a commission had discovered that the mortality rate among British soldiers in India from 1800 to 1865 had been 69 per 1000 while among European neighbours the rate was 10 per 1000. The committee also highlighted a worrying and burdensome aspect for the Crown. The commissioners had reported that in an Army of 70,000 men each year 4830 would die while 5880 would fall ill. For every soldier in India, the Government spent £100, which meant more than £1 million wasted every year. The same Army in Europe would have cost £800,000 less. The purpose of the commission was to highlight the usefulness of an Army of indigenous people and the futility in sending British soldiers meeting death and tropical diseases. The Sepoys, as the Indian infantrymen were called, were to remain a substantial part of the Raj's troops. This not only saved pounds, but also created a cohesion between the occupants and the employed. The Indian soldier served his country while the Indian civilian did not feel occupied by foreign troops. The command of the Army in the hands of British officers also allowed a continuous updating in the techniques of war and a control of the mood of the troops in order to avoid a new revolt. In 1881 the Indian Army consisted of 69,647 British soldiers and 125,000 indigenous soldiers. At home, the percentages between English and Irish were 65,809 and 25,353. In the entire imperial Army, Indian troops accounted for 62% of the total. Lord Salisbury went so far as to say that India was "*an English barrack in the Oriental Seas from which we may draw any number of troops without paying for them*" and he was right. In the 50 years before the Great War, Indian soldiers were

was also an ideological reason, since the *creator of* the concept of great game in Kipling's eyes looked almost like a martyr, Conolly took the burden of his race on his shoulders and lost his life in defence of his Empire. In addition, we can also find a reason and a mystical-religious aspect. The theme of faith in *Kim* is very strong and indeed in some places the Buddhism of Lama Teshoo is the real enemy of the protagonist who risks several times, to take him off the road.

A very interesting aspect of the novel as well as of the society of the time, is that related to education. It is not my intention to explain all the reforms for the school and the functioning of the complex British education system, but I want to dwell on some singular aspects of what can be called *Victorianism among the school desks*. In the novel we see how Kim is sent to a specific school for *Sahib* where he learns the *trade* of the spy. Leaving aside the fact that this specific type of school turns out to be an invention of Kipling, the model in force at home was not so different. The Victorian school was created to fight the comfortable world of family life. The children should not have grown up in the belief that everything was easy and affordable for everyone, but rather, everything should be conquered by sweat and sometimes even blood. The priest, and founder of several schools, Nathaniel Woodard wrote in 1848:

---

sent on twelve missions from China to Uganda. The Government relied so much on Indian troops that strong debates and criticism were stirred up in Parliament. Those who, like the liberal W. E Forster, accused the Government of not trusting national patriotism, preferring Muslims, Sikhs and Gurkha to British soldiers. Even a musical parody was born at that time: *We don't want to fight, But, by Jingo, if we do, we won't go to the front ourselves, We'll send the mild Hindoo.*

"The chief thing to be desired is to remove the child from the noxious influence of home"[118]

The school was to forge the future *leaders* of the Empire. Children were to be tempered, educated, and returned to the world as adults capable of fighting and leading the nation.

Thomas Arnold, dean of Rugby wrote:

"A thorough English gentleman Christian, manly, and enlightened is more, I believe, than Guizot or Sismondi could comprehend; it is a finer specimen of human nature than any other country, I believe, could furnish."[119]

A Christian gentleman. The spirit of the Empire in two words. Victorian education had two pillars: religion and sport.

Whilst the students had to be good Christians, attending all the religious ceremonies of the college, on the other hand the sport helped to build the body and form the character for the days when the cricket bat would be replaced by the rifle.

"Sport was the rock on which Britain's greatness was built"[120]

Sport was the winning weapon of imperial education.

---

[118] N. Woodard, *A Plea for the Middle Classes,* Joseph Masters, London 1848. p.13.

[119] T. Arnold, *The Life and Correspondence of Thomas Arnold*, John Murray, London 1845. p.391.

[120] Jeremy Paxman during an episode of *Empire* a BBC documentary

"Englishmen are not superior to Frenchmen or Germans in brains or industry, or the science or apparatus of war, in the history of the British Empire, it is written that England has owed her Sovereignty to her sports"[121]

In the face of such a strong interest in sport and fitness, the creation of the Boy Scouts by Sir Robert Baden-Powell in 1907 appears natural. The first 20 boys brought to Brownsea Island, in the bay of Poole, represented the heads of a movement that would take root in every part of the world. The advantage of Scouting was to build the *imperial* character even in those young people who had not attended the expensive elite schools. The Scout's life was not that different from a soldier. Hierarchies, uniforms, signals and order are still today, the hallmarks of this movement and it is not surprising that at the outbreak of the First World War, almost every scout voluntarily enlisted, after all they had been trained for that.

It is in this context that perhaps the most famous poem of the imperial era is inserted: *Vitaï Lamp* by Henry Newbolt.

There's a breathless hush in the Close to-night—

Ten to make and the match to win—

A bumping pitch and a blinding light,

An hour to play and the last man in.

And it's not for the sake of a ribboned coat,

Or the selfish hope of a season's fame,

But his captain's hand on his shoulder smote

---

[121] J. A. Mangan, *The Games Ethic and Imperialism: Aspects of the Diffusion of an Ideal,* Frank Cass Publishers, London 2003. p. 35.

"Play up! play up! and play the game!"

The sand of the desert is sodden red,—

Red with the wreck of a square that broke;—

The Gatling's jammed and the Colonel dead,

And the regiment blind with dust and smoke.

The river of death has brimmed his banks,

And England's far, and Honour a name,

But the voice of a schoolboy rallies the ranks:

"Play up! play up! and play the game!"

This is the word that year by year,

While in her place the school is set,

Every one of her sons must hear,

And none that hears it dare forget.

This they all with a joyful mind

Bear through life like a torch in flame,

And falling fling to the host behind—

"Play up! play up! and play the game!"

The last verse may remind you of something.

Peter Hopkirk is convinced that Conolly has taken from here the term Great Game on the other hand, he as a young man had attended the school of Rugby. We cannot know for sure.

War in the same way, it was nothing more than a game. The team became the battalion, the captain the general and the points the victories. Today it may seem ridiculous and perhaps childish but for the time the best way to create a good soldier was to create a good sportsman. Courage, team spirit, discipline, respect for rules and rituals, made a cricket game equal to a war against the Boers. Except for the dead. This may explain the fact that almost all modern sports were created in Great Britain.

But education looked back more than forward. In an 1899-time table from the Rugby school, we can see the lessons of a sixteen-year-old boy of the time. In 25 hours per week he attended 15 hours of classical studies. The Roman world was an example to the offspring of the Empire. The Empire had become great thanks to industry, but its model was the ancient one. Latin, Greek, classical literature and history were the main subjects and therefore it is not surprising that a visitor of the time could be struck by the fact that all the students of Rugby knew the names of the Roman Emperors, in chronological order but, hardly anyone, knew how to place the city of Birmingham on a map. Their job was not to find Birmingham but to lead the Empire.

That is what Kim learns in St. Xavier's. Kipling romances the story and creates a school for little spies but does not stray so far from the reality of the facts.

Criticism of the novel is divided into two positions: those who on one hand define Kipling as an imperialist racist, who tried to demonstrate British superiority over the Eastern peoples, and those who on the other, emphasise his ability to describe characters and religions in detail, putting aside his well-known prejudices[122]. The fact is that Kipling has been able to build a character who in some ways steals the scene from little Kim. Kipling build a Great Game, does not tell the real one, and

---

[122] For an in-depth analysis of Buddhism in the Victorian period I recommend the text by J. J. Franklin *the Lotus and the Lion: Buddhism and the British Empire.* An entire chapter is dedicated to *Kim.*

this, happens with the Buddhism in the book. The Teshoo Lama is not a normal Buddhist for India but rather is outside its place of origin. He is not Indian but Tibetan and wears a red headgear and this distinguishes him within the movement of the Lotus. *Yellow* Buddhism was the most widespread in India and therefore it would have been more sensible to use one of that sects as a guide for the protagonist but in a way, Kipling wants to untie the realities around his little friend from all over the world. Kim is not a real Indian but is the son of a *sahib*, the Lama is Tibetan, Creighton is an Englishman and the seller of horses an Afghan. The only Indian characters we meet are those who serve as the backdrop to the story. Characteristic and picturesque, noisy and disorganised. The contemporary Kipling reader could thus see how unfit they were for self-Government. Dozens and dozens of castes had transformed India into a pot of peoples and languages and above all religions. If religion cannot unite, politics would have thought of it. The novel gives a not negative but not even positive judgement on the East. The best that India can offer is chaos or at most a hybrid form of religious philosophy, or philosophical religion as Buddhism, whilst Europeans offer control, order, civilisation and especially the Great Game. The game described is a form of religion, a caste as mentioned above, suitable only for those who want an active life, whilst Buddhism is a haven for those who want to live their existence in a contemplative and relaxed way. Not a *British* way of seeing the world.

Kipling inserts in the novel a very British aspect but of which we have no testimony in the *real* Great Game: Freemasonry. Most likely many officials were affiliated to the lodges but not for this reason the whole apparatus had to be within the secret society.

Unfortunately, information on Freemasonry in India is very scarce and Kipling's relationship with the lodges is also shrouded in mystery, he was very attentive to his own privacy and the little information that has come to us is what we find in his works. One of the four short stories in the collection *The phantom 'Rickshaw and other Eerie tales is* entitled *The man who would be King* and deals explicitly with the subject; Kipling is present in first person in the plot. The work was published whilst still living in India and was born as a collection of texts to be read by train; it made up the fifth volume of the *Indian Railway Library* collection, librettos on sale in stations for a rupee and printed by A. H. Wheeler. The self-narrating the story is universally identifiable in Kipling and Freemasonry, its belonging to a lodge and rituals are a red thread throughout the story.

According to the official website of Indian Freemasonry, the first lodge was opened in Calcutta in 1774, but until the second half of the nineteenth century the Indians did not care about this umpteenth *thing* imported by the British. Kipling joined in 1885, when he joined the *Hope and Perseverance* Lodge in Lahore. Freemasonry for India was in practice the only place where young people or intellectuals could meet to discuss, completely ignoring all the prohibitions of relations between castes. In his autobiography, which came out after his death, he wrote:

"Here I met Muslims, Hindus, Sikhs, members of the Arya and Brahmo Samaj, and Jew Tyler, who was priest and butcher to his little community in the city. So yet another world opened to me which I needed"[123]

And he was convinced of the usefulness of a common place for all regions and Freemasonry offered all this:

---

[123] R. Kipling, *Something of unknown, Doubleday, Doran and Company, Garden City and Myself for my friends known*. Doubleday, Doran & Company, Garden City 1937. p. 78.

"Freemasonry offered a system that gratified both his craving for a world religion and his devotion to the secret bond that unites the men who bear the burden of the world's work"[124]

No wonder then that in his eyes the Great Game assumes almost a Masonic connotation. A mechanism made of courage, spirit of brotherhood, codes, secrets and amulets to recognise each other, the transformation of the game into a travelling lodge.

There are two aspects that highlight the strong influence of Freemasonry in the Great Kim Game: recruitment and initiation. If we read only the parts concerning these two aspects, we would hardly place them amongst the practices of an Indian Government department. The first consists in being presented by an elderly member and the second in a ritual that ends with the amulet of spies. It is still Mahbub Ali who convinces Colonel Creighton to accept Kim:

[Kim] has [experience] already, Sahib. As a fish controls the water he swims in"[125]

Kim is enlisted and then, before leaving for the first mission, undergoes a complex spiritual magic ritual. Once received the amulet is officially an agent of the Great Game.

Edward Said in his introduction to the Penguin edition of Kim, which later became a chapter of his work *Culture and Imperialism*, does not deviate from his certainties, not to say prejudices, always present when he speaks of the East and almost never confirmed by his statements. Said sins of presumption every time he treats authors

---

[124] C. Carrington, *Rudyard Kipling: His life and Work,* Doubleday, Doran and Company, Garden City. p. 55.

[125] R. Kipling, *Kim,* Norton Critical Edition, New York 2002. p. 147.

who mention, speak or describe the East in their works. The basic thesis, in every text, is that no Westerner can write something exact about the East because it is contaminated by prejudices, errors and beliefs that do not come close to reality. Said's theses and the criticisms of his theses are well-known, and this is not the place to take them up again, but I would like to point out what I think are the errors, often trivial, that the Palestinian scholar makes with reference to Kim.

Said writing the introduction to a book was supposed to prove that he had not only read it but also put aside his prejudices. He probably considered Kipling the umpteenth white and racist westerner, but this could not be because it would be difficult for him to explain his errors of judgement otherwise. Starting with the finale, he takes it for granted that Kim decides to become a British agent and not a Buddhist monk when it is easy to see that the book's finale remained open; nowhere does Kipling reveal his choice of character. He also writes with an immoderate certainty that for Kipling the Great Game was a political interest very similar to the Cold War for the control of Central Asia when, it is equally well-known that they do not know with certainty the reasons that drove Kipling to choose this subject. In my opinion, for Kipling the Great Game is not a nineteenth century *Cold War* as interpreted by Said, nor even less, a network of spies aimed at controlling the subjugated populations, not even the Department of *Survey of India,* nor even a colonial version of Freemasonry. All these aspects were just to create a frame. The content was the Empire. Kipling was a fervent believer in an ideal Empire led by men moved by a spirit of justice and honesty but unfortunately, he knew that the Raj was not so perfect. On the contrary, having grown up in Lahore, he knew well the limits of the officials and rulers of the Empire[126] and could not have told a true version but only an imperfect one, thus allowing the public to compare it with the

---

[126] Said tend to ignore this.

simple and perfect spirituality of Lama Teshoo. He has thus built an ideal, poetic, adventurous and simple imperial Government. The public knew full well that India was not like that, the chronicles and stories filled the pages of the newspapers all the time, so he gave the world a perfect version of the Empire and at the same time sent a signal to his friends in Government.

For this reason, it is difficult to accept a thesis that attempts to place the novel in a frame of comparison between East and West, pending in favour of the conquerors. Kipling had to invent in order not to disfigure with the East and that should be enough. If there is a comparison, it does not mean that it is automatically to be understood negatively, and where a comparison can appear, a suggestion of superiority of the West over the East cannot easily be highlighted. Kim plays inside himself, too. Mahbub Ali and Lama Teshoo try to attract little Kim to their side and we do not know how it ended because Kipling leaves the ending to the free interpretation of each one. The Great Game itself cannot be a good representation of the West because outside of Creighton and Kim all other agents are Indian or otherwise Asian.

The meaning of the Great Game for Kipling cannot be separated from that of Buddhism. They are two ways to build Kim's character and personality. In both you will find people with secrets not to be shared, both have to break free from their world to follow the path indicated, full of difficulties and obstacles. Kim must try to play with the dedication of Mahbub Ali and the detachment of the Teshoo Lama.

II

"Success is the ability to go from one failure to another with no loss of enthusiasm."

Winston Churchill

CHURCHILL

1896 - 1898

Chapter Three

Passage to... Westminster

A politician with a uniform

"In the closing decade of the Victorian era the Empire had enjoyed so long a spell of almost unbroken peace, that medals and all they represented in experience and adventure were becoming extremely scarce in the British Army. The veterans of the Crimea and the Indian Mutiny were gone from the active list. The Afghan and Egyptian warriors of the early eighties had reached the senior ranks. Scarcely a shot had been fired in anger since then."[127]

That is what a young Winston Churchill wrote. A Victorian soldier who felt like a beast in chains, willing to fight alone against all the enemies of the Empire.

The young Churchill was, in some ways, completely different from the way we know him today. There was not yet a *chubby* man in a black jacket and bow tie, always with a cigar between his fingers, with a difficult speech and rough and hasty ways. The political Churchill was yet to take over the soldier. Yet it was his experience as a soldier that shaped his political soul. Although he could not stand the Army, for all his life he maintained a high respect for the soldiers and the figure of the soldier, he even went as far as to order the candidates in the parliamentary elections, immediately after the Second World War, to be photographed and to present themselves amongst the voters wearing their uniforms.

----

[127] W. Churchill, *A Roving Commissione: My Early Life,* Charles Scribner's sons, New York 1930. p. 74.

Churchill's life was a succession of wars, clashes, battles, victories and defeats. Since he was old enough to handle a sword or gun, he occupied the scene in every war of the Empire. His role in the Great Game was marginal but interesting, especially for the implications in the Great War. Churchill travelled a great deal, especially as a young man, and unlike most of his contemporaries he did not see India as a stage but as a cage; when his regiment was sent to Northern India, he complained a lot with his mother. Lady Churchill was her son's right-hand man in most of her exploits. Churchill was astute, cheeky but lacking in something that belonged to his mother: a long column. His knowledge often helped his son, especially in periods when the family did not sail in water, economically, good.

The young Winston was aiming high, he wanted a political post at any cost, but he also wanted to be able to present himself to the voters as a war hero. His situation was complicated, especially because of his economic situation. He wanted to go where it was easy to make a career and earn fame, South Africa or Egypt not India. The days when a period in India would produce wealth and glory were over.

He tried in every way, especially using his mother's knowledge, to have a period of leave or a mission in another country but without success and so on the 11th of September 1896 him and his regiment set sail from Southampton to Bombay. He had left London in the middle of the Queen's Jubilee celebrations and was heading towards the suffocating heat of the Raj.

His arrival was certainly not one of the best, disembarked from the *SS Britannia*, he had to take a lifeboat to reach the port of Bombay, in the landing manoeuvres he received a tug on the shoulder, whilst holding on to the ladder, an accident that will cause him pain for the rest of his life, he could no longer practice sports such as tennis or polo, and often had to wear a leather harness under his shirt.

From Bombay the men were moved to Bangalore in the Presidency of Madras. It was a coveted destination because it was a thousand metres above sea level and that meant freshness. Churchill was now an officer and thanks to his position he had the allowance for housing, and this allowed him to stay in a real house rather than in the camp of tents, outside the city. The day passed between exercises, games and parades.

Churchill's main interest at that time was polo. He and his teammates wanted to be the first cavalry regiment to win the *Regimental Cup* of the Indian Empire. Above all, he wanted to be able to use the mighty Arab ponies that the regiment of Poona used. After a few years, they were able to get the right horses and the tournament was a success; Churchill proved himself by astounding everyone. After polo he dedicated himself to making his horse run, even if from England, even at the request of the Prince of Wales, he was advised not to trust that sector known for its lack of honesty in racing. As always, Churchill did his own thing, continuing with the races and becoming a jockey.

In India, Churchill noticed one thing, his ability to speak languages. His ability to make speeches by attracting everyone's attention.

"A liking for words and for the feel of words fitting and falling into their places like pennies in the slot. I caught myself using a good many words the meaning of which I could not define precisely. I admired these words, but was afraid to use them for fear of being absurd"[128]

In the winter of 1896 he began to study, not like his tutors or as they did at school. He wanted to understand everything around him, history, philosophy, economics and politics came into his life in a new way. In a short time, his main activity was the study, he read the great British authors, he had himself bought or sent the volumes he could not find, and he even went so far as to read more books at the same time, dividing the day. He had his mother send him the volumes in the *Annual Register*

---

[128] W. Churchill, *My earl life: 1874 – 1904,* Touchstone, New York 1996. p. 109.

that contained all the public facts of Great Britain. He began to learn about actions in parliament, debates, party choices, approved laws and debates. He developed a sympathy for Disraeli's work and a certain disgust for Gladstone.

"Woman suffrage was ridiculous, contrary to natural law and the practice of civilised states. Wives were adequately represented by their husbands [...] Spinsters would back religious intolerance and every kind of hysterical fad. Admits females to the polls and all power passes to their hands. Indeed, if you give women votes you must ultimately allow women to sit as members of Parliament. It was, he darkly prophesied, only the thin end of the wedge""[129]

In his letters to his mother he made an explicit request to go to war, the movements in the northern borders had generated in him an interest for action. He wanted to go down into battle. His mother did not agree at all and rejoiced when the conflict in Greece, in which Churchill was interested, ended before he managed to get himself sent as an envoy. He even wanted his mother to contact the King of Greece, his friend, and demanded a loan from Lord Rothschild.

Winston Churchill's first steps into politics took place during a three-month leave period. He returned to England and on the way, he discovered peace in Greece. He took a trip to Italy and then came home. He had been in London for a few days when he decided to visit St. Stephen's Chambres by Fitzroy Stewart, the secretary of the *Conservative Central Office,* to whom he expressed his desire to enter parliament. Since there were no seats available, he was sent to Bath for a speech. He received a lot of applause and newspaper articles, but it is curious to note that in that speech

---

[129] W. Manchester, *The Last Lion: Winston Churchill: visions of glory, 1874 – 1914,* Bantam Books Trade Paperbacks, New York 2013. p. 24; CV I/2 767, 768, 765.

Churchill harshly criticised the Liberal Party, a party to which he would join a few years later when he abandoned the Conservative Party.

Churchill's speech was a real defence of the Empire, he was very skilled in linking its glory to the success of the Tories.

"There are not wanting those who say that in this Jubilee year our Empire has reached the height of its glory and power, and that we now should begin to decline, as Babylon, Carthage, and Rome declined. Do not believe these croakers, but give the lie to their dismal croaking by showing by our actions that the vigour and vitality of our race is unimpaired and that our determination is to uphold the Empire that we have inherited from our fathers as Englishmen, that our flag shall fly high upon the sea, our voice be heard in the councils of Europe, our Sovereign supported by the love of her subjects, then shall we continue to pursue that curse marked out for us by an all-wise hand and carry out our mission of bearing peace, civilisation, and good Government to the uttermost ends of the earth"[130]

Whilst on leave, unrest broke out in the north of India. In 1893 an Anglo-Afghan border was created. For London, Afghanistan was the perfect element between the Tsarist Empire and the Raj. The problem, however, was that the areas on this side of the border were considered parts of the Raj but in fact there was no control because the tribes who lived there continued to maintain their autonomy. The British, however, never considered the risk of interfering in tribal situations, difficult to understand for a foreign observer. Over time, Raj's projects began to interfere with the independence of the tribes. Roads, railways, forts, telegraph offices and outposts were built. Trouble began when the Pathan tribe began to exert its holy influence that claimed to be immune to British bullets. Calcutta was aware of these things and

---

[130] W. Manchester, *The last...,* p. 249.

they immediately communicated the situation to London, so the Government immediately decided on a punitive expedition. Sir Bindon Blood oversaw the expedition. Churchill who was still in England when he heard the news, following the promise made by the general, was asked for help in case of war. Churchill then, sailed immediately to India.

Before leaving, Churchill had telegraphed the general to remind him of the promise he had made in the past, and throughout the voyage, at each port, he checked whether an answer had come to him; only in India he did receive a telegram, his glorious desires to fight were immediately broken as a result of the general's answer, but fortunately new, much more interesting doors opened for the young Winston.

"Very difficult. No vacancies. Come as correspondent. Will try to fit you. In B. B"[131]

He first had to divert to Bangalore, he needed a written permission from his colonel before reaching Blood's base camp. From London, his mother took care of finding him a newspaper willing to pay him for the articles. The *Times* was not interested but the *Daily Telegraph* offered to pay five pounds per article, whilst in India, the *Pioneer* was willing to pay for a 300-word daily telegram.

General Blood had located his headquarters at the Malakand Pass.

Every action of Churchill at the front was aimed at success, not military but political. Good action on the ground would have allowed him to campaign well. Unlike the various war correspondents, Churchill watched the war closely because instead of transcribing the official communiqués, he went to the front line, watched the battle

---

[131] CV I/2 775; RC 123.

and sometimes even took command of some campaigns, when the officers were killed.

"I shall get a medal and perhaps a couple of clasps, I should like to come back and wear my medals at some big dinner or some other function"[132]

That is what he wrote to his mother in those days.

Churchill risked a lot during a day in September, the Pathan had reached and surrounded a company that the young Winston was following. He was forced to join the battle, abandoning his role as an envoy and resuming his role as a soldier. At one-point during a violent attack he had been sent by a colonel to the rear, to warn that they were in need, but he, with a stratagem, stalled to avoid passing through the one who escapes in the face of danger, the way to Westminster, in fact, could not pass through that path.

The problem, however, was dictated by the fact that many of Churchill's accounts were not well received by the imperial military *establishment*. He told many things that the general public, and especially other countries, should not have known, and allowed himself to criticise some choices that were made such as the one in which he stressed that the Army was not able to cover the retreat of troops well, especially because they were based on selfish beliefs rather than certain data. The long marches were not supplied with adequate rations, the recruitment service was poor, and civilians were often put in danger.

"There will not be wanting those who will remind me that in this matter my opinion finds no support in age or experience. To such I shall reply that if what is written is

---

[132] M. Paterson, *Winston Churchill,* David & Charles Book, Cincinnati 2005. p. 111.

false or foolish, neither ager nor experience should fortify it; and if it is true, it needs no such support"[133]

On his return to Bangalore, however, Churchill made a bad discovery, consulting the *Daily Telegraph* he not only found out that his articles had been modified and cut but above all, they were not signed. He had created a figure and a thought, with the idea of spreading his personality in public opinion and suddenly he realised that he had simply become *a young soldier.*

But his mother from London undertook to bring the name of that young officer to all her contacts. They all knew of his writings in a short time, including the Prince of Wales. Churchill, however, had underestimated the Army and soon found himself blocked by his superiors. The high ranks of the Army in India still did not appreciate the words of young Winston. Although he had been appointed permanent correspondent by the *Daily Telegraph*, the battlefields had become a forbidden zone. He tried, as always, to bypass his superiors and asked his mother to put pressure on someone in London. At the beginning he received a *no* as an answer, also from his friend the Field-Marshal of Ireland, Lord Roberts, but later he managed to be nominated as a member of Sir William Lockhart's staff.

Churchill not only needed to make himself known to the general public, he also needed money. The articles did not yield enough to support themselves and would not be enough later to maintain an election campaign. He decided to have a report of his campaign published alongside General Blood's *The story of the Malakand Field Force,* released in March 1898. After a troubled editorial history, he entrusted everything to his mother and uncle who had tried, in every way, previously to write a book on the same subject. In a few weeks, he raised more money than his four-

---

[133] WSC I 349; CV I/2 830

year pay check as a subordinate. The book was a success. He even received compliments from the Prince of Wales who sent a copy of the text to his sister, Empress Widow of Germany. He advised Churchill to stay in the Army but Winston, despite wanting to watch the battles as an envoy and not as a soldier, hated the Army and did not feel carried away for the career that was to serve as a springboard for Westminster.

But India was no longer a continuous battlefield, the new horizon for soldiers was Africa. Kitchener had started his campaign in Sudan two years earlier to avenge General Gordon, killed in Khartoum. Churchill began again, trying every possible way to convince Kitchener to take him with him, but Kitchener simply hated the young Winston. He was a soldier loyal to the uniform and had felt terribly offended by the perpetuated attacks on the General Staff, in the articles in the *Telegraph*. Repeatedly, he refused to let Churchill arrive in Africa. His mother from England filled everyone she met with letters, organised dinners, afternoon tea and meetings in the gardens. She went to the *War Office* again and again and even went to Cairo personally to try to influence the general up close, but she always got a *no* in response. Meanwhile Churchill returned to England for a licence, his superiors were happy to take him away from the Raj. In London he moved all the strings known to him in order to succeed in his intent to reach Sudan, he even used the name of the Prince of Wales. The Prime Minister's secretary had read the text and arranged a meeting with Lord Salisbury, who wanted to congratulate him on his excellent work. Churchill used the influence of the Prime Minister to his advantage, as soon as the meeting was over, he wrote him a letter asking that Downing Street put pressure on the *War Office*. Salisbury saw nothing wrong and wrote to Lord Cromer, the British consul in Egypt, naming to him Churchill. Shortly after the arrival of the letter a British officer died and as usual it was the job of the *War Office* to replace him. Lord Cromer suggested Churchill and so eventually Kitchener had to surrender. He had power over the colonial troops but the control over the British soldiers was still under the authority of the *War Office*. Churchill was still in England and after having

153

borrowed a large sum and made an agreement with the *Morning Post,* for 15 pounds per article, he left for Egypt. He did not even wait for permission from his regiment in India, he had written to his superiors and had not received an answer. Convinced of the silent assent he left.

We will see the campaign alongside Kitchener later, but it should first be pointed out that Churchill used the situation to his advantage, once again, by creating articles that became the subject of debate at home and caused himself a great wound that he would show off in the election campaign. After his victory in Sudan, he returned to India at the invitation of the new Vicereine Lady Curzon, reunited with his regiment and resigned permanently from the Army.

Churchill had gone to India against his will, but India had given him a lot of money back, he had discovered his true path, the political one, and he had understood what his greatest gift was, the word and the writing. Now all he had to do was get a seat in parliament. In 1899 he had greeted the Army happy with his decision but could not know that the Army would return to him shortly, with a hard impact.

Another person, however, was willing to do anything to go to India, many efforts were made, and many obstacles still had to be overcome.

III

"The miracle of the world...the biggest thing that the English are doing anywhere."

Lord Curzon

CURZON

1888 - 1905

Chapter Four

Imperialism at teatime.

1. Victorian waltzes.

The years from Victoria's ascent to the throne in 1837 to the first Labour Government in 1924, stealing a well-known expression, represent the British *Short Century*. In a way Britain has carried on the nineteenth century beyond its natural end point. The First World War succeeded in undermining that set of values, rules, traditions, beliefs and prejudices that gave meaning to *Victorianism* but did not put it into deep crisis. McDonald's Government questioned not only the political system but also the Empire and its certainties, and there were many of them. Queen Victoria, summit of that national, international and imperial system, has had the ability to make the most of her influence on the court, on the people and above all on the Parliament. From the Viscount of Melbourne to the Marquis of Salisbury every week, no matter how powerful, each Prime Minister bowed before the Sovereign and received praise or reprimands for the policies adopted by his Government. In total 20 Governments and ten Prime Ministers have spent years in the corridors of Buckingham Palace, just completed at the beginning of his reign.

To say that the separation of powers has creaked under his reign is a euphemism. Her long reign had given her immense power. In London was the Prime Minister to draw the boundaries of the Crown but grey zone were, we can say, the territory preferred by Victoria. Strong of his fame amongst the people, she very often used her influence rather than her actual power to move the threads of politics.

Loyal to the nation and Empire the Queen never missed the opportunity to influence and often bend Governments to her will. During her long reign there were often institutional crises caused by her frequent presence on the political scene. More than one Prime Minister had to defend himself in Parliament against accusations of being

159

manipulated or subjected to the powerful Sovereign. Obviously, every Prime Minister knew how to use the matter to his advantage. For example, Disraeli[134] made her become Empress of India and she in return made him become Count of Beaconsfield and turned into hell the political career of his rival Gladstone[135].

The feud between the two politicians has indelibly marked the reign of Victoria. One conservative and the other liberal have turned the House of Commons into a battlefield for almost 20 years.

The British policy[136] between the end of the Nineteenth and the beginning of the twentieth Century has been a continuous mediation between the need and desire for

---

[134] R. Aldous, *The Lion and the Unicorn: Gladstone vs Disraeli,* Pimlico, London 2007; R. Harris, *The Conservatives — A History.* Bantam, London 2011; C. Hibbert, Disraeli: *A Personal History.* Harper Collins, London 2004; W Kuhn, *The Politics of Pleasure —A Portrait of Benjamin Disraeli.* The Free Press, London 2006; N. Alano, *Disraeli,* De Vecchi Editore, Milan 1967.

[135] R. Jenkins, *Gladstone: A Biography.* Random House Trade Paperbacks, New York 1995; D. W. Bebbington, *The Mind of Gladstone: Religion, Homer and Politics,* Oxford University Press, Oxford 2004.

[136] S. L. Steinbach, *Understanding the Victorians: Politics, Culture and Society in Nineteenth-Century Britain,* Routledge, London 2011; P. Adelman, *Gladstone, Disraeli and Later Victorian Politics,* Routledge, London 1997; J. Conlin, *Evolution and the Victorians: Science, Culture and Politics in Darwin's Britain,* Bloomsbury Academic, London 2014; P. Adelman, *Gladstone, Disraeli and Later Victorian Politics,* Longman, London 2010; I. St John, *Disraeli and the Art of Victorian*

internal reformists and the defence of the ever-expanding Empire. Disraeli, Gladstone, Cecil were the protagonists of the national political scene from 1868 to 1902. The two rivals fought over the chair of power, but both agreed to defend and hold the Empire together and in a Europe that was travelling ever faster towards extreme militarism Britain could no longer afford to remain without a real Army.

Disraeli during his first term expanded the electoral base hoping for an advantage for his party. The Queen tried in every way to support him, she advised Edward Smith-Stanley to resign, paving the way for Downing Street to her friend. He could not do much during the 11 months in power, with the new reform of the electorate new elections were necessary and at the end of 1868 the new electoral base proved to be a disaster. The *Reform Act*[137] of 1867 had not produced the desired results and the Queen was forced to assign the task of forming a new Government to William Ewart Gladstone. The policies of the liberal Prime Minister all went in the direction of the exaltation of personal freedoms and commercial autonomy. In his first term as Prime Minister Gladstone promoted a major reform of the British Army. Known as *Cardwell Reform*[138]. Britain was the only European nation not to have a system

---

Politics, Anthem Press, London 2010; I. St John, *Gladstone and the Logic of Victorian Politics,* Anthem Press, London 2010.

[137] C. Hall, *Defining the Victorian nation: class, race, gender and the British Reform Aalct of 1867*, Cambridge University Press, Cambridge 2000; J.B. Conacher, *Emergence of British Parliamentary Democracy in the Nineteenth Century: Passing of the Reform Acts of 1832, 1867 and 1884-1885*, John Wiley & Sons Ltd, London 1971.

[138] T. Royle, *Britain's Lost Regiments,* Aurum Press Ltd, London 2014; E. L. Woodward, *The Age of Reform 1815-1870,* Oxford university Press, Oxford 1963;

of conscription because it had always been convinced that civil rather than military officials were more useful to control the vast Empire, and in the worst case the *Royal Navy* was preferable to an Army. These beliefs began to creak as early as the Napoleonic Wars, but it was during the Crimean War that the alarms sounded loud in the ears of Westminster and Downing Street. The 25 thousand English soldiers sent to the front left the island without the protection of trained troops and the following year during the Indian uprising almost all British soldiers were used to quell the mutiny. In 1862, under the Conservative Government of Smith-Stanley, the committee put in charge or the matter was studying a solution and reported to Parliament the shortcomings of the Army and the *House of Commons* immediately attempted to act. The biggest obstacle to any reform of the Army was always the opposition of the Commander-in-Chief of the Army, the Queen's cousin the Duke of Cambridge, and especially the *East-India Company*. After the mutiny with the dissolution of the *Company* and the transfer of power directly to the Crown the reform of the Army could begin[139].

In 1870 the parliament, on the 2nd of August, voted to increase the armed forces. 20,000 men. The Army increased from 25 to 45 thousand men and £2 million pounds were allocated in credit for their maintenance. The following year, a booklet was

---

A. V. Tucker, *"Army and Society in England 1870-1900: A Reassessment of the Cardwell Reforms,"* in *Journal of British Studies*, Cambridge University Press, Cambridge 1963, 2. 2 pp. 110-141.

[139] M. Jasanoff, *Edge of Empire: Lives, Culture, and Conquest in the East, 1750-1850,* Vintage, London 2006. Trad It. *The company of the indies. the first multinational,* Il Saggiatore, Milan 2012.

published which became very popular the following year. *The battle of Dorking*[140] written by Colonel George Chesney. It was the first alarming text and gave the go-ahead to the *Invasion Literature*[141]. The work, which considers the reforms made to the Army, tells of how Great Britain suffers an invasion from a country without a name, but very similar to Germany, following a conflict very similar to the Franco-Prussian war. After several battles the enemy Army breaks the British lines in Dorking and conquered the island, splits the Empire with other nations and turns Britain into a highly taxed province. The intention was clear: the reform was not enough.

However, it was the Franco-Prussian War that stirred the consciences of politicians and soldiers who finally understood how far back the war techniques of their Army were. They saw how much more effective an Army of expert soldiers, well-equipped with modern weapons, was better than an Army of *gentlemen* available to the Crown at that time[142]. All power over the Army was placed under the control of the *War Office* and reserve forces were created and stationed in Great Britain with a fixed minimum period of service to be performed. The most sensational reform, however, was the abolition of the possibility of acquiring official positions in the Army. This custom, in vogue since Charles I, allowed anyone to be able to buy at a high price a

---

[140] Released in instalments on Blackwood's Magazine and then in the form of a booklet until it became a novel. H. G. Wells will be inspired to write his most famous novel, *The War of Worlds*, released in 1898. Published in Italian with English text. G. Chesney, *The Battle of Dorking: from Blackwood's Edinburgh Magazine May 1871*, Trad It. Riccardo Valla. Editrice Nord, Rescaldina 1985.

[141] It will be discussed in detail later.

[142] R. Ensor, *England, 1870-1914*, Oxford University Press, Oxford 1936, pp. 7-17

title from their superior in rank. The practice was allowed only in infantry and cavalry up to the rank of colonel. It was believed that this would make it easier to avoid coups d'état because officers were interested in maintaining the *status quo*, where they could hold a secure office, and to avoid abuse of officers because they risked losing their office without receiving any reimbursement.

The Cardwell reform also provided changes to the quartering and enrolment system. The *Army Enlistment Short Service Act* changed the enlistment system. From the beginning of the Napoleonic Wars until 1847, the enlistment was set to 21 years. The seven-year short enlistment was only in force during the wars. The enlistment, practically for life, combined with corporal punishment, put the Army on the same level as prisons. As time went by, the percentage of people enlisted dropped dramatically. In 1847 with the *Time of Service in Army Act* the years were reduced to ten then increased the following year to 12. At the end of the contract the soldiers could leave the Army without pension rights or sign another contract for a further 12 years and then have a leave of two months plus the military pension. The lowering of the duration of military service did not create problems as most of the soldiers were either re-arranged or returned after a few months. This system had the advantage of producing an Army of experts and veterans but did not provide for the reserves to be called back into service in case of need. The reserve system proved to be fundamental after the lesson learnt from the Franco-Prussian war, also because half of the military service was carried out in the colonies in climates completely different from the European one and back home the soldiers suffered from the climate change and turned out to be more a hindrance than a utility.

In 1870 Cardwell, with the full support of Gladstone, proposed to the parliament the short enlistment. Twelve years of service, six of which in reserve. The soldier could choose between the active service or the reserve, the latter paid four pence a day in exchange each year there was a period of recall and obligation of service in case of danger to the nation. Parliament and military officials strongly opposed this system and the Queen said she had signed the law *"most reluctantly".*[143] The system proved useful and the percentage of people enrolled increased considerably. The system remained in force until 1916 when the compulsory leverage was established to meet the needs of the conflict.

In 1871 the *Regulation of the Forces Act* became law, again within the *Cardwell Reform*. This law regulated the armed forces' quartering system. Before this law, the soldier could not choose the regiment under which to serve. The citizen enlisted in the general service that sorted the soldiers on the territory. As early as 1829, Lord Palmerston pointed out the problem of this system:

"...there is a great disinclination on the part of the lower orders to enlist for general service; they like to know that they are to be in a certain regiment, connected, perhaps, with their own county, and their own friends, and with officers who have established a connection with that district. There is a preference frequently on the part of the people for one regiment as opposed to another, and I should think there would be found a great disinclination in men to enlist for general service, and to be liable to be drafted and sent to any corps or station."[144]

With the '71 reform, the territory was divided into 66 districts based on the boundaries of the counties or population density. All infantry regiments were divided into two battalions. One was to serve abroad and the other at home whilst the reserve and the local militia formed a third battalion. This system helped to create a new, dynamic, homogeneous and cohesive Army. Allowed, especially during the war,

---

[143] J. A. Williamson, *The Evolution of England,* Oxford 1931, Clarendon Press, p. 107.

[144] W. L. McElwee, *The art of war: Waterloo to Mons,* Weidenfeld and Nicolson, London 1974. p. 79.

actions and offensives also of emotional impact on enemy troops and friends. You understand how useful it was to the cause of enlistment to ensure that new recruits have a familiar face in the middle of the battle. The reform risked a rejection until the Queen with a royal order forced the *House of Lords* to approve it. In 1874 Gladstone lost the elections and Cardwell lost his place but his reform, even if badly seen by the high spheres of the Army, remained in place.

With the return of the Conservative Government, Disraeli took the place of Gladstone at the head of the Government. The Cardwell Reformation remained and Disraeli, instead of abrogating it by giving reason to the requests of the Queen and the Army, decided to make the best use of the system created by the Secretary of Gladstone. Under his second term of office, Disraeli implemented a conservative policy aimed at the less well-off. He passed several laws that sought to improve the social reality of the country. In 1875, the *Public Health Act* sought to improve health by imposing, amongst other things, an archaic system of health insurance, running water in homes, a completely submerged sewage system, lighting and sidewalks in the streets. The *Artisan's and Labourers' Dwellings Improvement Act* of the same year required various local councils to clean up shantytowns and build council houses. The *Conspiracy and Protection of Property Act* legalised trade unions and the *Employers and Workmen Act* legalised contracts between employers and employees. Faced with these reforms, Labour MP Alexander Macdonald said: *"The Conservative party have done more for the working classes in five years than the Liberals have in fifty.*[145]

---

[145] W. F. Monnypenny, G. E. Buclke, *The Life of Benjamin Disraeli, Earl of Beaconsfield*. Volume I, 1804–1859. London 1929. p. 709.

The most interesting and best-known aspect of Disraeli's mandate, however, was his strong support for the imperialist cause. Under his rule, the Kingdom was very active on various military and diplomatic fronts.

He understood how important it was to maintain a secure trade route between the Motherland and the East. He was convinced that the Ottoman Empire was an important barrier against Russian expansion into Europe and Asia and that the *status quo* for his majesty's Government should last if possible. Russia, in fact, was in the middle of a period of strong industrial and territorial development and the years of the signing of the Triple Agreement were still far away and the Tsar was perceived as an enemy not to be trusted and therefore it was better to ensure control over the East, safe access to trade routes and an ally useful to counter Russian expansion especially now that India was under direct administration of London. In danger was the British rule over India and even if Disraeli wanted to avoid at all costs a war, he believed that in case of a conflict broke out *"would not terminate till right was done"*.[146]

The occasion presented itself in 1875. In order to face the bankruptcy of the region, the *Khedive* of Egypt decided to sell the shares of the Suez Canal, inaugurated in 1869. Disraeli without the support of the parliament and his Government decided to buy part of the shares[147]. The investment proved to be very cost-effective and allowed Great Britain to maintain direct contact with India and Australia, and it burned the French plans to control the Middle East.

1876 was a glorious year for Disraeli and his royal friend at Buckingham at Palace. With the *Royal Titles Act,* the title of *Empress of India was* added to the Monarchic

---

[146] R. Ensor, *England, 1870-1914*, cit. p. 46.

[147] R. Blake, *Disraeli*, St. Martin's Press, New York 1966. p. 586.

title and in exchange Disraeli was made peer with the title of Count of Beaconsfield. Disraeli's greatest success, however, was in foreign policy in the role he played during and after the Russian-Turkish war. The conflict broke out in 1877. Russia wanted to regain control of the regions lost during the Crimean War and stimulate the nationalism of the Balkan nations against the Ottoman Empire. The British Government immediately declared its neutrality if its interests in the region were respected. London, in fact, imposed on the Russians conditions to be respected so as not to force them to take sides with the Turks militarily. Freedom of transit in the Suez Canal, no invasion of Egypt and no siege of Constantinople. The Russian Foreign Minister accepted the British requests. After rapid Turkish victories the Russians decided to advance and when they reached Adrianople Disraeli ordered to move the Royal Navy from the Dardanelles to Constantinople and the Parliament voted to raise six million pounds for war expenses. The Government was shaken because Lord Derby and Lord Carnarvon resigned in disagreement with the Prime Minister. In the meantime, Russia granted the armistice to the Turks and the English fleet was brought back but later the Russians moved to Constantinople and Disraeli gave again the order to move the ships to Istanbul. At home everyone expected a war, the newspapers spoke of *outbreaks of war fever.* Disraeli did not accept the *Treaty of St. Stephen*[148] because of the strong Pan Slavism present. Disraeli absolutely wanted an international conference to re-discuss the clauses. In the meantime, the Indian recruits were called back to service and sent to the Mediterranean. Lord Salisbury, who in the meantime had occupied the post of Lord Derby as head of the Foreign Office, had close contact with Chancellor Bismarck and it was decided that the question of the Balkans would be discussed at the

---

[148] A. J. P. Taylor, *The Struggle for Mastery in Europe 1914-1918,* Oxford University Press, Oxford 1963.

Congress in Berlin[149] in the summer of 1878. Disraeli came out as the absolute winner of the congress. He imposed his foreign policy line and obtained great benefits for Great Britain. The Treaty of St. Stephen was scaled back, and Russia saw its control over the Balkans reduced. The independence of Romania, Serbia and Montenegro were confirmed, but Bosnia came under Austrian control and the great Bulgaria was dismantled. Shortly before the congress, the Cyprus Convention between the British and Ottoman Empires was signed. The Turks left the British control over Cyprus in exchange for support for the congress and defensive aid.

The Berlin Congress discussed the Eastern question, but when the treaty was signed, Europe was split. The future fronts of war were created in Berlin. Germany approached Austria-Hungary, gained prestige but lost Russian esteem whilst Great Britain and France came together, and the Ottoman Empire managed to postpone the dissolution and regain some territories taken from it in the Treaty of St. Stephen. Disraeli succeeded in his intent to break *the League of Three Emperors*[150]. The Alliance between Germany, Austria and Russia was not well seen in Great Britain

---

[149] W. Norton Medlicott, *Congress of Berlin and After*, Routledge, London 1963. R. Millman, *Britain and the Eastern Question, 1875–78,* Oxford University Press, Oxford 1979.

[150] The agreement between Wilhelm I of Germany, Alexandr II of Russia and Franz Joseph, however, was fragile from the beginning. The rivalry between Russia and Austria over control of the Balkans was not resolved within the League. With the Death of Alexander II, the Alliance of the Three Emperors was formed where the Russian and Austrian spheres of influence in the Balkans were specified. A. J.P. Taylor, *L'Europa delle Grande Potenze. Da Metternich a Lenin*, Laterza, Bari, 1961; H. Rogger, *La Russia Pre-Revoluzionaria 1881-1917*, il Mulino, Bologna 1992; Arthur J. May, *La Monarchia Asburgica 1867-1914*, il Mulino, Bologna, 1991.

because it was a compact front that could at any time question British supremacy and cut off links with India.

Shortly before the elections, when the Russian advance in Europe was blocked, it was necessary to stop it in Asia, the already mentioned second Anglo-Afghan war began. Control of Afghanistan was strategic for the security of India and the trade routes and Russia wanted to get its hands-on it as expansion into Europe had been blocked.

Despite victories in foreign and domestic politics, the 1880 elections brought the liberals back into Government. Gladstone took over from Disraeli, who died the following year. The Queen always remained his great friend, after having elevated him to the Chamber of Lords she honoured the body of the former Prime Minister by having a memorial built at the church of Hughenden Manor, a place of which Disraeli was Viscount.

With the death of Disraeli Gladstone had the road paved, despite winning the election the compact front between Disraeli and the Queen was a very difficult obstacle to overcome. The liberal Prime Minister was a convinced anti-colonialist. Contrary to imperialism in Africa and Asia, he led the last months of the war in Afghanistan and had to lead the Government during the Anglo-Boer war, the war in Sudan and completed the conquest of Egypt. In short, an anti-colonialist who fought four wars for colonies.

In 1880 he inherited the conflict in Afghanistan from his predecessor. At the end of the war the Asian nation was able to maintain its autonomy but had to give up control over its foreign policy to Great Britain. Afghanistan became basically an English protectorate[151] and the British controlled from that moment on the important Khyber Pass, at the time border between British India and Afghanistan today between Afghanistan and Pakistan.

Time to end a conflict that immediately arose another conflict. On 20th of December 1880 the First Boer War began. The conflict was almost a *European* war as it was fought between the British and descendants of Dutch settlers. The war, although the definition is exaggerated given the duration, the number of battles and soldiers deployed, was a kind of tail shot of the Anglo-Zulu War. The British, after a glorious victory against the Zulu Empire, were convinced that they were able to stand up to the Boers thanks to their intellectual and military superiority. The conflict ended at the end of March 1881 with a peace treaty signed in Pretoria. Great Britain granted autonomy to the Transvaal, a region north of South Africa with Boer self-Government. In 1881 the Sudanese Campaign began. Which will last until 1899. Sudan had been under the direct control of the Ottoman Governor of Egypt for almost 80 years. Here a religious leader, Muhammad Ahmad, fomented an armed revolt against Turkish rule. After a victory over the Egyptian troops, Ahmad's followers, the Mahdists, reorganised and the Egyptian soldiers withdrew to Khartoum. The British Government initially did not understand the power of the revolt and sent a weak expedition against the Mahdists barricaded in El Obeid. Here the British, led by William Hicks, were slaughtered. In the meantime, the English influence in Egypt became stronger and stronger, coming to control the entire administration and accounting of the land of the pharaohs. The high costs of the war alarmed the English accountants who suggested that to Khedive to withdraw its forces from Sudan. Charles George Gordon was appointed to lead the evacuation of

---

[151] W., P. Francis. *Afghanistan: A Short Account of Afghanistan, Its History, and Our Dealings with It*, Griffith and Farran, London 1881;

171

Khartoum. After some rebellions by local tribes the city fell despite being well stocked with food and ammunition. Gordon failed in his mission and Egypt lost Sudan, leaving it humiliated, but a few years later, thanks to the reports of some prisoners, escaped from the Mahdist nation, the British came into possession of valuable descriptions and military information that led in 1896 the Government to decide to invade Sudan. The expedition was led by Horatio Herbert Kitchener. One after the other he conquered the various Mahdist-style cities and fortresses. In 1896 his contingent rose to 25 thousand soldiers, half of the national Army. The Mahdists were definitively defeated in the battles of Omdurman and Umm Diwaykarat. The Muslim forces had Allah on their side, but Kitchener had the Maxim machine gun. The impact this weapon has had on modern warfare is equal to or greater than the introduction of gunpowder in Europe at the end of the Middle Ages. At first nobody wanted to believe it, the written and unwritten rules of the *gentleman's* war were hard to disrupt but an anomalous person took care of it, revolutionise the British Army. He managed to include an American invention in the armoury of the royal troops and was able to make the most of the opportunity by joining the board of directors of the Maxim Gun Company. He was not a military man, he was a banker. And not a simple banker, but The Banker. The banker of the Empire. Nathaniel Mayer. First Baron of Rothschild.

2. Jews in the City[152]

Few names manage to convey a strong intrinsic meaning, especially in history. Rothschild is one of them.

The story of the world's most famous dynasty of bankers is worthy a three-part novel. Their rise from the Frankfurt ghetto to business squares, parliaments and courts across Europe is extraordinary[153].

Frankfurt was not a welcoming city for Jews, the ghetto was a narrow neighbourhood wedged between the walls and a moat with houses crowding on a single alley. To access it the Jews had to cross the bridge and pay a toll and every time they met a Christian, they had to take off their hats, move to the side and bow, and in the evening heavy chains closed the *Judengasse*[154]. The Ghetto did not offer many opportunities for life or for profitable trade. A city ordinance forbade the Jews from farming, trading in noble goods such as fruit, arms or expensive fabrics such as silk and could

---

[152] They have written a lot about Rothschilds and I could list the various works by pages and pages, but I prefer to mention what I think is the best: N. Ferguson, *The House of Rothschild: Vol 1. Money's Prophets 1798 - 1848 - Vol 2. The World's Banker 1849 - 1999,* Penguin Books, London 1999 - 2000. The two volumes contain a very good and vast updated bibliography. See also N. Ferguson, *The Cash Nexus: Money and Politics in Modern History, 1700-2000,* Penguin Books, London 2002. I preferred not to mention pieces from Ferguson's works because although it is a very interesting subject, I did not want to go on longer than I had to.

[153] For the reconstruction of the rise of the family from Frankfurt to the whole of Europe I followed the order and chronology of F. Morton, *The Rothschilds,* Atheneum, New York 1962. pp. 21 - 62. Trad It. *I favolosi Rothschilds,* Rizzoli 1963.

[154] Jewish Alley.

not sell handicrafts. There were few areas left where to fit in: second-hand clothes, household utensils and an archaic form of banking finance.

Mayer Amschel did not even have a last name when he returned to Frankfurt. The family had sent him near Nuremberg to become a rabbi but after their death no one could pay for his studies and he first gave up a flourishing career in a Jewish bank in tolerant Hanover and then decided to return to his hometown. The Jews of Frankfurt were denied permission to have a surname, the families of the Ghetto were recognised by the sign above their door and in the past the family of Mayer had occupied a house with a red sign, in German *Rot Schild* means red shield. By now the family had moved to a humbler part of Judengasse but the *surname* had moved with them.

In a short time, Mayer started a business within the affairs of the two brothers. The trade of ancient coins. In a short time, the young Prince Wilhelm of Hesse-Hanau became his customer and with patience and gamble he was able to turn the Prince into his main customer and later into his springboard to global success. This was Mayer's dowry if he met a rich and famous client, he did not settle for it but used it to reach the next one and this became a sort of mantra within the dynasty.

The Prince was the richest man in Europe at the time. A small Kingdom but a great patrimony. George II's grandson and cousin of George III of England, in his family had two other Kings, the uncle King of Denmark and the brother-in-law King of Sweden. William traded soldiers. The most precious good in the Europe of wars. His subjects were trained according to a strict military system and sold to England. England had to keep the peace in the colonies and every wound or death increased Wilhelm's finances. The earnings were then lent to anyone. After him, only one family managed to create a larger private estate: the Rothschilds.

Mayer owes its fortune to Carl Buderus the young administrator of the Prince's private finances. The relationship between the two was prolific right from the start. Buderus allowed the *Wechselstube* founded by Mayer to cash in several London bills of exchange so that the name Rothschild came out of Germany for the first-time and entered the international banking system. Mayer had recently married Gute Schnapper, a matriarch and example of a female figure for all the women of the Rothschild family. The collaboration with Buderus grew more and more, he became a secret partner of the bank and increasingly hijacked Wilhelm's business on Judengasse.

Rothschild family became *The Rothschild* not thanks to Prince Wilhelm but thanks to Napoleon and especially thanks to his sons.

The first was Amschel who later became treasurer for the Germanic confederation, then came Solomon who in Vienna became the banker of the Empire reaching the rank of Baron, then Nathan who started the British branch of the dynasty, Kalmann who moved to Naples and put under control half of the Italian peninsula and finally Jacob who knew how to get rich in France both during the Republic and during the Empire.

When Napoleon brought the German territories under control, he forced the Prince to flee to Denmark[155]. The bank of Mayer and his sons allowed the Prince in exile to clog up his money through false registers, carriages with double funds, secret deliveries and private emissaries and the more time passes the more the destinies of the family were linked to those of the Prince but now Wilhelm is no longer the goal but the piece to achieve the next goal.

---

[155] A country that Wilhelm had saved from bankruptcy thanks to the Rothschild bank through a series of intermediaries. Since the two Kings were related, Wilhelm wanted to prevent the loan from becoming a gift. The intermediaries allowed a profitable interest rate.

The branch of the family that interests us most is the British. Young Nathan was the most important city banker in the world and his fortune, like that of his father, was once again linked to the Emperor of the French, more exactly to his defeat.

In 1804 Nathan had moved from Manchester, the textile heart of the country, to London, the financial heart of the world. It was Nathan who launched the family into the most profitable business, buying and selling currency. Textile trade, smuggling and lending did not yield as much as bills of exchange transactions. From 1810 onwards, the family would have devoted itself to that alone.

Two years after his arrival in London Nathan married the wealthy Hannah Barent-Cohen, daughter of the merchant and financier Levy Barent-Cohen. Nathan's wife's uncle was Salomon David Barent-Cohen, Karl Marx's great-grandfather. Oh, the irony.

Until 1809 Nathan traded only Government securities and foreign currency on the London Stock Exchange, but from 1810 he began the profitable trade in gold bars. Napoleon's fury around Europe had caused all economies and all finances except the British to tremble. The Government bonds issued by the London Government were solid and secure and Nathan saw them as an excellent source of income and obviously could not risk his own money. Prince Wilhelm had already invested in the country in the past and the Rothschilds were convinced that the time had come to have him pay out more money.

The landgrave was reluctant, but Mayer Rothschild had never disappointed him and had proved very useful immediately after the French occupation, and despite the Napoleonic soldiers occupying Frankfurt, he sent the Prince all his credits collected. The Prince was convinced, thanks to his partner and double-crossing Buderus. Nathan had cleverly given up a commission but would have been content with an eight per cent rate.

Between 1809 and 1810 Nathan, through his father, received £550,000 to invest in companies shares. Wilhelm had placed an average price of 72 pounds for each share.

Nathan immediately forgot about the Prince's requests, because he had first used the money as his own, invested it, made rapid profits and when, as he had foreseen, the price of the companies' shares fell to 62, he bought it. The ten pounds he saved for every share went into his pocket. Using Wilhelm's money every day on the stock exchange he speculated on the price of gold without ever missing a beat. The Prince from Denmark loudly asked for news, but the wise Mayer defended his son by unloading the blame on the intrusions made by the French. In 1811 Kalmann joined his brother in London and brought the first certificates to the Prince for a value of 189,500 pounds. But Wilhelm got tired of investing and decided to enjoy life sitting on his huge mountain of money. Nathan had never named the Prince in London and recorded all his purchases in his name, thus creating a huge reputation in a short time. Every time she showed up at the Stock Exchange, everyone hanged on every word he said.

In 1811 a new customer introduced himself to Nathan: The Duke of Wellington.

During the Napoleonic Wars the Duke of Wellington needed large amounts of gold to pay the troops, and the Government to pay aid to the Allies. Nathan sensing the situation that would arise had bought 800,000 pounds of gold bars sold by the *Company*. Since 1807 the Rothschilds had been at the service of the Government in order to send money to the Duke through their vast network in Europe, despised French enemies, but the task was also entrusted to others. Maltese and Sicilian bankers often managed to reach the Duke in Portugal or Spain. Nathan wanted to have a monopoly on these matters and was willing to do anything. The other bankers were offering smuggling and promises to pay, he was offering the gold of the Company straight from London to the Duke.

The astute Nathan had a weapon that other bankers could not have: his brother Jacob.

Jacob Rothschild had just arrived in Paris on the 24th of March 1811. He was helped by the Grand Duke von Dalberg, Mayer's client. Within a few hours, he had convinced the French Finance Minister to let English money pass through on French soil. How? By deceiving him. Jacob, who called himself James, had sent the minister false letters showing that England was frightened by the constant loads of gold that were leaving the country to the armies and allies on the continent. James convinced the minister that the best way to win the war and bend the wicked Albion was to let her spend her money on the continent. The minister took James's idea as his own and then allowed a cargo identified in Dunkirk to pass smoothly from North to South. In London Nathan sent ships loaded with gold napoleons, English guineas and Portuguese ounces to the French coast. There his brother James escorted everything to Paris and secretly changed the metal with bills of exchange at Spanish banks. After the operation Kalmann came into play and with the letters of exchange he left for Spain and then returned with the receipts signed by the Duke. Solomon made sure that the various points of exchange were secret and multiple. The price of the guinea never had to fall so as not to instil suspicion in the French. From Frankfurt, Amschel helped Mayer to defend the family fort and, if necessary, intervened where it was needed. The suspicions were many but if in Paris James enjoyed the protection of the Minister elsewhere it was the money that changed some suspicious official's mind.

The Rothschilds became the line of communication between England and the armies of the Duke, and later the same technique was used to bring money to the allies. Prussia, Austria and Russia received huge sums of money to deal with the joint effort against Bonaparte. In all, in the last years of the war Great Britain spent 15 million pounds in aid and Nathan and his brothers managed to move all the money so quietly and lightly that the pound never suffered a drop, even minimal. The commissions applied by the family are still unknown today.

However, the masterstroke and the mortal blow inflicted on Napoleon took place later: on 18th of June 1815.

With the victory at Waterloo, Great Britain became the greatest European, and global, power. But the victory was the result of a series of clever choices and a good dose of luck.

The brothers had a private mail service that they used to continuously exchange information useful for business. Rothschild's messengers travelled all the time. The family's carriages and ships travelled all over the continent and the globe, carrying all sorts of things wherever they were needed, but the most precious commodity were news. Knowing the outcome of a battle before anyone else, for example, could have had a major impact on business.

If Napoleon had won the battle in Belgium, the prices of English companies shares would have fallen and with them the pound sterling, whilst in the event of Wellington's victory the prices would have skyrocketed. On the 19th of June in the late afternoon after the battle a private messenger, Rothworth, set off very quickly from Ostend to England. On June 20, at the very first light of dawn, he arrived in Folkestone and found Nathan waiting impatiently on the pier. Rothworth had a freshly printed copy of a Dutch gazette. Nathan read the headlines carefully and then left in a hurry for London. He pre-dates Wellington's messengers by about 30 hours. He first informed the Government, which waited for the official messengers to be confirm, then he went to the Stock Exchange.

As soon as he entered Nathan leaned on *his* pillar and instead of buying up start selling. Hundreds and hundreds of shares below cost. On the stock exchange everyone trusted him and as soon as they understood what he was doing, they convinced themselves that Wellington had lost and what did they do? They started selling too. Leaning against the pillar he did not say a word but moved only one finger and each gesture lowered the price again and again suddenly before the news came, he bought as many shares as he could and immediately after the news of the victory arrived. The amount Nathan had earned that day was unknown and perhaps

179

he himself did not know the exact amount, but the fact is that after that day Nathan Rothschild became richer than everyone else. Even Queen Victoria.

The following years were difficult for the family. Peace had brought back old prejudices and old habits. The Rothschilds were ignored at the various peace congresses in Vienna and Aachen. They were Jews and they were not nobles. The various princes and rulers preferred to entrust their affairs to the usual bankers and friends. The Rothschilds could buy everything, but credibility was often of no use in the face of prejudice. Then they began to behave in the only way they knew: the financial way. They forgot about the dances, the sumptuous clothes, the expensive carriages and concentrated on the market and suddenly on the 5th of November 1818 the French Government's bonds and shares, those of the big loan of 1817 made without involving the Rothschilds, began to fall. Within a short time, the fall became dizzying and the concerned everyone, except Kalmann and Solomon. The family had bought for days stock tickets and bonds, issued by rival bankers, the noble and Christian bankers who had managed the loan, and then suddenly threw them into the market below cost. The message was clear: never ignore a Rothschild. The princes and rulers immediately understood the message and relations with Ouvrard, and Baring were severed and the Rothschilds were welcomed as conquerors amongst the palaces of Europe. Mayer's dream was fulfilled now in Europe there were the Rothschilds.

From then on, the rise of the Rothschilds to the Empire was marked by continuous success. It was not just them who got rich, though. The Empire grew out of all proportion, industry evolved, people grew rich and glory fell on every British citizen. The last years of the nineteenth century were marked by a deep sense of imperial hybris. Weapons and money allowed Victoria to look do at all the world's leaders. Great Britain was the banker and policeman of the globe and this allowed it to do everything, no one was able to hinder its plans, the other Empires were nothing compared to the great British lion. The Union Jack flew across every continent, the ships of the Royal Navy sailed the seas and oceans welcoming everyone as hosts and the newspapers always reported the decisions taken in London. A choice made in Westminster could mean life or death for individuals who were thousands of miles from the capital. Nationalism, militarism, economic power and faith forged over the years the conviction that no one could ever put an end to all that glory but then suddenly Africa made its voice be heard, giving a very strong blow to the fortress Empire.

Until the mid-nineteenth century, the few British possessions in Africa were mostly territories conquered during the wars for and against slavery. Within 20 years, 40 states were created, with over ten thousand tribes within them, 37 of which were under European control.

Weapons and money were the imperial pair. And if the Rothschilds in the figure of Nathaniel represented the money, the imperialist who absolutely represented the weapons was Cecil Rhodes.

Born in 1853 at Bishop's Stortford in Hertfordshire, his father was a vicar of the Church of England, who boasted that he had never given a sermon longer than ten minutes. He was the couple's fifth child.

At the age of nine he has been sent to the Grammar School of his city but in 1869 he was removed from the school because he had asthma. His father took the task of educating him at home but later decided to send him abroad because his health worsened rather than improved. His brother worked in South Africa, in Natal. After a seventh-day journey he arrived in Durban on 1st of September 1870.

After a failed experience as a cotton farmer, together with his brother at 18 he decided to move from Natal to Kimberley where there was a thriving diamond field. At the time, the area was under the control of about a hundred small companies that were fighting each other. Rhodes realised that the best way to make money, a lot of money, and at the same time be able to control the region politically was to keep the population under control. Obviously, he could not do all the work alone, to dismantle small businesses in favour of a single dominant company he needed a lot of money. Shortly afterwards, a Rothschilds envoy arrived in Kimberley in 1882.

The bank's project was simple: to make small companies merge, to create a single large company, to dominate the market. Funded by Nathaniel Rothschild, Cecil Rhodes managed to reduce the number of competing companies to three within three years. In 1886, thanks to the money of the Rothschilds, the Rhodes company and the De Beers Company merged with the Compagnie Française and shortly afterwards supervised the merger of the new company with the immense Kimberley Central Company.

The De Beers Company had two heads. Rhodes and Rothschild. Rhodes was not really the owner, as Rothschild owned more shares right from the start, and in 1899 its shares doubled those of Rhodes. So much so that in 1888 in a letter Rhodes could afford to say:

"I know with you behind me I can do all I have said. If however you think differently I have nothing to say"[156]

Nathaniel Rothschild had found in the young Cecil Rhodes his goose that laid golden eggs, the son of the reverend resembled King Midas. He never failed an intuition, earned and earned dizzying sums of money, conquered and controlled without opponents. Rhodes acted like a Rothschild.

In 1888, Rhodes wrote to his lender to offer him a new investment. This time in gold mines. He had identified an immense deposit beyond the Limpopo River. He had

---

[156] R. I. Rotberg, *The Founder: Cecil Rhodes and the Pursuit of Power,* Oxford University Press, Oxford 1990. p. 211.

obtained a concession from the King of Matabele, Lobengula, for the exploitation of the deposits but he needed money to start the new business. Rhodes immediately made clear his real intentions towards the concessionary tribe. For him, they were a simple obstacle to the control of Central Africa.

Rothschild obviously agreed to invest immediately. First Rhodes joined the Bechuanaland Company where he created a new Central Search Association for Matabeleland. Rothschild continuously increased its number of shares, in 1890 the company became the United Concessions Company. The year before, he had contributed to the founding of the British South Africa Company.

The two companies De Beers and British South Africa had a similar economic nature but a different way of interacting with the reality of the facts. The first behaved as if it was in Europe, the clashes and battles took place around the table of shareholders whilst the latter set aside all European scruples.

At some point, Lobengula realised he was circumvented by Rhodes. The concessions he had made had been misinterpreted, according to him, ignored. Determined to take back the territories, he sent his own warriors and Rhodes decided to take him out of the way definitively and sent his own personal soldiers against the troops. The Matabele were about 3000 whilst Rhodes had only 700 men but had entrusted them with a deadly weapon: The Maxim machine gun. The Maxim 0.45-inch model needed four men to make it work and in one minute it could fire 500 shots.

That was the first-time ever that the Maxim machine gun was used in a real gunfight, until then demonstrations had highlighted its speed and its usefulness but no one until then knew what impact it could have on a battlefield. On the 25th of October 1893, during the battle near the Shangani River, with four machine guns, Rhodes' troops killed 1,500 people. In a complimentary letter to Hiram Maxim, an eyewitness described the scene:

"The Matabele never got nearer than 100 yards led by the Nubuzu regiment, the King's body guard who care on yelling lie fiends and rushing on to certain death,

183

for the Maxims far exceeded all expectations and mowed them down literally like grass. I never saw anything like these Maxim guns, nor dreamed that such things could be: for the belts of cartridges were run through them as fast as a man could load and fire. Every man in the laager owes his life under Providence to the Maxim gun. The natives told the King that they did not fear us our rifles, but they could not kill the beast that went pooh! By which they mean the Maxim".[157]

The psychological impact on the enemy was devastating. The Matabeles attributed the creation of that terrible weapon to witchcraft, the soldiers of the Rhodes Company were invincible in their eyes. Rhodes, not wanting to lose credit for the conquests made, decided to make it clear who had conquered those lands. Since that day, that territory has been known as Rhodesia.

Weapons and money, Rhodes and Rothschild. The two of them worked as one. Where Nathaniel's money did not move things, Cecil's weapons would, together they redrawn maps.

The main concern within the financial dynasty was not so much the victims in the field but rather the fact that Rhodes preferred to move money from the profitable De Beers to British South Africa which served only for speculation.

Obviously, the couple were not free of criticism, even here not for the victims but for financial transactions. At the end of the century, a risky investment made a greater impact than a massacre of indigenous Africans.

Lord Randolph Churchill harshly criticised Rhodes after a trip to South Africa. In his eyes, an investment in mines was a risky and rookie operation and he considered Rhodes a braggart who could not *honestly* find the money to buy himself a mine.

---

[157] D. F. Goldsmith, *The Devil's Paintbrush. Sir Hiram Maxim's Gun.* Collector Grade Publications, Toronto 1989. p. 108.

Obviously, the attack on Rhodes was an attack on Nathaniel Rothschild who was very offended by the affront.

Hiram Maxim, inventor of the machine gun, developed his invention in London. He knew that the potential he would have on a well-armed and structured Army was very high. The American Army had just come out of the Civil War and the federal Government had several expenses to bear which made it very difficult to obtain an order. What better place, then, than London where to show off your creation?

When he managed to get a working prototype in his laboratory, he began to invite a lot of famous and especially wealthy people to Hatton Garden. All presented themselves: The Duke of Cambridge, the Prince of Wales, the Duke of Edinburgh, the Duke of Devonshire, the Duke of Sutherland and the Duke of Kent. The Duke of Cambridge was then the Commander-in-Chief of the Army and reserved absurd words for the new invention:

"Greatly impressed with the value of machine guns. [...] confident they will ere long, be used generally in all armies. [...] not think it advisable to buy any just yet. [...] When we require the we can purchase the most recent patterns, and their manipulation can be learnt by intelligent end in a few hours"[158]

In November 1884 Hiram Maxim founded the Maxim Gun Company and Nathaniel Rothschild was on the board. In 1888 his bank financed the merger between *Maxim*'s company and *Nordenfelt Guns and Ammunition Company*.

The imperialism of Rhodes, financed by Nathaniel Rothschild, had brought the Empire back to the first period before the Government's choices. In fact, Rhodes privatised colonialism. The British Empire was a corporation and he wanted to

---

[158] G. Mead, *The Good Soldier, A biography of Douglas Haig*, Atlantic Books, London 2007. p. 84.

secure the largest package. The wars for gold were not paid for by the taxpayers but were paid for by the shareholders of the two companies. In the event of bankruptcy, it was the board of directors that was to suffer the consequences, not the Government. In Africa, the British were to behave as they did in India. According to him, De Beers had:

"Every chance of making it another East-India Company" [159]

Rhodes dreamed of a large railroad from North to South, from Cape Town to Cairo. An imperial spine that would connect the black continent from head to toe. He himself had traced the route on a large map. From Cairo the Empire's locomotives would descend along the Nile leaving Egypt conquered and reaching Khartoum then down the Great Lakes region then crossing Nysaland, Rhodesia, Bechuananaland and finally Cape Town.

What was the *problem* with Africa? The same one that was in India. Conquer before the others. In the South Rhodes worked hard to colour red as much territories as possible, from the east others like him worked to subdue regions and tribes, but in the north the situation was quite complicated.

The proximity to Europe, and especially the Mediterranean coast, had always attracted European conquerors. In those territories, the French were the masters. France had a much more aggressive policy towards the Ottoman Empire. For the English, the sultan in Constantinople had to sleep soundly. A weak or dismembered Ottoman Empire represented a danger for India because of the always lurking Russia, whilst for the French trying to bring down the great sick man of Europe was always a skilful foreign policy plan.

---

[159] R. I. Rotberg, *The Founder...,* p. 212.

186

If in Egypt, the Royal Navy, had extinguished all Napoleonic *grandeur* wishes, in Algeria, a few years later, the French soldiers had conquered almost the entire country in a short time. The French, however, tried to conquer territories in Africa and the Middle East also with finance. At the end of the century, it was French investors who dictated the economic policy guidelines of Egypt and Turkey. The creator of the Suez Canal was a Frenchman, Ferdinand de Lesseps and French was also the capital invested. The work was inaugurated in 1869[160]. However, the British never wanted to leave the decisions on the Ottoman Empire in French hands. They believed that it should be the other powers to decide together.

Between 1862 and 1876 Egypt's public debt rose from 3.3 million to 76 million Egyptian pounds. Five times the tax revenue, also the personal debt of the Khedive Ismail amounted to 11 million pounds[161]. Debt expenditure amounted to more than half of the budget, 55.5%. Many other states were indebted to a greater extent, but

---

[160] It is erroneously believed that Verdi composed the *Aida* for the inauguration of the canal, but it was not so. The Khedive had offered the Italian composer eighty thousand francs for the composition of a hymn, but Verdi had refused. In 1870, however, he agreed to compose something for the inauguration of the new Cairo Opera House. Because of the Franco-Prussian war, the staging was very delayed because all the costumes and sets were in the Paris besieged by the Prussians. The theatre was then inaugurated with the Rigoletto and only later was the Aida performed.

[161] A. E. Crouchley, *Economic Development of Modern Egypt*, Hebrew University, London 1938. p. 374; C. Issawi, *Economic History of the Middle East 1800-1914*, University of Chicago Press, Chicago 1966. p. 439-445; Z. Y. Hershlas, *Introduction to the Modern Economic History of the Middle East*, Brill Academic Pub, Leiden 1964. pp. 99-122.

Egypt and Turkey were in a situation that was totally out of control. In 1874 the Government of Constantinople declared insolvency in October. Even before someone had even thought of convening yet another international conference Disraeli, as already mentioned, took charge of the situation and as often as he did decide in total autonomy. The Khedive offered the Government of his majesty £4 million in shares in the company that ran the Suez Canal. He knew full well, however, that the parliament would never approve such a move. This figure represented more than 8% of the total state budget net of debt expenditure. Disraeli therefore decided to turn to his, and many others', trusted friend Nathaniel Rothschild. The money was paid to the Government in a matter of hours. The Government now controlled 44% of the company's shares, but this gave neither London nor India peace of mind. The control was not a majority and above all the law that obliged the Company to keep the Channel open was not a certainty of operation. Moreover, the shareholders were only entitled to vote from 1895 onwards with ten votes. However, Khedive had made sure to pay 5% of the value of the shares instead of dividends. By the time each share was purchased it cost 22 pounds 10 shillings and four pence, by January 1876 it had already risen to 34 pounds 12 shillings and six pence, an increase of 50 percent. In 1898, the market value of the Government's shares was £24 million, rising to £40 million on the eve of the First World War and £93 million in 1935. Between 1875 and 1895 the Cairo Government paid the British Government £200,000 since Britain obtained voting rights on the shares, dividends became regular at market prices. £690,000 in 1895 £880,000 in 1901. With a masterstroke Disraeli had managed to put Egypt in his pocket once again without letting the taxpayers spend a penny. A private colonialism led by the Prime Minister and funded once again by Rothschild haven for any imperial financial action. In addition to the economic benefit, Rothschild obtained the symbolic benefit in 1885 because he was named a peer of the Kingdom and was welcomed into the Chamber of Lords. He was the first Jew to be a part of it, as Disraeli had converted to Anglicanism at a young age. It was a great victory for the family. Now all five descendants of Mayer's five sons could boast a noble title. His father, Lionel, had suffered a terrible humiliation when he tried his political career[162].

---

[162] The election of members from outside the Anglican Church in Great Britain was a very complicated matter. If the hated Catholics could sit in the House of Commons under the *Roman Catholic Relief Act* of 1829, the Jews had to wait a long time. In theory, no one was prohibited from applying, the problem came when you had to take the seat. In fact, an oath of Christian fidelity was imposed on the newly elected. When Lionel Rothschild applied, not even to say so to represent one of the four seats in the City, he was elected. It was 1847. But he refused to take the oath. At the time, Prime Minister Lord Russell had tabled a law to allow Jews the right to be elected by effectively cancelling the oath. The *Jew Relief Act* of 1848 was voted in favour by the Commons but was twice rejected by the Lords. At the time the bill was supported by Disraeli but not by his party. Lionel Rothschild could not therefore take his place among the chosen ones and resigned in 1849. He resurfaced for the by-elections of his constituency, to affirm his intentions, and rebutted again elected but in 1850 when he first appeared in the Chamber he asked if it was possible to swear only on the Torah, and was granted, but later refused to take the part of the oath that referred to the Christian faith (*upon the truth faith of a Christian*) In 1851 the law was resubmitted in view of the elections of 1852 but once again obtained a negative response from the Lords. Lionel was elected, but he did not swear the oath. Finally, in 1858, the Commons and Lords passed a law that left each chamber the right to decide on the oath to be taken by each new elected person. The House of Commons also allowed Jews to enter and on the 26th of July 1858 Lionel Rothschild was able to make his entrance among the MPs. He took an oath referring to Jehovah and not to Christianity and took his place later. He was re-elected in 1859 and 1865, defeated in 1868 but re-elected the following year. In 1874 he was defeated for a second time

The French were granted a consolation prize, we can say. A new institute, the *Caisse de la Dette Publique,* was created in 1876, controlled by the major creditor countries, i.e. not only Great Britain and France, but also Austria and Italy. The task of the Caisse was to supervise Egyptian finances through European representatives. In 1878, at the suggestion of the bank, Egypt completely relied on the Europeans and established an international Government. The Foreign Ministry was entrusted to an Englishman whilst a Frenchman was placed in charge of the Ministry of Public Works. Once again, the Rothschilds entered the business with a loan of £8.5 million divided between the British and French branches of the family. In France it was seen practically as an Anglo-French alliance. In fact, for the British, it was a choice of convenience and compromise.

"When you have got a faithful ally who is bent on meddling in a country in which you are deeply interested. You may renounce, or monopolise, or share. Renouncing would have been to place the French across our road to India. Monopolizing would have been very near the risk of war. So we resolved to share".[163]

Those were Lord Salisbury's words.

The new Government did not last long, however, because in 1879 the Khedive dismissed the Government. The four powers at the head of the Caisse removed him and put his more malleable son, Tewfiq, in his place. Tewfiq was far too malleable, however, because it was almost immediately deposed by the military led by the anti-

---

and retired from political life. In 1868 the Queen was asked to raise him to the House of Lords, but she refused, denying that it was because of a religious issue. But few believed her. In 1885 it was the turn of Lionel's son to enter the Upper Chamber.

[163] A. L. Al-Sayyid, *Egypt and Cromer: a study of Anglo Egyptian relations,* Frederick A. Praeger, New York 1969. p. 3.

190

European Arab leader Pasha. The European powers were very alarmed because an Egypt free from any European interference was not acceptable. With the Suez Canal, the country now had to remain in European hands at all costs. If Austria and Italy had no interests beyond North Africa, Great Britain and France always had to keep the lines of communication with the colonies in Asia active. For Britain, Egypt's autonomy was to be sacrificed in the name of India.

In London, however, there was a change at the top of the Government. At the height of the Egyptian crisis, the ballot boxes had handed over the keys to power to Gladstone. The liberal leader, however, although an extreme opponent of Disraeli's foreign policy choices, especially those in the Middle East first and foremost the purchase of shares in the Society of the Suez Canal, changed his mind once in Government. The double Anglo-French control was not feasible because France was experiencing the umpteenth crisis of the Third Republic. Great Britain could not allow Egypt to rebel and above all not to pay its debts. The rebels had fortified Alexandria. Gladstone consulted with the Rothschilds and obtained confirmation that the French would not oppose, On the 31st of July 1882, British ships bombed the port of Alexandria in Egypt. On the 13th of September General Sir Garnet Wolseley and his troops destroyed the rebels led by Arabs. The next day Cairo was occupied, Arabs were taken prisoner and sent to Ceylon. Formally Egypt continued to be independent and Great Britain assured the powers 66 times that this would not be a colonial domination but simply a temporary situation but in fact the power was concentrated in the hands of the British agent. The situation was similar if not the same as in the years before the dissolution of the Mughal Empire in India.

3. Vital Lamp.

The money of the Rothschilds and the cunning of men like Rhodes could not hold together such an immense Empire, however. Never have the people, the paying and voting people, needed symbols, gestures and motives to celebrate. If politicians were concerned with controlling the Suez Canal, defending India or increasing the navy, their subjects had other problems. The best thing to bring the two together was a national holiday and what better holiday if not a Jubilee.

On 23rd of September 1896 Victoria became the Sovereign with the longest reign in British history and the individual countries that were part of it. she outdid her grandfather George III. The Queen postponed the festivities by one year so that she could commemorate it all during her Diamond Jubilee for the 60 years of her reign.

That was the most joyful period for the Empire. The power of the *British race* seemed unstoppable. Empires that had dominated the world in the past were now just a memory. 1897 is not only a festive date but was the last moment of peace before the decline. Shortly after, the Boer war broke the imperialist spirit and the First World War besieged the fatal bite.

The Empire that wanted to equal the Roman Empire had surpassed it in size, power, wealth and technology but always lacked territorial logic. There was no real conquest plan for the territories. The goal was to conquer more than the others and with this goal in mind they found themselves in a situation where the Queen and Empress dominated 25 percent of the land on Earth. Under the bright colours of the Union Jack there were 400 million subjects. 41.5 million in Great Britain, 294 million in India, 6 million in Asia, 43 million in Africa, 7.5 million in the Americas and 5.25 million in Australia. The Empire covered an area of 11 million square miles, 28,589,000 km². From Buckingham Palace Victoria was the moral, religious and political symbol for territories scattered across all continents. In Europe it dominated Great Britain, Ireland, the Isle of Man and the Channel Islands, Gibraltar and Malta. In Africa British East Africa, Ashanti, Basutoland, Bechuanaland, Cape Province, Gold Coast, Gambia, Natal, Nigeria, Nysaland, Rhodesia, Sierra Leone, British Somalia, Uganda and Zanzibar. In America on Bahama Island and Barbados, Canada, Falkland Islands, Jamaica, British Guyana, British Honduras, Windward Islands, Windward Islands, Newfoundland, Tobago Islands, Trinity, Turks and

Caicos, Virgin Islands. In Asia there was the heart of the Empire: India but also Aden, Northern Borneo, Brunei. Ceylon, Hong Kong, Labuan, Malaysian Confederation, Papua, Sarawak and Singapore. In Australasia South Australia, Western Australia, New South Wales, New Zealand, Queensland, Tasmania Victoria. In the Indian Ocean it controlled the Mauritius Islands, the Seychelles and seven other smaller groups. In the Pacific Ocean they had gone as far as the Hellenic Islands, Gilbert, South Solomon, Union, Fiji, Pitcairn Island and 24 other groups of islands and coral atolls. In the Atlantic Ocean Ascension, Bermuda, St. Helena, Tristan da Cunha. In addition, there were territories under undeclared control such as the Transvaal where a controversy over indirect Sovereignty was ongoing. Egypt was under military occupation but formally free. Cyprus was administered by the British but at least nominally it was under Turkish Sovereignty.

Three times the French Empire, ten times the German Empire. According to *St James's Gazette,* the Queen oversaw

"One continent, a hundred peninsulas, five hundred promontories, a thousand lakes, two thousand rivers, ten thousand islands"[164]

Of course, there were not only political, military and image interests at stake, but also money. A lot of money. London in his double role as policeman and banker of the world was also present where other flags were flying. In 1914, just before the beginning of the decline, foreign investment amounted to £3.8 billion, between two-fifths and half of all foreign investment. More than twice as much as French investment and more than three times as much as German investment. Between 1870

---

[164] W. W. S. Adams, *Edwardian Heritage: A Study in British History, 1901-06,* Frederick Muller, London 1949. p. 18. Quoted in the St James's Gazette in 1901, *Census of the British Empire* 1901, *Parliamentary Papers* CII 1905.

and 1913, capital flows were around 4-5 per cent of gross domestic product and reached 7 per cent in peak years (1872, 1890, 1913). Between 1865 and 1914 the nation had invested more money in the American continent than at home. About 45 percent of the funds invested went to the United States and the White Colonies, one-fifth to Latin America, 16 percent to Asia and 13 percent to Africa. Only 6 percent were invested in Europe, showing once again how much Britain felt closer to the colonies than to the Old Continent. Very few public investments were made in new possessions, practically nothing. That was the ground for private colonialism. 1.8 billion was the investment made in the oldest colonies. In addition to investing in London, it attracted investment. And it did it like no other. Between 1865 and 1914, the average was 38 percent of foreign investments in the City and in the late 1800s the average rose dramatically to 44 percent.

Another solid stone of the Empire was trade. The Empire was born thanks to the merchants and continued to live thanks to them. Trade agreements were an important element. With an agreement the Crown was able to indirectly control those parts of the globe excluded from British rule. At the end of the nineteenth century, 60 percent of British trade was conducted in partnerships outside Europe. Developing countries were the best customers. Thanks to gains from overseas investment and hidden revenues in the folds of the system, such as shipping and insurance, the nation could afford to import much more than it exported. The ratio between export and import prices was about 10 percent between 1870 and 1914.

Britain forced the world not only to think, sell, buy and invest as and with her but also to use money. In 1868 only the United Kingdom and a handful of countries economically dependent on it used the Golden Standard but within 40 years only China, Persia and some Central American countries refused to adopt this system. Most powers, such as France, Persia and Russia, used the double gold/silver standard and the rest of the world used the standard calibrated only on silver. The Golden Standard was calculated on gold but in fact it was on the pound, that became the global currency.

The Queen could boast the greatest Empire in history and at the same time, if she wished, she could have flaunted even the smallest Army. The *Great* Napoleonic *Army* was far more numerous than all the British and indigenous soldiers scattered around the world. In 1898, 99,000 soldiers defended the country, 75,000 were stationed in India and 41,000 were those scattered in the other colonies. The Royal Navy was the main body and the largest, if we exclude the Indians, it reached 100 thousand sailors. India as always plays a role apart, it was in fact an Empire in the Empire. His Army of indigenous people reached 148,000. This kind of federal Empire earned a lot of money, dominated a lot and could afford to spend very little on military spending. In the 1898 state budget, only 2.5 percent of the net national product. Just over £40 million. Military expenses were always limited until the Great War. When the Government decided to modernise the navy, between 1906 and 1913, replacing the ships in circulation with 27 *Dreadnought*, steel beasts with twelve-inch guns and technological turbines, spent only 49 million pounds.[165]

In short, an Empire defended by savings. There were plenty of things to defend, though. During the reign of Victoria there were 72 military campaigns. The Victorian wars included a small number of men and most subjects heard the stories or read the reports in the newspapers. The percentage of the population in the armed forces never exceeded 0.8 percent before the First World War.

On the 22nd of June 1897, before going to St Paul Cathedral for the memorial service in her honour, Queen Victoria went to the telegraph room at Buckingham Palace and pressed a simple button. In a short time, an electrical impulse reached the Telegraphic Central Office of St Martin's le Grand and from there it reached the Empire in every corner.

---

[165] Much less than the interest on the public debt.

The message was a telegram in every sense:

From my heart I thank my beloved people. May God bless them

The St Martin's le Grand technicians reported that after the impulse came two more unexpected clicks that signalled a certain degree of nervousness in the old Sovereign.

The Queen had to attend the religious ceremony from her carriage parked in the churchyard, her health conditions made it difficult for her to travel on foot. The people came from everywhere to see her. From the death of Prince Albert, she had practically retired to private life, wearing mourning to death and reducing every public appearance to the bone.

It was a triumph for the people. Festivals, fairs, dances and sports. Everything was put in place to celebrate the Monarch, the Motherland and the Empire. An imperial chauvinism. The nineteenth century belonged to Great Britain and if we could have walked the streets of London on that June morning, we could hardly have contradicted such an axiom. The *British race* could do anything. It restored the wrongs, took away the evil rulers, surrounded the world with railways and submarine cables, lent money to everyone, populated the farthest lands, restored the balance, converted the pagans, freed the slaves, discovered lakes, established dynasties, won wars, kept the Turks and Russians at bay, built invincible warships and above all brought civilisation everywhere.

The last years of Victoria's reign were characterised by a neo-imperialism pushed to the extreme. The morality of imperialism as a principle did not find true opposition but only a handful of radicals critical of the idea of domination of one people over another, the submissive populations had not yet developed a national consciousness able to counter the ideal underlying the rulers. Public opinion was developed and active and very often embarrassed or upset some issues but even the most extreme points of view hardly ever questioned British superiority over other peoples. Politicians, choices, problems and solutions were questioned, but the Empire had forged a strongly imperialist *public opinion*.

196

History was of central importance and many began to feel the breath on the neck of decline, decay and fall. Previous Empires had collapsed because of the inability to mutate. The poet Matthew Arnold composed a very long poem, some of which were emblematic verses:

I chide with thee not, that thy sharp
Upbraidings often assail'd
England, my country--for we,
Heavy and sad, for her sons,
Long since, deep in our hearts,
Echo the blame of her foes.
We, too, sigh that she flags;
We, too, say that she now--
Scarce comprehending the voice
Of her greatest, golden- sons
Of a former age any more--
Stupidly travels her round
Of mechanic business, and lets
Slow die out of her life
Glory, and genius, and joy.

So thou arraign'st her, her foe;
So we arraign her, her sons.

Yes, we arraign her! but she,
The weary Titan, with deaf
Ears, and labour-dimm'd eyes,
Regarding neither to right
Nor left, goes passively by,
Staggering on to her goal;
Bearing on shoulders immense,

Atlantean, the load,

Wellnigh not to be borne,

Of the too vast orb of her fate.[166]

Many thoughts that the Empire needed a positive shock, a turn to a new course. They had to avoid the rocks of destruction.

We have already met John Seeley and his best seller *The expansion of England*. The political message from his book stirred things up for a long time. It was his idea that the Empire should abandon the *random* imprint that has always characterised its expansion. It was necessary to unite within to fight the nascent powers. Soon the white colonies would have surpassed in population the homeland and the telegram and the steam ships could unite distant unbridgeable until a few years earlier. These two factors were to become the basis on which to support the new imperialism.

"If the United States and Russia hold together for another half century, they will at the end of that time completely dwarf such old European states as France and Germany and depress them into a second-class. They will do the same to England, if at the end of that time England still thinks of herself as simply a European State, as the old United Kingdom of Great Britain and Ireland such as Pitt left her. It would indeed be a poor remedy if we should try to face these west states of the new type by an artificial union of settlements and islands scattered over the whole globe, inhabited by different nationalities and connected by no tie except the accident that they happen all alike to acknowledge the Queen's authority. But I have pointed out that what we call our Empire is no such artificial fabric, that it is not properly, if we exclude India from consideration, an Empire at all, that it is a vast English nation, only a nation so widely dispersed that before the age of steam and electricity its

---

[166] *Heine's Grave* from 1867.

strong natural bonds of race and religion seemed practically dissolved by distance. As soon then as distance is abolished by science, as soon as it is proved by the examples of the United States and Russia that political union over vast areas has begun to be possible, so soon Greater Britain starts up not only a reality but a robust reality. It will belong to the stronger class of political unions. If it will not be stronger than the United States, we may say with confidence that it will be far stronger than the great conglomeration of Slavs, Germans, Turcomans and Armenians, of Greek Christians, Catholics, Protestants, Mussulmans, and Buddhists, which we call Russia. "[167]

Greater Britain is the federal Empire with colonies such as Canada, Australia and New Zealand on the same level as Great Britain. Soon more works began to appear on this theme. *Oceana, of England and her Colonies* by J. A. Foude and *Problems of Greater Britain* by Sir Charles Dilke.

"[in a Greater Britain] Canada and Australia [to] be to us as Kent and Cornwall" [168]

Lord Rosebery in 1885 claimed that the Greater *Britain* was

"The same Imperialism... is nothing but this – a larger Patriotism" [169]

It was Joseph Chamberlain who turned these ideas into political initiatives, however. A liberal who after a few mishaps had landed in the ranks of the Tories. Chamberlain was the promoter of a kind of liberal Imperialism. Its springboard was a diatribe

---

[167] J.R. Seeley, *The Expansion...*, pe 75.

[168] E. Richards, *Britannia's Children: Emigration from England, Scotland, Ireland and Wales Since 1600: Emigration from England, Scotland, Wales and Ireland Since 1600*, Hambleton and London, London 2004. p. 229.

[169] E. Richards, *Britannia's...*, p. 229.

between Canada and the United States. Even though many Canadians were from Great Britain, they were happy to see a trade union with the Americans. He destroyed all similar ideas in the beginning, focusing on the importance of union within the Empire of the Anglo-Saxon races. In 1895 he became Minister of Colonies under the Salisbury Government. He wanted to get the Empire through its period of inactivity. Imperial federalism was the key to getting out of the grip of decline.

"The British Empire is based upon a community of sacrifice. Whenever that is lost sight of, then, indeed, I think we may expect to sink into oblivion like the Empires of the past, which ... after having exhibited to the world evidences of their power and strength, died away regretted by none, and leaving behind them a record of selfishness only".[170]

Chamberlain's idea was very similar to Rhodes' ideas. He had created an educational body that in his eyes was to be the imperial equivalent of the Jesuit Order. The purpose of the Rhodes Scholarships was to create a society of elected representatives for the good of the Empire. Rhodes made a bold statement:

"In considering question suggested take Constitution Jesuits if obtainable and insert English Empire for Roman Catholic Religion"[171]

His friend Rothschild, appointed executor of the will, created the funds that would finance the schools, thanks to the immense fortune accumulated by Rhodes.

Alfred Milner, an Englishman who grew up in Germany, had designed a similar instrument for the *Kindergarten,* which became Round Tables in London.

---

[170] N. Ferguson, *Empire...,* p. 178.

[171] R. I. Rotberg, *The Founder...,* p. 234.

"I am a British (indeed primarily an English) Nationalist. If I am also an imperialist, it is because the destiny of the English race, owing to its insular position and its long supremacy at sea, has been to strike fresh roots in distant parts of the world. My patriotism knows no geographical but only racial limits. I am an imperialist and not a Little Englander because I am a British race Patriot. It is not the soil of England ... which is essential to arouse my patriotism, but the speech, the traditions, the spiritual heritage, the principles, the aspirations, of the British race"[172]

The white colonies welcomed with great enthusiasm all forms of rapprochement between them and the Motherland. They were the first to establish *Empire Day* to be commemorated every year on the same day as the Queen's birthday. On the 24th of May 1901 in Canada, in 1905 in Australia, in 1910 in South Africa and only in 1916 in Great Britain.

The speech of *Greater Britain* and imperial federalism was shattered against the Irish cliffs though. Ireland was the big problem at the heart of the Empire. They were whites, Christians and Europeans. But Christians on the wrong side though. Irish Catholicism has always been a brake on national autonomy, a brake that has remained despite independence.

With the *Union Act* Ireland had lost its parliament and all issues were discussed and decided in Westminster. People like Chamberlain believed that if Ireland became a *dominion,*[173] the Empire would be in a dangerous situation. The same can be said of

---

[172] J. Morris, *Farewell the Trumpets: An Imperial retreat,* Faber & Faber, London 2012. p. 115

[173] Within the Empire some colonies were more important than others and some had exclusive privileges. We must therefore distinguish the colony from the domain, the

Scotland. At that time an idea of Scottish independence had practically disappeared because the country benefited greatly from the Empire and vice versa. Most of the bureaucrats, politicians and especially the soldiers in the colonies were Scots.

Gladstone tried twice to grant Ireland the *Home Rule,* but he failed both times. Chamberlain took the place of Disraeli as the one who had to put the stick between the wheels of the liberalist leader. However, the devolution conceived by Gladstone did not satisfy even the Irish independentists. In this period the first groups of armed rebels began to appear. For example, the Kenyan Brotherhood used the technique of attacks[174]. The Irish did not have much sympathy for the central Government as they had not been the cause but the culprits of the escalation of the famine of the 1840s which had left behind more than a million deaths from hunger and disease. The advocates of *Greater Britain* were convinced that a simple federalism and some concessions were enough to please the Irish whilst it was precisely the obtuseness of

---

enclave or the protectorate. As always, India has a category of its own. According to the Oxford Dictionaries, Dominion: *"Each of the self-governing territories of the British Commonwealth"* includes Australia, New Zealand, Canada and South Africa. Colony: *"A country or area under the full or partial political control of another country and occupied by settlers from that country".* All those areas controlled by an elite of whites sent from their motherland. Enclaves: *"A portion of territory surrounded by a larger territory whose inhabitants are culturally or ethnically distinct."* Gibraltar and Hong Kong. Protectorates: *"A state that is controlled and protected by another."* Some parts of the globe not controlled but under English influence. Like the gulfs and Oman.

[174] Another group, the Invincible, even killed the Minister for Ireland and his Under-Secretary in 1882.

their positions that forced the Irish to go towards the armed groups, making them become the majority.

But was there a form of *Greater Britain* aimed at the other colonies? Was there anyone in the Empire who was convinced that people and cultures should be mixed together? Yes, there was. And as he himself wrote:

My name is George Nathaniel Curzon,

I am a most superior person[175]

In Curzon defence, however, it must be said that he did not feel superior only to the lower *races* of the non-white colonies, he felt superior to all, including the white and Anglican English.

Lord Curzon had become Viceroy the year after the Great Jubilee. Lord Salisbury's nomination had been the crowning achievement of his dreams. As he himself stated during his speech at the Byculla Club in Bombay on November 16, 1905:

"The post of Viceroy of India is not one which any man fit to hold it would resign for any but the strongest reasons. When you remember that to me it was the dream of my childhood, the fulfilled ambition of my manhood, and my highest conception of duty to the State, when further you remember that I was filling it for the second

---

[175] These are the first two verses of a *Balliol Rhyme* satirical verses composed when he attended Oxford. The text continues as follows: *My cheek is pink, my hair is sleek, / I dine at Blenheim once a week.* The verses are also the title of an excellent biography of Curzon written by Kenneth Rose. Compared to Gilmour's work, Rose focuses on the first part of her life, travelling around the world and her rise to the post of Viceroy.

time, a distinction which I valued much less for the compliment than for the opportunity afforded to me of completing the work to which I had given all the best of my life, you may judge whether I should be likely heedlessly or impulsively to lay it down. No, Sir, there is not a man in this room who does not know that I resigned for a great principle, or rather for two great principles: first, the hitherto uncontested, the essential, and in the long run the indestructible subordination of military to civil authority in the administration of all well-conducted States, and secondly, the payment of due and becoming regard to Indian authority in determining India's needs."[176]

Curzon had already had connections with India and indeed represents an extraordinary bridge between the Great Game and the Great War.

Lord Curzon belonged to that generation of parliamentarians whose work in Westminster took just over half of a year. The rest of the time they spent in the countryside, on holiday or on a trip. Usually the parliament met in August or September and then until January or February it was not reopened. He was elected in 1886 as the representative of the Southport constituency. His first speech was against Irish nationalism and *Home Rule*. The speech was appreciated for his speaking skills, but he was criticised for his arrogance and too much self-confidence. The freedom given by his office allowed him to travel a lot around the world. Before being elected he had already visited all European countries and since 1888 he decided to undertake a series of trips to the Middle and Far East. Each trip was

---

[176]*Lord Curzon's Farewell to India. Being Speeches Delivered as Viceroy & Governor-General of India. During Sept.-Nouv. 1905*, Nabu Press, Charleston 2013. p. 13.

followed by a detailed report, so he could finance the next trip. The prestige of being a legislator ensured him hospitality and assistance that was always denied by officials to other travellers. In the eyes of the other members of his social class Curzon was poor, economically speaking. Until 1911 the parliamentarians received no salary and he himself opposed the various attempts of reform in that direction. He lived for many years with his father's income of a thousand pounds a year. The father was not a stingy man, he just did not have any money. The Kedleston estate was overwhelmed with maintenance expenses. 18,000 pounds a year was just enough to pay wages, pensions and to maintain and educate a large family. He himself spent only on hunting and some time on holiday in Bath. After years and years of sacrifice he was able to leave an inheritance at his death in 1916 of 450 thousand pounds.

To supplement his father's income Curzon had three main sources. The first was the £200 a year he earned from his Oxford scholarship. As a contributor to various periodicals he received from 200 to 300 pounds and then occasionally had one or two part-time jobs, in 1887 he became director of the *Clerical, Medical and General Life Assurance Society*, almost certainly got the job thanks to Lord Middleton, with a compensation not much higher than 200 pounds.

The following year he became director of *Hadfield's Steel Foundry Co. Ltd.* The new president wanted to relaunch the family business with an extensive programme of expansion and research. He was very interested in armaments. Curzon, with a pay of £250, dedicated himself to the new mission and had no qualms about writing to his friend St John Brodick, Financial Secretary to the War Office, asking him to increase Government orders for ammunition.

His first election campaign was paid for almost entirely by the Conservative Association of Southport. However, he struggled to put together the 50 pounds he had promised as his personal contribution. After the first six months of parliamentary sessions he began to save money and on the 4th of August 1887 he began his first trip outside Europe.

In December 1887, after a trip to the American continent, he arrived for the first-time in India. After a short visit to the country, he returned to Europe before February 1888.

"The strength and omnipotence of England everywhere in the East is amazing… no other country or people is to be compared with her. We control everything, and are liked as well as respected and feared"

He wrote to his father from Singapore before returning home.

This first contact with India left him with a feeling of magnificent certainty. He was certain that British rule in India would be favourable to both the British and the Indians. A sacred pact.

"For where else in the world has a race gone forth and subdued, not a country or a Kingdom, but a continent, and that continent peopled, not by savage tribes, but by races with traditions and a civilisation older than our own, with a history not inferior to ours in dignity or romance; subduing them not to the law of the sword, but to the rule of justice, bringing peace and order and good Government to nearly one-fifth of the entire human race, and holding them with so mild a restraint that the rulers are the merest handful amongst the ruled, a tiny speck of white foam upon a dark thunderous ocean?"[177]

---

[177] *Speeches on India, delivered by Lord Curzon of Kedleston, viceroy and Governor-general of India, while in England in July-August 1904*, John Murray, London 1904. p. 5.

He firmly believed that British rule in India was benign. This has nothing extraordinary about it, at the time it was the most common thought amongst rulers and administrators. The particularity of Curzon's thought was that he was completely blind to all forms of modern thought. According to him, in fact, the Indians would never have been able to govern themselves despite the Western education they received. In my opinion, there was no *racist* discourse in Curzon, but rather a targeted analysis of India's weaknesses. He recognised the merits of Indian culture and was fascinated by it, today we can admire his collection of artefacts preserved in Kedleston Hall, however, he believed that only few people were able to establish an autonomous Government usual and functional.

At this stage of his career Curzon placed at the top of the Empire's responsibilities the defence that the British gave to India against the Russians. For Curzon, slowing down the expansion of the Tsarist Empire was the main goal. The region between Central Asia, the Hindu Kush mountains, the Pamir area and the Himalayan and Karakorum mountains were the most endangered territory and the natural barrier against invaders.

In recent years Russian generals and explorers had revealed an eager interest in the trade routes that crossed the roof of the world region, where the borders of the Raj, Afghanistan and China met. The Russian explorers penetrated deeper and deeper into the region, taking advantage of the almost total lack of maps and therefore of control. Even Tibet began to become a territory of interest. Curzon's travels in the region convinced him that not only Afghanistan and Tibet but also Persia and its gulf were border territories and, in those places, as in the subcontinent the English had to move because they had to be defended and protected against Russian expansionist plans.

The trip to Russian Central Asia took place in the autumn of 1888 through Russia to Baku and through the Caspian Sea to Krasnovodsk.

The newly inaugurated military railway terminated there. The line crossed for 900 miles what is now the territory of Turkmenistan through the only nominally independent Canates of Bukhara and Samarkand. The frontier covered large portions of the Persian frontier. As Curzon himself wrote:

"It represented a sword of Damocles perpetually suspended above his (the Shah's) head"[178]

He was convinced that it was only a matter of time before the Russians decided to transport troops and armaments and occupy Khurasan militarily. Thanks to the railway, the Russians could have concentrated their troops in distant territories, such as Siberia and the Caucasus, and then quickly transferred them by trains. He was seriously concerned about London's general lack of interest in the matter:

"This railway makes them prodigiously strong. And they mean business"[179]

On his journey he discovered that all the railway staff were former soldiers injured in battle or retired veterans[180]. He did not believe that the Russian conquests in Central Asia were dictated by an elaborate plan originating from the aforementioned

---

[178] G. N. Curzon, *Russia in Central Asia in 1889 and the Anglo-Russian Question,* Longmans, Green & Co, London 1889. pp. 275-6.

[179] G. N. Curzon, *Russia...*, pp. 47-48.

[180] Ivi. p. 47.

will of Peter the Great, he was convinced that the Russians had simply taken advantage of the power vacuum left after the disappearance of powerful royal figures in the Canary Islands. The various Khan of the area had weakened and some, out of necessity, others, out of constraint, had approached the Tsarist Empire.

"In the absence of any physical obstacle and in the presence of any enemy [...] who understood no diplomatic logic but defeat, Russia was as much compelled to go forward as the earth is to go round the sun"[181]

When he wrote and published *Russia in Central Asia in 1889 and the Anglo-Russian Question* his intention was not to describe the region he visited from a historical, ethnographic or cultural point of view but simply to point out when it was different and how much the Trans-Caspian region has been changed, not to say revolutionised, since the construction of the trans-Caspian railway. Curzon was interested in culture and history, but he never wanted to pass on to his readers the things he had learnt in that field, since his main aim was to sound an alarm signal to the ruling class in his country, a ruling class of which he was a member and which he thought were not interested in the to the security of the Raj.

"So as to enable them to for a dispassionate judgement upon the achievements, policy, and objects of Russia, as well upon the becoming attitude and consequent responsibilities of England"[182]

His first trip to the Middle East ended in Tashkent where he was a guest of the Governor-General for Central Asia.

---

[181] Ivi, pp. 11-12, 314-19. Hopkirk, *The Great...*, pp. 445-456.

[182] G. N. Curzon, *Russia...*, Foreword, p. XI.

Curzon could not deny, in the face of the evidence, the extraordinary work of the Russian engineers. The Tsar's men had succeeded in building a mammoth work in an inhospitable desert. The thing that most frightened him, however, was the fact that the Russians by their very nature were more prone to the moral depravity of the court of the Emir of Bukhara. Sexual perversion and violence were, in his view, more common to the Russians than to the British and this put Russia at an advantage over the Empire.[183]

The Russian Government, according to Curzon capricious and pragmatic, always managed to keep the British suspicious. He was strongly opposed to General Annenkov's proposal to extend the railway as far as Afghanistan to connect Kandahar with the British railway line of northern Baluchistan. The Russians even already identified two routes that could become railway routes. One from the south starting from Dushak, taking advantage of the already existing line that from Sarakhs unfolded through the Heri Rud valley just above the Paropamisus mountains and from to Kushan and finally Herat, the other line had to pass further north from Merv up the Murghab valley to Panjdih, with a connection to Kushk and then again through the Paropamisus mountains to the Heri Rud valley. Curzon's opinion was:

"I shall not be surprised if many now living see a Russian railway station at Herat in their time"[184]

Even though this vision never saw its real counterpart, he did not stray far from reality when he ruled that a Russian railway in the heart of Afghanistan would flood the local markets with Russian goods, which were poorer but cheaper, to the detriment of British goods, and this would represent not only material and monetary

---

[183] Ivi, pp. 178-81, 184-5, 200.

[184] Ivi, p. 267.

damage but, above all, damage to the image of thee Empire. The railroad could also have carried weapons and ammunition and thus armed all tribes opposed to British domination by initiating riots at the gates of India, that could set the whole subcontinent on fire again. The skeletons of the soldiers who died during the retreat from Afghanistan and the physical and psychological scars of the mutiny were still a high warning against any form of revolt.

"Whatever be Russia's designs upon India, whether they be serious and inimical or imaginary and fantastic, I hold that the first duty of English statemen is to render any hostile intentions futile, to see that our own position is secure and our frontier impregnable, and so to guard what is without doubt the nobles trophy of British genius, and most splendid appanage of the Imperial Crown"[185]

After the trip he returned to London in time for the reopening of the parliament. The following year, in September 1889, after a brief vacation in Bayreuth and a participation in the Wagner Festival, he left for Asia. The period between one trip and the next was occupied by Curzon with the writing and sale of his book *Russia in Central Asia in 1889 and the Anglo-Russian Question.* He stayed in the Middle East for six months, four of which were in Persia.

This trip was completely different from the previous ones. Persia was not Central Asia or India. There were no hotels, comfortable railway carriages, palaces or carriages granted by the Governor-General. The maximum comfort was given by some British consulate or telegraph station and in rare occasions the hospitality of local tycoons.

The journey was long and expensive and to keep it he had to start writing articles for the *Times.* Seventeen items were paid £12.10 each. The drafting of *Persia and the*

---

[185] Ivi, pp. 13-14.

Persian Question, 1300 printed pages, and the preparation of the journey required over three years of preparation and over two hundred books read and consulted. No details were left to chance. Even an inflatable bath was included in his travel gear. Pots, pans, ovens and insecticide spray. The future viceroy, as a boy scout rather than a politician, embarked on this long journey and did not fail to describe, in typically romantic and Victorian colours, the positive aspects of the lack of *civilisation:*

"Tinned meats, soups, and biscuits can now be produced at European or Armenian shops in Teheran, Isfahan, and Shiraz; but it is a wise precaution to take them. Crosse and Blackwell's tinned soups are quite excellent, and besides being easily prepared, are almost a meal in themselves. Soup tablets or powders are good in their way in cooking Sardines, potted meats, chocolate or cocoa, Liebig's beef tea, and good tea of coffee, are useful adjuncts, which should be procured in Europe. Lump sugar can be bought in the humblest Persian village"

The journey took place in four parts. Two on the ground and two on water. The first step was 850 miles from Ashkhabad station on the Trans-Caspian Railway to Tehran via Khurasan. The most pleasant part was the 800 miles on horseback from Tehran to Bushire, then he climbed the rivers Shatt al-Arab and Karun to Shushtar and ended with the navigation in the Persian Gulf to India.

He immediately refused to travel within a caravan, more comfortable but slower and more tedious, and chose to use the Chapar system. He had three mares at his disposal for him and for his luggage, along with him were his Persian servant and interpreter and a boy who had the task of bringing back the mares once they had reached the end of the journey. The trip was a very brave gesture given his physical handicap, as a child he had fallen, and this had damaged his spine forcing him to wear a bust of iron and plaster throughout his life. Being standing for too long caused him atrocious pain, so much so that once he was appointed Viceroy, he had the sword modified so that if necessary, it could become a small seat.

Being able to personally counteract how deep the Russian influence in Persia was, he began to suggest to the Government to safeguard the trade route from the Persian Gulf to Khurasan, passing through Kirman and Quhistane to do this, he supported the appointment of deputy consuls and agents in the cities scattered along the road, Yazd, Abbas, Bandar to name a few. He also suggested the opening of a new trade route from Quetta to British Baluchistan via Sistan and Birjand, completely cutting Afghanistan off. In the book he also explains his idea to counter the Trans-Caspian Railway by building a railway line north just below the Afghanistan-Baluchistan border on the already existing Sind-Pishin line in the north of the region. He knew well that the Afghan Emir would prohibit an extension to Kandahar and Sistan he suggested a route that from Nashik, crosses Registan, or the desert to Sistan also assuming a trunk to Persia from Kiran to Kermanshah with connections to the Gulf, Gwandur and Chabahar.[186]

In the future no line was built for Sistan and Afghanistan remained for many years one of the few nations without railways. The line in the North of Bachustan during the Great War was extended westwards not for economic reasons but for strategic ones, by crossing the Persian border as far as Zahedan.

His journey continued through moments of boredom and interesting discoveries. Tehran showed him the contrast between East and West. Contrast that in that period could be found in every city in Asia connected in some way with European cities. It was a relief for him to be in a city after his long time in the desert. He wanted to visit the new museum that the Shah had built after his visit to Europe in 1873. There were placed all his jewels, gifts, *objets d'art* and all the curiosities that had bought or that

---

[186] Ivi, pp. 379-81; G. N. Curzon, *Persia and Persian Question,* Longmans, Green & Co, London 1892. pp. 205-20, 231-3, 236-41.

had been given to him. Curzon was not entirely satisfied because the museum contained, without distinction, valuable objects and junk.

Nasir al-Din Shah, the Shah of Persia, had returned from his tour of Europe a few weeks before when he granted a meeting to the British MP. The two used an interpreter even though the Shah proved to be an expert in French. An entire chapter was devoted to the Shah, his family and his Government. Curzon realised that he had a culture that was superior to the Europeans' beliefs about the Orientals, that he had foreign newspapers translated, and that he had a certain direct relationship with his subjects. However, there were also certain macabre and cruel aspects, such as the way in which prisoners and condemned people were treated.

Curzon was amazed that in Isfahan, the second national emporium, British goods were more common than Indian or Russian ones. The fabrics of Manchester and Glasgow flooded the stalls of the bazaar. The city had just been awarded a British consul.

As we have already seen, education in Victorian England was very much centred on the classical world, Eton and Oxford were not excluded and indeed there the culture, history and spirit of the past still flooded the minds of students. Curzon was therefore very amazed at the things he could see. Especially the region of Persepolis where he was able to remember, and later tell in the book, the stories of Xerxes, Darius and Cyrus and the campaigns of Alexander the Great. These characters represented the knowledge that those, excluding soldiers and diplomats, had of Persia. He did not escape a practice widespread at the time, and punished now, the personal graffiti on monuments, but rather took the defence of the *vandals:*

"A structure so hopelessly ruined is not rendered the less impressive-on the contrary, to my thinking it becomes the more interesting-by reason of the records graven upon it, in many cases with their own hands, by famous voyagers of the past,

214

with whose names and studies the intelligent visitor to Persepolis is likely to be almost as familiar as he is with the titles of Xerxes.[187]"

As one of his biographers, Kenneth Rose, tells us, he did not stop to think about what he would have said that a handful of Persian nobles had started to engrave their names on the stones of Stonehenge but:

"He merely took out his knife and in a stone niche of the palace of Darius the Great added his own epigraph to the History of Persepolis. 'G. N. Curzon 1889' he scratched"[188]

After visiting some Sassanid ruins, he headed towards the port on the Persian Gulf where five days after leaving Shiraz he arrived, seeing the English ships and enjoying the hospitality of the *British Residency.[189]*

The last part of the trip took place by river and sea. In 1887 Sir Henry Drummond Wolf persuaded the Shah to open the Karun to navigation and a service line started operating in 1888, managed by Lynch Bros. who already administered the Euphrates and Tigris Steam Navigation Co. but the service turned out to be uneconomic and soon after it was sold to the Persian Nsiri Co.

On the Tigris, Curzon met a British traveller famous for her adventures around the world. Isabella Bird Bishop[190]. She was crossing the country from Baghdad to Persia.

---

[187] Curzon, *Persia...*, pp. 156-7.

[188] K. Rose, *Curzon: A most superior person,* Macmillan Papermac, London 1985. pp. 226.

[189] Curzon, *Persia...*, pp. 197-230.

[190] C. E. Bosworth, *"The Intrepid Victorian Lady in Persia: Mrs. Isabella Bishop's Travels in Luristan and Kurdistan, 1890" Iran* XXVII 1989.

The two kept in touch even after the trip, in their letters you can find information and questions that then each in their own way merged into their books. After a trip from Bosra, Curzon returned to India and landed at Karachi. At the end of February 1890, he returned to Great Britain.

After a period of rest and convalescence he began to write his report of the trip.

The problem for Curzon arrived once at home. When in 1891 Lord Salisbury offered him a post in the Government at the end of the book, only one chapter was missing. He was offered the post of Undersecretary for India. Curzon was ambitious and was disappointed by position and discovered that the freedom of expression of a member of the Government was even more restricted than the one of a parliamentarian. Lord Salisbury claimed to check the book and censor any part that might damage Anglo-Persian relations. The most problematic chapter was the chapter on the Shah. Curzon complained a great deal to the Prime Minister, but he promptly replied:

"[...] your plea in behalf of your utterances, that they are true, is quite inadmissible. That is precisely the circumstance that will make them intolerable to the Shah [...] I do not think you are yet sufficiently officialised to be able to trust entirely to your own judgement as to particular phrases. It is not safe to handle the Shah with the truth and freedom which is permissible and salutary in the case of Mr. Gladstone"[191]

In the end only a few sentences were *censored.* The Shah's reign then went from being

Disfigured by one or two acts of great barbarity of which the black and insufferable stain could never be washed out"

a

---

[191] Salisbury to Curzon, 27th of November 1891.

"disfigured by one or two acts of regrettable violence".

Nasir al-Din was no longer described as

"petty economies and grudging gifts" ma

"Merchant ship intincsts[192]"

The changes were minimal but in diplomacy every word can trigger a war or a crisis.

Some *offensive* passages remained, especially those on the character of the Persians.

"The Persian character presents many complex features, elsewhere rarely united in the same individual. They are an amiable and a polished race and have the manners of gentlemen. They are vivacious in temperament, intelligent in conversation, and acute in conduct [...] On the other hand, they are consummate hypocrites, very corrupt, and lamentably deficient in stability or courage [...] Whilst, as individuals, they present many attractive features, as a community they are wholly wanting in elements of real nobility or grandeur. With one gift only can they be credited on a truly heroic scale [...] I allude to their faculty for what a Puritan might call mendacious, but what I prefer to style imaginative, utterance. This is inconceivable and enormous [...] I am convinced that a true son of Iran would sooner lie than tell the truth; and that he feels twinges of desperate remorse when, upon occasions, he has thoughtlessly strayed into veracity. Yet they are an agreeable people-agreeable to encounter, agreeable to associate with."[193]

Despite everything, Curzon's conclusion of the essay on her journey was very close to Bird's ideas.

---

[192] K. Rose, *Curzon...*, pp. 237-239.

[193] Ivi, Vol II, pp. 632-3.

"Above all we must remember that the ways of Orientals are not our ways, nor their thoughts our thoughts. Often when we think them backward and stupid, they think us meddlesome and absurd. The loom of time moves slowly with them, and they care not for high pressure and the roaring of the wheels. Our system may be good for us; but it is neither equally, nor altogether good for them. Satan found it better to reign in hell than to serve in heaven; and the normal Asiatic would sooner be misgoverned by Asiatics than well governed by Europeans." [194]

He was able to give a vision that was a long way from the classic interpretation that Westerners had of the East, but all lasted very little because when a few years later he became Viceroy all respect and attention to the situations of the indigenous disappeared. Until the day of his death he remained convinced that only under European control could the Asian states find stability and progress.

India under Curzon underwent a radical transformation. He acted more like an independent King than as a representative of the Government and the Crown and his battles against other officials led his dream of glory to clash with the reality of the facts.

Before embarking on the most important journey of his political career, not through deserts, rivers or mountains but through bureaucrats, administrators and the Indian people, Curzon went on what was perhaps his most important journey.

After Central Asia and Persia only two regions remained to be visited, two territories between British India and the Russian Empire: Afghanistan and the Pamir Mountains. Those two regions in the north-east of the border which, in the event of an invasion, would have represented the point of support for Russian troops. Curzon had long been eager to visit the region and asked both the former and the present

---

[194] Ivi, Vol II. pp. 630-631, Bosworth, *The Victorian Intrepid...*, pp. 92-93.

Viceroy for permission to visit the region, Afghanistan was a client state of the British Empire and diplomatic relations between London, Calcutta and Kabul were difficult and at risk of crisis with every sigh. An English parliamentarian could have triggered problems that the Crown did not need at that time. Permission was denied. Curzon, however, did not give up and, on the contrary, bypassing every chain of command, wrote directly to the Emir asking for an explicit invitation. In a letter full of flattery, he expressed his desire to see:

"The person of Your Highness which is in your dominions like unto the sparkle in the heart of the diamond"[195]

Without waiting for an answer in August 1894 he set sail for India. On his arrival in Bombay he received a letter from the Viceroy, Lord Elgin, reiterating the Indian Government's decision not to grant permission to travel. Curzon, however, did not give up and helped by his friends Rosebery and Lord Roberts, who had led the Indian Army until the year before, went to Shimla and managed to convince the Viceroy and his advice. He obtained the permission to pass for both journeys, the Emir in the meantime had responded with an invitation and, faced with this, Lord Elgin could not anything but imposed two conditions: avoid a district in the Pamir region and not complicate the situation in the region with the articles he should have written for the *Times*. Curzon only considered the first condition and sent the Viceroy on a rampage when he later printed some articles and when a Kashmir official failed to persuade him to destroy a critical article, on the shyness of the Indian Government.

Curzon perceived his success over Elgin as a personal victory, so much so that he came to write in his diary his desire to succeed him in 1899.[196]

---

[195] Gilmour, *Curzon...*, pp. 95.

[196] Curzon Diary, 1894 - 1895, CP (Curzon Papers) III/99.

Curzon was always able to describe with a poetic language what he saw and lived in his travels. The landscapes he observed along his way were described in the work he published after the end of the journey, he could see the power of nature that he showed:

"herself in the same moment tender and savage, radiant and appalling, the relentless spirit that hovers above the ice-towers and the gentle patroness of the field and orchard, the tutelary deity of the haunts of men"[197]

Travelling north from Gilgit, he crossed the Kilik pass after Hunza, and was the first westerner to see the source of the Oxus River. The geographical reports he made for the *Royal Geographic Society* earned him a gold medal and later the presidency.

After travelling along the Oxus, we head towards the Baroghil pass to the Yarkhun River.

Shortly afterwards Curzon met the frontier officer and explorer Francis Younghusband. The year before he had been appointed *Political Agent* in Chitral a small state in the Yarkhun Valley. Younghusband shared with Curzon concerns about Russian expansionist aims. Thanks to his experience in the region he was convinced that the Russians were aiming to create problems in those territories to destabilise India. Both were also convinced that Chitral should not fall under the Tsarist troops. The two talked to the Governor of the state who revealed to them that he feared for his life, his half-brother had long aimed to take power and two months after the departure of the British Mehtar was murdered.

Younghusband will later reveal that the days he spent with Curzon were days of pleasure and rehearsal. He felt a sense of respect and annoyance towards the parliamentarian. Whilst a parliamentarian's interest in frontier missions was a source

---

[197] Curzon *Leaves...*, pp. 130.

of pride for Younghusband, Curzon's endless speeches before coming to terms with his true ideas were a waste of time for him and his travelling companion. The explorer was convinced that Curzon's career would benefit with years in a regiment rather than his time at Oxford, but he could not deny the affection he felt for him. He even went so far as to say that he felt a very deep affection that he did not feel for any man outside of his family.

From Chitral Curzon returned to Gilgit and on a route further south he reached Peshawar and from there entered Afghanistan, via the Khyber Pass. The memory of the bad impression he made in Korea was still imprinted in his memory, he had caused amazement at the banal uniform of an undersecretary, so in London he had prepared himself by creating a dress full of ornaments, golden decorations, patent leather boots and a curved sword borrowed in India.

With an escort of Afghan knights, he entered the city and went to the Emir. At first the Sovereign put him in difficulty by asking several questions about the medals he wore, but he never doubted their authenticity. The Emir filled it with money, but Curzon very cleverly returned it all in the form of gifts to the King and the court. The Emir was positively impressed by Curzon and expressed his desire to meet other British aristocrats as soon as possible. In his autobiography he described him as a brilliant, witty and well-informed man. Curious to note how different it is from the widespread image that contemporaries had of Curzon. But Curzon was also fascinated by the figure in front of him. The Emir was a cruel and bloody person and was described as a kind of Afghan Henry VIII, but he could not deny that he possessed important and useful skills for the Government of that country. He was smart and clever and had managed to reconcile and unite the tribes of his country like never:

"The Emir at once a patriot and a monster, a great man and almost a fiend"[198]

Curzon was convinced that if he had lived in another era with his country uncrushed between the Tsarist Empire and the British Empire, he would have been able to create a vast Empire by putting Asia under his control. Curzon was fascinated by it, as he was fascinated by the Shah of Persia. He tended not to give so much importance to the cruel side of the Sovereign because he saw him with the eyes of the ruler and not with the terrified gaze of a subject.

Curzon stayed at court for two weeks and every day was summoned for long sessions of conversations that took place in Persian through an interpreter. They talked about everything from the tribes of Israel to cruelty as a deterrent, they even went so far as to discuss the Afghan's ability to be a dentist, watchmaker and painter.

He was concerned about the Russians and the threat they posed to his borders and wondered why the British were not worried about arming Afghanistan as a deterrent against the Cossacks. He explicitly asked Curzon why the Indian Government was concerned about defending its borders with Afghanistan rather than strengthening its borders with Russia. Obviously, the Emir never mentioned the war fought between the two countries 60 years before, the bones of the fallen of the retreat of Kabul were still unburied scattered between the mountain valleys and the wound was still bleeding in the collective and diplomatic memory of the Empire.

Sometime before the Government of His Majesty formally invited the Emir to visit Great Britain, he had not yet replied because he did not know what the reception would be given to an Eastern prince and especially what would happen to his country during his absence. After meeting with Curzon, he decided to respond and accept the invitation and gave him a letter addressed to Queen Victoria. Curzon expected to

---

[198] Curzon *Tales...,* pp. 9, 48 - 54.

personally deliver the letter to the Sovereign, but his personal secretary pointed out to him that such an important letter could only come from the hand of the Secretary of State. The Emir, however, never left his country, he was too worried about a coup d'état in his absence. Perhaps it was the best choice, in his eyes the English were not the masters but the neighbours with whom it was easier to talk. For his arrival in London he expected to find all the Government, the parliament, the Queen and the royal family to wait for him whilst for the English he was only a pawn in the Asian chessboard, probably he would only meet the Prince of Wales and the Foreign Secretary. The Emir also wanted a kind of ceremony of humiliation towards the Field-Marshal Lord Roberts, who in 1879 had brought troops to Kabul to punish the city after the murder of British residents. This is how Curzon described the conversation with the King:

" 'When I come to England and to London and am received by the Queen, shall I tell you what I will do?'

'Yes, Your Highness, I shall be glad to hear'

'I understand that there is in London a great Hall that is known as Westminster Hall. It's not that so?'

It is

'There are also in London two Mejilises [Houses of Parliament]. One is called the House of Lords and the other is called the House of Commons?'

It is so

'When I came to London, I shall be received in Westminster Hall. The Queen will be seated on her throne at the end of the hall, and the Royal Family will be around her; and on either side of the Hall will be placed the two Mejilises – the House of Lords on the right, and the House of Commons on the left. Is not that the case?'

'It is not our usual plan; but will Your Highness proceed?'

223

'I shall enter the Hall, and the Lords will rise on the right, and the Commons will rise on the left to greet me, and I shall advance between them up the Hall to the dais, where will be seated the Queen upon her throne. And she will rise and will say to me, 'What has your Majesty come from Kabul to say?' and how then shall I reply?'

'I'm sure I do not know'

'I shall reply: I will say nothing – and the Queen will then ask me why I refuse to say anything; and I shall answer: 'Send for Roberts. I decline to speak until Roberts come' And then they will send for Roberts, and there will be pause until Roberts come, and When Roberts has come and is standing before the Queen and the two Mejilises, then will I speak'

'And what will Your Highness say?'

'I shall tell them how Roberts paid thousands of rupees to obtain false witness at Kabul and that he slew thousands of my innocent people, and I shall ask that Roberts be punished, and when Roberts has been punished the will I speak'[199]

Curzon really hoped for a trip to London, it would be his personal victory over the entire establishment of the Indian Government. He even gave aesthetic advice to the Emir. One day during an interview he took off his turban to scratch his head and as Curzon said:

"In a moment he was transformed from the formidable despot to a commonplace and elderly man. I implored him when he came to London never to remove his turban or scratch his head; and, when I told him my reason, his vanity was at once piqued, and he promised faithfully to show himself at his best"[200]

---

[199] Curzon *Tales of Travel...*, p. 61.

[200] Curzon, *Ivi*, p. 50.

Abdur Rahman sent only his youngest son, Nasrullah, to England, who was benevolently received at court by the Queen.

The Emir, however, was offended by the continuing British refusal to establish a permanent diplomatic mission in Kabul, which only increased distrust in relations with Britain.

The Sovereign had secretly revealed to Curzon his plan to place Habibullah, his eldest son, as his successor, but Curzon knew well that in the eastern court's succession was never normal and peaceful. As Viceroy Curzon hoped to continue to enjoy the friendship, he had established with the Emir four years earlier, and to bring the transformation of the country into a more submissive state. But the intimacy granted to a traveller was not granted to the Viceroy of India. Curzon realised how difficult it was to deal with from his new position. Abdur Rahman:

"Was a very difficult person to handle and a very formidable opponent to cross"[201]

In 1901 Habibullah succeeded his father but still maintained a position of suspicion and distrust towards the English and their choice not to bear his country with arms.

4. Passage to India

The climb to the command of India was not easy and without obstacles for Curzon. In April 1897, whilst she was in Berlin on an un-official mission, he read in a newspaper that the Government was about to raise to peer the Marquis of Lorne, heir to the Duke of Argyll and husband of Princess Louise, the Queen's fourth daughter. All in view of an important assignment abroad. This in Curzon's eyes meant only one thing: the Government had chosen Lord Elgin's successor as Viceroy. He

---

[201] Curzon *Memoirs...,* II. p. 143.

decided to take pen and paper and write a long letter to Lord Salisbury setting out his point of view on the matter:

"[...]I have long, however, thought that were the post in India to fall vacant while I was still a young man — I shall be 40 by the end of Elgin's term — and were it to be offered to me, I should like to accept it. It may be thought that this argues undue temerity on my part and that I am singularly deficient in the requisite qualifications, Of this in many ways I am very conscious. But on the other hand it may perhaps be said for me that I have for at least 10 years made a careful and earnest study of Indian problems, have been to the country four times, and am acquainted with and have the confidence of most of its leading men.

If I have written books about its frontier problems — no doubt a risky venture — the views or forecasts I have been bold enough to express have I think on the whole turned out to be right: and I do not think, though my first book came out 8 years ago, I would cancel a single page in any one of them. I have been fortunate too in making the acquaintance of the rulers of the neighbouring states, Persia, Afghanistan, Siam, friendly relations with whom are a help to any Viceroy. At the India Office in 1891-1892, thanks to the appointment with which you honoured me, I learned something of the official working of the great machine.

I seem rather to have benne putting my wares, such as they are, in the shop window in this summary: but I have only done so to meet the obvious charge of presumption. It would perhaps be more pertinent to say that I believe a very great work can be done in India by an English Viceroy who is young and active and intensely absorbed in his work: who will at the same time try to do justice to the social part of his duties is the head of Anglo-Indian society (which Elgin certainly has not done) and will also establish the most friendly relations with the native chiefs and princes, and by keeping in touch with native feeling. For such a work a good deal of energy and application would he wanted and -— what very few men take to India — a great love of the country and pride in the imperial aspect of its possession.

For myself all experience in administration might be very useful as giving me knowledge of men and things which I lack, and as neutralising the youth which is always thrown in my teeth.

It may well be that, apart from apparent disqualifications, you may have other ideas as to the kind of work to which I ought to be set: and the few of my friends who have sometimes suspected me of Indian hankerings have pressed upon me that one should be unwise to leave the House of Commons.

All these are considerations which do not now arise, and which it would be absurd to discuss in relation to a contingency which may never even occur.

I have only decided to make this confession to you as my chief in great trust and humility, not with a view to soliciting from you any opinion or reply, but simply that you may know, if at a later date you are considering the disposition of the high post to which I have referred, and should there be any question between a number of possible candidates, that I would be grateful if my name were at least considered among the latter.

Please do not look upon this as implying any indifference to my present work, which is a daily delight to me and which I can never sufficiently thank you for having assigned to me. I should be intensely reluctant to give it up. But after all I am discussing a contingency that will not arise for another year and a half. Even should it arise then. Perhaps at a later date, should you not rule out my idea as vain and impracticable, you may be willing to let me discuss it with you. The fact of my having some day to go to the House of Lords has, of course, some influence on my own views, since I cannot in the nature of things look forward to a very prolonged House of Commons life- But my strongest impulse is, I can honestly say, not a personal one at all: it is the desire, while one is still in the heyday of life, to do some strenuous

227

work in a position of responsibility and in a cause for which previous study and training may have rendered one in some measure less unfit for the effort [...]".[202]

Lord Salisbury's response was polite, but he remained very evasive.

"In view of the Peerage to which you are destined – or doomed – I am not surprised at the turn your thoughts have taken. If the idea which you mention should be realised, India will be very much the richer and Foreign Office to poorer by the transaction. No one could say of such an appointment that it had put upon the roll of Indian Viceroys a man not fully worthy of those who have gone before. If it falls to my lot to criticise such an appointment, I shall heartily applaud it. But whether it will be in my power to make it is another question, to which I cannot even suggest an answer. A year and a half is a long way off and where shall we all be then?"[203]

A year after the first letter, when Curzon no longer heard of Lord Lorne's candidacy, he wrote to the Prime Minister again:

"It is just a year ago since I was writing to you about India; and the contingency that you discussed in your reply, viz. of having to make the appointment yourself, seems likely to arise. Perhaps, unless you have already made other and wiser arrangements, you may let me have a word or two with you about it when you return.

For 12 years I have worked and studied and thought – with a view should the chance ever arise – to fitting myself for the position. But I have also said to myself that I would not care to take it unless it were offered to me before I was 40: the reasons being that in my opinion the work is such as demands the energies of a young man in the prime life, and that no older man can do it in the way in which I am convinced,

---

[202] *Request for Viceroyalty. Curzon to Salisbury.* 18th of April 1897.

[203] *Evasive reply.* Salisbury to Curzon. 26th of April 1897.

from what I have seen in India, that it can and ought to be done: and in a less degree that I would like to get back to England while my father is still living, and before I am turned up into the House of Lords.

Then it seems too met that Viceroys as a rule can do nothing in their first year of two because they are new to the subjects and the work: and thus they are liable to be carried captive by the military men if the latter are strong in the Council, or by the financiers if they are to the front. My experience at the I.O. and elsewhere would to some extent relieve me of this source of weakness.

Trouble again must come when the Amir dies: it comes often enough with him while he lives. I think I possess to some extent his confidence and esteem. He constantly and regularly writes to me. I also know Habibullah, his successor. I think that while the father lives I could get on well with him; and that should he die while I was out there, there might be a little less change of trouble with his successor.

I cannot think that personal ambition is at bottom of any keenness I may exhibit in the matter. For many of my friends – talking to me on the slender suggestion of newspaper paragraphs – say to me that it would be folly to think of going away for five years, resigning a Parliamentary career and so on; and there is something to be said for this view, which I expect would be entirely shared by Arthur – to whom however I have never mentioned the matter. I can truly say that my anxiety in the case arises from the honest and not ignoble desire to render some service to a cause which I have passionately at heart.

On the other hand I frankly recognise the obstacles, the personal drawbacks and disqualifications and the strong reasons for a different appointment.

In that case I shall happily continue my work in my present post or any other that you may desire "[204]

Curzon in this letter as well as demonstrating a certain agitation and a hint of terror placed all his cards on the table. It shows his resume, qualities, and strengths. He never mentions it, but in practice he compares himself to Lord Lorne by pointing out how he was unsuitable for that role. Curzon knew very well that his rival was more than valid, however, married to a princess, even if the royal family was opposed to marriage, formerly Governor-General of Canada, where he had done more than exemplary work, clever and able man both in politics and with the people. The only stain on such an immaculate curriculum was the rumour that he was bisexual, as we shall see later homosexuality in Britain at that time was a thorny and complex issue, to say the least.

Lord Elgin, obviously aiming for a reconfirmation, had not been chosen by Salisbury and tried to discredit Curzon, in the eyes of the new Prime Minister, by sending him a very long letter, 16 pages, but with poor results. He had been a terrible Viceroy. He had not been able to solve several problems and the famine that broke out under his mandate had caused the death of almost five million people.

Curzon's letters were a calculated risk but had a useful advantage in reminding the Prime Minister of the qualities needed for a good Viceroy. Salisbury replied that the Indian question was in his thoughts but could not yet give a definitive answer.

In January 1899 the Prime Minister wrote to the Queen suggesting a name for her.

---

[204] *Second application.* Curzon to Salisbury. 18th of April 1898.

"He is a man in many respects, of great ability, as well as of extraordinary industry knowledge [...] his only fault is occasional rashness of speech in the House of Commons"[205]

In early June the Queen gave her provisional consent, a few days later the Prime Minister had a meeting to inform Curzon and revealed to him that it was his intention to offer him the office of Viceroy of India but first he would like to receive a certificate of good health.

Obviously, Curzon did not expect his back problems to be such an obstacle to his climb to the top of the Raj. Obviously, he could not undergo the visit immediately because he would have received a negative result, on the 19th of April he wrote to the Prime Minister a letter in pencil, revealing that he had written whilst lying down, thus unable to use pen and inkstand. The pain in his back forced him to long periods of rest whilst lying on his back.

Even the Secretary of State for India, Lord Hamilton, discussed Curzon's health in a letter dated 28th of September 1898. He wrote to Viceroy Lord Elgin:

"As to his health, I have my misgivings, so much so that when I knew he was to be appointed I pressed on the Prime Minister the necessity of a thorough medical certification and examination [...] The Indian climate suits him, and he is capable of greater exertion there than in England. He suffers from a slight curvature of the spine, and when greatly overworked he suffers pain and inconvenience, which I fancy affects his brain power, for he is obliged to lie on his back and do no work. The risk, I admit, is considerable, for a Viceroy being laid up in this way means a temporary stoppage of the Government of India; but he is a man of such high

---

[205] Salisbury to Queen, *Letters* III. p. 225.

courage and resolution that he will do all that a human being can to morally subordinate and override his physical failings"[206]

Curzon could not escape the visit and underwent a check-up with Sir Thomas Smith:

"I hereby certify that I have examined the Rt Hon. George Curzon and I can find no sign of disease about him and were I making report to a life assurance office, I should recommend him for insurance at the ordinary rate for a 1st class life"[207]

Curzon sent the certificate to the Prime Minister that same day. He could not resist and wrote another letter to Lord Salisbury:

"When you spoke to me the other day, I hardly found words with which to express my recognition of the compliment which your enquiries seemed indirectly to involve. Nor even now do I regard what you said as indicating more than a willingness to consider favourably my name in connection with the post of which we have spoken"[208]

Four days later, the Prime Minister replied:

"I am very glad to see that Sir T. Smith gives so favourable an account of your case. Probably work in another climate with better hour will rather do you good than harm. I shall send in my submission shortly to the Queen, and unless she has just changed in her view, I shall have no difficulty in getting her approval. I enclose a

---

[206] Hamilton to Elgin, 28th of September 1898.

[207] Medical Certificate. 20th of June 1898. Christ Church.

[208] Curzon to Salisbury. 20th of June 1898.

transcript from a part of one of her letters which she charged me particularly to show you"[209]

The Queen replied to the Prime Minister three days after her eightieth birthday. The letter is difficult to read, the uncertain calligraphy revealed the problems of sight from which the Sovereign suffered for some time:

"The Queen read with much interest Lord Salisbury's letter respecting the future Vice Roy and his account of his conversation with Sir Wm. Lockhart with whom she feels sure he will have be please. His opinion of Mr. G. Curzon is certainly of great weight and the latter's friendly feeling towards the Ameer and his knowledge of Afghanistan[210] are very important.

But that is not all; the future Vice Roy must really shake himself more and more free from his red-tapist narrow-minded Council and Entourage. He must be more independent, must hear for himself what the feelings of the Natives really are, and do what he thinks right and not be guided by the snobbish and vulgar, over-bearing and offensive behaviour of our Civil and Political Agents, if we are to go on peaceably and happily in India, and not trying to tramble on the people and continually reminding them and making them feel that they are a conquered people. They must of course feel that we are masters but if should be done kindly and not offensively which alas! Is so often the case. Would Mr. Curzon feel and do this? Would Mrs. Curzon who is an American do to represent a Vice Queen?[211]

---

[209] Queen's approval. Salisbury to Curzon. 24th of June 1898.

[210] *Sic*

[211] Queen Victoria to Salisbury. 27th of May 1898.

Lord Salisbury agreed with the Queen's words and stressed that:

"Putting aside the very un-official mode of expression, I entirely concur in the idea which is at the bottom of extract. Paper and "damned nigger" are threatening our rule in India: and unfortunately as we grow more contemptuous, the Indian natives of all races are becoming more conscious of it, and more sensitive"[212]

He asked Curzon to keep the news secret for the time being. The future Viceroy wrote about the Queen's letter in a long letter of thanks:

"I shall not fail to bear in mind her wise injunctions. They might furnish a Rule of Conduct to anyone about to occupy a position of authority over Asiatic races. In travelling I have seen something of these and have been thrown so much in their society that I hope I have lost – if indeed I ever had – the insular arrogance of the Englishman. One more likely to find this among men who have lived long – often too long – in the East, and have become hardened and sometimes almost brutalised by contact, in posts of power, with people of a lower social and mental organisation. I recognise that the newcomer, unwarped by these associations, ought to set a different example and to keep in control the sort of spirit that made the French writer say of our rule in India: "Its sont justes mais ils ne sont pas bons"[213]

It was the task of the Secretary of State for India to give the news to the Viceroy in office. Lord Hamilton hoped that Lord Balfour would be chosen:

---

[212] Salisbury to Curzon. 24th of June1898.

[213] Curzon to Salisbury. 25th of June 1898.

"He is a safe, reliable man, who has not committed himself in writing or speeches to any particular frontier views or policy"[214]

But as he himself admitted

"Curzon is a charming fellow, and whose ability, industry, and courage make him in some respects admirably qualified. The spirit of adventure is somewhat developed in him, and an adventurous Viceroy has too many vistas of exploration open him"[215]

On paper Lord Balfour was the perfect Viceroy: he possessed both the ability and the administrative knowledge to solve India's problems. Famine and plague had brought the subcontinent to its knees, and Lord Elgin was too shy and unprepared when it came to make important decisions. But Curzon had a trump card that made Salisbury decide in his favour: his interest in the Indian borders. The events of the last year made it clear in London that the situation was now unmanageable and the continuous sending of soldiers was not the best thing to do. Lord Hamilton believed that belligerence and ideas about Curzon's borders would be a handicap to his mandate whilst Salisbury believed that Curzon would extend the period of British rule over India.

But Salisbury forbade Curzon from releasing his latest book, On *the Indian Frontier*. The book was already in the printing phase and the author had to return a large sum to the publisher and pay some debts. When he returned home seven years later the book was not up-to-date with the times and was not published, despite everything Curzon was very angry with Salisbury for his excessive precaution.

---

[214] Hamilton to Elgin. 5th of August 1898.

[215] Ibidem.

The announcement to the world was made on the 11th of August. Every newspaper on the globe reported the news.

Congratulations came from everywhere; the Times was the only one not to fill it with praise. Before leaving for India, the trip was scheduled for the 10th of December, Curzon and his wife went to Strathpeffer, a spa in Scotland to seek relief from his back pain. On the way he was invited by Victoria and stopped at Balmoral. The Queen was enthusiastic about Curzon[216], wrote words of praise in her diary and a few days later congratulated Salisbury on her choice.

Before leaving for India, he still had a simple but complicated problem to solve. The title.

Curzon had discussed with the Queen herself that a mere member of the House of Commons could not represent the Queen Empress as Viceroy. In his years as a member of parliament he had tried to abolish the custom that required the abandonment of the seat to succeed him. Curzon therefore according to the rules would have to wait for the death of his father to sit in the House of Lords. Salisbury suggested a solution in half, Curzon would be made Peer of Ireland. The location gave Curzon two advantages. Under the Act of Union of 1800 Irish peers could elect 20 of them who would settle for life in the House of lords whilst others could stand for free for the House of Commons, so Curzon could be re-elected once back from

---

[216] *"Soon after luncheon saw Mr. Curzon, and talked of all the difficulties lying before him, but he knows India well and is free from red-tapism, so that I hope he will do well"*

236

India[217]. Where was the problem? Curzon had no connection with Ireland, he did not even have a blade of Irish grass and his English feet had never passed the *Irish Sea*, not to mention that it was from 1868 that a new Peer of Ireland was not created. For the designated Viceroy everything was forgotten and on the 24th of September the *Times* announced:

"The Queen has been pleased to confer the dignity of a peerage upon the Rt Hon. George N. Curzon, Viceroy designate of India, bye the name, style, and title of Baron Curzon of Kedleston, in Peerage of Ireland"[218]

On the 10th of December Curzon set sail for India. The trip lasted three weeks, on board the SS Arabia he arrived in Bombay with his American wife and two daughters, also in his retinue there was the old friend and now private secretary Walter Lawrence, expert connoisseur of India, thanks to his years of service at the Indian Civil Service.

As soon as they arrived, they were greeted by the Bombay Municipal Corporation, a festive crowd and a reception for 1400 people formed the backdrop to Curzon's first speech in India, speech given over a gold carpet. A trip with some unforeseen events led him along the country, the journey was honoured by the crowd at each station. On his arrival in Calcutta he was taken by carriage to the Viceroy's Palace. The new Viceroy was greeted with a thirty-one-shot salute as he climbed the steps of the building, a building that, by a curious case of fate, had been built on the model of Kedleston Hall. Lord Elgin was waiting for him at the top of the stairs. But official handover of power took place on the 6th of January in the Throne Room of the Palace,

---

[217] A well-known example is the case of Lord Palmerston, who from Peer of Ireland sat for 16 years in the *House of Commons*, 9 of which as Prime Minister.

[218] Everything had a price and for the title Curzon had to pay the Queen £290.

and later Curzon accompanied Elgin to his boat at the Hooghly River. 5 days before his fortieth birthday George Nathaniel Curzon became the fifteenth Viceroy of India and the thirty-fifth Governor.

5. The plagues of India.

The Curzon Government transformed India, indelibly. His work has created drastic splits between the British and the natives, splits that were momentarily strengthened in the First World War but soon after returned wider than before. He was able not only to increase the nationalism that was taking shape and idea at that time, but above all he succeeded where no one had succeeded before, he unified India under a single purpose: the hatred for him.

Curzon was a man who lived off hierarchies, chains of command and ancient rituals. An English gentleman with blue blood was used to believing that the good of *his* farmers depended on him, a loving father who administered everything with the aim of the welfare of his people. In Victorian Britain, only the foolish, and the imperialists, now had this feudal vision of command. England had not been that bucolic country of thatched cottages, little animals in the yard, hat- greetings and a Sunday fair for a long time. In a few years the country had passed from Jane Austen to Charles Dickens with virtually no interludes. Curzon knew all this but denied it, already in 1870, the majority of the population lived in cities with more than ten thousand inhabitants, and not in villages that grew up around the church.

Curzon went to look for that feudalism in India and found it in the various apparently autonomous principles but in fact under imperial control through an official sent to each court. In one of his last speeches as Viceroy, at the University of Calcutta, he said:

"I have always been a devoted believer in the continued existence of the native states in India, and an ardent well-wisher of the native princes. But I believe in them not

238

as relics, but as rulers, not as puppets but as living factors in the administration. I want them to share the responsibilities as well as the glories of British rule."[219]

On paper there is no puppet Maharaja but rather an important part of the British rule, in fact objects of furniture on the large Indian shelf.

Curzon was no stranger, all his predecessors felt the same way, the hierarchy had created the Empire and the hierarchy had to keep it alive and strong.

Curzon was ultimately chosen for his ideas on the question of the borders of the Raj but soon he had to deal with the problems that his predecessor had failed to solve, problems that upset not the borders but the whole country: hunger.

The famine that struck India under Elgin's rule and lasted under Curzon's administration[220] had the unfortunate task of reminding the British that what they thought were *Indian problems* were a breeze compared to drought and famine. A peasant cared nothing about the movements of Russian troops in Central Asia, he was more interested in surviving. The British with a bureaucratic cruelty took some decisions that led to the death of millions and millions of people.

---

[219] *Lord Curzon in India: being a selection from his speeches as viceroy & Governor-general of India 1898-1905.* Macmillan and co. Limited, London 1906 p. 42.

[220] I have extensively used the chronology and bibliography of Mike Davis' work. For more information see: M. Davis, *Late Victorian Holocausts: El Nino famines and the making of the third world,* Verso, London 2001. Trad It *Late Victorian Holocaust: El ino, famines and the birth of the third world.* I do not entirely agree with the author's conclusions, but the book contains a very good biography on the subject.

Previous famines had once again highlighted the biggest problem in India: distances. If a region suffered a famine you could get help from the neighbouring region or vice versa but the biggest problem was how to get food supplies. In 1880 the commission led by Sir Richard Strachey had put into force regional codes to regulate famine, controls and rescue in case of need. In 1878, two years after the famine, a relief and insurance fund were set up to ensure that Calcutta could finance famine and drought without compromising Government priorities, primarily the permanent military campaign on the north-west border. The measures taken were mainly two, the surplus of rice from Burma integrated into the imperial rations and the ten thousand miles of new tracks built, almost all built thanks to the fund against famine. With this system, each province could eliminate the food shortage by getting help from the others, Burma fed the Punjab and the north-western provinces or vice versa, Bombay and Madras helped each other and so on. All this allowed Lord Elgin to say triumphant to the Queen:

"The Improvement of the means of communications particularly by railway makes it possible to cope with scarcity now in a way that was out of the power of the officers of former days "[221]

In fact, it was all useless, and Lord Elgin never admitted that he was wrong, that he needed help, and in so doing he followed the same path as his predecessor, Lord Lytton, who was heading straight for the catastrophe[222]. A road that Curzon too went

---

[221] Rashmi Pande, *The Viceroyalty of Lord Elgin II,* Janaki Prakashan, Patna 1986. p. 131.

[222] Premansukumar Bandyopadhyay, *Indian Famine and Agrarian Problems,* Star Publications, Calcutta, p. 231.

on. In 1896 a very weak monsoon prevented sowing in Punjab, north-western provinces, Oudh, Bihar, Deccan and Madras. The rains did more damage in the central areas of the subcontinent, especially in Rajasthan and in the central provinces, where the region had been suffering from poor harvests for three years. The price of wheat went up and because of a bad harvest in England the reserves of grain suffered a greater export. In 1894 the British harvest amounted to 80 million bushels whilst in 1895 it was only 37 million[223]. The Elgin system only made it possible to democratise the price of grain even in areas for irrigation such as the Godavari delta in Madras. The railways did not guarantee food for everyone because even where stocks arrived, prices were prohibitive for most of the population. Part of the fund against famine, after having almost emptied it to create the railways, had been used to finance the second Afghan war, triggering the general anger. The Government also ignored the signs that were coming from all sides and alarming the vast amount of the population below the threshold of survival. The rise in prices had also raised the percentage of the poor, but just as in 1876 the Indian Office and the Government in Calcutta did not seem interested in the matter.

Imperial ignorance of the problem had turned drought into famine. Riots and unrest were happening every day, and the press was now accusing Elgin of inability. He, more concerned about the Afghans at the border, was not happy to open hospices and public relief yards in those districts most affected. Elgin, like Lytton, forbade the liberal governing bodies to help the population in any way, and forbade loans for the purchase of grain and the creation of solidarity emporiums. Burma was almost forced to export its surplus rice to Europe, the state coffers were being emptied

---

[223] M. de Cecco, *Moneta e Impero: Il Sistema finanziario internazionale dal 1890 al 1914,* Einaudi, Turin 1979.

because of the war and the fund to combat famine was being reduced. On his way to Jubbulpore, Elgin had the audacity to say:

"I can only say that travelling during the last few days in Indore and Gwalior and now in these Provinces up to the gates of your city I have been struck by the prosperous appearance of the country even with the small amount of rain that has come lately"

Elgin was convinced that the famine was not the fault of the drought but of the inability of the Indians to work. He imported *poorhouses* into India, hospices for the weakest, which were not well received because the population feared that those who lived there would be forced to convert or deported to Europe. An American official visiting a hospice reported that the diet was based on dry flour and water and the wheat was adulterated with soil. The death rate in that region went from 50 per thousand to 627 per thousand.

Ironically, the bloodiest riots took place in those regions not affected by the drought but only by the rise in prices, the press now told the facts by publishing also the photographs taken by the missionaries, the advent of the affordable Kodak One had spread the photograph. In the meantime, Elgin was more concerned with collecting taxes, which were obviously not paid, and to make the situation even worse in the summer of 1896, the bubonic plague arrived in Bombay from China. The city's ghettos offered fertile ground for disease, poor hygiene, sewage, mice and waste. Health authorities had been warning the Government for a long time and even the well-known Florence Nightingale had launched herself against the harsh hygienic situations in which the Indians were forced to live. The Empire was not inclined towards raising taxes to bring sewage and drinking water.[224] In short, the plague and

---

[224] F. B. Smith, *Florence Nightingale,* Croom Helm, London 1982. p. 125.

famine were joined by cholera and other diseases and together they killed a fifth of low-caste workers in the region of Bombay. Some ports began to impose a quarantine for grain from Bombay and a mass hysteria spread, the terror was that a general embargo would be imposed that would bring the already destroyed Indian economy to its knees. The Government fought the plague by burning the hovels and then sprinkling everything with quicklime and phenolic acid, the plague mice simply moved from house to house and over time the victims of disease were joined by homeless people. The railways of Elgin served only one purpose: to spread contaminated grain in the other provinces, so that the plague from Bombay spread to the Deccan.

"Even more important than travellers in bringing infectious rodent fleas to new locales was India's vast commerce, developed though the encouragement of free trade policies [...] The transport of rice, bajri, wheat and other grains across the famine-stricken country in the late 1890s, a traffic meant to be life-giving, particularly helped disseminate plague amongst India's malnourished population. Grain was he favourite food of the black rat, while the great plague vector [the flea], 'bred best in the debris of cereal grains' [...] When these fleas arrived at new towns or villages they often carried plague bacilli with them, fastened on local black rats as new hosts, began epizootics and then transferred plague to humans as alternate hosts"[225]

The Government, once again showing complete disinterest in its subjects, began preparations for the Queen's Jubilee. All this caused a series of attacks on Europeans everywhere, which risked leading to a second mutiny.

---

[225] I. Klein, *" Plague, Policy and Popular Unrest in British India" in "Modern Asian Studies"* 22. 4. Cambridge University Press, Cambridge 1998. p. 737.

Lord Hamilton and Lord Elgin were more worried about the plague, if the contagious panic had spread throughout the world the embargo would have held back the Indian and therefore imperial economy.

In June 1897, it was Elgin himself who admitted that 4.5 million people had already died. Behramji Malabari, the nationalist editor of the *Indian Spectator,* replied that the victims in their totality, adding also the deaths from the plague reached 18 million deaths.

The *Missionary Review of the World* abandoned its support for the British Government when the situation was now uncontrollable:

"When the pangs of hunter drive people in silent procession, living skeletons, to find food, dying by the way; the stronger getting a few grains, the feebler perishing, and children, an intolerable burden, are sold at from ten to thirty cents apiece, and when at best a heritage of orphaned children of tens of thousands must remain to the country – this is not 'impending' famine – it is grim, gaunt, awful famine itself"[226]

Cosmopolitan published photographs of starving Indians and compared the costs and glitz designed by the Government for the Jubilee celebrations. Lord Elgin did not make any difference when it came to spend over a hundred million pounds on the festivities whilst he was always reluctant to spend public money to stop the famine. The rescue yards looked more like a Nazi lager. The food was poor, the hygiene conditions were non-existent, the perpetrators were almost all thieves or racists and the survival rate was very low.

When the sky returned the monsoons in 1898, the Government decided to immediately close the shipyards and their occupants find themselves undernourished and without some means to exploit the rains. All of this caused another 6.5 million

---

[226] *"The Famine in India"*, Missionary Review of the World, April 1897. p. 286.

deaths, bringing the victims of famine to over 11 million. Unfortunately, however, despite the departure of Elgin a new drought hit the country and once again a Viceroy ignored all warning signs and soon there was a new famine even more devastating. The culprit? Curzon, of course.

In 1899 the new monsoon season came regularly at the end of May and lasted until June. Shimla's *season* was dominated by the presence of Lady Curzon, the Viceroy's wife was a Chicago heiress, but she behaved like a perfect English *High Society* woman. Receptions and balls were the order of the day but when it started raining in June it stopped immediately and for the whole of July no rain fell. Lord Curzon asked the chief of observers, Sir John Eliot, for an explanation, who predicted heavy rains from August to September. Rains that never came. A second drought in a few years was about to hit the country again.

In addition to the usual regions of Deccan and Rajasthan, this time the regions of Gujarat and Berar were also affected, which until then had been considered safe from any natural disaster.

The wells, irrigation canals and watercourses dried up completely in a short time and the lack of water and food was compounded by the lack of fodder for the livestock. The debts and problems of the previous famine were still present and burdened the shoulders of the surviving citizens and the surpluses of the abundant harvest of 1898 had served to pay loans taken out in the previous drought.

The drought brought economic insecurity, foreclosures and expropriations splashed, as the unemployed.

Curzon thought that:

"The Government had gone as far as it should in meeting Indian desires for participation in the public service and legislatures.

In order to avoid any problems, like those that broke out in Ireland after the famine, he decided to act in advance. He made the school system more rigid and severe, put

245

stronger control on the press, restored aristocratic prerogatives and managed to turn Hindus and Muslims against each other.[227]

Curzon did not want to give a cue to his opponents and therefore forced officials to proclaim in public that the crisis depended on drought and not misgovernment. He was convinced that helping the population would damage the moral fibre of the nation:

"Any Government which imperilled the financial position of India in the interests of prodigal philanthropy would be open to serious criticism; but any Government which by indiscriminate alms-giving weakened the fibre and demoralised the self-reliance of the population, would be guilty of a public crime"[228]

Curzon was able to overcome even Lord Elgin in absurdity, cut that rations calling them too abundant and tightened the requirements for asking for and obtaining help. With its new system, more than a million people were driven out of aid. He had managed to bureaucratise a famine by systematically organising a carnage.

Obviously, Curzon was not the primary culprit in all this, the war against the Boers forced the whole Empire to economise and Lord Hamilton had imposed new controls on the items of expenditure. Hamilton was the Secretary of State for India, but he was more concerned that India would fulfil its duties as a colony than the survival of the settlers who lived there. The minister refused to set up a charitable fund to raise money to fight famine but repeatedly insisted that Curzon set up a fundraiser for the war led by Kitchener and did not even raise an eyebrow when Curzon presented the project for the construction of a huge and expensive monument to

---

[227] J. McLane, *Indian Nationalism and the Early Congress,* Princeton University Press, Princeton 1977. p. 71.

[228] C. Ramage, *The Great Indian Drought of 1899,* Boulder Cole Habour 1977. p. 5.

Victoria in Calcutta but urged the Viceroy to put under strict control the rescue yards. Public opinion at home completely ignored the issue, preferring to focus on the tough war against the Boers.

To add to the absurdity when the population of Topeka in Kansas sent 200,000 sacks of wheat to the Indian people, the expeditions were taxed on their arrival in Ajmer.

Curzon's cuts also affected the workers in the rescue yards, the wages were calculated on healthy workers and on the number of hours and performance this led the malnourished Indians to earn a pittance, the rations were half of those reserved for prisoners.

Over time, in addition to drought and hunger, dysentery, cholera and diarrhoea increased the number of deaths. Curzon went further and decided to deport all the refugees who had illegally entered the *British Raj* territories from the autonomous realms. Of the 85 million people affected by the drought, only 42% lived in territories under direct British control. The others were citizens of the various autonomous realms. To send the needy back corresponded in fact to a death sentence and this Curzon knew it well but did not show the slightest hesitation. There were 688 independent states that had nothing to do with politics and economics, everything depended on British choices, and if the British did not make serious choices for their direct subjects, imagine if they would take care of someone else subjects. Except for a few charitable Maharajas, the majority followed Curzon's decisions to the letter.

The most absurd paradox is perhaps that of the merchants. They accumulated enormous amounts of grain and rice and moved them from the countryside to the cities. The grain was moved and placed under protection by armed men. Pierre Loti, the French traveller, on his tour of India, described the saddest and most grim scene of the whole matter, the journey of the grain in the wagons of the trains.

"At the first village at which we stop a sound is heard as soon as the wheels have ceased their noisy clanking – a peculiar sound that strikes a chill into us even before we have understood its nature. It is the beginning of that horrible song which we

shall hear so frequently now that we have entered the land of famine. Nearly all that is heard in the playground of a school, but there is an undefined note of something harsh and weak and shrill which fills us with pain.

Oh! Look at the poor little things jostling there against the barrier, stretching out their withered hands towards us from the end of the bones which represent the arms. Every part of their meagre skeleton protrudes with shocking visibility through the brown skin that hangs in folds about them; their stomachs are so sunken that one might think that their bowels had been altogether removed. Flies swarm on their lips and eyes, drinking what moisture may still exude [...]

'Maharajah! Maharajah!' all the little voices cry at once in a kind of quivering song. There are some who barely five years old, and these, too, cry 'Maharajah! Maharajah!' as they stretch their terribly wasted little hands through the barrier"[229]

The food was not for the poor but for the wealthy city dwellers who could afford the price of grain. The poor walked to regions not affected by the drought, Gujarat for example, but over time the famine also affected those territories.

In response to the drought, the central Government decided to increase taxes by 24 percent, sending orders everywhere to collect taxes in any way. The most affected were, of course, the farmers who were unable to pay and who saw their fields confiscated[230].

---

[229] P. Lotti, *India,* English translation by George Inman, T. Werner Laurie, London 1995. pp. 171 - 2.

[230] D. Hardiman, *The Crisis of Lesser Patidars: Peasant Agitations in Kheda District, Gujarat, 1917-34,* in D. Low (edited by), *Congress and the Raj,* Heinemann Educational, London 1977. pp. 55-56.

After two years of no one expected that the drought would last but the monsoon season of 1901 was almost as disappointing as the previous one, in addition an invasion of crickets and trestles has transformed the little work done in a useless effort.

Bombay kept the rescue yards open until Christmas 1902. The central provinces had to suffer a peak of mortality from malaria in 1900, which coincided with the return of the monsoons in summer.

The number of deaths varies according to the report or expert consulted. The official figures of the Indian Office say 1.25 million deaths but are not counted deaths from malaria. The calculations do not even consider the deaths in the independent states. The number is probably around 10 million dead.[231] *The Lancet* the well-known medical journal proposed an estimate of 19 million deaths, calculated based on the last census of 1901 removing the victims of the plague[232].

Another drought followed by a famine hit the country in 1907-1908, causing another 3 million deaths.

The damage to the economy was enormous and practically incalculable. The agricultural development obtained from the middle of the nineteenth century was completely zeroed, the draught cattle almost completely disappeared. Population growth slowed down, and infant mortality increased again after falling as a result of British reforms.

---

[231] A. Maharatna, *The demography of Famines: An Indian Historical Perspective,* Oxford University Press India, Delhi 1996. p. 15.

[232] *The Lancet,* 16th of May 1901.

The famines that struck the country never diverted the attention of the rulers from the *Great Game*, however, the imperial Government was more interested in Russia than in its subjects dying of hunger every day. For example, Lord Lytton, Viceroy during the famine of 1876-1878

"Burning with anxiety to distinguish himself in a great war"

He perfectly embodied Disraeli's imperialist ideas and in India he behaved like Salisbury and Disraeli wanted him to behave. Lytton, ignoring the starving deaths that surrounded him, started a new Afghan war and, as his budget adviser reminded him continuously of every war waged by the Viceroy, was to be paid not by the rich British taxpayers but by the poor, exhausted Indian subjects.

Lytton was appreciated by the Queen, not so much for his political work as for his poetic compositions, but even Lord Salisbury considered it extravagant. Lytton did nothing but use the theory of Adam Smith and Thomas Malthus to counter famine or do nothing. Smith was in fact convinced that:

"Famine has never arisen from any other cause but the violence of Government attempting by improper means, to remedy the inconvenience of dearth"[233]

The Viceroy was simply the perfect product of the Haileybury School that churned out the various administrators of the Raj. Malthus' theories mixed with social Darwinism created a solid basis for any defence at home of the Indian Government's choices. Malthus, who had been headmaster at Haileybury, argued that any public effort to combat famine would simply increase the number of deaths, man and politics should not intervene in any way in natural processes. The Lyttonian *laissez-faire* had been his trump card in getting the appointment, as the border issue had

---

[233] A. Smith, *An Inquiry into the nature and Causes of the Wealth of Nations (1776)*, Hackett Publishing, London 1930. pp. 27-28.

been for Curzon. The imperial Government would never give up its earnings to feed India, the Raj had to self-sustain.

This parenthesis on purely climatic and environmental issues appears important, especially if we analyse everything in the perspective of the Indian contribution to the First World War. The mortality of Raj's soldiers was very high, and not only amongst those hammered by bullets and explosions but amongst the wounded and the sick. After years of malnutrition with a weakened immune system and a climate unknown to them, such as autumn and winter in Flanders, even *simple* diseases contracted in the trenches could be an insurmountable obstacle.

6. "Curzonation"

The highest achievement for Curzon was undoubtedly the *Delhi Dubar* of 1903.

Delhi Dubar, the Court of Delhi, was a mass gathering held in Delhi's Coronation Park. The purpose of the event was to commemorate the Coronation of the King or Queen of Great Britain as Emperor or Empress of India. During the Raj period, the ceremony took place only three times.

The first Dubar was held in 1877 to celebrate the coronation of Victoria as Empress of India and set in stone the definitive transfer of power of the subcontinent into British hands. It was organised by Viceroy Lytton and for the occasion a banquet was organised for 68 thousand people amongst Maharaja, satraps and officials. The reception lasted a week and was the most colossal and expensive lunch in history.[234]

---

[234] *The Times,* 9th of January 1877; A. Harlan, *Owen Meredith,* New York 1946. p. 218-220; B. Cohn, *"Representing Authority in Victorian India"* in E. Hobsbawn, T.

The first Dubar had taken place during the famine. During Lord Lytton's mammoth lunch, about 100,000 people had died of hunger. What better gift to pay homage to the new Empress? A pile of dead bodies. Lytton was an opiate who most likely had inherited mental problems from his father. In order to organise this huge celebration, he had respected the dictates of the then Secretary of State for India:

"Gaudy enough to impress the Orientals [...] and furthermore a pageant which hid the nakedness of the sword on which we really rely"[235]

An amnesty was signed, and more than 16,000 prisoners were released, depriving them of the daily ration of food and forcing them to join the mass of hungry people. All exiles after the mutiny could return except Prince Firoz Shah[236].

"A truly Imperial Viceroy 237 " was defined by Curzon and observing the Dubar he had organised no one could contradict this definition. Curzon's unbridled imperialism managed to overshadow even the one organised by Lytton.

Curzon had made the whole of India observe a long period of mourning for the death of the Sovereign Empress, with the death of Victoria was gone an era and especially an ally. He did not have the same respect and admiration for her heir, especially as

---

Ranger, *The Invention of Tradition,* Cambridge University Press, Cambridge 1983. pp. 179-208.

[235] A. Roberts, *Salisbury: Victorian Titan,* Orion, London 1999. p. 215.

[236] R. Holmes, *Sahib: The British Soldier in India,* Harper Perennial, London 2006. p. 82.

[237] C. J. O'Donnell, *The Failure of Lord Curzon,* Forgotten Books, London 1903. p. XVIII.

he did not share the same concerns for his mother's India. The biggest obstacle for Curzon was the fact that the King did not intend to give much of his time to the Viceroy:

"Unless there was anything of importance or interest to relate"[238]

Curzon wanted the King to attend a coronation as Emperor in Delhi, the Queen had never set foot in the subcontinent and the Viceroy hoped that the new ruler would be more inclined to a trip. He had already calculated the timing of only seven weeks, but the Palace did not agree and in the end, Curzon had to be satisfied with the brother of the King whilst at the coronation in London were invited some Indian princes.

Curzon clashed with the imperial administration when they told him from London that because of the protracted Boer war the cost of the trip of all the guests to the coronation would be borne by the Indian Government. He pointed out that after all the effort and Indian contribution, economic and human, in the war in Africa the least that the central Government could do was to provide for the expenses and avoid rumours about the London Government. This time Curzon was on the side of reason, especially since at the same time Lord Hamilton had the audacity to announce to him that the costs of the Duke of Connaught's journey, the King's brother, would be borne by India and not by Great Britain. Curzon obviously did not let it go, he was already organising a very expensive party in which the King would not attend, and he did not want to have to pay for guests he did not want and for members of the royal family he did not want to receive. From London they made him understand when he was getting bored and shifting attention from more important things, but they were all afraid that the news would reach the press or the Parliament because they knew

---

[238] D. Gilmour, *Curzon...*, p. 236.

253

very well that the public would support the theses of India and not Great Britain. In the end the imperial Government surrendered and decided to pay all the expenses of the journey of the princes to England and the Count to India. Curzon even managed to escape the high bill of a reception at the Indian Office in honour of the seas princes and dignitaries representing the Raj.

"It is a great triumph, no one will know here how it has been obtained button One day it will come but how by a single strong despatch and by a little courage I defeated them all"

So, he wrote with a triumphant tone to his wife shortly after receiving the news whilst attending a coronation in Mysore.

Dubar's organisation took over a year. Every activity of 1902 was in the perspective of the big party, that Curzon wanted to organise himself in every detail. He knew very well what power the ostentation and ceremonies had in India and since the King would not be present the scene had to be occupied by the Viceroy. The protagonist of the party was Curzon himself, relegating even the brother of the Sovereign to the background. Shortly afterwards everyone starts talking about the *Curzonation*.

At the beginning of 1902 he first dealt with some border issues, his plans for glory could not be in any way ruined by some insurrection whilst the eyes of the Empire would be focused on his feast. Having settled the Berar issue in March he travelled to Agra and then inaugurated the North-West Frontier Province and then went to inspect the new *Imperial Cadet Corps.* The training of those who would become his bodyguard during Dubar was underway.

Curzon did not neglect any aspect of the party, from the programme of events to the new officers' uniforms designed for the occasion. He even took care of the decorations and architecture of the entire area used for the ceremony. Delhi underwent a dramatic change: in a relatively short time he electrified almost the entire city, a hospital and a new court, a post office and a telegraph station were built. New telephone lines were installed, and maps were printed to guide visitors. As usual, commemorative medals were produced for these events. The Viceroy even got involved in church business by personally choosing hymns for religious services.

The preparation of the feast was also the moment when Curzon's decline as Viceroy began. As we shall see in the next chapter, the reason that led him to resign was his defeat in the clash with the Commander-in-Chief of the Indian Armed Forces, Lord Kitchener, but the relationship with the imperial Government began to crack on an apparently marginal issue: Curzon was convinced that without a great novelty to be announced during his speech to Durbar the whole thing would seem to the eyes of the Indians as just a great and expensive event for a select few, he was convinced that the event needed a news bomb to be proclaimed and in this way satisfy all Indians and not only those present in Delhi during the two weeks of celebrations. He almost immediately rejected the idea of extending political privileges by increasing the number of natives in representative institutions, by increasing the number of Indians in the various local councils or by appointing some of them to senior positions in the national administration. After reflection he decided that the best way to present a new Emperor to the people was to announce a lowering of taxes, in this case the salt tax and the increase of exempt from income tax. He wrote to Lord Hamilton that he welcomed the idea but pointed out when the creation of a precedent was risky. The imperial Government should not and did not want to create the illusion that every new ruler would have to cut taxes. The Cabinet agreed with this fear and rejected Curzon's idea. He was not discouraged and wrote directly to the new King, in a telegram to the Private Secretary of the Sovereign he illustrated his idea and benefits. This gesture, considered by many to be unconstitutional, sent the Government on a rampage but in response the Private Secretary of Curzon stressed the fact that being a matter of coronation it was right to involve the Sovereign in a decision very closely related to him. A King who lowers his taxes would have been loved right from the start.

The new Secretary of State for India, Sir John Brodick, wrote indignantly to the Viceroy pointing out that for this intrusion the Government was even considering removing him from his post. In the end a compromise was found: taxes would not fall thanks to the King but thanks to the Indian Government and nothing would be announced during Durbar but 11 weeks later during the budget speech. After the compromise many members of the Government wrote to Curzon, first Lord Balfour, pointing out that their friendship had not been affected by the disagreements between Calcutta and London. Despite the relaxing letters something had broken between the two capitals and the rift was ready to widen and swallow it[239].

The opening ceremony confronted Curzon with another problem: elephants.

Curzon was the first Viceroy not to have his own elephant, he considered them uncomfortable especially for his back problems:

"One of the most horrible forms of locomotion"

He had used them other times during tiger hunts but not for ceremonies. The magnificence and extreme orientalism of *his* Durbar could not foresee the lack of elephants, in fact he had to borrow one from a maharaja.

The inauguration of the two weeks of festivities took place on the 29th of December, with a very long procession of dignitaries, maharaja, begum and of course the Viceroy with the Vicereine in her splendid pea cocktail dress.

"a magnificent sight, and all description must fail to give an adequate idea of its character, its brilliancy of colour and its ever-changing features, the variety of howdahs and trappings and the gorgeousness of the dress adorning the persons of the Chiefs who followed in the wake of the Viceroy [...] A murmur of admiration, breaking into short-lived cheers, rose from the crowd."[240]

---

[239] D. Gilmour, *Curzon...*, pp. 240-242.

[240] N. Ferguson, *Empire...*, p. 179.

Curzon's speech to the King contained his entire idea of what the historian Niall Ferguson called *Tory-entalism*, that is, the sum of feudal values of English power and the eastern power of autonomous principalities:

"His Empire is strong [...] because it regards the liberties and respects the dignities and rights of all his feudatories and subjects. The keynote of the British policy in India has been to conserve all the best features in the fabric of native society. By that policy we have attained the wonderful measure of success: in it we recognise an assured instrument of further triumphs in the future."

Here was the main political plan of the Curzon administration to make everyone understand that British and Indian interests coincided. His idea was that of an Indian federal Empire where the British dealt with a few important things and the princes had the rest of the power. The problem, however, was that Curzon did not show a conciliatory aspect but presented himself as a kind of teacher who wanted to educate the various princes and almost none of them endured all this, and he offended them deeply by not visiting each one after they had come to pay homage to *his* King. Under his Government, very few indigenous people advanced their careers in high-ranking positions in the Indian Civil Service. He did not consider them suitable for the task and preferred them to occupy minor and less important positions.

Curzon's most visible political choice, however, was to move the capital from Calcutta to Delhi. Calcutta had always been the British control centre, it was by the sea and it was in the richest region of the country, Bengal, but that region was the one that created the most problems for the Viceroys. Since the birth of Congress, the capital has been the control point of the country's political pulse.

Two years after the Durbar Curzon announced that Bengal would be split in two for better administration. In so doing, he set in motion a series of revolts and gave the impetus that Indian nationalism needed. Violent mouths of revolt broke out almost everywhere and several attacks were carried out against the Governor of the region. Soon the British administration discovered with horror that it was not the ignorant natives who were leading the way, but educated, wealthy bourgeois people who had studied in English schools and universities. Some, such as Aurobindo Gose, found themselves before the judges with whom they had taken the tests for admission to the ICS together. The division of Bengal put together, against the Indian Government, Muslims and Hindus who until then had been at war with each other.

Curzon reacted by throwing straw on the fire. He had a new capital built, a British imperial capital, in the historic heart of India.

New Delhi was nothing more than tents and sporadic palaces built for Durbar, Curzon in the guise of a new Augustus took over a city of cloth and returned it of stone and marble. *Britishness* oozed from every wall and every building but perhaps the most significant one is the message on the wall of the Secretariat:

LIBERTY DOES NOT DESCEND TO A PEOPLE.
A PEOPLE MUST RAISE THEMSELVES TO LIBERTY.
IT IS A BLESSING THAT MUST BE EARNE DBEFORE
IT CAN BE ENJOYED

Edwin Lutyens and Herbert Baker, the two architects, were able to create the most indelible sign of the British presence in India.

Curzon could not attend the inauguration of *his* capital, the official announcement of the change of capital was given only in 1911 but everyone knew that what was emerging outside the ancient capital Moghul was not just a new city.

The nationalists accused Britain of taking away all of India's wealth and it was Curzon himself who admitted that:

"Above all we must remember that the ways of Orientals are not our ways, nor their thoughts our thoughts. Often when we think them backward and stupid, they think us meddlesome and absurd. The loom of time moves slowly with them, and they care not for high pressure and the roaring of the wheels. Our system may be good for us; but it is neither equally, nor altogether good for them. Satan found it better to reign

258

in hell than to serve in heaven; and the normal Asiatic would sooner be misgoverned by Asiatics than well governed by Europeans"[241]

In fact, modern calculations allow us to break more than one lance in favour of the Empire. Net of the annual Indian domestic product from 1868 to 1930, only 1% ended up in British hands, compared with 10% in Indonesia ending up in the Netherlands. Whilst the British in India were investing huge sums of money. By the 1880s, the amount invested had already reached £270 million, one-fifth of all investments in the colonies. By the eve of the First World War, the figure had reached £400 million. Irrigated land had increased eightfold, under the Mughals only 5% of the country was irrigated, in 1947 a quarter of the entire national territory. The British created a coal industry from scratch, producing 16 million tonnes of coal a year in 1914. Jute producers multiplied by ten, causing a crisis in production in the homeland and the case of Dundee is an example. Life expectancy grew by 11 years, after several mistakes the quality of the cities improved with drinking water, sewage and a vaccination system that put a stop to cholera, malaria and plague. The Indian Civil Service with its incorruptible system has helped to create a well organised nation so much so that even today it exists with virtually the same rules set by the British.

Curzon's biggest mistake was to want better not India but British rule in India[242]. For him, the Maharaja who were lost in the meanders of their traditional rituals counted more than the vast patrol of Indians educated by the British, with a British culture and a knowledge of the state bureaucratic machine. Nationalism was not made up of a large section of the population who knew that without the British they would be

---

[241] G. N. Curzon, *Persia...,* Vol II. p. 630.

[242] N. Ferguson, *Empire...,* p. 185.

better off, but rather a small percentage of educated people who rebelled simply because they felt cut off.

Perhaps the simplest aspect of Curzon Government was Afghanistan because he simply decided, after two wars ended in a bad way, that it was better to forget the box of stones stuck between Russia and India. As we have seen, he tried in every way to shift his attention to Persia, but he was always hindered by bigger interests and above all by the grey eminence of India, Lord Salisbury. Soon we will see his two greatest risks, closely linked and destructive to his career in India and the homeland: Younghusband's expedition to Tibet and his rivalry with Lord Kitchener. Curzon set out to serve the Empire as Viceroy, but once in India he soon forgot about the primary task of being Whitehall's pawn in the eastern chessboard. He often behaved like an oriental ruler who stabilised his Kingdom and flaunted wealth and above all forgot that he was not the only Englishman with strong powers in that country. Besides the Viceroy in India, another figure reigned: The Commander-in-Chief of the troops and against the hero of Omdurman the superior George Nathaniel Curzon could do nothing but stand aside. This clash between two pillars of the Empire has determined not only the fate of their careers but has triggered a chain reaction that has in fact allowed Britain to definitively close the phase of the Great Game and specially to win the Great War.

IV

"A sense of solemn aspiration comes upon us as we view the mountain. We are uplifted. The entire scale of being is raised. Our outlook on life seems all at once to have been heightened. And not only is there this sense of elevation: we seem purified also. Meanness, pettiness, paltriness seem to shrink away abashed at the sight of that radiant purity."

Francis Younghusband

YOUNGHUSBAND

1903 - 1904

Chapter Five.

Lhasa

Viceroy and Dalai Lama.

Officially the Great Game ended on the 31st of August 1907 with the signing of the Anglo-Russian Convention in St. Petersburg[243]. Britain and Russia had been looking at each other in dog skin for so long that they had not noticed a new danger, this time not in Asia, which grew up near them. Germany. The agreement therefore aimed to release funds, attention and soldiers from Asia to shift attention to Wilhelm II and his expansionist aims. Obviously, Germany was never mentioned, the purpose of the treaty was to clarify the Anglo-Russian disputes in Persia, Afghanistan and Tibet. Persia is divided into three parts, the northern territories go under Russian control, the central ones become a free buffer state and the southern ones go under British control. Lord Curzon's plan to move the axis of interest from Central Asia to Persia never took hold, Lord Salisbury was always opposed to direct intervention, the maximum the Viceroy obtained was a handful of new officials and a few more contacts at court.

Afghanistan became a British protectorate and Russia made a commitment to cease all forms of communication with the Emir of Kabul.

What about Tibet?

---

[243] I. Klein, *"The Anglo-Russian Convention and the Problem of Central Asia, 1907-1914,"* *Journal of British Studies* (1971) 11. 1. p.126-147.

The Tibetan problem was almost as difficult and complicated as the Afghan problem. Once again, Lord Curzon was the author of the problem, but this time he succeeded in his intent. The British expedition to Tibet was the last major blow of the Great Game[244].

Once again, however, the British conviction of an elaborate Russian project of conquest led to the aggression of a Sovereign state, or at least on paper, the use of troops and the death of many people.

Lord Curzon was a licensed Russophobe, like much of his Government in India and the Government in London. Every entry about Russia was considered true no matter what. In India they were convinced that the Russians had their own espionage and conquest planning office to attack the subcontinent. Despite official denials, and those on the ground, the British never abandoned this belief. A belief that served more to justify the Raj than to defend it, the little information that the Russians obtained from inside the Dominion was produced by the British themselves and consisted of newspapers or reports of border campaigns. Throughout the Empire, every mission became synonymous of pride and pride. The British projected on the Russians and extensively on their *enemies* their mania for obsessive control and maniacal organisation and cataloguing.

In 1902 the Viceroy was more than convinced that Russians and Chinese had signed a secret agreement concerning Tibet. Curzon was certain that China had given the Russians free access to that territory. In the case of confirmation, this would not only

---

[244] A. Verrier, *Francis Younghusband and the Great Game,* Jonathan Cape, London 1991.

have posed a threat to the Raj but could have triggered a devastating war in Asia between the largest Empires in the region.

"Throughout the nineteenth century Russia's Asiatic policy had been canny, successful and (within a framework of opportunism) consistent"[245]

In a way it was not easy to blame him: The Tsarist Empire had conquered the Khanates of Khiva, Bokhara and Kokand, subjugated the Caucasian mountain tribes and forced the various Kingdoms scattered between the Black Sea and the Caspian Sea to recognise Russian control over that region. The issue was complex and intertwined with many other factors. It was undeniable that the Tsar aimed to expand its influence over much of Asia, Russia was still a reality deeply dependent on agriculture and trade and new territories meant new customers and new emporiums. What the British could not distinguish, however, was the Russian desire for expansion from their real capacity to invade the Raj. Except for Paul I's unsuccessful expedition in 1801, no other Sovereign had shown a desire to invade India. Most likely more than one Tsar was secretly hatching the desire to take possession of the Jewel of the British Crown, but in fact no one put that desire into practice. The Great Game was more of a British belief. The rulers of London and Calcutta were aware of the dangers of a military mission through the deserts surrounding the Caspian Sea, or through Afghanistan or Persia and knew the real conditions in which the Tsarist armies found themselves. Any raid on India would have ended in useless carnage. In the rosiest hypothesis, after several vicissitudes, the rest of the expeditionary corps would have arrived in Indian territory so exhausted that it did not represent a real threat. This time, however, the problem presented itself in a different light. Curzon did not fear an invasion from the deserts or the Khyber Pass but feared Tibet and its

---

[245] P. Fleming, *Bayonets to Lhasa: The First Full Account of the British Invasion of Tibet in 1904,* Rupert Hart-Davis, London 1961. p. 19.

unknown territories. At the time, knowledge of Tibet was closer to a fairy tale than to reality, it was a mystical and magical territory present in many literary works, but none of them approached the reality of the facts. Tibet had already caused a clash with British soldiers' years earlier and had lost miserably. But now Curzon was convinced of a secret pact and could not leave anything to chance or wait to find out how things evolved.

"What started as a quest for security, dictated by the need to drive back and contain the forces of Asiatic barbarism which had threatened Russia's very existence for so long, had become a gigantic foray into empty or ill-defended lands"[246]

The whole thing was based on documents of dubious origin. One of these was a letter from a Chinese citizen who had fled and fled to Darjeeling.

"Chinese Government seen his parties very weak and not so active, so he hand over Tibet to Russia Government and request him so help [...] The Russian Empire received the Tibet now and he helps the mother of Chinese Empire [...] All the mines of Tibet is in charged to Russian, and he can open railways etc [...] the Russian is allowed to put a fort at Tibet and also railway, but they are not to destroy those monastery of Tibet"[247]

A few days later Lord Curzon received a telegram from London informing him that:

---

[246] P. Fleming, *Bayonets to Lhasa...*, p. 20-21.

[247] P. Hopkirk, *Trespassers on the roof of the world,* John Murray, London 1982. p. 160.

"His Majesty's Minister at Peking reports that the Russo-Chinese Bank has designedly circulated rumours in the press that Chinese interests in Tibet may be transferred to Russia if the latter will undertake to uphold integrity of China"[248]

The *China Times* wrote a report on the secret pact but almost certainly its source was the author of the letter himself, Kang-yu Wai. Curzon took it all for granted, and he was not the only one, as he did every time he was dealing with facts about Russia. Other reports came to his desk from Nepal, England and Tibet itself. Randall Parr was the British customs agent at Yutong, just across the border with the Sikkim. Parr was the only British voice from inside Tibet.

Curzon had already found himself in the situation of having to talk to the Tibetans. Shortly before his term as Viceroy, the British had driven the Tibetans out of Sikkim and the Crown had entered into two agreements with the Chinese Emperor. The first was signed in 1890, the *Sikkim-Tibet Convention,* and its purpose was to delineate the borders between the two regions. Sikkim remained under British control and Tibet under Chinese influence. The other pact was signed in 1893 and had an economic purpose, was to facilitate trade between India and Tibet and it was decided to open an emporium in the city of Yutong, in Tibetan territory. The Tibetans tried to sabotage the two agreements in any way, not buying goods from the emporium, violating grazing rights, overthrowing border stones, imposing illegal tariffs and building walls. Calcutta complained to Beijing and the Chinese had to admit that they did not have the country under control. Curzon took office at that time and at the beginning decided not to show his power against them. He sent two letters to the Dalai Lama, but both returned with the seal still intact. His ego and office could not be insulted in this way and so it was that in 1903 he decided to intervene. The London Government was initially very sceptical about what to do, the Boer War had proved

[248] P. Hopkirk, *Trespassers...,* Ibidem.

extremely unpopular and another imperial conflict was badly seen. In April, the Government granted its permission for a small expedition just across the border to Gampa Dzong. The permission was far from Curzon's request, he wanted the green light for a mission to Lhasa, to deal directly with the Dalai Lama.

In May 1903, whilst he was in Shimla, Lord Curzon was bored of watching an equestrian race. Those who watched him saw him muttering with a moustache soldier in the shadow of the great Himalayan cedars. That soldier was Francis Younghusband and was receiving confidential instructions from the Viceroy on the secret mission to Tibet.

Claude White was chosen as Government representative for Sikkim and Frederick O'Connor as interpreter. The three left Kalimpong with two hundred Indian soldiers as escorts. On the 18th of July the group reached their destination. The Tibetans, however, proved to be complicated opponents to discuss with, the various representatives of the Dalai Lama kept repeating that they would negotiate on the British side of the border, the delegates withdrew to the fortress around the place, called *dzong*, and stalled all negotiations. After several months the group returned to India, apparently defeated.

Curzon was no longer willing to suffer further humiliation, when the mission had stalled, he had put pressure on London to obtain permission to bring to fruition not only a diplomatic mission but also a military one. The new envoys were to reach Gyantse, the fortified city halfway between the border and Lhasa.

The British ambassadors in Beijing and St. Petersburg informed the local Governments of the campaign and they immediately protested but the British Government immediately reminded them, especially the Russians, of the vast areas of Central Asia occupied without warning.

Curzon did not want to waste any more time and despite the bad time for a campaign he ordered that preparations should begin. Younghusband was promoted and made colonel. The problem, however, was that the mission, at least on paper, was a

270

diplomatic operation and a soldier could not present himself in a foreign country in the double role of diplomat and commander of the escort troops. The command of the military was entrusted to Brigadier General J.R.L. McDonald. The two distinct offices proved to be in fact a problem for the whole mission. Younghusband had a higher role than McDonald's but had a lower rank. Curzon never specified which of the two should have the last word in case of diatribes. In fact, the blame for this error lies with Lord Kitchener, who was the head of the *Indian Army* and oversaw the military choices. Curzon and Kitchener hated each other, and both had long been in a hidden war to destroy their opponent.

The expeditionary corps consisted of an escort of over a thousand men, four pieces of artillery and two Maxim machine guns. Along with soldiers and diplomats, correspondent journalists from the *Daily Mail,* the *Times and Reuters* also travelled.

On the 12th of December 1903, a soldier on horseback holding a *Union Jack* crossed the Jalap Pass and entered Tibet. He was Younghusband's forerunner. Following the armed escort there were ten thousand *coolies*[249], seven thousand mules and four thousand yaks, closed the column six camels carrying the luggage of the expedition. As a telegraphic line was laid along the way by a team of engineers. Snow was a difficult obstacle to overcome right from the start, the Tibetan winter was very reminiscent of the Russian winter against which Napoleon had surrendered a century earlier.

The passage of the pass was difficult, men and animals had to first climb to four thousand two hundred metres and then go down one thousand five hundred metres to reach the valley of Chiumbi. No one watched the pass, but the first resistance occurred in the valley floor. Captain Randall Parr accompanied by a local Chinese

---

[249] Indian farmers

officer and a Tibetan general appeared at the head of the men's column. The Tibetan request was the same as the first expedition, to go back and wait for Tibetan officials in British territory. Younghusband refused, pointing out that Gampa Dzong had already complied with the request but did not receive any response. His intention was to reach Gyantse through Yutong and Phari. Younghusband threatened to blow up city gates in case he found them barred. When they arrived in Yutong they found the city gates open and the leaders of the expedition were invited to Parr's house for a multi-ethnic lunch with typical English, Chinese and Tibetan dishes. The inhabitants of the Chiumbi valley noticed that the English had not shown themselves to be hostile and in turn behaved in a kind way, selling food and clothing. But the Tibetans had already attracted their enemies to the heart of the country before hitting them, the Sikhs and the Gurkha knew a little about it. Outside Yutong, a camp was built for the men to rest, whilst McDonald continued with some men to Phari, where he discovered that the Tibetans were organising themselves to create an armed resistance. McDonald did not find a resistance in the *Dzong* outside Phari. He had two Gurkha companies occupy the fort. He went back to report what had happened to Younghusband convinced that he had done a good thing occupying the fort without spilling a drop of blood. Younghusband got very angry because occupying the fort the population immediately realised that the peaceful intent was only a facade to a military mission. The mission for now was going quite well, but the first three stages had been passed without any problems so that the soldiers could celebrate Christmas eating food that had come specially for them. The problem did not take long to arrive, however. Shortly after, some monks came from Lhasa and imposed on the citizens a ban on all contact and collaboration with foreigners. The expedition was a serious blow, the supply lines were getting longer every day and the cold was a major problem for men and arms. Younghusband wanted to spend the rest of the winter at the village of Tuna to reach Gyantse in the spring but first had to cross the mountain of Tang La. The temperature reached minus 45 degrees and the men had to sleep embraced to the artillery pieces so as not to freeze them.

On the 8th of January they arrived in Tuna and found the resistance. The resistance was the city itself, it was dirty and inhospitable. McDonald wanted to return to the camp in Chiumbi whilst Younghusband was determined to stay in the city. McDonald proved once again unfit for his role and decided to abandon the expeditionary corps of which he was the protection. He and his men returned to the valley whilst Younghusband stayed in Tuna with four Sikh companies, a Maxim machine gun with their respective men and a piece of artillery. From that moment on McDonald's men started calling him *Retiring Mac*. In part, however, he was right because in the months spent in Tuna the men left with Younghusband suffered greatly: there were cases of snow blindness, frostbite and pneumonia, as well as hunger. It was precisely those very bad weather conditions that confirmed, once again, the absurd belief of the British of the risk of a Russian invasion from Tibet. Edmund Candler, one of the journalists following the expedition, in fact, wrote:

"The great difficulties we experienced in pushing though supplies to Tuna, which is less than 150 miles from our base railway station at Siliguri, show the absurdity of the idea of Russian advance on Lhasa. The nearest Russian outpost is over 1000 miles distant, and the country to be traversed is even more barren and inhospitable than on our frontier"[250]

Both Younghusband and Curzon believed that only in Lhasa in front of the Dalai Lama could they, somehow, resolve the matter.

Younghusband decided to make a reckless attempt to try to unblock the situation. He rode from Tuna to the Tibetan camp followed only by O'Connor who knew the language and another young officer who was studying it. When they arrived at the camp, they asked to be taken to the general for a meeting. The general welcomed

---

[250] E. Candler, *The Unveiling of Lhasa,* Edward Arnold, London 1905. p. 97.

them curious and amused but once in the tent Younghusband understood something that until then he had not framed well, along with the general there were three monks from Lhasa:

"I could from this in itself see how the land lay, and where the real obstruction came from"[251]

He knew the reality of Tibet well, he knew the power of Lhasa and the Dalai Lama, but he did not know the depth of the monastic power. Tibet was in fact a state that was very reminiscent of the medieval communities that had sprung up around the monasteries. The religious figure merged with the political and military.

The monks kept an eye on him in all his movements and threatened not to let him go until he revealed the date of return of his expedition to India, after a first moment of disorientation he managed to convince the monks to let him go with the promise that he would tell the Viceroy their requests.

The two leaders of the expedition decided that from that moment on all forms of Tibetan resistance had to be broken with guns. They had to get to Gyantse as soon as possible and then try to enter negotiations or convince London to let them go as far as Lhasa. The two bodies of the men's column only reunited on the 31st of March 1904, when the snows allowed McDonald's men to cross the mountains and re-join Younghusband.

The two had discovered that near the village of Guru there were more than one thousand five hundred Tibetans armed, but the two did not know if they were willing to open hostilities. The company advanced and several times emissaries came to try to stop them.

---

[251] F. Younghusband, *India and Tibet,* Gautam Jetley, New Delhi 2005. p. 164.

Once in Guru, the British found themselves with a wall built in the open countryside, about two hundred metres long and behind all the Tibetan forces ready. The Tibetan general reached out to his opponents and tried to convince them to retire once again. McDonald arranged for his men to put themselves in a position of attack, effectively surrounding the Tibetans. The orders were not to shoot but just to defend themselves. At 12 o'clock the men were ready, even on the Tibetan side the general had not given any order to fire. There was a moment of stalemate.

"The main body of the Tibetans were bewildered but not subdued. The whole thing must have been incomprehensible to these poor men. No order had been given to them to retreat, and seemed to have acquiesced in their friendly expulsion by the Gurkhas and Sikh Pioneers gathered in a dazed way. Gathered together in a body, their enormous superiority in numbers must have struck them. They had no idea, of course, of the advantage which we possessed, and there was a growing murmur as they discussed the matter excitedly behind the Wall"[252]

Charles Allen claims that a deception was also attempted, with a mannequin, to try to get the Tibetans to start the fight. They were badly armed, old guns and rifles. The Tibetans did not move from their positions, the monks arrived from Lhasa had brought pieces of paper engraved with the personal coat of arms of the Dalai Lama and according to them this amulet should have defended them from British bullets.

The testimonies on the facts of Chumik Shenko disagree on some points but in summary: *a useless massacre*. The Tibetan general refused any compromise and probably gave orders to attack fearing revenge in Lhasa if he surrendered. At first McDonald ordered the Sikhs to disarm the Tibetan fighters but later they started shooting and the British had no choice but to respond to the fire. The companies that

---

[252] P. Landon, *The opening of Tibet,* J. Jetley, New Delhi 1996. p. 81.

were positioned on the sides of the wall began to shoot with the machine gun Maxim, the Gurkha positioned themselves near the wall and opened fire, the Tibetans almost immediately stopped shooting and tried to escape but by now it was too late, in four minutes more than 700 of them were slaughtered. The British soldiers were surprised because the Tibetans, instead of running away simply abandoned their rifles and walked back.

"The most extraordinary procession I have ever seen. My friends have tried to explain the phenomenon as due to obstinacy or ignorance, or Spartan contempt for life. But I think I have the solution. They were bewildered... the impossible had happened. Prayers and charms and mantras, and the holiest of their holy men, had failed them, they walked with bowed heads, as if they had been disillusioned in their gods"[253]

In the letters at home and in the books that some of those present later wrote, there is always the sadness of the absurd massacre and, in a certain sense, the sense of guilt of the person who had to shoot.

Immediately after the fight the British set up a hospital in a hut near the village of Tuna and began to treat the wounded on both sides. The wounded Tibetans were very surprised by the treatment, they expected to be shot untreated. One hundred and 68 Tibetan wounded were transported to the improvised hospital and only 20 died from the injuries. Dr. Davys of the *Indian Medical Service* soon became famous amongst the Tibetan population, many citizens began to reach his hospital to be treated for various illnesses and wounds. He was now famous almost as a deity and tools took care of everyone for free.

---

[253] E. Candler, *The Unveiling of Lhasa...,* p. 109-110.

Younghusband ordered the march to Gyantse to continue, convinced that the Tibetans had now surrendered to all forms of attack but was wrong. The monks of Lhasa ordered the peasants on military service to attack every day, most of the time the soldiers withdrew as soon as they saw the English coming, but in the gorge of Red Idol Gorge McDonald's men had to kill another two hundred Tibetans before they could pass.

On the 11th of April 1904 the head of the column sighted for the first Gyantse. The rich city was defended by *Dzong* built on a hillside beside the city. As soon as he arrived under the fort, he discovered that the general who had been put in charge of defending the city was not willing to fight, he had neither suitable men nor weapons. Despite the death threat from Lhasa in case of surrender, he handed over the fort to the British. Once again, however, McDonald demonstrated his inability: since the fort was not supplied with water, he decided not to have it occupied by a garrison of men. The men were stationed about two kilometres from the fortress. McDonald decided to return to the Chiumbi Valley whilst Younghusband was waiting in the city for some response from Lhasa. Some doctors set up a sort of clinic for Tibetans and spent their time treating them. At the end of April, rumours arrived of new forces in preparation to drive the English out of the country. Younghusband sent Colonel Brander, who was now in charge of the remaining garrison in Gyantse, out on the advance. He discovered a contingent of over three thousand men waiting. In a clash at the Karo Pass on the way to Lhasa, other Tibetans were massacred. The technique was the same, the soldiers had built a wall the length of the pass and had barricaded themselves behind. Maxim machine guns and artillery pieces killed and dispersed the Dalai Lama's men. More than four hundred Tibetans lost their lives, whilst from the British side only five people died, and a dozen were injured. That was the clash fought at an altitude higher than any battle before and after that day. On his return to Gyantse, Brander discovered a Tibetan ambush against Younghusband's base camp. In a night clash eight hundred men had approached the British opening fire, after a few minutes of clash on the ground there were another one hundred and 40 Tibetans.

What started out as a diplomatic mission was now a real invasion. Also, in the night they had re-occupied the fort and McDonald had to return to Gyantse because all the heavy artillery was with him in Chiumbi. Fortunately, encouraging news came from London, the Government had in fact decided that in case of stalemate after a month in Gyantse the shipment had the order and permission to proceed to Lhasa.

Despite the ultimatum, the Tibetans continued their desperate resistance. The Kham fighters, the best soldiers in the country, were enlisted and by now the troops were led not by generals but by fanatical monks sent from Lhasa. The answer had to come by the 25th of June, the day before McDonald arrived in Gyantse with fresh forces from India. After several attempts to start negotiations on the 5th of July, McDonald gave the order to resume the fort before they moved to Lhasa. The assault on the fort was done at night and by surprise, after a first moment of difficulty the British troops managed to put under control the occupants and take back the fort. The press praised the British soldiers very much, the siege earned Lieutenant Grant a *Victoria Cross*. An ancient legend said that in case of fall of Gyantse's *Dzong* any other resistance to a foreigner would be useless. The news had a devastating impact on the population. The road to Lhasa was now flattened. In a few hours they regained control of Karo's step, after it had been re-occupied by the Tibetans. After crossing the mighty Tsangpo River the only thing between the English and Lhasa were the 70 kilometres that separated the two places.

The first words of Younghusband, who rode into the city with his friend O' Connor, were.

"Well O'Connor, there it is at last"

It was the 2nd of August 1904.

Lhasa was probably the most mysterious and unknown city on earth, the halo of secrecy that was lodged over the whole of Tibet became a solid block as soon as you approached Lhasa. The Dalai Lama, his palace, the monks and the mysticism of Buddhism filled the books in the West and the journalists who followed

278

Younghusband felt like the luckiest in the world, for the first-time they were written pages of truth and not fiction or supposition about the capital of Tibet.

"Today is probably the first-time in world history, that the dateline Lhasa has been prefixed to a news despatch"[254]

The positive impact of the city on the British, however, was short-lived, after the first reports of the magnificent Potala Palace journalists, soldiers and men of the retinue of Younghusband discovered the true face of the capital. A dirty city, uncomfortable, unattractive to Westerners and full of misery.

"Lhasa, like the Tibetans, is very dirty and there is little in it that will seem attractive to a native of the occident"

Candler was the one who was most shocked by the city:

"We found the city squalid and filthy beyond description, undrained and unpaved. Not a single house looked clean or cared for. The streets after rain are nothing but pools of stagnant water frequented by pigs and dogs searching for refuse"[255]

Landon undertook a sort of personal pilgrimage along the sacred road that ran through the city. The *Ling-kor* was about eight kilometres long and crossed the entire city, so Landon could meet the pilgrims who went to the capital, monks, peasants, desperate people and women. The street went through every part of the city including the poorest neighbourhoods, neighbourhoods that left a very sad image in the memory of the journalist.

---

[254] Those were the words of an excited *Daily* reporter in his first report from the capital.

[255] E. Candler, 23rd of September 1904, *Daily Mail.*

"From dawn to dusk along this road moves a procession, men and women, monks and laymen. They shuffle along slowly, not unwillingly now and then to Exchange a Word with a companion overtaken... but, as a rule, with a vacant look of abstraction from all earthly things they swing their prayer-wheels and mutter ceaselessly beneath their breath the sacred formula which shuts from them the doors of their six hells"[256]

The poorest neighbourhood was where the outcasts lived:

"It is difficult to imagine a more repulsive occupation, a more brutalised type of humanity, and, above all, a more abominable and foul sort of hovel than those which are characteristic of these men. Filthy in appearance, half-naked, half-clothed in obscene rags, these nasty folk live in houses which a respectable pig would refuse to occupy"[257]

The English, however, had a much greater problem, a problem that did not contemplate the poor people of Lhasa at all, but their God-King. What happened to the Dalai Lama?

The expedition had gone to Lhasa to discuss with the Dalai Lama but in a short time the British discovered that he had escaped shortly before their arrival. Moreover, the British found no trace of relations with the Russians, no hidden arsenal, no Tsarist adviser at the court of the Dalai Lama and above all no secret treaty. Suddenly all the reasons for the expedition collapsed like a house of cards. However, the British were not completely turned their backs on it. At the level of foreign policy for the London Government it was a real bad figure, but St. Petersburg did not start a smear

---

[256] P. Landon, *Opening the Tibet*, J. J. Jetley. New York 1905. p. 339.

[257] P. Landon, *The Mysterious City*, J. J. Jetley. New York 1905. p. 1905

campaign or a retaliatory action because they had got into a much more complicated situation: the Russo-Japanese war.

The Russians had been working for months in peace against the Japanese and they needed all the help available, including that of the British. The Russians did not in any way want to lose a conflict against what they considered to be a country inferior to their own. From their point of view, however, the British had immediately made it known that the expedition would return to India once they had achieved their goals. Even the Chinese could not make a big voice, they did not have a military force powerful enough to drive the British out of what they considered their protectorate and they were also convinced that a political-military beating against the fanatical monks of Lhasa would help future relations between Beijing and Tibet.

The thirteenth Dalai Lama[258] was a central figure in Tibetan history. Born in 1876 at only two years old, he was identified as the reincarnation of the twelfth Dalai Lama who had died young the year before. After his appointment as Dalai Lama, he was educated at the Potala in complete isolation from the world. He had a very strong personality, and from the very beginning he showed an above-average intelligence. Since he took power, his intention has been to allow his country to remain free and independent of the three Empires that fought for him, and he tried to implement social and political reforms to modernise the country.

---

[258] C. Bell, *Portrait of a Dalai Lama: The Life and Times of the Great Thirteenth*, Collins, London 1946; Gelek, Surkhang Wangchen. *"Tibet: The Critical Years: The Thirteenth Dalai Lama"*. *The Tibet Journal*. Vol. VII, No. 4. Winter 1982, pp. 11–19; Tamm, E. Enno. *"The Horse That Leaps Through Clouds: A Tale of Espionage, the Silk Road and the Rise of Modern China."*: Douglas & McIntyre, Vancouver 2010, chapters 17 e 18.

Before escaping to Mongolia, the Dalai Lama had given his personal seal to a regent who remained in the city, Younghusband met him and was struck by the person:

"More nearly approached Kipling's lama in Kim than any other Tibetan I had met"

The regent had no power to negotiate, the Dalai Lama wanted to create confusion for the British. He had fled the country in the hope that the British would be so forced to return to India but the Chinese, taking everyone by surprise, decided to remove all power from the hands of the Dalai Lama, accusing him of abandoning his people in time of need. Suddenly the problem with the Dalai Lama disappeared and above all the English noticed that they were not hated by the population; their respect for the sacred places, their pity for the wounded in Guru and the fact that they behaved as guests and not as invaders contributed to lowering the level of tension in the city. Younghusband was under pressure from London to conclude an agreement as soon as possible and return to India before the arrival of winter. The telegraph line that connected Darjeeling and Lhasa was fundamental for the expedition, Younghusband's despatches to the Viceroy and the London Government and the orders that arrived in Tibet dictated the pace of negotiations. The Tibetans were very intrigued by that mysterious thread that crossed the country, the English told that its purpose was that of a very long thread of Ariadne or a way to find the way home, in this way were avoided attacks and sabotage to the line: the worst nightmare in that delicate moment was to lose contact with the Raj and London. The Tibetans spoke so well of the line that 30 years later, during a visit by British officials to the country, they found the telegraph cable in its place again.

Younghusband had to deal extensively with the Tibetans before he could reach an agreement. He was a skilled diplomat but also a clever poker player, the Anglo-Tibetan Conviction was achieved both by his extensive knowledge of the Asian soul and by the threat of opening fire against the Potala. To demonstrate once again the intention of agreement and not invasion, the text of the treaty was written in three languages: Tibetan, English and Chinese. The regent affixed the private seal of the

Dalai Lama and Younghusband his signature. He requested that the seals of the regent, the representatives of the three main monasteries of the country and the seal of the National Assembly should also be placed at the bottom. The only one who could not sign was the Chinese official who did not receive permission from Beijing.

The treaty provided for the recognition of the border between the Indian Sikkim and Tibet, the opening of two commercial emporiums: one in Gyantse and one in Gartok, each with a permanent British commercial agent. The Tibetans also accepted the demolition of the fortifications between the border and Gyantse to make it easier for the emporiums to get there. They also undertook to pay a war indemnity of 562,000 pounds from annual instalments. A clause prohibited Tibetans from having any kind of relationship with representatives of foreign nations, excluding the British and Chinese. This clause was intended to avoid the nightmare of a Russian invasion. The Gyantse sales agent was given permission to travel to Lhasa if he so wished.

On the 23rd of September 1904, after seven weeks in the capital and almost a year in the country, the British took the road back to India.

Younghusband did not fail the expedition and got what he had gone there to get. The terms of the agreement did not satisfy either London or Calcutta, the orders were to re-discuss some clauses but Younghusband completely ignored the issue, he knew very well that for a Tibetan a treaty already finished and signed could not be modified at will so simply. Curzon was sick, and so was his wife, and he no longer had the power he had before, and he could not defend his friend. Younghusband was a hero to the public, the classic Victorian hero-conquerors, but for the Government he was nothing more than a soldier. The treaty that he had so painstakingly put together was in fact dismantled in every piece. The indemnity of that was reduced by two-thirds, the occupation of the Chiumbi plain, which originally was to last until the debt was paid off, was reduced to three years, the privilege of the Gyantse agent to go to Lhasa was revoked so as not to offend further the Russians. Younghusband after that mission began to devote himself to his interests in mysticism, and except for a parenthesis during the First World War, he left the political scene forever. Curzon's foreign policy proved to be a complete failure during his mandate, so much so that two months after Younghusband's return he resigned from his post as Viceroy. His secret war against Lord Kitchener had seen him defeated.

V

"Don't talk to me about atrocities in war; all war is an atrocity."

Lord Kitchener

KITCHENER

1902 - 1909

Chapter Six

Martyrs, warriors and sinners

1. Empire in doubt.

Horatio Herbert Kitchener was for the Army what Winston Churchill was for politics. A man for all seasons. The British Empire owes much of its glory to this man. He fought as a volunteer for the French in the Franco-Prussian War, reorganised the Egyptian Army and won at Omdurman in Sudan against the Mahdists, put an end to the Boer War, put the Raj's Army in order, took a Viceroy out of the way, became Baron then Viscount then Count, understood that the Great War would last more than a few weeks and organised the British Army for a long-term conflict and in fact allowed victory. If a mine had not sank *HMS Hampshire*, in 1916, with him on board, the chronology of the British Prime Ministers today would most likely have an additional name.

He joined the Imperial Pantheon thanks to the victory in Sudan. We have already seen how the victory in Omdurman had turned Kitchener into a national hero, having avenged the death of General Charles George Gordon was seen by all as a practically divine act, if Gordon in life had been described by many as a somewhat crazy officer after death he was certainly not treated in this way. The stories of his extreme defence of Khartoum[259] until his beheading had transformed his figure into a sort of imperial

---

[259] B. Burleigh, *Khartoum Campaign, 1898 or the Re-Conquest of the Soudan*, Chapman and Hall, London 1899; C. M. Snook, *Beyond the Reach of Empire: Wolseley's Failed Campaign to Save Gordon and Khartoum*, Frontline Books,

martyr. The mission in Sudan was one of the many cases that show us the power that public opinion had in the Empire. Gordon had been sent to Sudan to evacuate the British forces, but he disobeyed orders and decided to stay and stand up to the men of the *Mahdi* convinced that he could beat them as a Christian man and soldier. This resounding blow of the courage reached London, and there the newspapers, all of them began to attack the Government of Gladstone. Everyone was now accusing the Prime Minister of abandoning a brave British soldier. The Premier did not want a war at all, but he was forced to satisfy the people who asked him out loud. But it was too late. After ten months of siege, the city was doomed. Gordon never gave up, he kept holding his positions and every night he would retire to his room lighting candles, his soldiers reminded him that in this way he became an easy target for the snipers, and he responded every time:

"When God was portioning out fear to the people of the world at last it came to my turn and there was no fear left to give me. Go tell all the people of Khartoum that Gordon fears nothing. Because God has created him without fear"[260]

The final battle was bloody, and Gordon was killed and beheaded by the *Mahdi.*

The whole figure of Gordon is perfectly described in the famous painting, *Gordon Last Stand* by George W. Joy. We see the general in front of the enemy, the sword in the scabbard and the gun abandoned in one hand, a figure bristling at the top of the stairs that looks at the enemy in the eyes without running away. Not a heroic death in battle but a martyrdom. An imperial martyrdom.

London 2011; D. C. Boulger, *Gordon: The Career of Gordon of Khartoum,* Leonaur, London 2009

[260] J. Paxman, *Empire...*, p. 180.

The figure of Gordon is very important to understand the figure of Kitchener. He had grown up in the myth of Gordon, first as a simple officer then as an imperial hero. He had met Gordon in Egypt and was initially attracted by his asceticism but later became a kind of rock, insensitive to everything. He was a soulless man. On the 1st of January 1897, after strong pressure on the Government, an expeditionary corps left from Egypt for Khartoum. Kitchener's objective was to avenge Gordon's death. The column of men advanced a mile and a half a day, so slowly because in the whilst advancing, they were building a railway line. The opportunity was too tempting to be wasted. The investors threw themselves obsessively into the business.

The battle demonstrated once again how skilled British engineers and scientists were. They could build different, deadly ways to kill people every time. Progress could never walk without the war at its side.

The battle lasted about five hours, Churchill, as mentioned before, was present and described it to the press. The men of the *Mahdi*, who had already died, had arranged themselves in a single row about eight kilometres long. In all, there were 52,000 of them. Whilst the British were about 20 thousand willing in the usual square formation with heavy artillery at its centre. Kitchener followed the whole fight on his horse.

"The Maxim guns exhausted all the water in their jackets, and several had to be refreshed from the water bottles of the Cameron Highlanders before they could go on with their deadly work. The empty cartridge cases, tinkling to the ground, formed small but growing heaps beside each man. And all the time out on the plain on the other side bullets were shearing through flesh, smashing and splintering bone; blood spouted from terrible wounds; valiant men were struggling on through a hell of whistling metal, exploding shells, and spurting dust – suffering, despairing, dying

[...] The charging Dervishes sank down in tangled heaps. The masses in the rear paused, irresolute "[261]

The result was an overwhelming victory: 10,000 dead, and almost all others wounded or escaped. *Only* 48 British soldiers have fallen.

Kitchener desecrated the tomb of the *Mahdi* and took his head away as his body was thrown into the Nile. The message was simple: Eye for an eye.

The war had, in the long run, a negative effect on British troops. Foreign observers were present in the field. One of them, Major Von Tiedermann, of the German Imperial Army. He immediately returned to Berlin and told the Kaiser about the power of the Maxim machine gun. Thanks to Lord Rothschild, the arms manufacturer Ludwig Loewe began producing the Maxims, and by then every German infantry regiment had a machine gun. Kitchener himself would have sent hundreds of Britons to their deaths against German weapons years later.

Kitchener was now ready for the glory of the Empire. The problem, though, was that he was alive. He won, but Gordon was the hero of Khartoum. The Empire was to feed its offspring with dead heroes not with those who could speak, make speeches and publish books. For politics Kitchener was useful but for the propaganda Charles George Gordon or Captain Cook, who died against the Hawaiians or Sir John Franklin who died frozen whilst looking for the way to the Arctic or the men of the *Light Brigade* who charged the enemy without fear ending up as food for the cannons of the Crimean War. All these heroes have played the game. Not the Great Game but

---

[261] W. Churchill, *The River War, An Account of the Reconquest of the Sudan,* Courier Corporation, Cambridge 2006. p. 274.

a game even more extensive and important. The game of the Empire. Where you either live as strangers or you die as hero.

To fully understand both the figure of Kitchener and especially the British behaviour in the First World War one must understand the Second Boer War, the Vietnam of the British Empire[262].

The Boers were the only white tribe in Africa. They had already fought a war against the British Empire and emerged victorious. And the Empire never forget its defeats.

The Cape region was very important for the survival of the Empire, just look at a map of the colonies to understand why. Most of the colonies were in Asia and in case of sudden closure of the Suez Canal the circumnavigation of Africa was the only way to reach the Raj and other territories. During the Napoleonic Wars, the London Government decided to set up a military base in Cape Town. In a short time, it became a colony but the immigration of British people to South Africa was very low and the local indigenous people, especially *Afrikaners*, remained the majority[263].

In 1834 the Governor of the colony, Benjamin d'Urban, put an end to slavery in those territories. The decree infuriated the Boers and over 5 thousand of them decided to leave the territories and retire beyond the rivers Orange and Vaal, there they created a new society based on racial segregation and agriculture. In order to do that, they had to have violent clashes with the local tribes. The Boers were of Dutch origin, in 1652 the Dutch East-India Company had placed a stopover at Cape of Good Hope and in a short time the arrival of Dutch, Protestant Germans and French Huguenots

---

[262] A. Caminiti, *La Guerra Anglo-Boera. Anche l'Impero Britannico ebbe il suo Vietnam,* Frilli, Genoa. 2008.

[263] T. Pakenham, *The Boer War*, Abacus, London 2006. pp. 13-14

293

had enriched and enlarged the region. As time went by, the poorest left the coastal region and retired to the hinterland.

Little by little the British authority on the spot convinced the central Government of London to change its mind on the Boers until the war arrived. On paper, the reason for the clash was the impossibility for foreigners, in large numbers British, living in the Boer territories to vote. The Boers were few and granting citizenship and the right to vote to immigrants would in a short time have reduced most of the minority in their state. The real reason for the fight, however, was the money. In 1870, in the Kimberley, a territory on the border between the State of Orange and the colony, the largest diamond deposit in the world was discovered, the Empire built railways and infrastructures useful for the extraction and finally the white immigration had a surge. In 1872 the colony was given the right for an autonomous Government. In 1877 the new Governor made a proposal for a federal union of the white settlers to the two republics that at that time were going through a serious economic crisis[264]. Obviously, for the British, political and military control had to be British. Two years later the imperial troops invaded the Transvaal, winning the wars against the Zulus, which for a long time had encroached on the Boer territories.

In London, however, the South African question became the ground of conflict between the parties, Gladstone disagreed with the federal union and blocked all development projects in South Africa. The Boers had meanwhile rebelled and won the short war, the first Boer war. Independence was granted and the Boer president, Paul Kruger, decided to grant control over foreign policy to the British, he knew well that in the long run the British would bend their resistance. [265]

---

[264] T. Pakenham, Ivi. p. 32.

[265] T. Pakenham, Ivi. pp. 32-33

In 1886 the situation changed, completely unexpectedly. In the Witwatersrand a gigantic gold deposit was discovered that soon transformed the Transvaal into the richest nation in the area. British immigration moved to the Boer Republic and in a short time the number of foreigners exceeded that of the Boers. A new city, Johannesburg, was founded. The British took control of the deposits by exploiting the powerful contacts and especially the economic structure already used elsewhere.[266] On the Boer side, however, the situation became worrying, despite the high earnings that the republic obtained from the rights of extraction the growing number of foreign whites was destabilising the country, President Paul Kruger refused to grant full political rights to foreigners, in 1888 promulgated a law that granted the right to vote to foreigners after 15 years of residence.[267]

The stalemate broke in 1895 when the Prime Minister of the Cape, Cecil Rhodes decided it was time to end Boer independence.

Rhodes initially, in agreement with the Minister for Colonies, Chamberlain[268], wanted to cause a revolt of foreigners within the Boer territories and in this way be "forced" to intervene in their aid but the raid was a failure and at first London decided to forget about the Boers ignoring the requests for intervention. Chamberlain was able to stay in office but had to keep it down. But it did not last long. From the European point of view, the question made the relations between Germany and Great

---

[266] T. Pakenham, Ivi. p. 14.

[267] T. Pakenham, Ivi. pp. 10-11.

[268] T. Pakenham, Ivi. pp. 43-46.

Britain even more difficult because Kaiser Wilhelm II congratulated the Boers, with a telegram, for the victory and supported their positions at an international level.[269]

In 1897, Alfred Milner was appointed as the new Governor of the Cape Colony. A convinced Imperialist, friend of Rhodes and extreme defender of British expansion in the Boer territories. The London Government on paper was not interested in a further difficult issue with the Boers whilst Milner was willing to put in place an aggressive policy.[270]

Milner was convinced that time would only strengthen Kruger to the detriment of the British, so not only did he secure Chamberlain's support, but he also ensured that the public was on his side by frequenting the good lounges, councillors, journalists and especially the wives of the main politicians.[271]

In the meantime, Kruger strengthened the relationship between his republic and the other Boer republic, the Orange Free State led by Martinus Steyn. The two nations began a process of administrative renewal and in 1897 they signed a military alliance.[272]

The situation changed dramatically on the 23rd of December 1898. That day the Boer police in Johannesburg killed, in circumstances still obscure today, a foreign worker Tom Edgar. Milner did not miss the opportunity, still in London he began to direct an uprising against the Government of Kruger led by the leader of foreigners, James

---

[269] T. Pakenham, Ivi. p. 46.

[270] T. Pakenham, Ivi. pp. 37-38.

[271] T. Pakenham, Ivi. pp. 38-39.

[272] T. Pakenham, Ivi. pp. 58, 60-62.

Percy Fitzpatrick. He worked together with the capitalists of the mines who were aiming for a discount on extraction taxes[273], a discount promised by the British in the exchange for support. From the inside, foreigners propaganded against Kruger's Government, pointing out how the Boers were violent towards foreign whites abroad, the news bounced off the newspapers that supported Milner's aims. In an attempt to block the crisis in the bud, Kruger proposed lowering extraction taxes and promoted a law for the right to vote after only five years of residence.[274] Entrepreneurs obviously had no interest in pursuing these proposals so they began to raise the stakes knowing full well that Kruger could not accept, the request that blew the table definitively was to assert the five years of resident retroactively, in this way the foreign voters would suddenly become the majority of the country.[275]

Milner managed to get the full support of the Government.[276] On the 19th of May 1899, the executive meeting in London decided to support the expansionist aims of the Governor. A conference was organised between Milner and Kruger. The British proved calm and moderate but was ready to deny any request of the Boers, Kruger on the other hand tried to avoid the direct confrontation trying to make compromises but it was all useless, the meeting ended on the fourth day with nothing.[277]

---

[273] T. Pakenham, Ivi. pp. 65-71.

[274] T. Pakenham, Ivi. pp. 72-74.

[275] T. Pakenham, Ivi. pp. 76-81.

[276] T. Pakenham, Ivi. pp. 81-82, 87.

[277] T. Pakenham, Ivi. pp. 82-83.

Milner after the conference was even more convinced of his imperialist ideas, wanted not only to increase a crisis but pointed to a military threat, the commander of British troops in South Africa, William Butler, however, was not convinced of this need and indeed pressed for a peaceful solution with the Boers. He also believed that there was no need to increase the troops because the ten thousand soldiers stationed in the territories controlled by the Crown were more than enough in the event of a Boer attack. In spite of this, Milner presented three requests to the London Government: the first was to replace Butler, considered pro-Boer, with a more authoritarian and imperialist figure; then he requested expert officers to be sent to train and prepare for the defence of the border cities and finally an increase of soldiers, another ten thousand, to be placed in Natal with the aim of being on the precautionary paper but in fact intimidating.[278]

These requests were accepted at home in a contrasting manner. The Minister of War, Lord Lansdowne, rejected such warlike plans as inappropriate whilst on the other hand the commander of the British Army Field-Marshal Garnet Wolseley proposed to mobilise the whole Army to impress the Boers and their likely allies, in all it was a movement of thirty-five thousand soldiers between infantry and cavalry. The Minister of War simply asked General Butler to control the Boers more and sent ten officers and equipment to the troops already in place to defend the borders. He appointed General William Penn Symons as commander of the troops stationed at Natal.[279] On the Boer front, in the meantime, after the failed conference of Bloemfontein Kruger tried to enter into other agreements with the British. In London Lord Chamberlain was now publicly in favour of Milner's ideas and was not

---

[278] T. Pakenham, Ivi. p. 96.

[279] T. Pakenham, Ivi. pp. 99-102.

interested in the concessions of the Boer president,[280] the Government of Kruger proposed a package of concessions in favour of foreigners but the London Government instead of accepting them immediately requested a committee of inquiry to see if the concessions went in the way foreigners in the Boer republics would like it or not.[281] Kruger proposed other even more convenient requests to foreigners, but by then Chamberlain was intent on triggering a conflict and sent back all concessions to the sender.[282] Kruger withdrew all diplomatic requests and returned to his ultra-conservative positions. During the diplomatic crisis the Government was split with the Minister of War and the Chancellor of the Exchequer, Michael Hicks Beach, in favour of a diplomatic resolution whilst the Minister for Colonies Lord Chamberlain and Field-Marshal Wolseley were in warlike positions. At the meeting on the 8th of September 1899, Chamberlain came up with it and obtained that Wolseley was sent to South Africa with ten thousand men, coming mainly from India, Cyprus, Alexandria and Crete, Butler was called back home and General George Stuart White was appointed head of Natal's troops. Funds were allocated for the mobilisation of the first Army under the command of General Redvers Buller.[283]

The top brass of the Army were optimistic about British military power at the expense of the Boers whilst General Buller in a meeting with the Minister of War revealed all his concerns and doubts about the war plans, he was convinced that the

---

[280] T. Pakenham, Ivi. pp. 105-107.

[281] T. Pakenham, Ivi. pp. 108-109.

[282] T. Pakenham, Ivi. pp. 112-121.

[283] T. Pakenham, Ivi. pp. 124-126.

troops should be increased to avoid surprises in case of a sudden attack by the Boers whilst Lansdowne was convinced that no preventive measures were needed, in case of a Boer attack the Army would adapt to the situation and move otherwise.

On the 16th of September the troops left for South Africa and arrived in Cape Town on the 3rd of October. Then they reached Durban by sea and arrived there on the 7th of October. The Government in London, meanwhile, learnt that all diplomatic relations had been broken and the manoeuvres to send the whole of General Buller's First Corps of Armies had begun.[284]

The Boers had by then accepted the idea that a war was practically inevitable. Their military forces were completely unprepared for a clash with the greatest Empire in history. The Boers hoped, however, that for the time being the imperial troops at the borders were very small. The British had five hundred irregular soldiers in Mafeking, five hundred in Kimberley and two thousand under the command of General Penn Symons south of Natal. Jan Smuts then proposed to attack immediately catching the British by surprise, the Boer Army in all counted on 40 thousand men. The military and political leaders of the Transvaal decided, however, that such a choice was imprudent, but shortly afterwards they repented when they discovered that eight thousand men were travelling to South Africa and that an entire Army corps had been mobilised.[285]

On the 29th of September the Transvaal Republic issued the order to mobilise its troops and the Orange Free State did the same on the 2nd of October. On the 9th of October the Boers presented to the British agent in Boer territory an ultimatum where

---

[284] T. Pakenham, Ivi. pp. 129-130, 134.

[285] T. Pakenham, Ivi. pp. 133-134.

an arbitration was proposed in which Great Britain was requested the immediate withdrawal of its troops arrived in South Africa after the 1st of June and to return home those on their way. After a large military parade in Joubert on the 12th of October the Boers entered Natal starting the war.[286]

The fact that the Boers had started the conflict was of importance for British public opinion, despite the fact that the escalation had started by the British. From their point of view theirs was only a preparatory manoeuvre in case of attack, and all the defenders of the Boers at home lost power when the news of the beginning of the war reached the newspapers, those who for years had pointed the finger at the whites of Africa were now considered visionaries because their fears had become reality, especially those characters who from the beginning aimed at a mobilisation of soldiers to defend their citizens in Africa became in the eyes of most people of the perfect examples of smart and able imperialists.

The Boer ultimatum arrived in London on the same day that Chamberlain prepared a British document to be sent to the Transvaal where it was required that foreigners be granted the right to vote after only one year of residence. The ultimatum would have lasted 24 hours but when the Boer arrived, he in fact tore up his own and blamed the Boers for the beginning of the hostilities.

On the 9th of October the troops arrived in Durban and found out about the ultimatum, the generals immediately began to mobilise the soldiers. On the 14th of October the British corps led by General Buller, who had 47 thousand soldiers, embarked.[287]

---

[286] T. Pakenham, Ivi. pp. 134-139.

[287] T. Pakenham, Ivi. pp. 139-146.

Until June 1899 the British Army in South Africa had only ten thousand men with 24 Maxims, after the arrival of the Indian and Mediterranean reinforcements the number had risen to 22 thousand with 60 Maxims of which 14 thousand in Natal under the command of General White.[288] The British were still outnumbered by the Boers but the 47 thousand men in command of Buller had not yet arrived. The entire expeditionary corps consisted of 37 infantry battalions, seven cavalry regiments and 19 artillery batteries that had been organised by mobilising the reservists who made up half of the contingent.

The British Army relied on their experience of imperial wars, had the best weapons, well-trained soldiers and above all excellent officers. At least that is what they were convinced of. The facts, however, let another reality to be known.

The Army was still stuck to strict rules of war, the clashes had to take place in compact ranks and a strict discipline regulated everything. The new weapons were praised and used but no one thought to instruct the troops in case even the enemy had those deadly weapons. A mistake that cost a huge number of lives.[289]

The Army, as we have already seen, had already undergone a revolutionary reform a few years earlier. The reform conceived by Cardwell was, however, a reform half done, modernising the imperial troops ended in 1881 with the reform of Childers.[290] Hugh Childers was the Secretary of State for War in those years and wanted to complete the work begun 20 years earlier. His reform regulated the infantry regiments. According to the reform, each regiment should have had two regular battalions and two militia battalions. The battalions of each regiment were recruited

---

[288] T. Pakenham, Ivi. p. 39.

[289] T. Pakenham, Ivi. pp. 27-28.

[290] *The London Gazette*: no. 24992. pp. 3300-3301. 1st of July 1881.

from the same geographical area. The traditional bright red jackets that have distinguished the colonial wars for years were withdrawn and gave way to khaki uniforms, and the characteristic Pith helmet became part of the equipment of soldiers and not only officers. The supplied rifles were changed, the Lee-Enfields and the Lee-Metford were adopted, each battalion was equipped with two Maxim machine guns. The reform came into force on the 1st of July 1881, not without protests, mainly because the regiments lost their local name and simply took on a number as a name.[291]

During the war cavalry and artillery revealed all their shortcomings. The cavalry was trained only for direct confrontation but was not able to perform simpler tasks such as control of the territory, coverage, explorations and raids. The Boers had skilled infantry corps mounted instead. The artillery had a lower firepower than the Boers, the whites of Africa had imported the best weapons that French and Germans had managed to sell. The British had to improvise during the conflict by creating naval artillery units capable of withstanding the firepower of the Boers.[292]

The Boer forces were inferior to the British soldiers but were organised in a different way and consequently more able to fight. The two republics did not have a regular Army to send on the spot in case of war but relied on the city militias recruited in case of war, the *commandos* were organised according to the various administrative districts, all men between 16 and 60 years were recruitable and had to get their own clothes and animals to mount, the state distributed only the weapons. Since the Boers had built their two states making room between indigenous tribes quarrelsome had

---

[291] T. Pakenham, Ivi. pp. 24-25.

[292] I. Knight, *Colenso 1899, the Boer War in Natal*, Osprey, London 1995. p. 28.

become skilled in the fight and riding, over time they developed the technique of trenches, so even in case of numerical inferiority they could avoid direct collision by bombing or firing from long distances.[293]

All British beliefs about a quick and easy war were shattered during the first months of the campaign, the Boers managed to inflict several defeats on the troops of his majesty so that public opinion and Government alarmed a lot at home.

The British soon found themselves besieged both at Ladysmith and Kimberley and the troops in Natal were not doing well. Redvers Buller, British supreme commander spent a lot of money to try to free the two cities and the region and at Milner's urgent request he took care of organising a defensive line in case of attack on the Cape colony. In a raid on an armoured train on the 15th of November several British soldiers were taken prisoner, including the young Winston Churchill.

The British counter-offensive failed one after the other, the Boers were able to retire before ending up in a trap and knew better than the English the territory and this was an advantage in a territory rich in hills and rivers, often were the natives to choose the battlefields, by positioning themselves on the tops of the hills and hitting the other British departments. The Boers were also advantaged on the front of the supply lines the English moved many men into enemy territory whilst the Boers moved with the *commandos* that were usually made up of about a thousand men, this combined with the help they received from the population contributed to the war effort.

The second week of December 1899 was called *The Black Week* at home. There were three battles, Stormberg, Magersfontein and Colenso with a total of 2,776 deaths, injuries and prisoners. The strongest impact of it with the Battle of Colenso

---

[293] I. Knight, Ivi. p. 28.

since it was defeated the supreme commander of the troops, Buller.[294] At home, the Commander-in-Chief of Ireland Field-Marshal Frederick Roberts wrote to the Minister of War on the 16th of December recommending a change in tactics and submitting his candidacy to lead the imperial Army in South Africa. Prime Minister Lord Salisbury wanted Kitchener to be there with Roberts, who had[295] strong support at home after his recent victory in Omdurman.

The Government, to avoid another defeat and especially losing the war, decided to reorganise the troops and supplies by creating new departments, especially cavalry, formed by British volunteers coming from the White Dominions. The Boers did the same later trying to convince the volunteers from the opposing powers to Great Britain to join the Boer cause but as much as the whites of Africa had international support, because seen as those who defended their land against the London imperialist barbarians, the number of foreign volunteers did not exceed five thousand units throughout the conflict.

Roberts' arrival did not pay off right away. The British were heavily defeated during the battle of Spion Kop[296] for the first-time in history the Maxim machine gun was used against the Queen's soldiers.[297] The English, led by Charles Warren, who had led the investigation against *Jack the Ripper* two years earlier in London, were deceived by the fog and convinced themselves that they had conquered the Spion

---

[294] T. Pakenham, Ivi. p. 254-256.

[295] T. Pakenham, Ivi. p. 292-295.

[296] J. Grehan, M. Mace, *The Boer War 1899-1902: Ladysmith, Magersfontein, Spion Kop, Kimberley and Mafeking (Despatches from the Front)*, Pen & Sword Military, London 2014.

[297] I. Knight, Ivi. p. 64-79.

Kop hill without a fight, but when they realised that they were not high up but low down it was too late: as soon as the fog dissolved, the carnage began. Hundreds of soldiers were mowed by machine guns. A thousand and four hundred people killed and wounded. At the foot of the hill the English had prepared a hospital camp but most of the wounded died in the newly built trenches. Amongst the stretcher men present on the spot there was also a young Indian member of the *Indian Ambulance Corps:* Mohandas Gandhi better known as the Mahatma. Churchill, meanwhile, freed, witnessed the battle as a war envoy and survived by miracle.

"Thick and continual stream of wounded flowed rearwards. A village of ambulance waggons [sic] grew up at the foot of the mountain. The dead and injured, smashed and broken by shells, littered the summit till it was a bloody reeking shambles [...] the scenes at Spion Kop were among the strangest and most terrible I have ever witnessed"[298]

Roberts' change of gear radically changed the conflict. The year 1900 was the turning point. He managed first to free Ladysmith then Kimberly and finally to conquer Pretoria. On the 13th of March 1900, he triumphantly entered the capital of the Orange Free State, Bloemfontein.[299]

In public opinion, however, the most well-known fact of the Boer war is undoubtedly the siege of Mafeking. An insignificant town on the border between the Cape Colony and the Transvaal. A bank, a court, a Masonic lodge, a post office, a monastery, a library, a station, a hospital, a prison and a handful of houses. That was Mafeking. Here, however, they fought a lot not only in the field but also in newspapers, living

---

[298] W. Churchill, *The Boer War: London to Ladysmith via Pretoria and Ian Hamilton's March,* A&C Black, London 2013. p. 121.

[299] T. Pakenham, Ivi. pp. 379-380.

rooms, history books, children's magazines, war bulletins and letters. In Mafeking there was not just anyone but Robert Baden-Powell. The failed Rhodes raid started here and many, including Milner, feared that if the city fell into Boer hands the many Boers living in British territories would join their cousins from the two republics. The defence of the city had become an indispensable fact for the very victory of the war.

Mafeking became the perfect combination of Great Play, Scouting and Greater Britain. Cricket and not war, a game not a clash, a public and not two enemy nations. But the blood was real, it was not just sweat.

The spirit of the English colleges' playgrounds presented itself in all its magnificence during the siege of the city. Baden-Powell fed the idea of a city of warriors, boys ready to die for the Queen and the Empire without question. *Play up! Play up! and Play the game.*

Cricket was so imprinted in the mind of the British man that in an exchange of communications between the Boer commander and Baden-Powell they speak of the siege as a game:

"Dear Sir,

I see in the Bulawayo Chronicle that your men in Mafeking play cricket on Sundays, and give concerts and balls on Sunday evenings. In case you will allow my men to join in, it would be very aggregable to me, as he, outside Mafeking, there are seldom any of the fair sex, and there can be no merriment without them being present. In case you would allow this we could spend some of the Sundays, which we still have to get through round Mafeking, and of which there will probably be several, in friendship and unity. During the course of the week, you can let us know if you accept my proposition and I shall then, with my men, be on the cricket field, and at the ballroom at times so appointed by you.

I remain, your obedient friend,

307

Sarel Eloff,

"Commandant"

"Sir,

I beg to thank you for your letter of yesterday, in which you propose that your mean should come and play cricket with us. I should like nothing better – after the match in which we are at present engaged is over. But just now we are having innings and have so far scored 200 days not out against the bowling of Cronje, Snyman and Botha, and we are having a very enjoy able game.

I remain,

Yours Truly,

RSS Baden-Powell."[300]

In the city they even managed to print stamps with the face of Baden-Powell instead of that of the Queen, there was talk in the newspapers of the Independent Republic of Mafeking. The city was besieged for 217 days, inside there were about one thousand five hundred British out of seven thousand Boers. Baden-Powell was able to establish a regime of order and calm in the city, even though the telegraph cables had been cut, isolating the city from the rest of the world, he managed to keep in touch with his countrymen thanks to indigenous educated who managed to escape the control mesh of the Boers. In the city all the men were enlisted and the boys over seven years old were enlisted to carry out the functions that the men had abandoned in order to be able to fight, especially postmen, lookouts and auxiliaries. He even

---

[300] N. Cawthorne, *The Beastly Battles of Old England: The misguided manoeuvres of the British at war*, Hachette, London 2011. p. 202.

devised a clever bluff: every day when men went out for the patrol they had to, in certain places, pretend to climb over a sort of non-existent barrier, so the Boers who watched from afar with telescopes were convinced that the city was well defended by trench or ditch. Any wire mesh would have been impossible to see from afar. He regularly sent small groups to attack groups of Boer soldiers, all this did not serve either to open an opening or to exhaust them but simply to convince the Boer commanders of the thirst for blood of the British. Life in the city was obviously not all pink and flowers, almost half of the men died or were injured. Baden-Powell had recruited more than seven hundred black natives, they were not used to fight but when the time came the commander had no qualms about reducing the food rations of blacks to feed the white minority. Milner sometime after commenting on the facts as well:

"You have only to sacrifice "the nigger" absolutely, and the game is easy"[301]

On the 17th of May 1900 the city was liberated. For many, it was a sign that the war was won. In fact, it was, not only thanks to Mafeking though. Roberts had won several victories and made several prisoners. Despite the fact that the war councils of the two republics were inclined towards a clash to the bitter end, the morale of the Boers had been broken so much so that in November of the same year Roberts decided that his task was over and communicated to London his desire to return to his homeland leaving the last skirmishes in the hands of Kitchener[302]. On the 25th of

---

[301] D. Harrison, *The White Tribe of Africa,* University of California Press, Oakland 1983. p. 45.

[302] T. Pakenham, Ivi. p. 551.

October he had declared the annexation of the Transvaal, but more than 30 thousand Boer soldiers were still free in the Orange.[303]

Kitchener soon discovered that the war was over but a more exhausting one, the guerrilla war, had begun. The Boer *commandos* refused to surrender and continued current sabotage and violent raids against isolated columns of soldiers, railroad tracks, telegraph poles etc..[304]

Kitchener knew that the only way to completely break the last Boer hopes was to hit not the soldiers but their families. The displaced people had become many and the Boer soldiers knew that they represented a burden for the English but stupidly they were convinced that being white they did not run any risk but unfortunately, they had not considered the total lack of humanity of Horatio Herbert Kitchener. He decided to rake the Boer territories not yet conquered and send women, children and elderly people to camps, concentration camps.

It was not the first-time, the first to use them were the Spaniards in Cuba five years earlier, but these were the first to end up on the front pages of the newspapers. In all almost 28 thousand Boers died in the English concentration camps, the majority were children. The number of dead children exceeded the number of dead soldiers on both fronts. Deaths in the camps accounted for 14.5% of the Boer population. The deaths were mainly due to malnutrition and poor medical care. Amongst the 115,700 inmates, 14,000 died, in separate camps. Of those 14,000, 81% were children.

Whilst Kitchener was amassing the Boers in the concentration camps, in the capital Bloemfontein they were dancing in the presidential palace. The festivities went on for a long time which forced the officers to replace the floorboards that had worn out

---

[303] T. Pakenham, Ivi. p. 551-552.

[304] T. Pakenham, Ivi. p. 562-563.

and had caused more than one fall amongst the officers' wives. The disused parquet was sold to the Boer women, each board cost 1 shilling and 6 cents, with that wood they could build coffins for their children whilst the husbands were buried in mass graves in the battlefields. Despite everything the Boers continued to fight but when Kitchener decided to build everywhere forts and barbed wire barriers the last rebel *commandos* stopped and decided to sign the Treaty of Vereeniging, on the 31st of May 1902. The two republics disappeared and became all territory of the British Empire. The problem was that it was now up to the British to rebuild everything they had destroyed. The right to vote for black people was postponed to a future hypothetical autonomous Government. Exactly ten years after the signing of the treaty they created the Union of South Africa that included the old British territories and the two former republics, to become Prime Minister was an old Boer commander, Botha, and in his Government entered many former combatants. In fact, after ten years the English delivered not only their old territories but also the British ones to the Boers. The Boers ignored the clause on the right to vote for blacks in the treaty and shortly after promulgated a new law that forced them to settle for the less fertile portions of arable land. In fact, South African *apartheid* was born there at that time.

The strongest impact of the war was produced at home more than in South Africa. The Empire was hit too hard and was unable to absorb it, especially for 12 years after the end of the war the Great War broke out. In all, the taxpayers spent 250 million pounds and 45 thousand deaths and injuries were the tribute of blood. Public opinion did not forgive the various leaders for their role in the war, Kitchener carried the stain of the concentration camps forever and escaped a stain of eternal infamy thanks to his role in the First World War. Emily Hobhouse, one of the first activists of the twentieth century, fought in South Africa and at home to improve the conditions of prisoners in concentration camps, succeeding in establishing a Government commission with the task of investigating the real conditions of the people concentrated there. The report of the commission was very violent and in a short time the camps scattered around the country had to adopt new hygiene rules that reduced the percentage of deaths from 34% to 2% in a few months. The Hobhouse was obstructed in every way by Kitchener who tried to ban her from visiting the concentration camps and managed to keep her out of the commission that she wanted. Despite this, the media impact of the issue was very high and everywhere associations were created for the collection of funds and goods to send to the Boers left homeless. Politically, it was an earthquake, and the liberals took the opportunity to break with the Tories once and for all, putting an end to Chamberlain's twenty-year control over imperial politics. David Lloyd George, whom we will soon learn to know, in a famous speech to the Communes hurled himself against the Boer war with words of fire:

"A war of annexation [...] against a proud people must be a war of extermination, and that is unfortunately what it seems we are now committing ourselves to – burning homesteads and turning women and children out of their homes [...] the savagery which must necessarily follow will stain the name of this country."[305]

The war gave to a vast number of scholars, historians, economists, political and scientists the opportunity to produce a vast literature against the Empire. The most famous work of that period is certainly *Imperialism* by John Atkinson Hobson. In the book, he hurls himself against the circle of a few chosen ones who are enriched by the imperialism paid for with money and blood by the British. In the eyes of the people, Rothschild and Rhodes were no longer the imperial heroes who could extend the Queen's rule but represented a leech that fattened at the expense of the others.

---

[305] R. Hattersley, *David Lloyd George: The Great Outsider,* Hachette, London 2010. p. 43.

"As speculators or financial dealers they constitute [...] the gravest single factor in the economics of Imperialism [...] Each condition ... of their profitable business [...] throws them on the side of Imperialism [...] There is not a war ... or any other public shock, which is not gainful to these men; they are harpies who suck their gains from every sudden disturbance of public credit [...] The wealth of these houses, the scale of their operations, and their cosmopolitan organisation make them the prime determinants of economic policy. They have the largest definite stake in the business of Imperialism, and the amplest means of forcing their will upon the policy of nations [...] [F]inance is [...] the Governor of the imperial engine, directing the energy and determining the work"[306]

This shifted the axis of British politics to the left, causing not only damage to the Empire but also to those nations that looked to Britain with more than one eye on the matter.

2. Titles, Viceroys and Resignations.

Immediately after the end of the Boer war Kitchener, after a short stay in his homeland, where amongst many things he was appointed Viscount, was sent to India as new Commander-in-Chief. On the 28th of November 1902. His task was to reorganise the devastated Army of the Raj.

The Indian Army dates to the dissolution of the *Company*. Before the 1857 mutiny, the Company had three armies stationed in the Presidencies of Madras, Bombay and

---

[306] J. A. Hobson, *Imperialism,* Cambridge University Press, Cambridge 2011. p. 64.

Bengal.[307] The company used its profit to equip and pay the soldiers it enlisted. In 1858, when the British took direct power, the situation changed radically.[308] Until 1894, British India did not form a real regulated Army, but merely used the previous armies of the three Presidencies by simply uniting them. This Army still maintained a strong indigenous imprint, the British enlisted mainly in what they called the Sikh, Gakhars, Awans, Punjab Muslims, Gurkhas, Mohyals, Yadavs, Kumaonis, Garhwalis, Marathas, Pashtuns, Bunts, Baloch, Dogras, Jats, Rajputs, Sainis and Nairs *martial races*. Each Army kept its own commander-in-chief, although general control was in the hands of the commander of Bengal[309] as he was formally the commander of the East Indies. After the Second Anglo-Afghan War a commission of inquiry proposed to abolish the three armies of the Presidencies.[310] The administrative and military personnel, previously divided into three *Presidential Staff Corps,* were also united into a single *Indian Staff Corps.* In 1893 Bombay and Madras lost their commander-in-chief and all the power came under the control of Bengal but in 1895 the three armies were completely abolished and a new system was created, the Army was a single large body divided into four commands: Bengal, Madras and Burma, Bombay with Sind, Quetta and Aden and the Punjab including

---

[307] Harold E. Raugh, *The Victorians at war, 1815–1914: an encyclopedia of British military history* ABC-Clio Inc, Santa Barbara 2004. p. 173–79

[308] J. Gaylor, *Sons of John Company – The Indian & Pakistan Armies 1903–1991.* Parapress. Turnbridge Wells 1996. p. 2.

[309]B. Robson, *The Road to Kabul.* Spellmount. Stroud 2007. p. 55.

[310] D. Jackson, *India's Army,* Sampson Low, London 1940. p. 3.

the North-West Frontier and the Punjab Frontier Force.[311] The choice was made by the Indian Government with an ordinance dated to the 26th of October 1894 and the new system was to enter into force on the 1st of July 1895. In this way a unique Army was presents in each of the cardinal points of the subcontinent. The Army also played the role of armed police, working with the civil authorities in the fight against banditry and the outbreak of revolt. The most important moment in the history of this Army was when it was sent to China to quell the Boxer revolt from 1899 to 1901. Outside of this system were still the British units stationed in India and the local bodies and contingents of Hyderabad.

With the arrival of Lord Kitchener, the system was disrupted and changed for the last time. The reforms of the hero of Khartoum were maintained, with small measures, until the end of the Raj in 1947.[312]

Kitchener concluded the union of the armies of the Presidencies and incorporated into the new system all the regiments previously excluded. In this way his *Indian Army*[313] also included the minor and local bodies, the contingents of Hyderabad, the armies of the autonomous states and especially the British regiments stationed in India.

It may be absurd but until then the Army had no specific task, it was born in an era when the British had to make room for themselves with carrots and sticks but now,

---

[311] J. Gaylor, *Sons of John Company...*, p. 5.

[312] M. Barthorp, *Afghan Wars and the North-West Frontier 1839–1947*, Cassell, London 2002. p. 142-143.

[313] G. Pastori, *Dall'Indian Army all'Army of India*, Centro di Cultura Italia - Asia "G. Scalise" Asian Notebooks. N° 75. Milan September 2006. p. 83 - 99

they controlled the entire Indian subcontinent, but no one had thought of writing down rules and priorities. The four basic points decided by Lord Kitchener were:

1) Defending the North-West Frontier from foreign invasions. This was the main task of the Army in India, the British phobia of losing the Raj was projected into every sector of the society, Army included.

2) All units forming the Army had to have training and experience at that border.

3) The organisation of the Army had to be the same both in times of peace and in times of war.

4) The internal security of the Raj was a secondary task. The police should be delegated as much as possible. The Army's efforts had to be poured into the defence against the external enemy.

When he arrived in India, Lord Kitchener found himself at the head of an Army scattered over almost five million square kilometres. The troops were scattered in 34 forts and stations throughout the country. Kitchener set up a system called *Kitchener test* in which each battalion in India was subjected to careful examination and control. The test caused not a few mumbles and lamentations but later all the officers admitted that it had been useful. His plan was to gather all the men together and place them in new places along the northern border. There should have been nine divisions divided into two axes, five divisions in the axis that connects Lucknow to the Khyber Pass, passing through Peshawar and the other four in the axis from Bombay to Quetta crossing Mhow.[314] This idea was rejected, however, because the cost of dismantling almost all the forts scattered around the country to rebuild them in the north was too high. The compromise was found in 1905 when it was decided

----

[314] M. Barthop, *Afghan Wars...,* p. 143.

to reduce the existing controls from four to three. Ten stable divisions plus four independent brigades were created. The 9th division was under the direct control of the Commander-in-Chief's Headquarters, forming what was called the *Army Headquarters*.[315]

The divisions had been created and numbered so that in case of use they could deploy a complete infantry and cavalry division and an unspecified number of troops for internal security and for the defence of internal borders in case of need.

Northern Command: 1st Division Peshawar, 2nd Division Rawalpindi, 3rd Division Lahore, Kohat Brigade, Bannu Brigade and Derajat Brigade.

Western Command: 4th Division Quetta, 5th Division Mhow, 6th Division Poona, the Aden Brigade.

Eastern Command: 7th Meerut Division, 8th Lucknow Division.

Army Headquarters: 9th Division Secunderabad, Burma Division.

At the end of its mandate in 1909 the Indian Army was now organised as the British Army even though it had less up-to-date weapons and equipment. Each division of the *Indian Army* consisted of three Indian battalions and one British battalion. The whole Army could count on one and a half million volunteers to defend a population that in those years was estimated at 315 million individuals. Regime battalions were not permanently placed within a division or brigade to prevent them from taking on a localised footprint, which was the case with divisions. All this allowed each division to always receive experienced men who had served in each territory of the two axes.

---

[315] T. A. Heathcote, *The Indian Army – The Garrison of British Imperial India, 1822–1922*. David & Charles, Newton Abbot 1974. p. 31.

All the previous regional denominations have been abolished to highlight the presence of a single large Army, once enlisted the men hardly ever served in their territory of origin. This allowed a mixture of castes and religions until that time reduced to large cities or movements dictated by famine. The numbering order started with the regiments of Bengal followed by the *Punjab Frontier Force*, then the regiments of Madras, the contingents of Hyderabad and finally Bombay.

A General Staff was created to manage the military policy.[316] In peacetime it had to supervise the training and in case of war the conduct of military operations, the distribution of forces for internal and external security at the Raj, plans for future campaigns and especially intelligence activities. According to the British form, the staff was divided into two sections: *Adjutant-General*, which was responsible for personnel, training and discipline, and *Quartermaster-General,* which was responsible for managing supplies, housing and incoming and outgoing communications. In 1906, a separate department for planning and intelligence was created.[317] The various leaders of the herds responded to the *Chief of the General Staff,* a Lieutenant-General. In 1907 a special College for the training of officers was established in Quetta.[318]

Lord Kitchener's reform did not provide for an intermediate chain of command and this lack weighed heavily on the work of the Division Commanders who were forced to take care of the voluntary troops and the internal security of their areas of reference. Since, in case of mobilisation everyone had to serve, the ordinary administration remained without men, this problem arose when it came to enlist and

---

[316] B. Robson, *The Road to...,* p. 57.

[317] T. A. Heathcote, *The Indian Army...,* p. 26.

[318] T. A. Heathcote, p. 139.

sending troops to Europe and the Middle East during the First World War. The police forces were insufficient, and this led to the forced choice not to move some troops from their old stations in the country, some soldiers never joined their divisions allocated to the north. Lord Kitchener's reform not only regulated the Army but in fact created three distinct entities in symbiosis with each other.

The Indian Army: was the national Army, with recruits from all castes on a local basis with British officers.

The British Army: it was the Army formed by the British troops temporarily stationed on Indian soil. This Army was flexible and changing all the time, the departments were sent to other parts of the Empire or to their homelands.

The Army of India: It was the union of the two armies.

Lord Kitchener, who was aiming for Lord Curzon, did not share the fact that he had to submit to the orders of a civilian. Especially when one considered the fact that the Commander-in-Chief did not have a seat on the Viceroy's Council. That role was held by a representative of the Military Department. Lord Curzon, when it came to choose the new Chief Commander for India, made a serious naive mistake: he wanted the best men in the Empire to do his job as well as possible, and when he heard of the end of the war in South Africa, he did not hesitate for a moment and expressly asked London to have Kitchener by his side. Kitchener had wanted that role for a long time. Curzon's mistake, however, was not to calculate the personal ambitions of the man who wanted so much.

Shortly after his arrival Kitchener proposed to Curzon to appoint him a member of the Council but the Viceroy rejected the request because he did not consider it necessary since the Military Department, representing the Army, was already present. In May 1903 Kitchener presented a new request to place the Military Department under the control of the Army and not above it. Curzon, who had by now understood where Kitchener wanted to go, also rejected this request. The following month Kitchener proposed to reduce the powers of the Military

Department, Curzon did not take an immediate position but shortly afterwards during a period of leave at home he discovered that the request had been submitted by Kitchener first to the Imperial Defence Committee and then to the Viceroy. Kitchener was willing to climb over Curzon and Curzon knew that in London it was the Commander-in-Chief who had more political connections.[319]

In September 1904 Kitchener, taking advantage of the interlude between Curzon's first and second terms of office, attempted his resignation. From April to December, Lord Ampthill, former Governor of Madras, led India. The acting Viceroy knew very well the reason for that request and even if reluctantly had to reject his resignation. In London, meanwhile, the Government decided to set up a commission for the study of Military States and the Military Department, the two things that Lord Kitchener wanted to reform. He had not wasted time and whilst the commission was working the newspapers supported his idea of reforming the Indian Army. In April 1905 John Brodrick left the commission and transformed it into a working committee managed by himself. Brodrick was a Kitchener supporter and wanted to help him. A Commission was independent of the Government, a working committee was not. On the 30th of May the Government approved Brodrick's report, which provided for the abolition of the position of the Military States and the Military Department by the Council, the division of his former powers between the Commander-in-Chief and a new figure for Military Food with a seat on the Council but reduced to a consultative role. With this move Kitchener had deprived the Viceroy of any military adviser outside the Commander-in-Chief and not only by doing so had concentrated in their hands all the executive and administrative power of the Army and military matters.

---

[319] S. P. Cohen, *Issue, Role, and Personality: The Kitchener – Curzon Dispute.* In *Comparatives Studies in Society and History.* Vol. 10, No. 3. Cambridge University Press, Cambridge April 1968, p.337-355.

As already mentioned, the diatribe had occurred in the Tibet question when it came to appoint the two leaders of the mission.

Curzon resigned in the face of this decision by the London Government. He was probably convinced that they would be rejected but unfortunately for him on the 16th of August 1905, Lord Balfour accepted his resignation and Curzon left the Office. It took the Government only three days to find a replacement, and on the 21st of August Brodick announced the new Viceroy: Lord Minto.

In this clash between titans both were defeated[320], Lord Curzon did not have enough support in London to support his theses at the expense of Kitchener, he wanted him close to him, but he realised too late of the mistake. For his part Kitchener was convinced that with the resignation of Curzon the Government would choose him as successor but had not calculated that a soldier for that position had little chance of victory and his knowledge, and fame, were high but not so high. Not to mention that the issue of concentration camps was still burning in public opinion. He was reconfirmed in his position and kept it until 1909 when he returned to Egypt.

The two major defenders of the thesis *The Russians want to invade us* had found themselves shoulder to shoulder in the Raj for a few years but had not managed to live together. Ambition had finally prevailed over reason of state and both had come out with broken bones. However, in a few years' time, they both found themselves united to collaborate for the victory of the Empire in the First World War.

---

[320] P. King, *The Viceroy's Fall: How Kitchener destroyes Curzon.* Sidgwick and Jackson, London 1986.

Part Two

GREAT WAR

Intermezzo

"Bring me a cup of tea and the 'Times."

Queen Victoria

Chapter Seven

Grandmother of Europe

1. A Victorian War

The First World War was in fact a Victorian war, the fighters were born under Queen Victoria, weapons and armaments were created under her reign, the political and military leaders had served under her and above all, in fact, the conflict can be reduced to a family war since in almost all fronts there were heirs of Victoria and Albert. European diplomacy was a kind of family drama.

Victoria and Prince Albert had a total of nine children[321]. Five females and four males. Everybody became husbands or wives, from a very young age, in various European royal families, joining their family with the strongest Empire of the time was a good reason to give one of the children as a wife or husband.

The eldest daughter, Princess Victoria Adelaide Mary Louise[322], born in 1840, married Friedrich, the future Friedrich III, son of the Crown Prince of Prussia, the future King of Prussia and Kaiser of the German Empire, Wilhelm I. She became the Crown Princess and later Empress. Queen Victoria had pushed for a marriage between the two royal families because she saw in the future couple a bulwark for the birth of a united Germany, liberal and above all pro-British. It was a union of love and national interest. The couple was ten years apart, they met in 1851 during

---

[321] C. Erickson, *Her Little Majesty,* Simon & Schuster, Cambridge 2002

[322] H. Pakula, *An Uncommon Woman: The Empress Frederick, Daughter of Queen Victoria, Wife of the Crown Prince of Prussia, Mother of Kaiser Wilhelm,* Touchstone Press, Cambridge 1995.

the opening of the *Great Exposition* in London. On the 19th of May 1857 the engagement was officially announced, the following year they married in St. James Palace. In 1861 Friedrich's father became King of Prussia and Victoria Adelaide's husband became heir to the throne. The couple, however, was immediately in contrast with the strong and authoritarian politics of Chancellor Otto von Bismarck. The couple's eldest son, Wilhelm, the future Kaiser Wilhelm II, was educated in the English way but he preferred to his English guardians the German ones and nourished throughout his life a hatred and love for his mother. Victoria Adelaide fought for the rights and goals of her new nation, often going against the interests of her Motherland. Within the British imperial family there was a lot of coldness during the German unification wars, in fact the wife of the Prince of Wales, Alexandra, was the daughter of the King of Denmark who reigned over territories disputed by Germany. After the Franco-Prussian War Wilhelm I was appointed Emperor at Versailles. When the first Kaiser Friedrich died, he took his father's place on the throne despite a tumour in his throat that had deprived him almost entirely of his voice. The imperial couple hoped to impose a liberal imprint on the Empire after the years of the powerful Chancellor, but the reign of the second Kaiser lasted only 99 days, his death was expected but was still a lightning bolt in the clear sky, the rebellious son who had moved away from his mother over the years and from his British upbringing was now the new Emperor. Victoria Adelaide's German experience was a failure, she was isolated from Bismarck during her time as a princess, the education to her first son was a failure and only increased in him a hatred and envy for the nation of her mother, when finally, her husband became Emperor he died shortly after.

The first male son of Victoria and Albert[323], born in 1841, became the future King and British Emperor Edward VII, also known as the Uncle of Europe. He married Princess Alexandra of Denmark in 1863. We will return to the figure of Edward shortly.

The third-born of the imperial couple was a princess, Alice[324]. Born in 1843. By the Queen's wish, all her children, like her, would have to marry out of love and not for national interest. Obviously, however, love had to be confined to the royal families of Europe. Victoria's anti-Catholicism precluded from the list all principles related to the Holy Roman Church, including her cousin the King of Portugal Pedro V. The two Protestant princes identified by Alice's older sister, Victoria Adelaide, were Prince Wilhelm of Orange and Albert of Prussia, cousin of the Prince Consort. Both were discarded despite pressure from each other's royal families. Victoria Adelaide finally proposed to Prince Ludwig of Hesse - Darmstadt. With the excuse of finding a wife for her brother, the Prince of Wales, she went to Germany and met Ludwig and his brother Heinrich there. The two princes were in turn invited to England where the Queen was able to meet her future son-in-law. At the end of her stay Alice had chosen Ludwig. In 1861 the engagement between the two was announced. On the 14th of December 1861, the world sadly welcomed the news of the death of Prince Albert. Despite the tragedy, Queen Victoria wanted to continue the preparations for her daughter's wedding, which took place in the dining room of Osborne House on the 1st of July 1862. The wedding was mostly a funeral, except during the ceremony all the guests and the newlyweds wore black mourning clothes in memory of the

---

[323] G. Brook-Sheperd, *Uncle of Europe,* William Collins Sons & Co Ltd, Glasgow 1975.

[324] G. Noel, *Princess Alice: Queen Victoria's forgotten daughter*, Constable and Company Limited, London 1985.

Prince. The marriage went on between ups and downs, for Germany it was not a rosy period. During the Austro-Prussian War Alice even found herself on the opposite front to her sister in Prussia, the Grand Duchy of Hesse had sided with Austria. After the birth of the German Empire the situation improved because during the Franco-Prussian War Ludwig had sided with the Prussians. In 1877, after his father's death, he became the Grand Duke of Hesse. In November 1878 the whole family fell ill with diphtheria. The first to die was his daughter Maria and later, on the 14th of December, the same day her father, the Grand Duchess Alice died too. Ludwig will remarry in 1884 with Alexandrina Hutten-Czapska, their marriage was morganatic. Alexandrina was married to the Russian ambassador to the Grand Duchy of Hesse. After the news of the wedding there was a lot of embarrassment at court and the following year it was cancelled. On the 13th of March 1892 he died leaving the throne to his son Ernst Ludwig.

The couple had a total of seven children. The children's marriages were used to establish alliances within Germany and with Russia. The most famous heir is undoubtedly Alix Viktoria Helena Louise Beatrice, better known as Aleksandra Feodorovna Romanova,[325] the last tsarina of Russia. Aleksandra, a name she took after her conversion to the Orthodox Church, met Nikolaj Aleksandrovic Romanov[326], and married him on the 14th of November 1894 in the Winter Palace. Queen Victoria, her grandmother, wanted at all costs her to marry the eldest son of the Prince of Wales, the Duke of Clarence, Albert. Albert is linked to the most famous scandal and news event in late nineteenth century London: the Cleveland

---

[325] C. Erickson, *Alexandra*, St. Martin's Griffin, London 2002.

[326] A. Solmi, *Nicola II and Alessandra di Russia*, Rusconi, Milan 1989; A. Morrow, *Cousins Divided: George V and Nicholas II*, Sutton Publishing, Phoenix 2006.

Street scandal[327] and the murders of Jack the Ripper. In 1889 the London police discovered a male brothel on Cleveland Street. The police put all the boys who worked there under pressure and they eventually revealed the names of all their clients. The most famous client was Lord Arthur Somerset, head of the stables of the Prince of Wales. Somerset was homosexual, and in Victorian England everyone knew about it, but no one spoke of it. He lived separated from his wife from[328] the day she caught him having sex with his own servant. At the time, male homosexuality was prohibited and punishable by law even if both men were of age, consenting and in a private place[329]. The maximum sentence for the crime was two years of forced labour. The Cleveland Street brothel was arranged in such a way that the rich, *reversed* aristocrats would disguise their young lovers as telegrapher messengers. Immediately after the discovery of the brothel amongst the upper classes spread the word of the involvement of a member of the royal family. We do not know for sure before or after these rumours but at one-point Arthur Newton, Lord Somerset's lawyer, threatened to drag Prince Albert into the mud of the process. Today, thanks to the letters exchanged between the lawyer of the Treasury, Sir Augustus Stephenson and his assistant the Honourable Hamilton Cuffe we know of the threat of Newton. Shortly after the Prince of Wales intervened in the investigation

---

[327] T. Aronson, *Prince Eddy and the homosexual underworld,* John Murray, London 1994.

[328] Lady Georgiana Charlotte Curzon, relative of Lord Curzon.

[329] M. Cook, *London and the culture of homosexuality, 1885 – 1914.* Cambridge University Press, Cambridge 2003; C. Lane, *The ruling Passion: British colonial allegory and the paradox of homosexual desire,* Duke University Press, London 1995; A. L. Rowse, *Homosexuals in History,* Carroll & Graf, New York 1977; R. Hyam, *Empire and Sexuality,* Manchester University Press, Manchester 1990.

and everything was silenced, Lord Somerset could leave the country and he settled in Florence where he soon became known to all as *Lord Gomorrah*. Several historians and biographers have written about this fact and the Prince, saying that it was probably true that he was homosexual or bisexual but even today we have no confirmation. In letters from Lord Somerset to his friend Lord Esher he states that he knew nothing about Albert's involvement but hoped that the gossip would serve his purpose.

"I can quite understand the Prince of Wales being much annoyed at his son's name being coupled with the thing but that was the case before I left it [...] we were both accused of going to this place but not together [...] they will end by having out in open court exactly what they are all trying to keep quiet. I wonder if it is really a fact or only an invention of that arch ruffian H[ammond]"[330]

Harold Nicolson, biographer of King George V 60 years after the facts learnt from Lord Goggard, then a simple twelve-year-old student, who

"Had been involved in a male brothel scene, and that a solicitor had to commit perjury to clear him. The solicitor was struck off the rolls for his offence, but was thereafter reinstated"[331]

During the trial none of the lawyers were convicted of perjury or disbarred but Arthur Newton was convicted of obstruction of justice, after it became known that he had helped his client escape abroad, by being sentenced to six weeks in prison. In 1910

---

[330] H. Hyde Montgomery, *The Cleveland Street Scandal,* Coward, McCann & Geoghegan, New York. p. 122.

[331] J. Lees-Milne, Harold *Nicolson: A Biography. Volume 2: 1930-1968*, Chatto & Windus, London 1965. p. 231.

he was suspended for 12 months because he had falsified letters from a client, Newton was in fact defending the infamous Dr. Harvey Crippen involved in the notorious murder of Hilldrop Crescent[332]. Crippen will end up hanging on charges of killing his wife, whilst modern science has shown that the remains found in the house were not those of Cora Crippen. In 1913 Newton was suspended for good and sentenced to three years in prison for lending money illegally. We do not know whether what Lord Goggard said was true or not, but there is still an aura of mystery of doubt on the matter. The other case in which Prince Albert was involved was that of the murders of Jack the Ripper, in the autumn of 1888 in the Whitechapel district. Jack the Ripper was the first serial killer in history and needs no introduction, as Shakespeare or the Mona Lisa his figure is known in every corner of the world. The cold and skilful killer who terrorised London for an entire season by killing prostitutes in the dark of the night and removing organs and body parts. At the time, public opinion was terrified and Scotland Yard, the investigative police, did not. The most famous cartoon of the time was that of a blindfolded *bobby*[333] groping in the dark, published in the *Punch* of 22nd of September 1888. Much has been said and written about the figure of Jack, the crimes were five, all women and all prostitutes: Mary Ann Nichols killed on the 31st of August in Buck's Row, Annie Chapman murdered on the 8th of September in the courtyard of number 29 Hanbury Street, Elizabeth Stride died on the 30th of September in Berner Street that same night was also found Catherine Eddowes body in Mitre Square. It is thought that that night the Ripper was disturbed immediately after the first murder and could not rage on the corpse, so he chose another prostitute the same night. The latest murder historically

---

[332] E. Larson, *Thunderstruck,* Broadway Books, New York 2007.

[333] This is the name given to the London policemen in memory of Sir Robert Peel, who was the founder and organiser of the London police force in 1828.

attributed to Jack the Ripper is that of Mary Jane Kelly discovered on the 9th of November at 13 Miller's Court. Several other subsequent murders were matched to Jack the Ripper's hand. The last murder was the most brutal, the victim was literally reduced to pieces and this made everyone think of a kind of last chapter of a tragic serial novel. During the months of the crimes Jack took the trouble to mock the police by sending several letters, in one of these, the most famous one is the one called *Dear Boss Letter,* dated 25th of September, in which the author signs himself as Jack the Ripper. Subsequently, on the 1st of October, the *Saucy Jack Letter* arrived in which he announced a double murder at a short distance from each other. *From Hell Letter* was received on the 16th of October. In the letter the address was *From Hell* and together with the letter a piece of kidney preserved in ethyl alcohol was sent. The coroner's examination revealed that the half kidney looked like the missing part of the one left on Eddowes body. As we know, the murderer was never captured, and we will never know who committed those crimes. Prince Albert's name was connected to Jack in the first few months of the investigation. According to the theory the prince had contracted syphilis from a prostitute, and this had caused in him a hatred for women and especially prostitutes. The royal family years later released evidence that Albert was not in London at the time. Another theory is that one known as *The Royal Conspiracy* where the murdered prostitutes were nothing more than witnesses of a secret marriage between Albert and a Catholic prostitute. The marriage would have produced a daughter. According to the theory, Queen Victoria could not accept to have an heir to the throne with a Catholic daughter and ordered to all witnesses to be killed.

The Prince was certainly not the best candidate for a woman like Aleksandra, who wanted a happy marriage and especially love. The Queen wanted the union but appreciated the nephew's courage to stand up to her and say no. In fact, Aleksandra had already fallen in love with the heir to the throne of Russia, the young Nikolaj. Nikolaj's mother was the sister-in-law of Aleksandra's uncle, the Prince of Wales, and her uncle, Sergej Aleksandrovic, Grand Duke of Russia, was the husband of

Aleksandra's sister, Elizabeth. The two were second cousins. It only took two meetings, one in 1884 and the other in 1889, to make them fall in love. Tsar Aleksandr III, Nikolaj's father, did not agree with this union. He demanded a higher-ranking bride for his son. His first choice was Princess Hélène of Paris, but she did not want to abandon her Catholic religion. The other choice fell on the daughter of Kaiser Friederich III, Margarete, but Nikolaj hated her and even she was not willing to change religion. In the end, when the Tsar was struck by an illness, he decided to consent to the marriage. In April 1894 they got engaged. Despite the death of their father on the 1st of November, the marriage between the two was held on the 14th of November of the same month. She became a devout orthodox woman. Her sister Elisabeth also became her aunt because she was married to Nikolaj's uncle. The Tsaritsa had inherited haemophilia from her mother, who in turn had inherited it from Queen Victoria. The women were healthy carriers of the disease but the sons of all three suffered from it. The best-known is certainly the zarevic Aleksej.

The fourth son of Victoria and Albert was Alfred, Duke of Edinburgh. Born in 1844. He was a skilled diplomat, good-looking and well-liked and he also was in the Navy. In 1862 he was the ideal candidate for the throne of Greece after the revolt had forced the Sovereign to abdicate, but the succession was blocked by the English Government itself. He was the first member of the Royal Family to visit Australia, New Zealand, India and Hong Kong[334]. In 1874 he married Marija Aleksandrovna Romanova, daughter of Aleksandr II and aunt of Nikolaj. The two of them had a total of six children. Alfred inherited her father's titles, Mary later became Queen of Romania as she married Ferdinand I. Ferdinand became King after her father and older brother renounced the title. He thus became heir to his uncle Karl I in

---

[334] B. McKinlay, *The First Royal Tour, 1867–1868*, Robert Hale & Company, London 1970.

November 1888. He became King of Romania on the 10th of October 1914. Although he was a member of the Hohenzollern family when his nation went to war in 1916, he did so alongside the nations of the Entente. Victoria, the third daughter, married the Grand Duke of Hesse Ernst Ludwig, son of Alice and Ludwig. In 1901 she divorced to marry the Grand Duke of Russia Kirill Vladimirovic Romanov. Alexandra, the penultimate daughter, married Prince Ernst of Hohenlohe-Langenburg. Their eldest son, Gottfried, married Margaretha of Greece and Denmark in 1931. The last daughter of Alfred and Marija, Beatrice married the Infante of Spain despite being in love with Michail Aleksandrovic Romanov, but they could not marry as first cousins and marriage between first cousins was forbidden by the Orthodox Church. Their fathers were brothers. Alfonso d'Orleans was a cousin of Alfonso XIII King of Spain. The marriage was celebrated with a double Catholic and Lutheran rite. The couple had to live in exile for several years because the King did not accept the marriage and only in 1912, he consent to their return. Alfonso XIII was a womaniser and rumours began to spread that he was having an affair with Beatrice, the Queen did not like it and the King had to send Beatrice into exile. They returned to Spain but had to suffer the humiliation of the Spanish Civil War.

The fifth one of the imperial couple was a girl, Helena[335]. Born in 1846. She was the most active member of the royal family, always present at public ceremonies and very attentive to volunteerism, she was one of the founders of the Red Cross. Queen Victoria wanted her daughter to stay with her so when it came to choose her husband, she did not aim for a high-ranking member. Shortly afterwards the choice fell on the fallen Prince Christian of Schleswig-Holstein. This caused quite a few problems within the royal family. The Prince's territories were disputed by Prussia and

---

[335] S. Chomet, *Helena: A Princess Reclaimed*, Begell House, New York 1999.

336

Denmark, according to the wars fought between Prussians and the Danes those territories were now Prussian but disputed by the King of Denmark. To take the news very badly was the Princess of Wales Alexandra, daughter of the King of Denmark Christian IX. Half of Victoria's children were against the union and the other half supported it. Despite all this, the wedding took place in Windsor in 1865. The Prince was 15 years older than his new wife. In all they had six children and their marriage, despite their age, was happy and they were faithful to each other.

The fourth daughter and sixth of the nine children was Louise. Born in 1848. When it came to choose her a husband, the Queen began to examine the various offers from the families of Europe. She did not want another Danish wedding, so she discarded Alexandra's offer to marry her to her brother. Victoria Adelaide proposed Prince Albert of Prussia, but the Queen did not want another Prussian in the family and Albert did not want to move to England. Wilhelm of Orange was discarded because of his bad reputation. Louise, however, did not want to marry a royalty so she chose John Campbell, Marquis of Lorne and heir to the Duchy of Argyll. A member of the royal family had not married a royal since 1515. The Prince of Wales was opposed to the wedding mainly because the Duke of Argyll was a supporter of Gladstone. The two married in 1871, on the 21st of March, in Windsor. For the first-time since her husband's death, the Queen did not wear mourning. The couple moved to Canada in 1878 because Lorne had been chosen by Disraeli as the new Governor-General of Canada. They only returned to their homeland in 1883 after having left an excellent reputation behind. They never had children. Louise died as Duchess.

Victoria's seventh child, and third son, was Arthur, Duke of Connaught and Strathearn. Ever since he was a child, he wanted to take up a military career. He served in different parts of the Empire, especially in Canada. Despite the contrary opinion of his mother Arthur married in 1879 Louise of Prussia grandson of the German Emperor. He performed various tasks for the Empire: he was in South Africa for the first meeting of the New Parliament after the merger of the colony and Boer territories and contributed to the creation of a monument for the British fallen of the

Second Anglo-Boer War. In 1911 King George V chose him as the new Governor-General of Canada. The family was very popular during their period in Canada. Expenditure was made in the war years on better preparation of Canadian troops. The couple had three children, Margareth was born in 1882 and married Gustav VI of Sweden. Arthur, born the following year, married Princess Alexandra, Duchess of Fife in 1913. Patrizia the third-born married Sir Alexander Ramsay in 1919 even though she had many heirs to the throne or brothers of Sovereigns to choose from as suitors.

The eighth and penultimate son of Victoria and Albert was Leopold, Duke of Albany. Born in 1853. He inherited haemophilia from his mother and suffered continuous bleeding all his life. His mother wanted to keep him with her whilst he saw marriage as the only way to escape maternal control. Because of his illness it was difficult to find a wife, after trying with several princesses he finally married, in 1882, Helena Frederica daughter of George Viktor of Waldeck and Pyrmont. The marriage lasted only two years, he died in 1884 after a fall in Cannes. They had two children.

Albert and Victoria's last son was Beatrice,[336] born in 1857. In 1885 she married Heinrich of Battenberg, a family with excellent relations to the Grand Duchy of Hesse, who had long been linked to the British royal family. He was born out of the morganatic marriage of his father, Alexander, to Julia Hauke. The Queen allowed the marriage with the promise that the couple would live in Windsor with her. In 1896 her husband died leaving Beatrice a widow at the age of 38. She became Governor of the Isle of Wright instead of her husband. The mother had asked her to review her diaries before she had them archived, Beatrice took 30 years to check

---

[336] M. Dennison, *The Last Princess: The Devoted Life of Queen Victoria's Youngest Daughter*, Weidenfeld & Nicolson, London 2007.

them all, transcribing only the parts that had been reviewed or censored. The originals were burned by Beatrice. The couple had four children, the best-known being Victoria Eugenie who became Queen of Spain as the wife of Alfonso XIII.

This complex web of kinship and marriage was supposed to serve in theory as a defence for the European *status quo*, family members would never move war against each other, especially at that time when we saw everywhere only new technologies, industries and positivism. In fact, however, the crowned heads of Europe were friends only in the family, everyone had to respect their national interest, and if you calculate that many Sovereigns were foreigners in their Kingdom you understand the diversity in respecting the wishes of the people and the family. European diplomacy was an intricate network, complex and difficult to satisfy. Victoria, even after her death, continued in some way to steer global decisions. In addition to the largest Empire in history, she bequeathed nine children, 34 grandchildren and 64 great-grandchildren to the world. Together we can say that they were the best ambassadors of the Empire. Or at least they tried.

At this point, we must ask ourselves a question that is essential in order to understand not only the reason for the conflict but also the reason that led Britain, and its colonies, to wage a risky war that could have called into question, or worse, destroyed everything it had built in three centuries. Was British intervention necessary?

2. Bullets and inkwells.

The British playwright Alan Bennett in his most famous work puts the following speech in the mouth of a professor of history.

"The truth was, in 1914, Germany doesn't want war. Yeah, there's an arms race, but it's Britain who's leading it. So, why does no one admit this? That's why. The dead. The body count. We don't like to admit the war was even partly our fault cos so many

of our people died. And all the mourning's veiled the truth. It's not "lest we forget",
it's "lest we remember". That's what all this is about - the memorials, the Cenotaph,
the two minutes' silence. Because there is no better way of forgetting something than
by commemorating it."[337]

Is Professor Irwin, right? Should Britain have stayed out of the conflict? or was the conflict inevitable, British intervention necessary and the victory of the Triple entente indispensable?

England was the cradle of mass journalism. The newspaper, which was merely a tool used by the local lords to learn about the news from the City, gradually became a social channel for the masses. The British population has enjoyed, in a relatively short period of time, an unprecedented increase in literacy in history. Through a series of measures ranging from the creation of schools, not only in large cities but also in small villages, through the foundation of educational institutions, *mechanics institutes*, dedicated to teaching crafts, up to the *Public Libraries Act* of 1850, with the establishment of public libraries, the population was able to access reading and writing and this led the publishing market to a real boom. Prices fell and the State stopped taxing it allowed even the poorest of workers to buy and read a booklet, a book or a newspaper. Since the advent of mass publishing, the British, and the Europeans, began not only to create their own national culture, but also *public*

---

[337] A. Bennett, *The History Boys*, Faber & Faber, London 2006. p. 55. Trad It. *Gli student di Storia,* Adelphi, Milan 2012. pp.76-77.

opinion, which became increasingly influential and politics did not take long to understand its hidden potentials.[338]

In 1922 Walter Lippmann, a journalist, former Undersecretary of War, and adviser to President Wilson, published his most famous work, *Public Opinion*, in which he reported a curious and useful episode for our investigation:

"There is an island in the ocean where in 1914 a few Englishmen, Frenchmen, and Germans lived. No cable reaches that island, and the British mail steamer comes but once in sixty days. In September it had not yet come, and the islanders were still talking about the latest newspaper which told about the approaching trial of Madame Caillaux for the shooting of Gaston Calmette. It was, therefore, with more than usual eagerness that the whole colony assembled at the quay on a day in mid-September to hear from the captain what the verdict had been. They learned that for over six weeks now those of them who were English and those of them who were French had been fighting in behalf of the sanctity of treaties against those of them who were Germans. For six strange weeks they had acted as if they were friends, when in fact they were enemies.

But their plight was not so different from that of most of the population of Europe. They had been mistaken for six weeks, on the continent the interval may have been only six days or six hours. There was an interval. There was a moment when the picture of Europe on which men were conducting their business as usual, did not in any way correspond to the Europe which was about to make a jumble of their lives. There was a time for each man when he was still adjusted to an environment that no

---

[338] R. Altick, *Writers, Readers and Occasions: Selected Essays on Victorian Literature and Life,* Ohio State Uni Press, Columbus 1988. Trad It. *Democrazia fra le pagine,* Il mulino, Milan 1990.

longer existed. All over the world as late as July 25th men were making goods that they would not be able to ship, buying goods they would not be able to import, careers were being planned, enterprises contemplated, hopes and expectations entertained, all in the belief that the world as known was the world as it was. Men were writing books describing that world. They trusted the picture in their heads. And then over four years later, on a Thursday morning, came the news of an armistice, and people gave vent to their unutterable relief that the slaughter was over. Yet in the five days before the real armistice came, though the end of the war had been celebrated, several thousand young men died on the battlefields".[339]

Lippmann uses this event to highlight how public opinion was, directly or indirectly, controlled by the media, but it takes on a different meaning in the light of what has been said above, that is, it highlights how in the summer of 1914 it was not so obvious for the continent to go to war. We cannot take this fact as a universal truth because we are talking about an island in the middle of the ocean. In old Europe, things were different. But as we will see later, the reality of that island in the middle of the ocean was not so different from that of the continent.

If a war in 1914 was not sure, one thing was, that in the end, a war would break out, eventually. But against whom? The United Kingdom wanted to keep the Empire out as much as possible of any "continental" issue, France had an open wound for over 40 years, since the Franco-Prussian war, Germany wanted to expand, Austria-Hungary wanted total domination over the Balkans, Russia wanted to prevent it, Italy wanted to end unification and the Ottoman Empire wanted to avoid implosion. Treaties and alliances had been signed in the decades before and months after the Sarajevo attack, but not all of them were respected. In Britain, and in other countries

---

[339] W. Lippmann, *Public Opinion*, Greenbook pubblications, New York 1922, Trad It *L'opinione Pubblica*, Donzelli Editore, Rome 2004. p. 5.

with less influence, the population had somehow been "prepared" for the conflict. A preparation that had been going on for years and that had taken place in the simplest and most widespread way of the time: literature.

There is a widespread belief that the *culture* of militarism was the cause of the war. Men and women were so well prepared and informed about the conflict that the declaration of war was only an act of routine. If we replace militarism with printed paper, the phrase takes on a much more truthful meaning, in my opinion. Books and newspapers have shaped the mind of British society. In a sense after steam, trains and ships at the base of the pillars of the Empire there was the printed paper, and led to a mistaken belief in the scope, duration and intensity of any future conflict. Talking about war was a great way to make money. Lord Northcliffe, director of the *Daily Mail* at the beginning of the century, was once questioned about the sale of his newspapers and what made them sell. The answer was, *"The first answer is "war." War not only creates a supply of news but a demand for it. So deep-rooted is the fascination in a war and all things appertaining to it that [...] a paper has only to be able to put up on its placard "A Great Battle" for its sales to go up"*[340] With the end of the Boer wars there was a vacuum in war journalism. A void that should be filled as soon as possible. Thus, was born the literary vein of texts that did not speak of an ongoing conflict, but suggested a war in the future. The enemy par excellence was the German Empire. Russophobia was part of the past, now Russia was a friendly and allied state. A granddaughter of the Queen had married the Tsar. Germany was also a friendly country on paper, Victoria's eldest daughter had married the future Kaiser, but her son wanted at all costs to establish himself in the world and own an Empire more important and vast than that one of his grandmother. The newspapers,

---

[340] H.D., Lasswell, *Propaganda Technique in the World War*, London, 1927, p. 192.

and especially the *Daily Mail*, were so "guilty" of stirring up the population that in 1914, at the beginning of the war, the real war this time, a German official in Berlin refused to issue a passport to a journalist of the *Daily "because he believed he had been largely instrumental in bringing about the war"*[341].

In England, the first novel to suggest an Anglo-German conflict was Headon Hill's *The Spies of Wight*, published in 1899, with a plot centred on the conspiracies of German spies in England. Three years later, Albert Charles Curtis' *A New Trafalgar* was released and here the action moved to the sea, where a German invasion is hypothesised, a danger averted by the arrival of a secret super battleship of the Royal Navy[342]. The following year Erskine Childers' novel *The Riddle of the Sands is* published. In the book the two protagonists discover by chance the plans to invade the island to be carried out using barges loaded with German soldiers[343]. In the same year we have *The Boy Galloper,* by Lionel James, where the protagonist is forced to wear his cadet uniform after a[344]German invasion. In 1910, William Le Queux's bestseller *The Invasion of 1910*[345]appeared in episodes on the *Daily Mail*, in which we discover that 40 thousand German soldiers have invaded the island; Lord

---

[341] H.A., Innis, The press: A Neglected Factor in the Economic History of the twentieth century, Oxford, 1949. p. 31.

[342] I. F., Clarke, *The Great War with Germany, 1890-1914* a cura di, Liverpool University Press, Liverpool, 1917. p. 129-139.

[343] E. Childers, *The Riddle of the Sands,* Smith, Elder & Co, London 1903, p. 248. Trad it.: *L'enigma delle sabbie*, Bariletti, Rome, 1989.

[344] I. F., Clarke, *The Great War...*, p. 326.

[345] I. F., Clarke, p. 139-152.

Northcliffe personally modified the path of the German invaders by making them pass through cities full of readers of the *Daily Mail*. Three years earlier, Patrick Vaux had printed *When the Eagle Filies Seaward*[346], where the number of soldiers was as high as 60 thousand. In the same year *The Death Trap,* by Robert William Cole, was released, where the Japanese[347]came to the rescue the English. Also, in 1907, the first novel that narrated a German victory over the armies of his majesty, Alec John Dawson's *The Message*[348] was published. In Dawson's and Edward Phillips Oppenheim's volumes, in *A Maker of History*, published in 1905, it was assumed that thousands of Germans had infiltrated British society:

"Each have their work assigned to them. The forts which guard this great city may be impregnable from without, but from within — that is another matter..."[349]

A veritable *psychosis of spies* covered the island from south to north and from east to west.

For Walter Wood in *The Enemy in our Midst* there was a German commission for secret preparations, where a real putsch was planned in London. In 1909 Captain Curties' *When England Slept*[350] and Le Queux's *Spies of the Kaiser*[351] were released.

---

[346] I. F., Clarke, p. 153-166.

[347] I. F., Clarke, p. 168-178.

[348]I. F., Clarke, Ivi, pp. 339-354.

[349] C. Andrew, *Secret Service*: *The Making of British Intelligence Community*, London, Guild Publishing, 1985, p. 77.

[350] I. F., Clarke, *The Great War...*, p. 356-363.

[351] W. Le Queux, *Spies of Kaiser*, Frank Cass, London 1909.

The first one talks about an invading Army that secretly entered within a few weeks in the second there is a story of a German spy network in England.

Spies' psychosis was not just limited to novels. Theatres, poems and periodicals were invaded by such texts. Poets and playwrights filled pages and pages on German terror.

The verses of Charles Doughty[352], *The Cliffs* and *The Clouds*, published in 1909 and 1911 whilst in theatres, in the same year as *The Cliffs,* the audience could enjoy the comedy of Guy du Maurier, *An Englishman's Home.* Students from all the schools of the Kingdom from 1913, to the dawn of the real conflict, could read on *Chums*[353] a series of stories about an Anglo-German war. There were even those who[354] believed that in 1930 England would be "*a small island off the western coast of Teutonic*"[355].

Saki, Hector Hugh Munro, published the novel *When William Came: A Story of London under the Hohenzollerns* in 1913. In a sadistic, sharp and grotesque way, he described an England that had been defeated and incorporated into the German Empire. The protagonist, Murrey Yeovil, who came to Europe to visit England, found a Germanised country with the royal family in exile in India. A curiosity of the novel is that Yeovil discovered that English Jews were pro-German. A

---

[352] I. F., Clarke, *The Great War...,* pp. 377-381.

[353] S. Hynes, *A War Imaginated: The First World War and English Culture*, Random House, London 1990. p. 46.

[354] The magazine of the Aldeburgh Lodge school.

[355] I. F., Clarke, *The Great War...,* pp. 179-180.

widespread belief, especially in British conservative circles. Ernest Oldmeadow a few years earlier in *North Sea Bubble* had already talked about the subject by describing the horrors of a Germanised England; Sausage and Sauerkraut for All, Autonomous Ireland and the name of Händel correctly spelled[356].

The so-called *Psychosis of spies* was not only a British phenomenon, on the contrary, it spread with the same vigour in the continent too.

In Germany, just at the beginning of the century, the public could taste the version of the conflict that came out of the pen of Karl Eisenhart. *In Die Abrechnung mit England,* where a United Kingdom defeated in the Boer war was attacked by France. Great Britain in response implements a naval blockade that triggers war with Germany that wins the conflict thanks to an electric battleship and conquers the booty of the colonies of his majesty. For August Niemann, in *Der Weltkrieg deutsche Traume*, in conflict would be between Germany, Russia and France united against Britain that dominated the world. In *100 Jahre deutsche Zukunft* by Max Heinrichka an Anglo-German war breaks out for Holland.

But as in Great Britain, not everyone in Germany was confident in a German victory. In *"Sink, burn, destroy": der Schlag gegen Deutschland* by an unknown author, the British navy defeats and invades Germany from the port of Hamburg.

However, not always the sworn enemy was Germany, the first texts to come out had France as their adversary.

In 1891 a text, to say the least, prophetic, came out. *The Great War of 1891.* Published in the weekly *Black and White*. According to the authors, the war began in the Balkans after the assassination of a royal, in this case Prince Ferdinand of Bulgaria, by the hands of Russian agents. The escalation leads Serbia to declare war

---

[356] I. F., Clarke, Ivi, p. 364-398.

on Bulgaria, Austria-Hungary decides to occupy Belgrade by bringing the Russians into war. Germany respects the treaties with Vienna and enters war against Russia whilst France, because of the treaties, enters into war alongside Russia against Germany. After a declaration of neutrality, Great Britain helps Turkey and France and Russia declare war on it.[357] In 1893 *The Final War* came out, where Germany and France were plotting to conquer England but at the end Germany changed sides and the English even entered triumphant in Paris. William Le Queux, whom we met above, began his career with two books about France. *The Poisoned Bullet* of 1893 and *England's Peril: A Story of the Secret Service* of 1899.

The Campaign of Douai, London's Peril, The Great French, War of 1901, The New Battle of Dorking, The Coming Waterloo and Pro Patria all by Max Pemberton. It appeared during the Boer War. Louis Tracy's *The Invaders* reports the same Franco-German plot seen before[358]. Even in France writers did not miss the opportunity and *La Guerre avec l'Angleterre*[359] was very successful. In the German Empire, *Berlin-Baghdad*, 1907, attracted the attention of its readers as it recounted a prophetic war in the skies between post-revolution Russians and Germans.[360]

But not everyone was so sure of a future war. Satire was also used as a *weapon* against the first-hour alarmists. In *The Swoop! Or How Clarence Saved England: A*

---

[357]I. F., Clarke, Ivi, p. 29-71.

[358] I. F., Clarke, *Voices Prophesying War, 1763 - 1984*, London - New York, 1992. pp. 102-108.

[359] C. Andrew, *Secret Service: The Making of British Intelligence Community*, London, Guild Publishing, 1985, p. 69.

[360]C. Andrew, Ivi, pp. 233-247

Tale of the Great Invasion, 1909, Wodehouse takes every aspect of a conflict to the extreme and describes how Britain was simultaneously invaded by Germans, Russians, Swiss, Chinese, Monegasques, Moroccans and the mad Mullah. The protagonist of the novel, a boy scout, must carefully read in the newspapers the cricket page to find information about the landing in Surrey. In short, a good example of *reductio ad absurdum*. Le Queux was mocked by Milne in *The Secret of the Army Aeroplane*, in 1909, published in the satirical magazine, *Punch*. *"Last Tuesday a man with his moustache brushed up the wrong way alighted at Basingstoke station and inquired for the refreshment-room. This leads me to believe that a dastardly attempt is about to be made to wrest the supremacy of the air from our grasp"*[361]. In 1910, 11 cartoons by Heath Robinson appeared in *The Sketch,* another satirical magazine. Here we find the Germans disguised as birds in the trees, in bathing suits as they invade a beach and even disguised as statues in the British Museum[362]. In Germany a map became famous in which the British Empire was reduced to Iceland leaving everything else to Germany[363]. In 1908 Siwinna published *Guide for Fantasy Strategist* in which, with much effort, he demolished, or at least attempted, the various British and German war plans[364].

The science fiction writer Herbert George Wells in 1908 with *The War in the Air* described an apocalyptic scenario. A mainly aerial war with bombardments and

---

[361] N. Hiley, *Introduction*, in Le Queux, *Spies of the Kaiser*, Frank Cass, London 1909. p. IX-X.

[362] I. F., Clarke, *The Great War...*, pp. 282-292.

[363] I. F., Clarke, Ivi, p. 214.

[364] I. F., Clarke, Ivi, pp. 296-313.

destruction throughout Europe. All this leaves only *"blown up" by bombardments from airships, leaving only `ruins and unburied dead, and shrunken yellow-faced survivors in a mortal apathy"*[365].

None of the authors could *guess* the exact period or produce a story that came close to what was the war in 1914-1918, the most represented scenario was a German invasion of Britain, but the scenario was completely alien to the strategic plans of Germany. Almost all the authors we have seen reveal complete ignorance of the real preparation of the armies and their technical limitations.

The writer who perhaps came closest to reality was the lesser-known father of communism, Friedrich Engels:

"world war of never before seen extension and intensity, if the system of mutual outbidding in armament, carried to the extreme, finally bears its natural fruits [...] [E]ight to ten million soldiers will slaughter each other and strip Europe bare as no swarm of locusts has ever done before. The devastations of the Thirty Years War condensed into three or four years and spread all over the continent; famine, epidemics, general barbarisation of armies and masses, provoked by sheer desperation; utter chaos in our trade, industry and commerce, ending in general bankruptcy; collapse of the old states and their traditional wisdom in such a way that the crowns roll in the gutter by the dozens and there will be nobody to pick them up; absolute impossibility to foresee how all this will end and who will be victors in

---

[365] I. F., Clarke, Ivi, p. 233.

that struggle; only one result absolutely certain: general exhaustion and the creation of circumstances for the final victory of the working class."[366]

An exact description, to say the least, of what will become the Great War.

In 1890, Von Moltke pronounced prophetic words in a speech at the Reichstag:

"The age of cabinet war is behind us — all we have now is people's war [...] Gentlemen, if the war that has been hanging over our heads now for more than ten years like the sword of Damocles — if this war breaks out, then its duration and its end will be unforeseeable. The greatest powers of Europe, armed as never before, will be going into battle with each other; not one of them can be crushed so completely in one or two campaigns that it will admit defeat, will be compelled to conclude peace under hard terms, and will not come back, even if it is a year later, to renew the struggle. Gentlemen, it may be a war of seven years' or of thirty years' duration — and woe to him who sets Europe alight, who first puts the fuse to the powder keg".[367]

Von Moltke's speech is even more impressive when you consider that it was delivered in the same place where Germany would later declare war to Britain. The Kaiser and the Reichstag will put the fuse under the gunpowder. Fuse that Von Moltke wanted to keep as far away as possible.

The person who managed to create a more detailed war forecast, however, was a Warsaw financier. Ivan Stanislavovic Bloch. In his work, released in England under

---

[366] S. Forster, *Dreams and Nightmares: German Military Leadership and the Images of Future Warfare*, 1871-1914, Essay presented at the Conference of Augsburg, 1994.

[367] S. Forster, Ibid, p. 4.

the title *Is War Now Impossible?* in 1899, he claimed that a conflict would be devastating for three specific reasons. The military technology of the various nations had eliminated the possibility of waging a fast war. No more bayonets and cavalry, then. With the evolution of artillery men would be forced into a trench warfare and no longer into open field battles having close combat. According to Bloch's calculations, a European war would have mobilised at least 10 million men who would be fighting on an immense front, even with high mortality rates, the war would still have lasted many years. The last point is the economic aspect on which Engels was based.

"Entire dislocation of all industry and severing of all the sources of supply ... the future of war [is] not fighting, but famine, not the slaying of men, but the bankruptcy of nations and the break-up of the whole social organisation".[368]

Bloch's analysis was correct but, in some parties, outdated. He claimed, in fact, that a future war would break out between Russia and France against Germany, with the Austro-Hungarian Empire and Italy on the other side. They are outdated if we think of a war in the second decade of the twenty-first century, but they are current if we think of the period in which the book was written. He also believed that since the conflict would become a trench war in a short time the soldiers of the most organised nations, Great Britain, Germany, France, would not be able to endure for long the hardships of a war of attrition whilst he believed that Russian farmers would adapt more easily. Another mistake he made was overestimating the British Navy. He believed that no inferior navy would be useful in a war against Great Britain. The

---

[368] I. S. Bloch, *Is War Now Impossible? Being an Abridgment of 'The War of the Future and its Technical, Economic and Political Relations'* London, 1899. p. LX.

biggest mistake, however, was to believe that an economic crisis caused by the conflict would have made a long-lasting war unsustainable.

Bloch is also linked to a curious event. In 1899 the English journalist William Thomas Stead interviewed him about his book. Stead was not only a great investigative journalist, but he is also known for starting tabloid journalism. He was also a great pacifist. It was precisely about his investigative journalism that he began to write his first articles in 1870. In 1876 he published a series of articles on atrocities committed by the Ottoman Empire. In 1880 he became director of Pall Mall Gazette. He began a strong campaign against child prostitution, *Maiden Tribute of Modern Babylon,* which cost him a three-month sentence. In 1890 he left Pall Mall and founded his own magazine, Review of Reviews, where he gave vent to his pacifism and spiritualism, typical of the Victorian era. He will also participate in the Hague conferences as a reporter. On the 22nd of March 1886, he published an article. A shipwreck at sea that had caused many deaths due to the lack of lifeboats on board. In 1892 he published a story, *From Old to New World*, in which he imagined a shipwreck in the middle of the Atlantic. A White Star Line ship rescues the survivors of a ship that sank after colliding with an iceberg. For a joke of fate Stead booked a ticket for the Titanic. He went to America to attend a peace conference at the request of President Taft. Stead died on the ship, after donating his life jacket and helping women and children get on the few remaining lifeboats, he then went to the first-class reading room. Another curious note: a clairvoyant friend advised him not to travel on the Titanic. Most likely, if he had not died, he would have been awarded the Nobel Peace Prize. It was precisely his pacifism that brought him closer to Bloch and, thanks to his very strong personality, the monumental work of the Polish statesman was also published, albeit in a reduced version, in English.

Bloch in his work concludes that a war would not have been possible because the nations in his opinion were not so *crazy:*

"The war [...] in which great nations armed to the teeth [...] fling themselves with all their resources into a struggle for life and death [...] is the war that every day becomes more and more impossible [...] A war between the Triplite [Germany, Austria and Italy] and the Franco-Russian Alliance ... has become absolutely impossible [...] The dimensions of modern armaments and the organisation of society have rendered its prosecution an economic impossibility, and [...] if any attempt were made to demonstrate the inaccuracy of my assertions by putting the matter to a test on a large-scale, we should find the inevitable result in a catastrophe which would destroy all existing political organisations. Thus the Great War cannot be made, and any attempt to make it would result in suicide."[369]

It should also be noted, however, that Bloch added a post scriptum:

"I do not [...] deny that it is possible for nations to plunge themselves and their neighbours into a frightful series of catastrophes which would probably result in the overturn of all civilised and ordered Government."[370]

The book was particularly appreciated in Russia. Nicholas II in a letter admitted that reading *"a book by a Warsaw banker named Bloch"*[371] He had the inspiration for his *Appeal to the Governors* later merged into the Hague Peace Conference.

---

[369] I. S. Bloch, Ivi, p. X-XI.

[370] I. S. Bloch, Ivi, p. XXXI.

[371] G. Gooch, H. Temperley, British Documents on the Origins of the War, 1898-1914, volume 1, London 1926, p. 222. *"The book was referred by the Emperor of Russia at my request to the Minister of War, with the request that it should be subjected to examination by a council of experts"* l'esito fu: *"No book could*

Where did Bloch got it wrong? He ignored the fact that it was practically impossible for revolutions, like those described by him, to take place simultaneously in all the belligerent states. He also never considered the fact that one of the engines of the conflict was precisely the attempt to bring down the enemy before collapsing.

After Bloch's death in 1902, his predictions fell into oblivion, also thanks to changes in alliances. In 1909 Norman Angell published *Europe's Optical Illusion* revised, expanded and republished under the title *The Great Illusion*. Angell tried to carry on Bloch's pacifist ideas. He argued that a war would never break out because the economic damage would be so great that it would stop any intention of war. In support of his thesis, he filled the book with statistical data, tables and economic accounts. Angell's appeal was even less prominent than Bloch's, although the book was very successful, and the nations continued the arms race. At a time when value and courage were the cornerstones of European men, pacifism was seen and described as a mere act of cowardice. Angell tried to undermine the ethical ideal of war with economic data, but this irritated more than one part of the Government. Criticism also came from all over Italy. On the pages of La Voce, a magazine founded in 1908, the philosopher Giovanni Amendola, with an article of May 2, 1910, turned against the theses of Angell. According to Amendola Angell may have been right but he did not consider the fact that the most varied and irrational motives could cause a war. "It *is thanks to this simple, unconscious, but healthy crowd that books such as Norman Angell's will serve no purpose, and that, thanks be to God, men will continue to slaughter themselves rather than run aground [...] to the philosophy of gain they (peoples) still prefer that of risk and struggle. [...] (Angell)*

---

contribute so much to the success of the Conference" Bloch, *Is War Now Impossible?* p. XIII

imagined portraying humanity from war, imprisoning it in the economy. [...] (the economy) would have pushed men, in droves, in flocks, towards a social barracks that for many, democratic or conservative, does not matter, is the historical goal to be achieved"[372] Amendola was against pacifism because he saw in it the ruin of man. He was convinced of the need for the *"man of war"*. Only he possesses *"the virtues of sacrifice, fortitude, and audacity, which constitute the bottom of the fighter and make the man of war, with all his excesses and all his brutalities, a type infinitely superior to that of the shrewd sybarite who finds in the cult of peace the best expression of his voluptuous convection of life*[373]. Amendola was certainly not the only one who believed in the man of war; on the contrary, this feeling was imprinted on all the peoples of Europe. Wherever the skills of the soldier and of war were exalted. Technology was the perfect tool for the exaltation of the martial man. We can therefore understand the reason for the fortune of *alarmistic* authors and philosophers such as Nietzsche. The war even got into children's books. The most famous children's text in Britain at that time is full of references to rivalries between European powers.

Peter Pan's story was a literary phenomenon. The character first appeared in 1902 in an adult book written by Barrie. *The Little White Bird.* The story was so successful that the publisher decided to publish chapters 13-18 under the title *Peter Pan in Kensington Gardens.* Barrie decided to adapt the opera and on the 27th of December 1904 he staged, in London, Peter *Pan, or The Boy Who Wouldn't Grow Up.* In 1911 the novel *Peter Pan* was finally published. In Peter Pan's story we find all the elements dear to the writers of the time. War, death, patriotism, courage and *britishness.* Peter is a kid who keeps waging wars with his gang on the Island of

---

[372] G. Amendola, *La grande illusione*, in *'La Voce'*, 2 March 1910, p. 1.

[373] Ibidem.

Neverland. His enemy is Captain Hook. A man with a climbing moustache and an atrophied arm. We can see a faithful caricature of Kaiser Wilhelm II. Hook even goes so far as to imagine a *"children's holocaust"*. In another scene, we find Peter on a rock, the tide is about to swallow him, and he exclaims: *"Dying will be a great adventure"*. Wendy, the little girl who became the mother of Peter's gang, stands as a British matron and shortly before Hook gives the order to kill the children, in a speech she says: *"Dear boys, I feel I have to tell you a message from your real mothers and it is this: 'I hope that our children will die like real English gentlemen'"* and the boys, like real patriots, face the threat of death by loudly singing *God save the King* above the noise of pirates[374].

About 300 books were written between the end of the nineteenth century and the beginning of the twenty-first century. Those mentioned above are only a small percentage of that vast "war" literature that has romanticised conflict in every possible key. We can say, almost with certainty, that a war was expected, the more difficult it is to explain why no one foresaw the duration and tragedy.

Alarming literature caused an increase in fear of the foreigner. Spies and foreigners began to be placed on the same level. Many people were clamouring for a restriction on immigration.[375]

In 1914, many politicians, businessmen and soldiers understood the economic and human danger of war and supported peace, but it did not have the same seductive charm as the *madness* of war. Young people, students, intellectuals, women, traders,

---

[374] M. Barrie, *Peter Pan. The child who didn't want to grow up*, Mondadori, Milan 2007.

[375] In *"A maker of History"* di Oppenheim il protagonista afferma: *"This is what comes of making London the asylum for all the foreign scum of the earth"*

farmers and peasants. Everyone was intoxicated by the call to arms. In the name of patriotism, pacifism ended up out of the window and European nations turned against each other. Even Freud lost all moral restraint in the face of the declaration of war, he behaved like a child on Christmas morning: *"All my libido pours out on the Austro-Hungarians"*.

After the signing of the Treaty of Frankfurt on the 10th of May 1871, which ended the Franco-Prussian war, Europe entered the longest period of peace before the Cold War. 43 years old. In this long period of time, however, the powers on the one hand made alliances, as large as possible, but inside they increased armaments and Army.

Britain kept two feet in a shoe, metaphorically speaking. It always tried to avoid a European conflict, different discourse should be made with the colonies, but was the most active power on the front of the arms race. The *spy psychosis* launched into literature not only served to fill the reading afternoons of the factory worker or the country lords, but it also led to an alarmism on the defence front that caused a massive militarisation campaign. The most prolific author, Le Queux, was very successful amongst the high offices of the Army. In his book *Invasion of 1910* there was no problem in advertising a proposed national recruitment system made by Lord Roberts:

"Everywhere people were regretting that Lord Roberts' solemn warnings in 1906 had been unheeded, for had we adopted his scheme for universal service, such dire catastrophe would never have occurred"

Roberts even resigned from his position as field-marshal to promote his cause.

Great Britain and Germany pursued two different ways to achieve the same goal. Control over the old continent and the world. Great Britain wanted to maintain the world *status quo* that saw it at the head of trade and global hegemony, Germany instead, especially after the rise to the throne of Kaiser Wilhelm II, wanted to undermine the British primacy, reach it and in the future overcome it.

Germany was the last European nation to be created. With the Congress of Vienna, a Germanic confederation was created in Central Europe. 39 states including Prussia and the Austrian Empire. The confederation never surpassed this embryonic form. In fact, the commando was almost always in the Austrian hands, which tried in every way to block the unification. Prussia, on the other hand, was very attentive to the Unionist thrusts because it saw in a strong German nation a motor for industrialisation and trade. With the war of 1866 between the Austrian Empire and Prussia the confederation broke up and began a long journey that will lead to the creation of the German Empire after the Franco-Prussian War.

Ken Follett, a well-known British writer, put the following words in the mouth of a Prussian general in March 1914:

"Admirable people the British in many ways. The King is governed by ministers, ministers are subject to parliament and members of parliament are chosen by ordinary people. What a way to govern a country."[376]

With a sentence, even if in a novel, we have the description of two ways of understanding a constitutional Monarchy.

Great Britain and Germany had essentially the same form of Government. A parliament elected by the people, a Government and a Sovereign head of state. In fact, however, Victoria and Edward VII on the one hand and Wilhelm I and II on the other behaved in opposite ways. It was the English Sovereign who exerted less influence on the Government whilst the Kaiser had disproportionate power over his own cabinet.

Wilhelm was not subject to anyone and could pilot foreign policy at will, the problem came when it had to work with the chancellors, especially Bismarck. The role of the

---

[376] K. Follett, La Caduta dei Giganti, Mondadori, Trad It. Milan 2010. p. 155.

Kaiser was in practice to create the limits within which the chancellery could move. The clash came about when the chancellor tried to get out of his area of responsibility. More needs to be said when it comes to Britain. Victoria's long reign had given her immense power. She saw the Governments rise and fall and gradually gained more and more powers until she reached a situation opposite to that of Germany.

3. Gods and Titan(ic)s

Despite the vast amount of literature, as we have seen, the new century had begun in peace and this situation seemed destined to last over time. If we had been in some European capital, it would have been difficult for us to see a feeling of hatred towards another European nation. In London, German products were sold in the department stores, Paris was a melting pot of populations, Rome was a must go for every noble or wealthy European, in Florence there was a vast community of English so that the city still has the Cemetery of the English in which are buried amongst the many also Elizabeth Browning and the last descendants of Shakespeare. The English nobility loved to spend a period of rest in thermal resorts in Germany or France. Above all, there were the royalty who dominated almost all European countries, related to each other, exchanging visits and holidays, transforming the old continent into a single large ballroom.

In Great Britain politics and court dictated the pace of social life, Victoria had passed the century and despite age and disease she ruled the Empire with the moral rigour that had spread throughout the country. By now she struggled walking, she almost always moved with a sedan chair or a wheelchair, she was almost blind and had practically disappeared from public life, delegating almost everything to her heir.

The period of the *Belle Époque* can be enclosed between two symbolic events. The 1900 Paris Universal Exhibition and the sinking of the Titanic in 1912.

The Paris Expo[377] was an unprecedented event and for 70 years, even afterwards, the number of participants was exceeded only with the Osaka Expo of 1970. It was the most glorious period for Europe. From the Congress of Vienna, a climate of European peace had been established, Empires despite misunderstandings and mistrust maintained a peaceful situation for a very long time, often waging war in the colonies but avoiding transforming once again their continent into a battlefield.

The Universal Expositions that were held in those years were all marked by a sign of glory and pride, each country wanted to show others how strong, powerful, rich and prepared they were. Ever since the first Expo, in London in 1851, conceived and desired by Prince Albert, the world has been looking to that event as a showcase for the powers. France had wanted to match Britain in 1855, London had responded in 1862 and Paris again in 1867 then the time had come for Vienna to show itself with the Expo of 1873. Philadelphia was the first exhibition held outside Europe in 1876. Melbourne was the first in a colony in 1880, then it was Barcelona in 1888 and again Paris in 1889, Chicago in 1893, Brussels in 1897 and finally Paris in the first year of the new century.

Every Universal Exposition has its own history, many of the monuments that we can see today in the great cities of the world are remnants of Expo. The most famous symbol is in Paris: the Eiffel Tower, which was built for the 1889 Expo and then left in place after the event closed. There were also particular cases that today would be absurd to understand, such as Belgium, for example, where during the Expo of 1897 in a pavilion dedicated to the Congo there was a real human zoo with indigenous black Africans transported to Europe and forced to live there for months. Many of them died.

---

[377] M. Macmillan, *The war that ended peace,* Profile Books, London 2013. Cap 1.

The Paris Expo was the event of modernity, industry and technological progress. In fact, at its inauguration no one would have expected a very high success, on the 14th of April when the French President Émile Loubet inaugurated the Exhibition the site chosen for the event was still a construction site, almost none of the pavilions were complete. At the entrance, a female statue in the guise of Sarah Bernhardt was despised by everyone. The press was not lenient with the Government and the organisers, it seemed that it had to end with a failure and not a success and yet by the end of the months of exhibitions more than 50 million people had visited the site. Each country went back in time and chose its best period and then recreated it in Paris. The European countries were reflected in the Gothic or Renaissance period, China rebuilt part of the Forbidden City, the Ottoman Empire brought with it a cornucopia of different styles with Christian churches, mosques and synagogues, the German Empire had redeveloped the library of Federal the Great. Between France and Germany there was bad blood, not far from there at Place de la Concorde the statue depicting Strasbourg was still veiled in black after the defeat in the Franco-Prussian war with the annexed loss of Alsace. The Germans, however, behaved well in avoiding symbolising in some way in their pavilion their military victories. The Kaiser, however, wanted to send a message to another country, his grandmother's, with his pavilion. In fact, on one of the facades there was a very large painting depicting a stormy sea with sirens recalling the sailors. The motto engraved on the panel, wanted by Wilhelm himself, recited:

" *Der Stern des Glücks lädt die tapferen, die Anker zu segeln zu erreichen, um die Wellen zu erobern*"[378]

---

[378] The star of fortune invites the brave to set sail and to launch himself to conquer the waves.

But that was not the only signal that the Kaiser wanted to send out, in the grandiose Palace of the Electricity a gigantic crane of German manufacture was on display, capable of lifting to 25 tonnes.

Vienna had two pavilions, one for the Austrian side and one for the Hungarian side of the Empire. In the middle a small pavilion representing Bosnia, officially part of the Ottoman Empire but in fact under Austrian rule since 1878.

The place of honour was reserved for Russia, the strongest ally of the *République*. Nicolaj II had a giant map of France, made of precious stones, built and donated to the French people. An entire pavilion was dedicated to the Tsaritsa mother and a Kremlin-style palace was built on the site. A bridge was also built in Paris, the Alexandre III, in memory of the alliance between the Tsar and France. The first stone was laid by Nicolaj and the bridge was inaugurated during the Expo. The bridge is still there.

Great Britain was not amongst the allies of France at that time, which is why the British pavilion was not sumptuous and imposing. A simple Tudor-style country manor was built, which mainly housed paintings by English authors, and many collectors refused to lend their paintings to the Government.

The Expo was to glorify every single country but to show the world how strong and powerful Western civilisation was. New discoveries in the medical, hygienic, metallurgical, chemical and mechanical fields were everywhere in the various pavilions. The most fascinating novelty of all was certainly electricity. Everywhere there were new electric instruments. An automatic sidewalk that allowed visitors to observe a large part of the exhibition standing still on an electric roller, a futuristic 360° cinema and a building lit by 5,000 light bulbs. Electricity was the guest of honour.

At the same time as the Expo in the nearby Bois de Boulogne, the second Olympics of the modern era were held. De Coubertin had been forced to hand over the organisation of the event to the French Government. It was very complicated to organise everything; the Government was more interested in the Expo. Funds were cut and many athletes retire in protest, for the first-time women could compete, even if De Coubertin was against the fact that he had banned the participation of women during the first Olympics four years earlier in Athens. More than a thousand athletes took part in the event engaged in 28 different disciplines. The winners were not awarded medals but umbrellas and books. The most curious discipline disputed during this edition and without a shadow of a doubt the most weird one was the Live Pigeon Shooting, the race consisted in freeing a certain number of pigeons from some cages and then trying to hit as many as possible before the animals escaped, several races were interrupted and the sport was no longer proposed because almost always the pigeons exploded in flight whilst they flew over the public making rain, on the spectators, blood and the remains of the animals.

Education was a pillar within the Exhibition. The organiser of the event, Alfred Picard, advised everyone to start by visiting the Palace of Education where there were educational models for all ages. Governments between the end of the 19th century and the beginning of the twenty-first century had by then learnt a simple truth: an educated nation was synonymous with more wealth. Everywhere in Europe, evening courses were organised for workers or workers' associations to train not only from an educational point of view, but also from a moral one, the millions and millions of workers who formed the work base of the countries. The percentage of citizens working in the countryside was getting smaller and smaller, the continent had received a sharp demographic increase that depended on two fundamental factors: the long period of peace and new medical discoveries: life was getting longer. At the end of the nineteenth century, the European population was 400 million. Cities such as Budapest, which in the mid-nineteenth century had just over 200 thousand inhabitants at the outbreak of the war reached almost a million. Paris grew from 600,000 during the revolution to 4 million at the beginning of the century. Trade unions were a reality recognised by states in every country now. In France alone, there were more than a million registered workers. A country like Russia, one of the most undeveloped powers in the world, expected to have a fully literate population by 1922. The reading and dissemination of books and newspapers was a fait accompli, public libraries grew, and publishing houses seized the opportunity to access an audience that had been excluded from the market until few years earlier. Comics for boys, love stories novels for women, yellow and western novels and adventures for men. The spread of mass education had already begun in Britain at the beginning of the 1800s, and the serial novels that had made the fortune of figures such as Dickens and Thackeray were born there. Step by step the other powers had also discovered the advantages of an educated and prepared working class. In this way, the *nation* entity that until then had been little diffused was created. Until recently, the European citizen identified himself as a citizen of a city or a region and the great revolutions had always started from a few educated minds who knew how to attract the attention of the people with heated speeches. Now anyone could create their own opinion, get information on the progress of the Government, follow that case in the news or take sides against or in favour of a war. The working class was finally entering public opinion. The most famous case of public opinion becoming an integral part of a public fact occurred in France, *The Dreyfus Affair*[379].

The scandal broke out in 1894 when on the 6th of October the French Army accused the artillery officer Alfred Dreyfus of espionage in favour of the Germans. Dreyfus was a wealthy Alsatian Jewish family. After the defeat of 1871 and the loss of Alsace and Lorraine, he decided to maintain his French identity, and preferred the French

---

[379] M. Dreyfus, *Dreyfus, mio fratello*, Editori Riuniti, Rome 1980; A. S. Lindemann, *The Jew Accused. Three Anti-Semitic Affairs: Dreyfus, Beilis, Frank. 1894-1915*, Cambridge University Press, Cambridge 1993; B. Lazare *L'Affaire Dreyfus. Un errore giudiziario.* Curated by Paolo Fontana, Mobydick, Milan 2001; R. Harris, *the Officer and the Spy*, Mondadori, Milan 2014.

Army to his career in the family business. According to the prosecution he had written a letter to Maximilien von Schwartzkoppen the German attaché at the embassy in Paris with the intention of passing on military information to the enemy. The French Army had discovered a leak and they needed a scapegoat. Dreyfus was the perfect candidate, especially since he was Jewish. He was imprisoned, tried secretly and then after a public ceremony in which he was degraded and humiliated he was sent to Devil's Island, a French penal colony in Guyana. The news rebounded in all French and foreign newspapers and immediately began to appear accusations against Jews and defence of Dreyfus according to many unjustly accused. If it had not been for another officer, Dreyfus would probably have died in South America serving a convicted felon for a crime he had not committed. Colonel George Picquart was appointed head of military espionage after Dreyfus was convicted and did not take that much to realise that the overwhelming evidence, he had been convicted of was actually a smokescreen. He also began to investigate and concluded that it was not Dreyfus the traitor but Ferdinand Walsin Esterhazy, a major of the French Army from a noble and ancient family burdened with gambling debts. The calligraphic report made showed that the letter sent to Schwartzkoppen was written by Esterhazy. Picquart had also discovered a secret relationship, during his investigations he discovered that Schwartzkoppen was the lover of Alessandro Panizzardi, his Italian Pari grade at the Italian embassy in Paris. The two exchanged love letters full of affectionate female nicknames. Some people argue that the relationship between the two was probably already known at the time of Dreyfus' first trial and had helped to create a terrible image of him: Jewish and sodomite. The accusation against Dreyfus started from a letter from Panizzardi to Schwartzkoppen, intercepted by a French spy inside the German embassy. Picquart presented a report to his superiors but was not accepted and was later removed from office and sent to a war zone in Africa. On his return to France he fought to prove the innocence of what had been a pupil of him at the Military Academy. By now the nation was divided between *Dreyfusarde* and *antidreyfusarde*. The best-known aspect of the story is probably the letter of Émile

Zola to the French president, *J'Accuise* came out on the front page of *L'Aurore* on 13th of January 1898. The next day a long list of intellectuals signed a manifesto in defence of Dreyfus. The nationalistic press sided with the Army and sounded the alarm of a Jewish plot to destroy the nation. Picquart and Zola were arrested and later pardoned. In August, Major Hubert J. Henry, of French espionage, who had always been against Dreyfus, declared that the letter in which Dreyfus was mentioned had been created by him, to indict him. Henry committed suicide in prison soon after. The Army was forced to reopen the case and a new trial was held in Rennes. Shortly before the trial, news came out in the newspapers that Esterhazy had confessed to having written the letter with the list of information passed on to the enemy. The letter known as *Bordereau*. Esterhazy was not indicted but simply removed from the Army, left France and fled to England without ever paying for his betrayal. Everyone at this point expected in a release of Dreyfus but in a completely unexpected way the court of Rennes confirmed Dreyfus as a traitor. The court had been forced by the General Staff to sentence Dreyfus again so the Army would not be humiliated again. The sentence was reduced from life in prison to ten years. The popular reaction showed its face at the new elections of 1899, the citizens voted in masse for the liberal-radicals who had fought so hard to defend Dreyfus. The new President-in-Office of the Council proposed to Dreyfus that he should apply for a pardon, in this way he would have been released. Dreyfus was tired of the prison and decided to accept the proposal even though he was completely innocent. In September 1899 he was pardoned by the president. Only in 1906 will it be fully reintegrated into the Army after the sentence of Rennes was cancelled.

The Dreyfus Affair is still a wound in the French past, the event was for the time a striking fact that upset the country and Europe. The echo of that injustice was felt everywhere and some kept, despite the cancellation of the sentence, his idea of Dreyfus' guilt and his role in a Jewish plot. Queen Victoria, for example, spoke in her diary about Dreyfus and the injustice he suffered.

Europe had shortened, new means of transport had made great strides, the continent was now caged in a vast railway network, 290,000 kilometres, electric trams raced in the cities, in Paris was inaugurated during the Expo the first underground line in the country, Londoners travelled underground since 1863. The Paris Expo was the first event marked by mass tourism, during the summer many visitors came to Europe from abroad, especially Americans. Crossing the Atlantic was no longer an undertaking.

All these innovations were visible during the Paris Expo. What began with a series of disasters in the end turned out to be one of the most successful editions of all those past and those to come. The event was intended in a sense to sanctify European peace, but a smart observer could already have glimpsed the future sides, whilst the people were celebrating peace the leaders were already planning the war, whether they knew it or not is a question that will remain unanswered. Each village also showed off its own war power alongside the latest kitchen appliance. On the other hand, even on the Hachette guide dedicated to the exhibition there was talk of war as:

A natural inclination of mankind[380].

France tried in every way to maintain its alliance with Russia, the Germans had allied themselves with the Austro-Hungarians and war plans were already being prepared in the event of a clash on two fronts, the new German Chief of Staff, Alfred Von Schlieffen, was the father of the plan that bears his name and that in practice described how to act in the event of an attack on France. The only great power that had not yet taken sides was the British Empire. The period of the Paris Expo was not particularly happy for the nation. For almost two years the Queen's soldiers had been

---

[380] E. Weber, *France: Fin de Siècle,* Harvard University Press, 1988.

fighting in South Africa against the Boers, the war had brought out all the global discontent towards the Empire, every nation spent words of praise and admiration for the Boers fighting for their land. In Paris a pavilion was dedicated to the Transvaal and the crowd visiting was always large, the statue of Kruger always covered with flowers and every occasion was good to emphasise the support to the whites of Africa.

Throughout Europe, Queen Victoria and Kitchener were targeted with caricatures and articles of complaint for the treatment they reserved to Afrikaners. The Prince of Wales out of disdain refused to visit the exhibition, despite being a frequent visitor of Paris. It was precisely from these events that the Empire decided to abandon its *splendid isolation*[381] and try to forge alliances with other powers. The Boer war had made the institution lose prestige and now the enemies saw it less strong and less organised than in the past. But it was precisely this idea that in a way caused a European short circuit that led the continent to put aside arms diplomacy.

4. Bertie the Uncle of Europe

On the 22nd of January 1901, at the age of 81, Queen Victoria died at Osborne House on the island of Wright after 63 years, seven months and two days of reign. This marked the end of the second longest reign in British and English history. Queen Elizabeth II is now the longest reigning Monarch. At her bedside there was the heir, the Prince of Wales and his eldest nephew the Kaiser Wilhelm II. The funeral, military as the Queen wanted it to be, was a magnificent event. Almost all the rulers of Europe took part. Everyone had gone to London to pay homage to the one who

---

[381] M. Macmillan, *That war...,* Cap 2.

had dominated the largest Empire ever for over 60 years. Victoria's death was a shock to the country. The funeral was held in Windsor, in the coffin the Queen wore a white dress[382] and the wedding veil. She wanted to bring with her some objects in memory of family, friends and servants[383]. A robe and a cast of Prince Albert's hand were placed on her left, in her right-hand, hidden under a flower decoration, there was the engagement ring and a lock of hair of John Brown, her friend, and perhaps secret second husband[384], children's memories and photographs. On the 2nd of February, the funeral procession passed through London where an immense crowd could pay tribute to the beloved Queen. At a certain point in Windsor, the horses were no longer able to pull the cannons with their coffins and some sailors dragged the Queen's remains to the mausoleum of Frogmore. Victoria was buried next to her husband and during the ceremony a dusting of snow covered the whole area[385].

Victoria's long reign had forced her son to wait 60 years before ascending the throne. Edward, or Bertie as he was called in the family, was the opposite of his mother, he loved the worldly life and the fun. He practised many water sports, frequented opera and clubs a lot and was always surrounded by beautiful women, causing more than one scandal.

---

[382] E. Longford, Victoria *RI*, Weidenfeld & Nicolson, London 1964. p. 563.

[383] C. Hibbert, *Queen Victoria: A Personal History*, HarperCollins, London 2000. Pe 497; E. Longford, Victoria *RI*..., p. 563.

[384] C. Hibbert, *Queen Victoria...*, p. 498.

[385] E. Longford, Victoria *RI*..., p. 565; G. St Aubyn, Queen *Victoria: A Portrait*, Sinclair-Stevenson London. 1991. p. 600.

His reign did not begin in the best possible way, 20 days after burial his mother, he sailed to Germany because his older sister, Victoria Adelaide, was seriously ill with cancer. Edward arrived in Holland and from there travelled by train to Friedrichshof Castle. During the journey, the new King was able to touch with his own hands the anti-English feeling widespread in Germany, the convoy on which he travelled was welcomed almost everywhere by insults and mockery. The visit to his sister was a torment, Wilhelm was constantly present and never left the two brothers alone. After a few days Edward left for England, his sister did not have much time left, less than a year according to doctors. He had promised to return to her, but on the 5th of August he received news of her sudden death.[386]

The coronation ceremony was planned for the 26th of June 1902, but an operation of the appendix forced him to postpone until the 9th of August. Although he was a lover of pomp and ceremony in honour of the Monarchy, his ceremony was very sober[387].

Edward's reign is very important despite its short duration, he stood on the throne in fact only 9 years. He was probably one of the most political of the British Monarchs. During his years as Prince of Wales and as a Monarch, he was able to build relationships and friendships that proved to be incredibly useful for the good of his country. His declared intention was to unite the country with the greatest number of nations through alliances and treaties. Before taking the throne, he travelled far and wide in Europe and the world and this contributed to making very important friendships, especially after becoming King.

---

[386] G. Brook-Sheperd, *Uncle...*, pp. 102 - 108.

[387] G. Brook-Sheperd, *Uncle...*, pp. 119 - 124.

Bertie pointed out to all his diplomatic skills during his trip to Russia for the wedding of his sister-in-law, who had married Zarevic. During his stay in St. Petersburg he wrote to Prime Minister Palmerston in which he stated:

"I should be only too happy to be the means in any way of promoting the <u>*entente cordiale*</u> *between Russia and our own country [...] I am very good traveller so that I should not at all mind the length of the journey [...]"*[388]

This statement was not very well received by the Government, at that time between Russia and Great Britain there were not good relationship, many at Whitehall saw in the Tsar the most dangerous enemy to the Empire. No wonder the letter was ignored altogether. About 20 years later, in 1881, Edward wanted at all costs to represent his mother during the funeral of Aleksandr II after his assassination, he also remained for the coronation ceremony of his successor and in fact imposed on the Government and his mother the decision to award the new Tsar with the Order of the Garter[389], the highest British honour. Edward made another trip to Russia for the coronation of Nikolaj II. The new Tsar was doubly related to the future King. The new Prime Minister, Lord Rosebery, was more inclined towards an Anglo-Russian alliance and encouraged Edward to make friends with Nikolaj[390]. However, the time was not ripe for such a fast approach after years in which the countries had looked at each other like lions ready to fight. However, the newspapers praised the initiative and the Minister defended his choice in parliament.

Edward, unintentionally, is guilty of a fact that has cracked the already difficult relations between Great Britain and Germany. Although the two imperial families

---

[388] G. Brook-Sheperd, *Uncle...,* p. 72.

[389] G. Brook-Sheperd, *Uncle...,* pp. 72-74.

[390] G. Brook-Sheperd, *Uncle...,* p. 74.

were linked, family relations were still worse than diplomatic ones. The Kaiser in England was described as one not to be mindful of, a belief that found supporters at every level of society starting with the Prime Minister. This belief was probably not entirely unfounded. Wilhelm had a personality that we can define as *special*. Some of his letters, recently found, reveal a sexual obsession with her mother, especially her hands:

"I have been dreaming about your dear soft, warm hands, I am awaiting with impatience the time when I can sit near you and kiss them but pray keep your promise you gave me always to give me alone the soft inside of your hand to kiss, but of course you keep this as a secret for yourself."

In another letter he stated:

"I have again dreamt about you, this time I was alone with you in your library when you stretched forth your arms and pulled me down. Then you took off your gloves and laid your hand gently on my lips for me to kiss it...I wish you would do the same when I am in Berlin alone with you in the evening."

Dr. Brett Kahr, psychologist and collaborator of the Freud Museum on this *disorder* expressed himself as follows:

"Wilhelm is devoting his sexual energies to his mother and in particular to part of his mother's body, her very beautiful hands. So I think he's using his mother as a way of testing out these burgeoning erotic feelings in a way that almost borders on the incestuous."

The Kaiser had a fetish for the female arms, his most exciting desire was to slowly take off a woman's glove and kiss her from the tip of her finger of her elbow.

Because of the mother's refusal, or rather her being affectionate but not as he wanted it, grew in him a hatred for his mother and her country of origin. This feeling became more profound when an English doctor failed in his attempt to heal his father from throat cancer. His experience with English doctors was very bad, before giving birth

373

her grandmother had sent a doctor to help Victoria Adelaide during childbirth, but complications had arisen and after a difficult breech delivery Erb's paralysis had developed and the future Kaiser was born with an atrophic left arm. This disability deeply marked Wilhelm since he was a child, his arm was 15 centimetres shorter and for the rest of his life he tried to hide the problem wearing gloves or resting his hand on the hilt of the sword or on a walking stick.

"An English doctor crippled my arm and an English doctor is killing my father!"

If they wanted to look for a good description of Wilhelm, we would probably find it in Churchill's words:

"Just strut around and pose and rattle the underdrawn sword. All he wished was to feel like Napoleon, and be like him without having had to fight his battles. Surely less than this would not pass muster. If you are the summit of a volcano, the least you can do is to smoke. So he smoked, a pillar of cloud by day and the gleam of fire by night, to all who gazed from afar; and slowly and surely these perturbed observers gathered and joined themselves together for mutual protection. [...] but underneath all this posing and its trappings, was a very ordinary, vain, but on the whole well-meaning man, hoping to pass himself off as a second Frederick the Great"[391]

During Edward's visit, when he was still Prince of Wales, a family crisis arose in Vienna[392] with Wilhelm, we must be careful of all the signs that Wilhelm has scattered along the way from when he ascended the throne to when they threw him off it.

---

[391] Kissinger, Henry. *Diplomacy*. Simon & Schuster, New York 1994. p. 121.

[392] G. Brook-Sheperd, *Uncle...*, pp. 84 - 85.

Edward visited Vienna before going on holiday to Hungary and Romania. Before leaving, he had written to the Emperor Franz Joseph asking about his nephew, the Kaiser, in Vienna at the same time. That way he could make the visit coincide and meet Wilhelm. Not receiving an answer, he did not get too worried and arrived in Vienna on the 10th of September 1888. Edward went to see the Emperor, and this gave him a plan for his time in the Austrian capital. According to this programme, the visit would be extended until the 3rd of October. Edward, as usual, accepted the programme without saying a word. He discovered on the same day that the Kaiser would arrive in town on the same day he would leave. At that point the Prince of Wales was convinced that a change to his programme would not harm anyone and asked it to be extended by a few days so that he could meet his nephew. The next day, the British Ambassador to the Viennese court was responsible for communicating the bad news. The Austrian Foreign Minister, Count Kalnocky, had revealed that it was the Kaiser himself who asked for his arrival to coincide with his uncle's departure; the reason for the request was that Wilhelm wanted to be the only prominent guest in the capital, without anyone who could steal the scene from him. The Queen immediately intervened by calling her nephew and taking the side of her son. Wilhelm ran to the shelters denying that his intention was not to meet his uncle on purpose but soon after he was betrayed when he complained that he did not appreciate the fact that Bertie treated him as a grandson and not as the German Emperor. Such behaviour only worsened Wilhelm's image in the face of the British establishment. Lord Palmerston was convinced of his madness and even the Queen diplomatically expressed a similar opinion:

"As regards the political relations of the two Governments' she wrote 'the Queen quite agrees that that should not be affected if possibly by these miserable family quarrels; but the Queen much fears that, with such a hot-headed conceited and

wrong-headed young man, devoid of all felling, this may, at any moment, become impossible "[393]

Unfortunately, however, it was not only the accident in Vienna that caused the problems between his uncle and grandson and between Great Britain and Germany. The two of them kept poking their noses for years. Wilhelm longed to visit England in his new role as Emperor[394], he had taken the throne in the summer of 1888. His uncle was still offended by the Viennese treatment, but he put the matter aside and in August 1889 the Kaiser went to England for five days. During that brief stay, the Queen appointed him Honorary Admiral of the Royal Navy and had Spithead organise a military parade in his honour. Wilhelm was excited to be able to wear the uniform of a grade that was Nelson's. He spent most of his time in Cowes and on the Isle of Wight. The Queen was as happy that the family crisis had been shelved but in reality, a careful eye could show how the horizon was dark. First of all, Wilhelm was escorted by a small fleet, then he allowed himself to recommend technical improvements to English ships. The British admirals were amazed at the Kaiser's ability to speak the technical language of the ships perfectly and Bertie was alarmed and angry because he did not understand it. The Prince of Wales participated every year in the Cowes' regatta, because of the interest of his nephew Bertie was forced to invite him to join. Bertie got very angry when his steamer, *Britannia*, was beaten by his nephew, *Meteor I.,* in those waters the last attempts to make the two countries friends were wrecked. The worst came in 1895 during the week of commemoration for the victory over the French. The Kaiser included in its escort two new cruisers that bore the names of the victorious battlefield locations for the Prussians, Worth and Weissenberg. The British newspapers did not forgive him, his chauvinist speech

---

[393] G. Brook-Sheperd, *Uncle...,* p. 85.

[394] G. Brook-Sheperd, *Uncle...,* pp. 86 - 94.

to the crew of the Worth was considered an affront and an offence. Wilhelm got very angry and never came back to England for the races. Before leaving the country, he commissioned a new yacht from the same designer as Bertie's. *Meteor II* was even stronger than its predecessor. If Edward had been of the same character of his nephew, he would have immediately ordered a new ship but instead he simply withdrew the *Britannia* from every race. In 1899, during the race, again won by the Emperor, the Prince of Wales toasted to his grandson but complained of his absence. But rejoicing in the tranquillity between the two states. The Kaiser's peace of mind was made to disappear by an English telegram in which he complained about the referees and the English public during the race.

Everything could be touched but not the sport and especially not the renowned *British fair play*. The fate of a friendship between the two countries did not fall sheer into the waters of the Solent but embarked on a lot of water. It was clear to everyone that if the Kaiser allowed himself to mock the rules of a race only because he was in a bad mood nothing could stop him from doing the same in politics or in war. Shortly after the events of Cowes broke out the Boer War which opened a terrible furrow in British foreign policy. London was terribly aware of how isolated it was in Europe, if until then it was not a problem now it was terribly tragic not to have an ally or supporter in its own cause in South Africa. Chamberlain, the powerful Minister for the Colonies, was a pro-German and in the manoeuvres within the Government he managed to get the upper hand. This position statement coincided with a new trip of the German Imperial Family to England. Most of the Government saw in this gesture a turnover between the two nations and were ready to bet in a treaty of alliance. Great Britain was coming to the alliance table very late in the day. At the centre of Europe since Bismarck's time, the Triple Alliance with Germany, Austria and Italy pulsed, more as a symbolic figure than a power, which supported each other. At the opposite ends of the continent, France and Russia were linked to each other since 1894. There was more than one reason for confrontation between France and Germany, and Russia and Austria had been competing for control over the Balkans for decades.

377

Whilst France dominated the alliance, mainly because of the large loans made to the Russians, Germany controlled it all. London found itself having to choose between its long-standing enemy, allied with its enemy in Asia, or its crazy nephew. The sequel to the Kaiser could be practically the same questions but they added the problem that Wilhelm only needed a few hours in England to become an Anglophile, so they feared that he discovered the German cards too quickly. Germany was aware that the only one in Europe who could gain from an English defeat was her, time was on her side and she did not want to ruin the game. The main task of Von Bulow, Foreign Minister, was to test Chamberlain's real power to find out if he would be able to take the whole Government with him into the German case. The meeting ended with nothing but a victory from the family side, Wilhelm left without offending any Englishman. And that was already a great achievement.

Chamberlain fought for the alliance with Germany, he said that not only political-military factors, but also racial factors played a part in the affair. This time it was not Wilhelm who blew it, but Von Bulow. During a speech in Parliament, he spoke with fire on the future of Germany, without mentioning any alliance with Great Britain.

"Without strong forces on land and sea, there is no other way for a nation like ours – soon to be sixty millions strong, living in the centre of Europe but also stretching out its economic feelers in all directions – there is no other way so far discovered to fight the battle for existence in this world. In the coming century, the German nation will either be the hammer or the anvil"[395]

---

[395] G. Brook-Sheperd, *Uncle...,* p. 91.

Public support for the Boer cause was also involved, and all-English politicians and newspapers remembered the telegram of the Kaiser to President Kruger after a victory over the British.

Wilhelm, perhaps because he did not stay, but most likely because he thought he was right, wrote a long letter to his uncle as a New Year's gift. He had just learnt about *Black Week* and felt obliged to dispense unsolicited advice. Unfortunately, however, it did not stop there, a week later came another letter in which the Kaiser used the metaphor preferred by the British to explain the defeats: sport. Unfortunately, however, the British did not like the sport when they were the ones to lose. In addition, the Kaiser had brought into play the heaviest defeat suffered at home, not a battle but a game. On the 28th of August 1882 for the first-time the national cricket formation lost at home, Australia won. The impact was so strong that even obituaries of English cricket appeared in the newspapers. From that event was born the oldest tournament in history, *The Ashes*. Wilhelm should never have dared to remember that event, especially now that the Empire was playing an even more difficult *game* in Africa. Edward's answer was lapidary.

"The British Empire' he wrote, 'is now fighting for its very existence [...]. we must therefore use every effort in our power to prove victorious in the end"[396]

Thanks to the opening of the Tsarist archives, we now know that at a time when the Kaiser was trying to approach Great Britain, he was also trying to convince Russia to wage war against India by promising to keep the British occupied in Europe, and he was trying to attract France to the deal as well. It is from these speeches that we best understand Wilhelm's personality, not only a double player but totally detached from reality. His thirst for glory and power far exceeded his real strength and it was

---

[396] G. Brook-Sheperd, *Uncle...*, p. 92.

only by chance that those proposed to the Russians and the French did not come to light before, if it had happened Britain would have hardly let such an affront fall.

What in fact rocked the last pale hopes of an alliance was the revolt of the *boxers* in China. When Baron von Ketteler, the German Plenipotentiary Minister in China, was assassinated in broad daylight in Beijing on the 18th of June 1900, the Kaiser almost declared war on China. He did not know very well whether to be a crusader or a saviour, and when in doubt, he played both. He wanted to teach the Chinese a lesson and, in the meantime, show Europe what he really was in charge of. In his thoughts:

"No great decision would be made in the world in future without the German Kaiser"[397]

But the speech he sent out on all the rage to half of Europe and made the German Government ashamed was the one he gave on the 28th of June 1900 on the pier in Bremerhaven, from there would set sail the German contingent for China:

"There will be no quarter, no prisoners will be taken! As, thousand years ago, the Huns under the Attila gained for themselves a name that still stands for terror in tradition and fable, so may you imprint the name of a German for a thousand years on China, and so deeply that never again shall a Chinese dare so much as look askance at a German"[398]

Von Bulow tried unnecessarily to censor the speech but ended up in the newspapers and soon the whole of Europe became aware of it. By adding offence to offence, the Kaiser took it for granted that a German soldier should lead the international

---

[397] G. Brook-Sheperd, *Uncle...,* p. 93.

[398] G. Brook-Sheperd, *Uncle...,* p. 93.

contingent in defence of Europeans in China. He named Count Waldersee a Marshal and sent him to Beijing. The German people lit up with nationalist pride. Unfortunately, however, where Wilhelm did more than just damage, he always made fun of it and the expedition was not exempt. The contingent that should have behaved like Attila by inculcating terror in the Chinese entered Beijing six weeks after the international mission had already solved everything. However, his uncle could not enjoy this international figure because his mother's condition had worsened: The crown was about to land on his head.

Bertie was convinced that he could manage his mother's last days and then take the throne in peace but forgot about his grandson. As soon as Wilhelm heard of his grandmother's condition, he immediately left by train for England, leaving the whole Berlin court in the lurch, celebrating with great pomp the two hundredth anniversary of the Hohenzollern dynasty. Wilhelm held the old Sovereign hostage in his arms, or rather arm. He was the one who took her last breath. It was he who wanted to measure the Queen to decide the size of the coffin and wanted at all costs to deposit his body, but Edward had enough and refused to accept this interference, in a bad way he put his nephew back in line and took the trouble to lay his mother in the coffin. However, Wilhelm presented himself shortly after with an enormous flag with which he wrapped the whole thing, and which was then held as a trophy. Whilst the two were escorting, on the *Victoria and Albert* the body from Osborne House to the shore the Kaiser had all the ships in the area put up their flags at half-mast. Including the royal yacht. This sent the new King on a rampage and he asked for explanations:

"The Queen is dead, Sir"

"But the King of England lives"

Since that day and throughout its reign, that flag has never moved from the top of the flagpole.

Edward surprised everyone when he announced to the *Private Council* that he would not reign with his father's name but that he would take the throne as Edward VII. All his life he had made his mother believe he was going to be called Albert. This was not a simple choice dictated by chance but was part of a set of gestures and changes aimed at de germanising the British Monarchy. The new King wanted to feel English and not German and wanted the nation to be perfectly reflected in the reigning Monarch. Albert was too attached to Germany, Edward was an English name that connected to the great Monarchs of the past. Plantagenets and Tudor.

The Kaiser, who extended his stay in England until 5 February[399], was of a completely different opinion. He not only aimed at an alliance between the two nations but also wanted his uncle to exalt his Germanic origins and wanted the British people to accept him as an ally and German friend. Wilhelm wanted to enter the heart of public opinion but his ways of doing things, his obsession with militarism and especially his speeches rode against him. Wilhelm was also affected in his homeland by what his subjects call *rednerische Entgleisungen* or oratory derailments. The new King had not hidden his intentions of rapprochement with his nephew's nation, but more importantly everything had to take place with calm and caution. The British had been away from the European dance floor for decades and now Wilhelm wanted them to jump straight into the fray to dance a waltz whilst Edward was more inclined to stay on the edge beating time with his foot. On the morning of the departure of the Kaiser he made a speech that bounced off all the newspapers and in fact laid a stone on all the progress made so far:

---

[399] Not entirely unfounded gossip said that the Kaiser wanted to recover all the money his mother had lent to Edward when he was Prince of Wales.

"We ought to form an Anglo – German alliance, you to watch over the seas while we would safeguard the land. With such an alliance, not a mouse would stir in Europe"[400]

The Kaiser was an actor lent to politics, his whole existence was a continuous change between comedy and melodrama. What for him was a gesture of reconciliation and a metaphorical diplomatic embrace for most of the English was an arrogant, naughty, ampulous extravagance. Wilhelm's love and hate for Britain came out at the worst of times. When Chancellor von Bulow went to see him, immediately after his return home, he discovered that the Sovereign wore only London fashionable civilian clothes, wore a brooch with the initials of his deceased grandmother and addressed everyone in English. This triggered a series of protests, far from the imperial ears, by officers who did not consider respectful of the decorum of a commander-in-chief.

Edward's first trip as a Sovereign was to Germany, his sister was dying of cancer, as we read earlier, and he went to his bedside a few weeks after his mother's death. Wilhelm was completely disinterested in his mother, whilst he was in London, he received news from her but refused to move. Knowing that his uncle would go to his country, he took the opportunity to resume negotiations and decided to visit his mother. He specialised in macabre funeral diplomacy. Very Victorian of course.

The King left on board the *Victoria and Albert* and crossed the Channel to the Dutch port of Flessinga. They had a nasty surprise there:

"When we were alongside the jetty at Flushing, we heard a large number of people apparently singing hymns. I thought this a very proper way of spending Sunday evening. But what I could not understand was why they sang the same hymn over and over again ad nauseam. I asked Sir Henry Howard, His Majesty's Minister and

---

[400] G. Brook-Sheperd, *Uncle...*, p. 102.

The Hague, who came on board as soon as we arrived, and he explained that it was the Boer National Anthem, and that the mass of people who were sing in had originally intended to sing it on the jetty but that owing to his representations, the authorities had kept them outside' as Ponsonby drily added: 'I got to know this hymn very well'"[401]

The train trip was a disaster. Crowds of Germans waited for the King in the stations to sing and shout anti-British songs. It was only in Düsseldorf that a teacher had her students lined up on the canopy and together they sang *God Save the King*. Unfortunately, however, there was no stop in that city and in the few moments when the train crossed the station the only result obtained by the girls was to wake-up the King as it was two in the morning.

Von Bulow resented the treatment very much, so much so that he was convinced that it was that bad reception that had ruined international relations between the two countries.

"Politically the King's journey had an unfavourable effect on his future attitude to Germany. Indeed, his entire judgement of German conditions was influenced by it. Contrary to the theoretical Germans, who like to derive their judgments from books, or from the depths of some ethical conviction, the English base their judgement directly on what they observe themselves"[402]

The British Monarchy had undergone a profound change with the birth of the Empire. At the base of all this was the political-institutional changes and a new relationship between the motherland and the colonies. With the decisive parameterisation of the political system the Crown had lost much of its effective

---

[401] G. Brook-Sheperd, *Uncle...*, p. 104.

[402] Ibidem.

power, between 1870 and 1914 the Monarchy became a symbol of the Empire, its cohesion and its vastness. The Monarchy lost its power but gained the popularity of its subjects. The citizens did not identify the Monarch with the *parliamentary establishment,* and this allowed the Monarch to assume upon itself an imperial and national symbolism. It is therefore not surprising that the symbolism of the various ceremonies, the coronation in the first place, made extensive use of medieval symbols, gestures and representations. In the Middle Ages the Monarch was always the father of the nation and represented it, this aspect had been lost after centuries of social, political and economic changes. In the Victorian and Edwardian era, they began to reappear again. In Great Britain it was more suited than other countries to a *revolution* of this kind. The social changes that the country had undergone had made the fertile ground for a new form of Monarchy: the extension of suffrage, the creation of trade unions, the most advanced forms of communication, the growth of literacy, the spread of high circulation newspapers at low prices, trains that went everywhere. As we have already said, the Empire was based on telegraph wires, the postal system and the railways.

By the absurd, the Monarchy resumed the scene at its most shadowy moment[403]. Queen Victoria had slowly withdrawn from the public scene, especially after the death of Prince Albert, leaving the field free to politics. It was the astute Disraeli who brought the throne back to the centre of attention of the nation and the Empire. By appointing the Queen Empress of India, the royal ceremonies were no longer limited to the national public but took on global importance. Princes and dignitaries of the colonies began to travel to reach the Monarch at home, wherever the *Union Jack* waved the British Monarch was inserted into an existing system of values and

---

[403] J. Leonhard, U. von Hirschhausen, *Empires and nation states in the 19th century.* The mill, Bologna 2014. pp. 20 - 28.

powers. The British did not want to be the conquerors, although in fact they were, but as the normal continuers of previous power. So, in India the Monarchy was nothing more than the normal heir of the Mughal Empire, in Africa it was even simpler because Victoria was a woman and, in many areas, controlled by the British there were still matriarchal rules. In the White *Dominions* the problem was almost inexistent because they felt more part of the motherland than of the Empire, their autonomy helped both. The Monarchy became a fundamental part of Government in the Empire. The royal family was a perfect basin from which to take the names with which to baptise cities, rivers, territories. Disraeli also began the habit of appointing the Sovereign's siblings or minor children as Governors. In some places the portraits of the Sovereign became objects of worship and even the Anglican cults took on a new aspect where references and hymns composed to pay homage to the Crown and those who wore it. For the Queen's Jubilee the *Imperial March* was used and the ode composed for the coronation of Edward VII became the famous patriotic anthem *Land of Hope and Glory* that still today is the guest of honour during the final evening of the *BBC Proms*. Even architecture became a way to glorify the Monarchy and by reflection the Empire. The Victoria monument in front of Buckingham Palace is one example. The colonies celebrated with great pomp every visit of a member of the royal family. Victoria never set foot in India, but the Indians held the 1877 *Durbar* in her honour and the Prince of Wales was there representing his mother.

During his reign Edward VII did nothing but increase and encourage this new course of the Monarchy. It was his intention to continue to weave the diplomatic flag that he had already waved before he became King. The year after his coronation, 1903, he undertook a very important journey to three capitals: Lisbon, Paris and Rome. He had organised everything in great secrecy and presented to the Government the plan already decided and prepared. The Government had to submit to his will.

In Lisbon the King was welcomed by Carlos I. during a reception organised in his honour in the speech given by Edward he expressed himself in defence of the Portuguese colonies against the German threat:

386

The speech was very much appreciated and was greeted by an ovation. It arrived in Berlin almost immediately, unleashing his nephew's wrath.

After a stop in Gibraltar, Syracuse Naples the King finally arrived in Rome where Vittorio Emanuele III was waiting for him at the station. The journey to Italy was rich in meaning; first of all, Italy was part of the Triple Alliance, then it was a Catholic nation and in Rome there was the Pope. It was since the time of Knut I that an English royal did not set foot in Rome. During a toast at the Quirinal Palace, the English King delivered a speech that struck the Italian Sovereign and his entire court very hard:

"We both love', he told his host in an improvised speech, 'liberty, and free institutions [...] and have marched together in the paths of civilisation and progress [...] it is not long since we fought side by side, and, although I am confident that another occasion will not present itself, I am certain that we shall always be united for the cause of liberty and civilisation"[405]

However, it was a completely unexpected gesture, even if prepared in secret, that completely captured Vittorio Emanuele. During a carriage ride through the streets of Rome, on the 28th of April, King Edward stopped the procession in front of Porta Pia, went down and gathered in a moment of recollection with his head down. King Vittorio Emanuele was moved by that gesture and immediately got out of the carriage and stood at next to the King. The gesture will be remembered by the King years later during a meeting with the Italian Prime Minister immediately after the outbreak of the war. The next day Edward decided to visit the elder Leo XIII. The

---

[404] G. Brook-Sheperd, *Uncle...,* p. 171.

[405] G. Brook-Sheperd, *Uncle...,* p. 180.

King refused to kiss the ring to the pontiff and the two agreed to an anonymous handshake. Despite Lord Balfour's fears, the meeting turned out to be productive as the Pope congratulated Edward on his freedom and treatment of English Catholics. The day after he left for Paris. He arrived there on the 1st of May. The city was celebrating, Edward was practically at home in the *Ville Lumiere*. The streets of the city were decorated with the colours of the two nations, not a great effort for the organisers since they are the same ones.

This was probably the most important of the three trips. First the King delivered a warm speech of rapprochement to the British Chamber of Commerce

"The days of conflict between our two countries are, I trust, happily over [...] England and France may be regarded as the champions and pioneers of peaceful progress and civilisation and as the homes of all that is best and noblest in literature, art and science [...] A Divine Providence has designed that France should be our near neighbour and, I hope, always our dear friend. There are no two countries in the world whose mutual prosperity is more dependent on each other"[406]

Then he spent his time discussing with President Émile Loubet and Foreign Minister Théophile Delcassé how to get the two nations back on the same side. The two Frenchmen were of the same opinion as the King, especially when he pointed out that he was more than in agreement with a threefold alliance with Russia as well. Edward's words years earlier during his stay in St. Petersburg were heard again.

Loubet returned the visit shortly after, it was during his permanent in London that the rapprochement between the two nations took a more articulated form and after weeks of negotiations between Balouf and Delcassé finally came to a signature on the 8th of April 1904 in London. In the treaty, the two countries solved their colonial

---

[406] G. Brook-Sheperd, *Uncle...*, p. 193.

problems. Egypt became British and the French would no longer make any claims and the same argument was made for Morocco. The Fascioda crisis had been shelved. Before the treaty was signed, the Russian-Japanese War broke out in Asia. This could be a problem as Japan was an ally of Great Britain and Russia of France, but Edward asserted his family relationship with Nikolaj and informed the Russian ambassador that in no way would Great Britain go to war alongside Japan.

In Germany Wilhelm did not welcome the signature of the *Entente Cordiale*[407] at all. For years he had tried to sign a similar agreement with Great Britain and now he had seen the opportunity slip away and moreover because of the historical enemies. The nephew decided to invite his uncle to Germany, to Kiel. For the occasion, the Kaiser had the entire German war fleet stationed in the port. During his visit, Edward was able to see for himself how far the Kaiser had detached from his Government. Von Bulow did not want the whole fleet in the port, and they did not want to force the hand with the British, because they knew that an agreement with France did not necessarily preclude an alliance with Germany. The Kaiser also wanted to intervene in Asia to stop the *yellow danger* whilst neither the Chancellor nor the King believed seriously in the danger posed by Japan in Europe. After a brief visit to Hamburg, Edward returned to England.

The tranquillity with Germany did not last long, however, as soon as France asserted the role in Morocco, the Kaiser decided to make his voice be heard. On the 31st of March 1905 Wilhelm personally went to Tangier, during his conversation with the French ambassador he told him that Germany considered Morocco an independent nation. Loubet was more for dialogue whilst Delcassé was for a hard line against Germany. The Minister, however, was isolated in the Government and the National

---

[407] MacMillan, The war..., Cap 3.

Assembly and had therefore decided to resign, Edward, bypassing his own Government, wrote personally to the French Minister urging him to remain in his place[408]. The King went to Paris where he met the President and the Minister of Foreign Affairs and the German Ambassador. Germany threatened war if France did not decide to hold a conference on Morocco. Delcassé was now completely isolated and finally resigned and France had to bow to the German request. Edward was able, however, to maintain the Anglo-French treaty in force.

The King was not content to have entered into several international agreements. There were other nations left to talk to. If we look at a map of Europe, we immediately realise that one of the interests of the Sovereign by now was to isolate the nation of his nephew, making agreements with his neighbours Edward hoped in his heart to force the Kaiser to lower its tone. Spain was settled by a marriage between Alfonso XIII and Edward's niece, the daughter of his younger sister. The two fell in love during a ball in London and the following year, 1906, they married[409].

The last nation left to talk to be the Austro-Hungarian Empire. The Greatest Protestant Empire with the Greatest Catholic Empire.

Officially, the two Sovereigns only met once in Vienna in August 1903. The trip lasted only 4 days and was in fact only an exchange of courtesy, although Edward tried to put the Macedonian question on the table. The country had been placed under Ottoman control, which behaved disrespectfully to the various ethnic and religious realities of the region. This fact had triggered on one hand Austria and on the other

---

[408] G. Brook-Sheperd, *Uncle...*, pp. 246 - 247

[409] G. Brook-Sheperd, *Uncle...*, p. 277.

hand Russia. In the meantime, the Austro-Hungarian Emperor and the Tsar met to discuss the matter and decided on a common policy against the Ottomans.

However, the two Emperors met four more times[410] unofficially at Bad Ischl. A spa they have both been visiting for a long time.

The first informal meeting took place in August 1905. In August 1907 the two met again and it was again about Macedonia. Edward was convinced that the only way to resolve the issue was to force the Turks to stop all abuse in the region, but Franz Joseph was convinced that any action too harsh against the Ottoman Empire should cause a crisis and the collapse of that Empire would trigger many other problems. The third meeting served only to simplify the mistrust between the two foreign ministers. The last meeting between the two took place in 1908, this meeting was wanted by Edward. The King wanted the Emperor to persuade the Kaiser to slow down the German arms race. Edward had failed on that side during a direct meeting with his nephew. Franz Joseph, however, had categorically refused to do so, Germany was his most important and strongest ally.

Edward was planning to visit his cousin Nikolaj but after the defeat in the war against Japan and the revolution that broke out in the country, the King preferred to postpone it. On the 31st of August 1907, as we have already seen, the Anglo-Russian Agreement was signed between the two countries[411]. It put an end to the Great Game in Asia and although it was not a treaty, it was perceived as such. The following year the two finally decided to meet. Since the situation in Russia was not yet under control, the visit was held at sea, at the port of Reval. Edward appointed Nikolaj Honorary Admiral of the *Royal Navy*. Before leaving, King Edward had a

---

[410] G. Brook-Sheperd, *Uncle...,* pp. 289 - 296.

[411] G. Brook-Sheperd, *Uncle...,* pp. 316 - 330.

conversation with Lord Rothschild which had brought to the Sovereign's attention the treatment of Russian Jews. During his visit to Reval, the King had asked the Russian Prime Minister, Pëtr Arkad'evič Stolypin, for clarification.

After the voyage, Germany went on a rampage and the Kaiser decided at that point that the only way to interfere with the encirclement that Britain had put in place was to increase the Army and navy.

"We must now overhaul our state finances! Heavy indirect taxation; a strong navy, astrong Army and our powder dry!"[412]

In 1908 the relationship with Austria, which in fact was near easy, became more complicated because of the annexation of Bosnia-Herzegovina. On the 6th of October of that year Franz Joseph announced the entry of the region into the Austro-Hungarian Empire. The region has been under Austrian control since 1878, although it was in fact a piece of the Ottoman Empire. Edward did not know that Vienna and St. Petersburg had reached an agreement, the Russian disinterest in Bosnia in exchange for the free movement of the Russian navy in the Turkish straits. After the annexation Vienna did not respect its part of the pact and Russia turned to Great Britain for international aid. The King expressed himself publicly in favour of the Russian cause. In fact, Austria was lost.

Edward decided to go to Berlin, he wanted to meet his nephew before another crisis broke out. On the 9th of February he arrived at Lehrter Station in the capital of the Reich. The two of them in an open carriage crossed the city direct the royal palace.

During the visit the King was slightly ill but decided to attend a reception at the British Embassy. The two Sovereigns only discussed the important facts shortly before their departure. He has received a note written by the Kaiser to his Chancellor

---

[412] G. Brook-Sheperd, *Uncle...,* p. 330.

in which he illustrates the short conversation, it is words that are hurriedly thrown down on a sheet of paper but that have a very important meaning.

"H. M. King Edward VII held his first political talk with me in the last minute before his departure. He expressed his thanks and deep satisfaction with his reception here. The day in the Town Hall had pleased him very much. Then he came to the relations between our two countries which, he hoped, would henceforth move into safer and calmer channels of mutual trust. On the naval question he said:

I hope people will grow sensible [...] and take a quieter view. We are in a different position from other countries, being an island, we must have fleet larger than all the other ones. But we don't dream of attacking anybody, only we must make sure that our shores are quite safe from danger.

I: It is perfectly natural that England should have a Navy according to its interests and to be able to safeguard them and its shores. The same thing is with us. We have laid down a naval Bill [...] adequate to our interest. This implies no aggressive against any Power, certainly not against England.

HE: On quite so, quite so, I perfectly understand it is your absolute right; I don't for one moment believe you are designing anything against us.

I: This Bill was published 11 years ago; it will be adhered to and exactly carried out, without any restriction.

He: Of course that is quite right, as it is Bill voted by the people and their Parliament. I know that cannot be changed.

I: It's a mistake on the part of some Jingo's in England that we are making a building race with you. That is nonsense. We only follow the Bill.

He: Oh, I know that is quite an absurd notion, the situation is quite clear to me and I am in no way alarmed; that is all talk and will pass over[413]

In 1910, after his usual holiday in Biarritz, the King returned to London where he had to deal with the appointment of the new Viceroy of India. On the 1st of May, whilst he was in Sandringham, he was struck by bronchitis. The King's situation only got worse and he died on the 6th of May. The solemn funeral was held on the 20th of May in London. A host of crowned heads paid homage to the deceased Sovereign. In a silent film of the time we can see the procession on horseback, and you can see the Kaiser next to the new Sovereign George V. Alexander of Serbia, Nikolaj II, Franz Ferdinand of Austria-Hungary. In one photograph we see all the other Kings, and the ever-present Wilhelm, around the new King. There we find Haakon VII of Norway, Ferdinand of Bulgaria, Manuel II of Portugal, Georg I of Greece, Albert I of Belgium, Alfonso XIII of Spain and Frederick VIII of Denmark.

King George was not destined for the throne, he was Edward's second son, but between him and his brother, Albert Victor, there was only a 17-month difference. The two were then both raised as royal heirs. Both grew up in the navy until his older brother embarked on the career that would lead him to the throne. As we have seen, the Duke of Clarence was more famous for his scandals than his role at court. Most likely, despite the pain of losing his granddaughter, Queen Victoria breathed a sigh of relief when she learnt of his death. Albert Victor died of pneumonia on the 14th of January 1892, leaving his place on the line of succession, and his fiancée, to his younger brother. George married his brother's betrothed. The two of them were engaged six weeks before the King death. Despite the recycled marriage they loved each other very much.

---

[413] G. Brook-Sheperd, *Uncle...*, p. 345.

The death of his father struck George very hard, in his personal diary expressed the whole tragedy of the news:

"I have lost my best friend and the best of fathers ... I never had a [cross] word with him in my life. I am heart-broken and overwhelmed with grief, but God will help me in my responsibilities and darling May will be my comfort as she has always been. May God give me strength and guidance in the heavy task which has fallen on me"[414]

George immediately showed his personality when he refused to pronounce the text of the *Accession Declaration* for the opening of the new parliament. According to the Sovereign, the anti-Catholic tone was disrespectful to the British subjects who followed that faith. A new text was created.

The coronation ceremony was held in Westminster, as per tradition, on the 22nd of June 1911. The following month the King and Queen went to India. For the first-time since the birth of the Raj, a reigning royal went to the territories of the Empire. For the occasion was organised a high *Durbar* that was held from the 7th to the 16th of December. The presentation of the Sovereigns was held on the 12th of December, a Tuesday. For the occasion, the King wore the new crown, the *Imperial Crown of India,* which had 6170 diamonds arranged on eight arches and was covered with sapphires, rubies and emeralds. After the celebrations the Kings looked out from the Jharokha of Red Fort. It was not as sumptuous and expensive as the *Curzonation*, but it was a huge success. It took a year to prepare the whole thing, 200,000 visitors were expected and in all it cost £1,000,000. Three bakeries were built, and 20,625 loaves of bread were baked every day. 2941 sheep and 2220 cattle were slaughtered for the occasion. Two railway lines were built specifically to allow visitor traffic to easily reach Delhi. The organisers wanted to distance themselves from the 1903

---

[414] King George V's diary, 6th of May 1910, Royal Archives.

Durbar, sumptuousness organised by Curzon. The 1911 one did not strike for its splendour but for its meaning. The King chose to make his entrance on horseback and not on an elephant, as the Viceroy had done 8 years earlier. The Standard Motor Car Company supplied 70 cars to royalty and officials. Painted in royal blues with red lines covered in blue leather and with the stylised crown along the side and a miniature crown on the bonnet. For the occasion, the new King and Emperor had the capital moved from Calcutta to Delhi. The King wore the military clothes of Field-Marshal to pay tribute to the backbone of the Empire: the military. All guests were accommodated in 233 camps. Only the King's camp covered 85 acres.

"Every tent was lighted by electricity, enormous marquees formed the living and reception rooms, and these contained large brick stoves for fires in the evening, which, at Delhi, were bitterly, though healthily, cold."

This was also the *Durbar* of the press. There were 90 journalists, as we would say today, accredited. Everyone received a fee of 120 pounds not many given the five weeks of media coverage, but in return they were housed in a camp very close to that one of the King who thanked them personally for the services rendered. Even the cinematography did not miss the event. From 1903 it had made great strides and for the immense sadness of Curzon the *Durbar* that the whole Empire could see was that of 1911. The Gaumont Company was the first to reproduce the images shot in Great Britain. Charles Urban, the American pioneer, filmed it all in kinema colour. One of the first colour movies in history. *With Our King and Queen Through India* known to all as *The Durbar in Delhi.* The docufilm was first shot in black and white, and was released immediately in this version but on the 2nd of February 1912 at the Scala Theatre in London, for the occasion decorated like the Taj Mahal, was screened a two-hour version in colour, distributed by the Natural Colour Kinematograph Co. The King made his entrance preceded by 824 British and Indian veterans of *Mutiny*. The *Coronation Park* was organised in a semi-circular way, around the royal stage there was room for 12 thousand, then behind a cordon of soldiers and pavilions on a hill there was room for 60-70 thousand people. The order

396

in which the Indian princes paid homage to the King was established based on importance. The five chiefs of primary importance received 21 saves of cannons, the others were divided to climb. Sixteen garments with 13 blanks, 30 with nine and so on. The only note out of tune was when Maharaja Sayajirao III presented himself to the King without any jewel and after a simple bow turned and went away. This gesture was interpreted at the time as a protest the British power. Unfortunately, it was filmed by the cameras and that gesture of disrespect to British pride became very famous. *The Gaekwar Bob* became a way of saying that he referred to both the fact and the gesture. He was the only one though. The 1911 *Durbar* is best-known for combining central power, princes and the population, and this was later made known by India's contribution to the First World War. The King-Emperor concluded his visit to India with hunting trips to the north.

Durbar was for the British Empire what the Paris Expo was for Europe. The showcase of power, magnificence and glory. What had begun as an era of wealth and prosperity seemed destined to continue for other years, but the end of the *Belle Époque* came like a bolt of lightning in the clear sky. His death date was the same as his birth date. 14th of April 1912. The sinking of the Titanic.

Titanic was the physical version of the *Belle Époque*. The existing example of all the years of European glory. Indestructible, unsinkable, imposing and luxurious.

"It is unsinkable. God Himself couldn't sink this ship"

That was the recurring phrase. We all know the Titanic. The nobility, the maiden voyage, the orchestra that played to the end, the dead.

The memory of the Titanic is linked to that of the dead. Europe had forgotten to die in the glory years of the beginning of the century. Tragedy plunged the powers back into chaos. Stefan Sweig called Dream Castle had woken up.

The Titanic was built in Ireland, but it was a British ship and its owner was American. It was part of a series of three ships, the *Olympic*. The Titanic was the second. *Olympic*, *Titanic* and *Britannic*. It is easy to imagine what the newspapers would have written if the *Britannic* had sunk. The ship was built to compete with the steamers of the rival company *Cunard Line*. In the true spirit of the time everything was better if it was bigger. The Titanic was part of that, breaking a record. The longest, widest, highest, heaviest, fastest and obviously most luxurious ship.

269.90 metres long, 28 metres wide, 10.54 metres draught, 46,328 tonnes gross tonnage, 53.3 metres maximum height. Four funnels, 29 boilers capable of burning 728 tonnes of coal a day. 23 knots an hour. It could carry 3547 passengers and crew. The paying public, of course the first-class ones, could enjoy a 9-metre long and 4-metre wide indoor pool, a gym, a Turkish bath and a squash court. There were 34 suites on the first-class decks. Each with a living room, smoking room and reading room. Each had its own personal style, precious woods, marbles and carpets. Three lifts in first-class, and for the first-time a lift in second-class. The third-class was practically the equivalent of a second-class in any other ship. The ship was equipped with a radio station that could reach 400 nautical miles, the two antennas were placed on two masts 60 metres high masters and placed 180 metres apart. In the event of technical problems, the electric motors could be replaced by a diesel engine. These two stations, which amongst other things have the primacy of using SOS code, were mainly used to send and receive personal telegrams. The various signs of iceberg sightings were almost completely ignored. The ship had modern Welin cranes that could support 32 lifeboats and if necessary lower 64. The problem, however, was that at the time, and this may seem rather absurd today, the number of lifeboats was not calculated on the number of passengers but on the tonnage of the ship. The Titanic, therefore, with 16 lifeboats plus four inflatable dinghies was even in surplus according to the law. It did not matter, however, whether the 20 lifeboats were enough for only half of the passengers. The original design included watertight bulkheads from keel to stern, but this would have disturbed the layout of the first-class lounges, so the compartments were made only up to deck E. The ship could float with two intermediate compartments or with the first four flooded.

Liberty style was everywhere. The famous first-class staircase was a masterpiece of inlay and wrought iron. The clock was embedded in an inlay depicting the Honour and Glory. An immense dome of iron and glass overlooked the staircase. In addition to the dining room there was an *A la carte* restaurant. Managed by an Italian. There were four funnels on the ship but only three connected to the engine room; the fourth was for pure aesthetic taste of symmetry.

The ship cost 7.5 million dollars at the time, about 167 million today. One-way ticket to New York cost $3100, 40,000 today. First-class apartment $4350, $83,200 today. The cabin cost 150 dollars, in second-class 60 and in third-class from 32 to 40 dollars, about 6-8 pounds. A ten-word telegram cost $3.12. A first-class passenger in a single day with a telegram, and the reply back, spent the cost of the third-class ticket. 50 cents for a game of squash and $1 for a Turkish bath. Captain Smith made £105 a month, a simple five-door sailor. A lookout five pounds plus five shillings. A hostess earned 3 pounds and ten shillings whilst the workers who had built it earned about 1 pound a month. Telegraphers could get 4 to 2 pounds per trip.

All this wonder of power and modernity left for its first voyage from the port of Southampton on the 10th of April 1912 at 12pm. A special train departed from London that morning with the most illustrious passengers including John Jacob Astor IV, the richest man on the planet at the time. The industrialist Benjamin Guggenheim, Washington Roebling, his father had built the Brooklyn Bridge, Archibald Butt presidential adviser who travelled with his partner Francis Millet. Isidor Straus, owner of Macy Shopping Centres. Steel magnate Arthur Ryerson, George Widener, heir to the American tram industry. The Countess of Rothes, actress Dorothy Gibson, journalist William Thomas Stead, writer Helen Churchill Candee, Jacques Frutelle, film producers Henry and Irene Harris. Sir Cosmo Duff-Gordon and Lady Duff-Gordon, John Thayer and millionaire Molly Brown. The ship was also carrying the managing director of White Star Line, the company owning the ship, Joseph Bruce Ismay, who cowardly saved himself and gave the world the news. The designer Thomas Andrews who first understood the damage of the collision and sank with the ship he had created.

At 11:40 p.m. Frederick Fleet and Reginald Lee, the two lookouts, saw an iceberg straight ahead in front of the ship. The manoeuvres did not avoid contact. Five compartments were flooded condemning the ship. At 2:20 a.m. on the 15th of April 1912, the ship finally disappeared. Of the 2223 passengers, only 706 were able to escape thanks to the lifeboats. 1518 people died that night in the icy waters of the North Atlantic.

The news shocked the world. From the Carpathia, the ship that came to help the lifeboats, Ismay sent the sad telegram:

"Deeply regret to advise you Titanic sank this morning fifteenth after collision with iceberg resulting serious loss of life. Further particulars later"

Queues were created in London and New York in front of the White Star Line facilities. The newspapers spoke of nothing else, in the United States and Great Britain commissions were formed to review the rules of the sea. The Titanic was the symbol of glory of the Western world and its sinking was the equivalent of a breath of breath against a house of cards. After years of peace, serenity and tranquillity, Europe woke up from a dream that had lasted too long.

5. Iceberg

World War I began that April night when the side of the Titanic touched the iceberg. From that day on, Europe, and consequently the world, changed forever. It may seem strange and risky to use a simple accident at sea as the cause of a conflict that cost the lives of millions of people but in fact the sinking of the Titanic has created a small crack in the European mask, crack that over time has expanded to swallow the entire continent.

The journey we made was aimed at achieving this goal. We went way back in time and it served to reconstruct the complex diplomatic and military puzzle of the British Empire without which understanding the wound left after 1918 is, in my opinion, practically impossible. This was to understand the *Company,* because there were the Opium Wars, the Boer Wars, Mutiny, the *Durbars,* the kinship of Queen Victoria, the psychosis of spies, the obsession of Curzon, the coldness of Kitchener, the useless mission of Younghusband, the first steps in politics of Churchill and the web of alliances of Edward VII. A red thread binds all these events and that fragile and thin thread in the hands of Elizabeth I has gradually become stronger and stronger over the centuries, passing through Prime Ministers, Kings, Queens and soldiers until they get lost and break through the mud of the trenches in Belgium and France, the sand of the deserts of the Middle East, the waters of Jutland and the dark rooms of the Whitehall. That thread over the years has drawn an inscription, small and small then always larger until it almost suffocates the Empire. That word? India.

The red thread that binds all British history begins and ends in India. Without India the Empire would never have existed and because of India the Empire ended.

Officially the Empire ended in 1953, in fact it still exists today in a different form thanks to the Commonwealth, but the fatal blow that wounded Britain letting it bleed for years before perishing definitively was not exploded in its direction but rather was directed against another great Empire. On the conscience of Gavril Princip were not only Archduke Franz Ferdinand and his wife Sophie but also the very existence of the greatest Empire of the modern era. He just did not know that.

6. The last days of mankind[415].

Contrary to what we think and what has been said, it is not true that everyone expected a war. The European diplomatic situation was not perfect, but was still doing a good job, the friction between Germany and Great Britain kept many officials awake in Berlin and London, France looked at the Reich in doge's eye, Austria-Hungary had a thousand problems both within its own articulated Empire and outside, Russia had for some time no longer aimed at Asia but at Europe and the Ottoman Empire could not decide whether to disappear or fight for its survival. All these facts, however, were carefully kept under control by treaties and alliances that on paper had the task of damping any warlike idea. At least that was the idea. If in the rooms of power there were thoughts of a conflict, for years now, the population was not of the same idea. *Selfridge's* warehouses in Oxford Street were full of German goods, the economic policy of free trade reigned undisturbed across the Channel and this allowed German industries to challenge British products in the field both on the domestic market and on the imperial square. The spa resorts in Germany were popular destinations for stays of the English nobility, despite the eccentric Kaiser the two royal families were still on good terms and moreover the English royal family was anything but English: *Sachsen-Coburg und Gotha* was not really a typical British surname.

Germany was rivalling Great Britain, and, in many respects, the young European state had made giant strides overtaking the British Empire in several areas, but the central problem was another, finance not industry.

---

[415] For a better understanding of the diplomatic issue dealt with in this chapter see Niall Ferguson, *The Pity of War*. Chapter 2.

The German unification took place within a year, for European politics it corresponded to a day. This not only upset the balance but allowed the new-born nation to make a leap forward by overcoming different powers and placing itself at the head of the continent.

"There was nothing wrong with the conclusion [...] that Germany and continental Europe west of Russia would only be able to hold their own [...] alongside the coming giant economic and political power blocs [...] if Europe pulled together. And a united Europe would fall almost automatically under the leadership of the strongest power – Germany"[416]

Most politicians, journalists and historians said, and some still say, that the only way for Britain to maintain its supremacy was to oppose German technological, economic and military advancement. This created a very defective reading key for the analysis of the years 1870 to 1914. Assuming or implying that it was Germany that wanted to overtake Great Britain, that it was the Kaiser who led an arms race, that it was the Germans who hated the British. In fact, however, all this happened, but on the contrary.

Between 1890 and 1913, German exports grew at a higher rate than those of other European powers. In addition, Germany's gross domestic capital was the highest on the continent. The country had an annual population growth rate of 1.34%, the gross national product grew by 2.78%, steel production was 6.54%. Numbers way beyond France and Great Britain.

However, what had to be considered was not so much economic growth as the financial power of the European powers. In that area no one could stand up to Britain.

---

[416] I. Geiss, *"The German version of Imperialism: Weltpolitik"*, in Schollgen, a cura di, *Escape into war? The Foreign Policy of Imperial Germany*, Oxford 1990.

In the middle of the previous century, Britain was investing around £200 million overseas. In the second half of the century there were three great waves of exports that reached very high figures and never reached again until the 90s of '900. In 1861 and 1872, net foreign investment rose from 1.4% of GDP to 7.7%. In 1877 it fell to 0.8% then in 1890 it rose to 7.3% and returned below 1% in 1901. In 1913 a level unthinkable until then was reached, 9.1%. In terms of accumulation of foreign goods, the increase compared to 1860 was of ten times, going from 370 million pounds to 3.9 billion in 1913. Almost a third of the state's total wealth. Compared to other countries, Great Britain was the undisputed leader, if we put together the figures for Germany, France and the United States, they did not reach British levels.

On the eve of the war the country could count on a total of investments that occupied 44% of global investments. The other peculiarity of the country was that despite the vast Empire the colonies were not the main destination of investment. In the period from 1865 to 1914 only a quarter of the investments went to the colonies, 30% were invested at home and 45% in foreign economies. Great Britain was not only the first country to make loans in the world, but it was also the bank of the world, the *Bank of England* was the last source of credit used by the international monetary system. In 1868 only two countries were based on the Gold Exchange Standard, England and Portugal. By 1908, the whole continent had adopted the system.

The Empire was useful but not essential to British supremacy. Some factors played in favour of London's power over the world. In 1860 the Empire extended for 25 million square kilometres, in 1909 it reached 33 million. In the summer of 1914, 444 million people lived under British rule, almost all of them Indians. Only 10% were real British citizens. The British supremacy also resulted from its emigration combined with its export of capital, whereas Germany had stopped exporting

Germans and capital.[417] The high rate of emigration of British citizens has helped to create links with the *Dominions*. This has allowed the establishment of solid relations of loyalty between the colonies and the motherland[418]. Germany, on the other hand, has suffered a decline in birth rates and a higher rate of labour migration from Eastern Europe. British trade was threatened by German trade, but the main enemy for German growth was Germany itself, because in the event of high export growth, European and colonial markets could have turned towards protectionist policies, effectively eliminating all German productive growth. The UK could afford to take the risk that if it could no longer place its products on the market, it would have a large financial portfolio. German banks have preferred to make domestic investments by focusing on domestic industries, but this did not serve to increase the Germanic power in the global chessboard. France and England, on the other hand, maintained a high influence even in times of crisis in trade. This explains, therefore, why France managed to provide economic help to Russia after the alliance, despite the not glorious French economy of that period. French banks were able to invest and lend mountains of money to St Petersburg without risking a negative effect on the internal market. Germany was growing but remained limited in its movements, the threats of the Kaiser and its desires for revenge were substantially devoid of real political value. His military education did not allow him to understand how obsolete the combination of power and Army was. In the Europe of the financial economy a nation needed more than a large Army to dominate and Britain was an example.

[417] V. Hentschel, *Wirtschaft und Wirtschaftpolitik imwilhelminischen Deutschland: Organized Capitalism and Intervention State?* Stuttgart 1978. p. 134.

[418] A. Offner, *The First World War: an Agriarian Interpretation,* Oxford University Press. Oxford 1989. pp. 121 – 135.

During the Second International of Socialist Parties in Stuttgart in 1907 a document was approved, the resolution on "militarism and international conflicts".

"Wars between capitalist states are as a rule the result of their rivalry for world markets, as every state is not only concerned in consolidating its own market, but also in conquering new markets [...] further, these wars arise out of the never-ending armament race of militarism [...] wars are therefore inherent in the nature of capitalism; they will only cease when the capitalist economy is abolished"

After the outbreak of the war this thesis became in practice a dogma for the European left. Lenin was convinced, and not just him, that war was a product of capitalism. At first glance, it may seem reasonable to entrust the blame for the conflict to companies that supplied arms to the Powers, a war would have caused an excessive increase in the number of orders and earnings. For example, one of the families that would have made the most money in Europe would have been the Rothschilds. Lord Rothschild had shares of the Maxim-Nordenfelt who supplied the machine guns to the British Army[419]. The Viennese branch of the family supplied the Emperor with bullets and ships via their Witkowitz steelworks. Thanks to the naval programmes wanted by Alfred von Tirpitz, Grand Admiral, the German shipyards did great business. Between 1898 and 1913 86 ships were commissioned, 63 of which were assembled by private companies. In Hamburg, the Blohm & Voss shipyards used more than a fifth of their production for the navy.

Faced with these figures, the Socialists were right, but unfortunately there is no piece of evidence to show that capitalist investors are genuinely interested in a European conflict. The London bankers were trembling at the idea of war because this could

---

[419] N. Ferguson, *The World's Banker: A History of the House of Rothschild*, Penguin, London 1998. Cap 29.

have led to the bankruptcy of all the institutions that financed international trade. The Rothschilds were active on the Anglo-German front, trying at all costs to avoid a conflict between the two nations. In Germany the situation was no different. Owner Albert Ballin and banker Max Warburg were against the war during the July crisis. Warburg tried to convince the Kaiser that the nations he wanted to fight against, France, Russia and England, already had several problems within themselves and this could be an advantage for Germany, they had to leave them quiet for a few years and see them wear out on their own. A war would have recompacted all the internal fronts.

In 1913, the director of the Deutsche Bank, Karl Helfferich, published a brochure on this subject. The president of the Allgemeine Elektrizitats Gesellschaft, Walther Rathenau, unsuccessfully tried to persuade the officials of the Reich to build an economic staff. On the 18th of June 1914, Rudolf Havenstein summoned the directors of the eight largest share-capital banks to the Reichsbank to advise them to increase their reserve shares, thus avoiding the risk of liquidity problems in the event of war. The eight directors told him to not interfere.

Socialist theory therefore lacks any foundation.

Despite the differences between the Kaiser and his uncle, relations between Great Britain and Germany were much better than those with the other powers, as we have already seen. Between the end of the nineteenth century and the beginning of the twenty-first century, a war against France or Russia was more likely. In fact, even though literature feared a war, the two nations maintained many relations, far from the spotlight.

The British had kept aside during German unification, had not moved a finger during the war between Prussia and France and above all had not put themselves sideways when Bismarck began to plant flags on non-European territories. The English satisfied the Germans during their colonisation of Southwest Africa, Cameroon and East Africa. In 1890 the two nations exchanged two territories, Germany had no interest in Zanzibar and gave it to Great Britain demanding in return the island of Helgoland in the North Sea and the so-called *finger of Caprivi*, a strip of land that connected the possessions in south-west Africa to the river Zambezi. However, the most profitable factor for the two countries was their co-operation in China. Since 1874, the Chinese Government's main lenders have been two Hong Kong-based English companies, *Jardine Matheson & Co.* And *Dent & Co.* The British also controlled maritime customs. At the beginning of 1885 the German banker Adolph Hansemann contacted the two comrades and made them a proposal to share financing, and risks, with the Government and the Chinese railways. In February 1889 a *joint venture* of 13 German banks[420], the *Deutsch-Asiatische Bank,* was created. After the 1894-95 war between Japan and China, Lord Rothschild and Hansemann spent their time working with *Deutsch-Asiatische Bank* and the *Hong Kong & Shanghai Banking Corporation* (HSBC) to prevent Russia from expanding its influence over China. Both were sure to have strong support from their respective Governments, but that was not the case. In Berlin, many diplomats saw an alliance with the British as a bad thing and preferred to spend words of praise for Russia and France. In May 1896, China's announcement[421]that the indemnity to Japan would be paid out with a Russian loan destroyed every project by Hansemann and Rothschild. In London they were even more worried because they knew very well that Russia could not lend money to the Chinese, they themselves had debts to pay, the money came from France. The benefits of the deal were shared between Russia and France. Russia was granted permission to transit its Trans-Siberian Railway in Manchuria,

---

[420] B. Barth, *The German Finance and the Imperialisms: Banks and foreign policy before 1914.* Stuttgart 1995.

[421] R. Poidevin, *Les Relations Èconomiques et financières entre la France et l'Alemagne de 1898 à 1914.* Paris 1969.

whilst France was granted concessions for the construction of railways in China. A new Russian-Chinese bank was created, financed by French money. The two bankers decided to join forces anyway, but this time with the intention of putting an end to the competitions in China by creating a single international lending organisation, as already done with Turkey and Greece. In 1898 they succeeded in doing so by making a new loan to the Chinese Government. However, Salisbury did not grant the Government guarantee on the loan, which made it difficult to place the British shares on the market. In 1898, at a London conference between bankers and politicians, China was divided into areas of interest. The Yangtze valley was placed under English control and the Shantung under German control. The collaboration continued for other years, in 1902 the problems related to railway concessions were solved with another conference in Berlin.

In 1898 the German ambassador in London, Paul von Hatzfeldt, proposed an Anglo-German alliance to Chamberlain during a dinner party.

"Joe is very impulsive and the Cabinet discussion of the preceding days (about Port Arthur) hard forced on his attention our isolated and occasionally therefore difficult diplomatic position. He certainly went far in the expression of his own personal leaning towards a German alliance; he combated the notion that our form of Parliamentary Government rendered such an alliance precarious (a notion which apparently haunts the German min), and I believe even threw out a vague suggestion as to the form which an arrangement between the two countries might take"

The then Foreign Minister, Bulow, replied almost immediately

"His telegraphic reply [...] dwelt again on the Parliamentary difficulty, - but also expressed with happy frankness the German view of England's position in the European system. They hold, it seems, that we are more than a match for France, but not more than a match for Russia and France combined. The issue of such a contest would be doubtful. They could not afford to see us succumb, - not because they loved us, but because they know that they would be the next victims – and so on.

The whole tenor of the conversation (as represented to me) being in favour of a closer union between the countries"[422]

The two Governments began to take the matter seriously, and meetings were held. Especially between Chamberlain and Hermann von Eckardstein, first secretary of the embassy with the task of linking the two nations. He proposed on behalf of the Kaiser an agreement between the two countries:

"A possible alliance between England and Germany [...] the basis of which would be a guarantee by both Powers of the possessions of the others"[423]

Chamberlain talking to Salisbury spoke of the treaty as of:

"A Treaty or Arrangement between Germany and Great Britain for a term of years [...] of a defensive character based upon a mutual understanding as to policy in China and elsewhere"[424]

The British, however, especially Salisbury, never showed any real interest in the matter. This is not just because the Germans ran a little too fast or because the Kaiser offended the British every other day. The explanation that is often given is that of a blame between the two countries because of their colonies and the interests of one

---

[422] B. Dugdale, *Arthur James Balfour, 1st Earl of Balfour, 1906 - 1930,* Vol I. p. 258f. London 1928.

[423] J.L. Garvin, *The Life of Joseph Chamberlain, Vol III. 1895 – 1900.* London 1934.

[424] R. Jay, *Joseph Chamberlain: A political study,* Oxford University Press, Oxford 1981. p. 219.

on the possessions of the other and vice versa. In 1899 Hans Delbruck said in an article:

"We can pursue colonial policy with England or without England. With England means peace; against England means – thought war"[425]

The truth was, however, that Germany was building its own Empire thanks to Great Britain. One example is China, but also the dispute over Portugal, Germany and Portugal were also on course for a colonial issue. Great Britain and Germany joined forces to help the country by lending money and sharing the influence over the Portuguese colonies. In 1902, despite criticism from the British public, the two countries joined together to secure Venezuela's public debt[426].

The most strategic region for the two countries, however, were the territories of the Ottoman Empire. The Germans had strong interests in the region. In 1889 the Kaiser had made a visit to Constantinople and had made a friendship with results, as we shall see later. After the Greek defeat against Turkey in 1897, the two countries decided to help the debt of Athens. In 1898 the Kaiser made a second trip to the Ottoman capital. The following year presented an incredible opportunity for the two countries. Georg von Siemens, of the Deutsche Bank, had the idea of building an imperial railway to Baghdad. Siemens, and its successor Arthur von Gwinner from the beginning had thought of a collaboration of English and French in the deal. The

---

[425] J. Steinberg, *The Copenaghen Complex,* Journal of Contemporary History. 1966.

[426] P. Kennedy, *Rise of the Anglo-German antagonism,* London 1980.

City, however, was not interested in that region[427], the weakness of the Ottoman Empire was not a source of certainty.

In 1903, the British and Germans reached an agreement to extend the line to Basra, 25% of the shares would be British, but when the public learnt that 35% of the shares would go to German investors, Prime Minister Balfour was forced to withdraw from the deal[428].

The already mentioned telegram of the Kaiser to the Boer President after the victory over the English troops in Jameson made the British very angry. The support of the Germans for the Boer cause was certainly not a good business card in view of an alliance. The agreement on Portugal was done precisely for discouraging the Germans from taking an interest in the Transvaal. In fact, German banks had no problem exploiting English loans to the Transvaal after the war. The war, however, had highlighted the impossibility for England to defend itself and the Empire at the same time. The lack of alliances in Europe could no longer continue. Even during the war, it was possible to hypothesise that Great Britain would enter the Triple Alliance in London.

In 1901 England even tried to please Germany by proposing a division of Morocco into areas of influence. London was worried about Gibraltar; the Spaniards had built new fortifications in Algeciras. According to the draft treaty the English would go to Tangier and Germany to the Atlantic coast, in this way the two countries would have avoided France to put its hand on the country. The treaty ended in nothing by the simple fact that Berlin never really expressed an interest in Morocco.

---

[427] B. Barth, *The Germans...* p. 134.

[428] G. W. Monger, *the end of isolation: British foreign policy 1900 – 1907.* London 1963.

The alliance between Britain and Germany appeared several times during those years but the main reason why nothing ever happened was the German weakness. London did no really consider it a real problem because it did not consider it a real power. When the problem of alliances arose and the end of the *Splendid Isolation* other powers in Europe worried London. Even Chamberlain, who had repeatedly put forward the idea of a London-Berlin pact, was the first not to be fully convinced of his idea.

The main purpose of the British was to avoid costly and risky conflicts. They only fought when necessary because they were more interested in France and Russia because in those years, they were their most dangerous enemies, the Russian and French fleets combined could reach almost the same of the British firepower. Not to mention that in a hypothetical conflict with Germany in Europe or elsewhere, England would have found itself in difficult relations with France, its neighbour and neighbour in other parts of the world and Russia with which its shared borders in Asia: fighting the Germans without first ensuring the security of India was unthinkable. In London they were sure: despite its continuous hustle and bustle, Berlin was weak on the world stage.

The *Entente Cordiale* was in fact a colonial barter to appease the difficult relations between the two countries. In this way England solved the problem of Egypt and France the problem of Morocco. In addition, England approaching France could kill two birds with one stone because the excellent relations between French and Russians would allow an improvement between English and Russians[429]. This led to a series of manoeuvres: the conciliation on the issues in Manchuria and Tibet, the abandonment of harmful ideas in the Black Sea, Persia and Afghanistan, sending

---

[429] K. M. Wilson, *The Policy of the Entente: Essays on the Determinants of British foreign policy,* Cambridge University Press, Cambridge 1985.

413

Curzon, at the time still Viceroy, on all the rampage. The Russo-Japanese War was a turning point. In case of victory England would most likely have put back in place a pact with Germany, Russia powerful in Asia was a threat to both. If the war had not taken place, London and St. Petersburg would probably have signed an Anglo-Russian equivalent of the Anglo-French *Entente Cordiale.* With Russia's defeat in the conflict on the international political scene, Japan appeared, it was the first-time that a European power had lost against a non-European power. Japan was allied with Great Britain and now represented an excellent Asian bulwark against Russia. In addition, a second stronger power than Germany had appeared in Asia: The United States. There was no good relationship between London and Washington, although the last war fought was in 1812, the Americans had not yet forgiven the support of the British for the Sudist cause during the Secession War. The Americans had secured several properties in Asia, the Pacific and the Atlantic. The Philippines, Puerto Rico, Guam, Hawaii, the Philippines and Samoa and some slices of China. With the construction of the Panama Canal, Great Britain was presented with the opportunity to make peace with the Americans, the fact that 4800 kilometres of Canada bordered the federation was a good reason to stay on good terms. In 1901 the treaty of Hay-Pauncefote was signed, with which Great Britain declared its agreement with the fortification of the Channel by the Americans. The following year the British naval presence in the Caribbean was reduced. The two countries came closer together when in 1904 they established a financial control over the Dominican Republic and over Nicaragua. When Wilson took over Haiti in 1915, the Dominican Republic in 1916 and overthrew the Mexican Government in 1914, London said nothing.

British foreign policy changed dramatically between 1900 and 1906. His primary interest was to secure the friendship of the powers that could put his global position in crisis, and France, Russia and the United States filled those boxes. To please these three nations, it was necessary to fight against the minor powers and Germany occupied that position.

7. Fish and Chips

With the resignation of Balfour on the 5th of December 1905, imperial politics was handed over to the liberals. He hoped that his rival, Henry Campbell-Bannerman, would fail to form a Government but managed to form a minority executive that led the party and the nation to new elections. CB's position, as everyone called it, was quite shaky within its own party. Against him were the three *Relugas Compact*. Herbert Henry Asquith, Edward Grey and Richard Burton Haldane. The pact between the three was sanctioned in December 1905 at the Grey fishing hut in Scotland, in the village of Relugas. The purpose of the pact was to speed up CB's transition to the *House of Lords* by turning him into a puppet Prime Minister and taking power in the *House of Commons*. Campbell-Bannerman understood the danger he was running within the party and, playing in advance, called new elections and decided to offer Asquith the role of *Chancellor of the Exchequer,* Grey that of *Secretary of State for Foreign Affairs* and Haldane the post of *Secretary of State for the war.* The three of them agreed. The campaign slogan was *peace, retrenchment and reform.* In his first speech during the election campaign, the new Prime Minister said:

"Expenditure calls for taxes, and taxes are the plaything of the tariff reformer. Militarism, extravagance, protection are weeds which grow in the same field, and if you want to clear the field for honest cultivation you must root them all out. For my own part, I do not believe that we should have been confronted by the spectre of protection if it had not been for the South African war. Depend upon it that in fighting for our open ports and for the cheap food and material upon which the welfare of the people and the prosperity of our commerce depend we are fighting

415

against those powers, privileges, injustices and monopolies which are unalterably opposed to the triumph of democratic principles"[430]

Thanks also to an alliance with McDonald's Labour, he was able to win the elections and strengthen his position in parliament and especially in the party. CB is in fact the father of the British *welfare state*. His Government fought hard to improve the living conditions of its citizens. Continuing the work begun by Disraeli. He introduced in order: free school canteens, social security, legislation in favour of trade unions, public health care, in 1907 a law allowed judges to serve the sentences inflicted on young criminals in community recovery and not in prison, regulated child labour, made illegal the purchase of tobacco, alcohol and fireworks to minors and made mandatory health inspections in places where children resided.

If CB was the father of the *welfare state* Edward Grey was the architect of the dissolution of the British Empire. During his nine years as Foreign Minister the country underwent a political upheaval, especially at the foreign level, which led to the country to take sides and then fight the last imperial war, the Great War.

The previous Governments of Salisbury and Balfour that had contributed to the disappearance of the *Splendid Isolation,* had already begun a so-called reform of imperial foreign policy but the diplomatic legacy of the Tories in 1905 did not include in any way binding agreement for a descent into war in favour of France or Russia or both in the case of a German attack. If anything, they defined the order in which the English would deal with foreign powers: France, Russia, Germany. At first it was even thought that a liberal Government would be much less inclined

---

[430] Sir H. Campbell-Bannerman at the Albert Hall, *The Times,* 22nd of December 1905. p. 7.

towards an alliance with France or Russia to the detriment of Germany. According to Lloyd George the CB Government had fought at first to:

"Reduce the gigantic expenditure on armaments built up by the recklessness of our predecessors"

The problem with that Government, however, was not its ideas but its components. For a series of knock-on effects, the internal problems of the liberal Government brought the country to the edge of the abyss.

The main architects were Grey and Asquith. Edward Grey was not an unscrupulous imperialist like Chamberlain or Rhodes, he was part of a current of the liberal party, the *Liberal Imperialist*, which aimed to counter the ideas spread by Gladstone within the party and wanted to turn it into a real national party by winning back the votes of the workers and centrists. Grey's appointment was the first step in that direction. Grey was a character covered in a thick layer of tragedy. This is how it was described in the *Daily News in* 1908:

"The inflexibility of his mind, unqualified by large knowledge, swift apprehension of events or urgent passion for humanity, constitutes a peril to the future. His aims are high, his honour stainless; but the slow movement of his mind and his unquestioning faith in the honesty of those on whom he has to rely render it easy for him to drift into courses which a more imaginative sense and a swifter instinct would lead him to question and repudiate"[431]

The words of Alfred George Gardiner were confirmed several times. In 1916, Lloyd George doubled his dose:

---

[431] P. Rowland, *The Last Liberal Government,* Vol II: Unfinished business, 1911 – 1914. London 1971. p. 361.

"a high intelligence but a [...] commonplace texture. His speeches were clear, correct, and orderly but characterised by no distinction of phrase or thought. He lacked the knowledge vision, imagination, breadth of mind and that high courage, bordering on audacity, which his immense task demanded. He was a pilot whose hand trembled in the palsy of apprehension, unable to grip the levers and manipulate them with a firm and clear purpose, waiting for public opinion to decide his direction for him. Truly magic at heart a philanthropist, a man of peace; as high-minded an apostle of the moral law as ever was. Could deal with questions that had rational answers; when faced with the inexplicable, he tended to retreat"[432]

Grey's intent was to

"To pursue a European policy without keeping up a great Army"

But since 1902 Grey's main intent has been to field his country against Germany. In 1903 to the author of *Vitae lamp* Henry Newbolt said:

"I have come to think that Germany is our worst enemy and our greatest danger [...] I believe the policy of Germany to be that of using us without helping us: keeping us isolated, that she may have us to fall back on"[433]

In mid-1905 he declared to a parliamentarian:

"If any Government drags us back into the German net, I will oppose it openly at all costs"

---

[432] C. Barnett, *The collapse of British Power,* London 1973.

[433] G. L. Bernstein, *Liberalism and Liberal Policies in Edwardian England,* London 1986. p. 182.

And in 1905, just before joining the Government.

"I am afraid the impression has been spread either some success by those interested in spreading it, that Liberal Government would unsettle the understanding with France in order to make up to Germany. I want to do what I Can to combat this"[434]

But Grey was the only one within his Government to reveal such a strong Germanophobia. Most of his party friends did not share an *Entente Cordiale*. Most of the Liberal Party at that time was more inclined to an alliance with the Germans. CB was very skilled and could move between the two currents so that neither prevailed over the Government policy but when in 1908 he gave way to Asquith Grey found himself advantaged for his friend thought as he did. Asquith had very little knowledge of foreign policy and this allowed Grey and Foreign Office officials to splash around in British diplomatic affairs keeping the Prime Minister, Government and parliament almost unaware of everything. Grey's main advantage in parliament was not his party but the opposition. The conservatives, although they were gaining ground compared to the liberal majority, which in all years in Government never managed to increase its consensus but did the opposite, had ideas in accordance with those of Grey. Compared to Lloyd George, Chancellor of the Exchequer in the Asquith Government, and Asquith Grey himself enjoyed not so much esteem as communion of purpose. The Chancellor's tax policy and the Irish question of the Prime Minister did not have the same approval. Grey therefore had less trouble getting his ideas approved or pursuing his intentions than his colleagues. Lord Balcarres, leader of the Tory minority in 1912 said:

---

[434] K.M. Wilson, *Policy...,* p. 35.

"Had supported Grey for six years on the assumption that he continues the Anglo-French Entente which Lord Lansdowne established and he Anglo-Russian Entente Lord Lansdowne began"[435]

Grey was a fly-fishing lover, he even wrote a book about the practice. Unfortunately for Britain he was more experienced in fishing than in foreign policy. And no matter how hard he tried to appear important and authoritative, on the foreign political scene he was the fish. Especially the Russians used it for their own purposes. His policy of relaxation with Russia, culminating in the already mentioned agreement of 1907, infuriated almost the entire party because they did not consider it right to spread the prosperity at home and ally with an authoritarian regime. Compared to his previous ones, however, he knew how to do something else, using Russian weakness after his defeat against Japan, he cut off funds for the defence of India, proving that Russia was no longer an enemy but an ally and in doing so, at a stroke, he took away the voice and strength of those in the Ministry of War and in the Government of India who were constantly sounding alarms about Russia. He opposed and even got the support of Colonel William Robertson when it came to decide on an increase in armed efforts in Persia and Afghanistan.

"For centuries past we have thwarted [...] each and every power in turn which has aspired to continental predominance; and concurrently, and as a consequence, we have enlivened our own sphere of imperial ascendancy [...] a new preponderance is now growing, of which the centre of gravity is Berlin. Anything [...] which would

---

[435] K.M. Wilson, *Policy...*, p. 17.

assist us in opposing this new and most formidable danger would be of value to us "[436]

All the historical diatribes with the Russians, Afghanistan, Persia, Tibet, the Dardanelles etc. were cancelled at a glance with the agreements of the 31st of August 1908. How did Eyre Crowe get to say:

"The fiction of an independent and united Persia had to be sacrificed for the sake of avoiding any quarrel with Russia"[437]

Grey was so terrified of Germany that he even went so far as to support, albeit not officially, Russian ambitions in the Balkans. However, he had rightly identified the region as a possible powder keg for a large-scale conflict. In November 1908, in a letter to the English Ambassador to Berlin, Sir William Goschen, he wrote:

"A strong Slav feeling has arisen in Russia. Although this feeling appears to be well in hand at present, bloodshed between Austria and Servia would certainly raise the feeling to a dangerous height in Russia; and the thought that peace depends upon Servia restraining herself is not comfortable"[438]

The problem for Grey, and for most of the Government, was that at that time a minister was not always consulted on his ministry on business. And this happened in 1910 when he discovered that his country had made agreements with the Germans

---

[436] Pro Fo 800/102, Robertson Memorandum of Understanding with Russia, 29th of March 1906.

[437] K.M. Wilson, *Policy...*, p. 83.

[438] PRO FO 800/61, Grey in Goschen, 5th of November 1908.

on the future of the Ottoman Empire and Persia. Just the same year the Russian Foreign Minister had said:

"The English, in pursuing political aims of vital importance in Europe, will abandon in case of necessity certain interests in Asia simply in order to maintain the convention with us which is so important for them"[439]

Grey even wanted to resign, but he did not do so because he was afraid that a pro-German member of his party would take his place. Grey was even willing to accept the idea of the Russians to take Constantinople, *appeasement* at every level, all in order to cut off from any question the Germans and above all to keep in good relations with his neighbours.

As far as France was concerned, however, it was easier for him to maintain a Francophile policy. The previous conservative Government, supported as we have seen by the King, had made friendly arrangements. He made a secret military clause part of the pact. The General Staff had long had secret plans to help France in the event of war against Germany. The first floors provided for a deployment of forces to be disembarked in France to help. The central problem, however, was Belgium. Since 1839 Great Britain had signed a treaty in defence of the neutrality of the country. Belgium was not just any country, its King, Leopold I, was the uncle of Victoria and Albert and had organised their wedding. At that time the treaty had been signed by Great Britain, Austria, France, Prussia and Russia together and on the other side the Netherlands. In 1870 it was renewed in London. The British strategists did not consider the country in danger in case of outbreak of war but did not exclude an invasion in case of continuation of the conflict. They agreed that two Army corps

---

[439] A. J. P. Taylor, *The struggle for Mastery in Europe, 1848 – 1918.* Oxford University Press, Oxford 1954.

would be sent within 23 days in case of need. From their point of view, this would also have increased Britain's weight compared to standing aside and observing. This idea practically only whispered in the corridors of the Foreign Office began to take hold after the birth of the CB Government in 1905. These two political and military plans concluded that in the event of an invasion of Belgium Great Britain would be *kept* but not *obliged to* intervene.

"Britain had the right to intervene in the case of violation of Belgian neutrality, not the obligation"[440]

In 1906 Grey stated

"if there is war between France and Germany it will be very difficult for us to keep out if the entente and still more the constant and emphatic demonstrations of affection (official, naval, commercial, municipal)[...] have created in France a belief that we should help her in war [...] all the French officers take this for granted [...] if the expectation is disappointed France will never forgive us [...] the more I review the situation the more it appears to me that we cannot keep out of a war without losing our good name and our friends and wrecking our policy and position in the world"[441]

Grey's ability, if you can speak of ability, was to keep every commitment on the hypothetical level, every conversation was not binding every meeting never had an official value. He communicated the British aid to the French in case of French need

---

[440] PRO CAB/38/11/4 military conference on actions during the war with Germany, 19 December 1905 – 1st of June 1906.

[441] PRO FO 800/92 Memorandum of Grey, 20th of February 1906.

but almost nothing was received in writing at Downing Street. In 1906, the General Staff *promised* the French 105,000 well-armed soldiers in the event of help.

By now a conflict with Germany was not only felt but almost taken for granted, the problem was that from Germany there were no signs so obvious for such an advanced scaremongering.

In 1906 Grey succeeded in estimating five points that were added to the other articles of *Entente.*

A) The despatch of a large expeditionary force to the Baltic would be impracticable until the naval situation had cleared. Such a plan of operations could not take effect till after great battles had seen fought on the frontier.

B) Any military co-operation on the part of British Army, if undertaken at the outset of war, must take the form either of an expedition to Belgium of direct participation in the defence of the French frontier.

C) A German violation of Belgian territory would apparently necessitate the first course. The possibility of such violation taking place with the consent first course. The possibility of such violation taking place with the consent of the Belgian Government must not be overlooked.

D) In any case, the views of French would have to be considered, as it is essential that any measure of co-operation on our part should harmonize with their strategic plans.

E) Whichever course was adopted, a preliminary landing on the French north-western coast would be advantageous.[442]

---

[442] PRO CAB 38/11/4 military conference: actions during the war with Germany. 1st of June 1906.

In little more than six months he had succeeded in transforming an agreement for the resolution of colonial diatribes into a defensive pact.

On 25 August 1911 the *Committee of Imperial Defence* promulgated a document stating that it was a good thing:

"In the case of our remaining neutral, Germany will fight France single-handed. The armies of Germany and the fleets of Germany are much stronger than those of France and the results of such a war can scarcely be doubted [...] in a single-handed war France in all probability would be defeated"[443]

In fact, the spark of the First World War is found in those words, spark that caused the explosion, i.e. the sinking of the Titanic with all the consequences, and then the shock wave i.e. the facts of Sarajevo.

That document contains all the facts, and as convinced as they were of British superiority, the imperial strategists had weighed up well the prospect of conflict: in the long run it would be the Germans who would lose out. From a British perspective, the six imperial divisions would have represented the needle of the balance compared to the 40 German and 39 French divisions. The Navy failed to respond with a different plan, their idea of a naval blockade and an invasion of German territory did not satisfy anyone.

Field-marshal Sir William Nicholson in his criticism of the CID plan sadly caught all the tragedy of the conflict and all the obtuseness of the British commanders:

"The truth was that this class of operation possibly had some value a century ago, when land communications were different, but now, when they were excellent, they

---

[443] PRO CAB 38/19/50 Memorandum of Churchill.

were doomed to failure [...] would the Admiralty continue to press that view even if the General Staff expressed their considered opinion that the military operations on which it was proposed to employ this division were madness?[444]

In December 1912 during a new meeting of the CID Lloyd George came to affirm:

The geographical position of the Netherlands and Belgium made their attitude in a war between the British Empire in all either France and Russia against the Triple Entente. One of immense importance. If they are neutral, and accorded full rights of neutrals, we should be unable to bring any offensive economic pressure upon her. It was essential that we should do so"

The problem would have arisen if the Netherlands and Belgium had granted transit permission to German troops, in this regard Nicholson's successor, Sir John French (nomen omen):

"In order to bring the greatest possible pressure to bear upon Germany, it is essential that Netherlands and Belgium should either be entirely friendly to this country, in which case we should limit their overseas trade, or that they should be definitely hostile, in which case we should extend the blockade to their ports[445]

In summary: Great Britain was allied with France and Belgium, in the event of a German conflict against France Great Britain would need the pretext of breaching Belgian neutrality to intervene in favour of the French and if Germany had not breached the country's neutrality she would have done so. It goes without saying that the extolled moral superiority of the Government of His Majesty, which boasted of fighting for the neutrality of Belgium, collapses in every point.

K. Wilson, *Policy...*, p. 64.

[445] PRO CAB 2/3 CID meeting, 6th of December 1912.

Belgium was not entirely secretive about these agreements and as time went by Brussels began to fear a British naval violation as much as a German land-based violation. In 1912 in London they were not sure whether Belgium would activate the clause requesting aid in case of German violation, especially if the Germans invaded a small portion of territory and when Holland announced the construction of a new fortress in Flessinga the *Royal Navy* was concerned because this would deny British ships entry to Antwerp.

In one of the many cases in which Grey did not know what was going on in the affairs of his Minister, it was learnt that on the basis of the agreements between the two admirals, the defence of the Mediterranean would be entrusted to the French, thus allowing Great Britain to concentrate on the naval blockade, the British Admiralty in fact had not put aside the Navy's ideas because they considered them compatible with the plans by land. Despite the historical differences between the Navy and the Army, the two war plans could coexist, and so it did.

In the light of all these facts, the German idea, denounced in the Reichstag by Bulow, of encirclement of Germany assumes a no longer paranoid but truthful thought. Not to mention that the *famous* war council convened by the Kaiser in December 1912 was caused by a phrase by Haldane

"Britain could not allow Germany to become the leading power on the continent and it to be united under German leadership"

For a psychopath like the Kaiser, it was shining gold.

British politics later absolved itself of its responsibilities in the conflict by pointing out that the *Weltpolitik* was the reason for its arms race and alliances. Fear of seeing one's own interests in Africa, Asia and the Middle East interfered by the Germans would have led the axis of the balance to shift towards the warlike aspect. In fact, however, as we have seen, Germany was not a real danger, the British did not care who they had as a neighbour around their colonies. Germans were interested in the Portuguese colonies and the English had no problems on that front, the problem was more of an image, it meant ignoring the word given to the Portuguese years earlier. Not to mention that the oldest alliance, still in force today is the treaty of Windsor or Anglo-Portuguese Alliance signed in 1368.

At the pick point of the conflict, relations between the two countries were going through a period of strong positivity. Grey did not think it was wrong to oppose German policy on the Portuguese colonies, and when the Germans showed an interest in Turkey he did not publicly complain of any affront. The German behaviour in the Balkan wars of 12-13 was not criticised, the appointment of Liman von Sanders as Inspector General of the Turkish Army was not seen as a threat and the question of the Berlin-Baghdad railway was never felt as a threat since its creator wanted in the deal also English and French. In March 1914, a few months before the war, Lord Rothschild met the German Ambassador in Tring and exchanged some points of view with him

"As far he could see and as far as he knew, there was no reason for fear of war and no complications ahead"[446]

The day before Franz Ferdinand's assassination, the Foreign Office praised the Germans.

The most difficult issue between Germany and Great Britain is undoubtedly that of the naval arms race. The growth of the German navy was considered for decades one of the main causes of the outbreak of conflict, most historians, however, did not consider the troubled negotiations that went on for years with the search for a naval pact, the two countries had developed a complex and modern state system and the maintenance of a large fleet began to weigh on the coffers of the state.

---

[446] Rothschild Archive, London. 16th of March 1914.

428

In December 1907 the Germans proposed a North Sea convention with Great Britain and France, in February 1908 the Kaiser wrote to Lord Tweedmouth that Germany did not aim to exceed the size of the British navy, in July of the same year he met in Kronberg the Permanent Undersecretary of the Foreign Office Sir Charles Hardinge, in 1909 and then in 1910 Bethmann-Hollweg proposed a naval pact to limit naval expenses, in 1912 Haldane went to Berlin and met the Kaiser, Tirpitz, and Bethmann-Hollweg and discussed a naval and colonial pact of non-aggression, in 1913 Churchill proposed to stop building new ships and in 1914 Sir Ernest Cassel and Albert Ballin made an attempt to reach an agreement. None of these attempts were successful. The main reason? German stubbornness. In exchange for a naval agreement, the Germans wanted Great Britain to sign a solemn promise of non-intervention in the event of a Franco-German conflict:

"The high contracting powers [...] will not either of them make any umprovoked attack upon the other or join in any combination or design agaisnt the other for the purpose of aggressione [...] if either [...] becomes entrangled in a war in which it cannot be said to be the aggressor, the other will at leat observe towards the pore so entangled a benevolent neutrality"

It was Bethmann-Hollweg's words in the written draft that never became a treaty. Grey was only willing to promise a non-intervention in case of German non-aggression of France. The problem of any alliance, however, also had to consider the Kaiser. On the one hand, his ministers and collaborators talked to the British and on the other hand he and Tirpitz increased their naval expenses. This was the case, for example, on the eve of the meeting with Haldane in 1912. The Germans wanted a naval pact but in return they demanded British neutrality, neutrality that the greatest power in the world could not afford to offer. The other major obstacle to any agreement with the Germans was represented by France and Russia. Since the pact with the French was very weak and the borders not well-defined any agreement with Berlin would in fact represent a break with Paris and break with Paris meant giving up good relations with St. Petersburg. Grey's mistake, however, was to think that a break with France and Russia would automatically provoke a war in an undefined period of the future. In 1912 he told a newspaper:

"That if France is not supported against Germany, she would join with her and the rest of Europe in an attack upon us"[447]

A very imaginative perspective, to say the least.

"If [...] by some misfortune or blunder our Entente with France is to be broken up, France will have to make her own terms with Germany. And Germany will again be in a position to keep us on bad terms with France and Russia, and to make herself predominant upon the Continent. Then, sooner or later, there will be a war between us and Germany"[448]

The *appeasement* against France and Russia had caused a situation of possible conflict with Germany, *appeasement* that had precisely the aim of avoiding a conflict. Grey was now convinced that Germany was the new Napoleonic threat to the European continent and every effort was made to counter this plan. But he ignored the causes of his phobic German policy, the British arms race has had the same effect in Germany, alliances with France and Russia have developed the encirclement syndrome. In 1907 Esher, who had hardly ever shared ideas with Grey, said without much thought:

"German prestige is more formidable to us than Napoleon at his apogee. Germany is going to contest with us the command of the sea [...] she must have an outlet for her teeming population, and vast acres where Germans can live and remain. These

---

[447] Manchester Guardian

[448] G.M. Trevelyan, *Grey of Falloden,* London 1937. pp. 114 - 115.

acres only exist within the confines of our Empire. Therefore 'L'enemì c'est l'Allemagnè'[449]

However, we must not make the mistake of stating that it was Grey's policy that made the conflict inevitable. His theories and choices led to a settling of the situation, he preferred an agreement with the French and Russians and found himself in a certain sense obliged to pass all the blame on the Germans. At parliamentary level, however, the situation was quite different. He had kept almost everyone in the dark about his new commitments to France. Even CB. Each report remained un-official and already in 1908, the choices of intervention or not were entrusted to the Cabinet in case of need. In so doing, however, he did not give the country the opportunity to choose where to stand, the parliament would most likely have supported his position, but some might have demanded a greater interest in an alliance with Germany stressing when it was false the belief that an agreement with Germany automatically broke that with France. The alliances with Paris and St. Petersburg were born at a time when they were the threats to the Empire and on the one hand the Foreign Minister was convinced of the new German threat and on the other hand, he persisted in maintaining a dubious position on a probable alliance, as already done before. According to Grey, keeping the Cabinet in the dark was a way to free it for every decision, but in fact they made it unable to decide. When some articles on the matter began to appear in the radical press, especially the commitment to send troops to France, the ministers threw themselves at their colleague. The idea was branded as ridiculous by Lewis Harcourt and Sir Walter Runciman. Asquith, as usual, went in favour of the wind and alerted Grey. In November 1911, during a Government meeting, he found himself outnumbered when it came to whether to support the

---

[449] P. J. Cain, A. G. Hopkins, British *Imperialism,* Vol. I *Innovation and Expansion 1688 - 914.* London 1993. p. 450

agreements. The president of the *House of Lords*, Viscount Morley, reported with these words:

"The question of [...] conversations being held or allowed between the General staff of the War Office and the General Staff of foreign states, such as France, in regard to possible military co-operation, without the previous knowledge [...] of the Cabinet"

Asquith defended Grey by reassuring Morley that any military policy issue should first be cleared from the Cabinet. Haldane was convinced that this was enough to calm the situation but when the Prime Minister reported the meeting to the King, he did so with words that were anything but reassuring:

"No communications should take place between the General Staff and the Staffs of other countries which can, directly or indirectly, commit this country to military of naval intervention [...] Such communications, if they related to concerted action by land or sea, should not be entered into without the previous approval of the Cabinet"[450]

Grey was then forced to give a speech in Parliament in which he reassured the MPs that there were no secret articles between His Majesty's Government and France. At the sitting of the 24th of March 1913, Asquith found himself having to confirm once again:

"As has repeatedly been started, this country is not under any obligation, not public and known to parliament, which compels it to take part in any war. In other words, if war arises between European Powers, there are no unpublished agreements which

---

[450] K. Wilson, *Policy...*, p. 28.

will restrict of hamper the freedom of the Government or of parliament to decide whether or not Great Britain should participate in a war"[451]

Grey first informally informed the Governments of France and Russia, announcing that his Government had decided to have free hands-on the matter in case of conflict but then admitted to both that a situation in which Germany became a strong continental force would be very unpleasant for his country.

A few days after the attack in Sarajevo, on the 11th of June, the Foreign Minister said in parliament:

"If war arose between the European Powers, there were no unpublished agreements which would restrict or hamper the freedom of Government of or parliament to decide whether or not Great Britain should participate in a war. No such negotiations are in progress, and none are likely to be entered into as far as I can judge"[452]

With this Grey wiped out the only trump card he had in the deck: the possibility of an English intervention in favour of the French would have dissuaded Berlin because in the long run it would have been at a disadvantage.

Grey's mistake was not so much that of not wanting to ally with the Germans, he was not obliged to do so in any way, but he was that of never wanting to advance the alliances with France and Russia to an official level. An agreement could be overlooked, whilst a formal mutual aid treaty would more easily have been an obstacle to Germany in the event of a conflict.

---

[451] P. Rowland, *The Last...,* Vol II. p. 263.

[452] Hansard, *The Parliamentary Debates.* 4°. 1892 – 1908. E 5° 1909 – 1980.

"The fundamental fact [...] that the Entente is not an alliance. For purposes of ultimate emergency it may be found to have no substance at all. For an entente is nothing more than a frame of mind, a view of general policy which is shared by the Governments of two countries, but which may be, or become, so vague as to lose all content"[453]

France was by now convinced that in the event of an attack, the British would have acted to help them, but in reality, this conviction had no legal cover. The only thing they had was Grey's word, which would only become a fact if he convinced the Cabinet to act.

In fact, the three *Relugas Compact* had led the country to a situation of diplomatic and political uncertainty, British uncertainty had made it much more likely that a conflict on the continent rather than driving it away. This led the Germans to consider the idea of a preventive attack, exploiting the absence of a concrete commitment of intervention between the British and the French. On the other side the continuous denials and the continuous backward steps brought the country to a standstill, the inevitable intervention as a deterrent was never revealed leaving the field open to any German choice. The enormous number of deaths, the sense of guilt and especially the events of World War II have covered the British responsibilities of a thick layer of oblivion, having won the war the British have forgotten, or have wanted to forget, the fact that it was practically them to cause it.

---

[453] K. Wilson, *Policy...*, p. 37.

434

VI

Only the dead have seen the end of war."

George Santayana

KHAN

1914 - 1918

Chapter Eight

The Old Lie

1. The Last Season

The summer of 1914 was a period of total frenzy. The London *Season* went on quietly, at court the young blue-blooded debutants were presented to the royal couple and to the British *high society*. Cricket, polo, fox hunting, horse racing and regattas filled the agendas of the rich society. Not to mention the many receptions, the plays, the Opera. British society did not expect any conflict, politics had spread the false belief that everything was kept under control.

The Kaiser, the Tsar and the King had all met for the last time six months before the outbreak of the conflict, when all three met in Berlin during the month of May 1913. Wilhelm had invited the two cousins on the marriage of the only female daughter of the Emperor of Germany. According to the British ambassador in Berlin the reception was a resounding success, from the stories the royalty of Great Britain had a lot of fun, banquets and dances were very sumptuous[454].

In the private of his palace in London, however, the King had complained about his German cousin, he had never been able to talk to Nicolaj alone, every time the Kaiser would eavesdrop behind the doors or stop the meetings. Wilhelm also complained to his cousin about his country's alliances with France and Russia:

---

[454] M. Macmillan, *The war that ended peace,* Paperback, London 2013. Chapter 7.

439

"There you are making alliances with a decadent nation like France and a semi-barbarous nation like Russia and opposing us, the true upholders of progress and liberty"[455]

Just a few signs to understand, however, that the facade of tranquillity and joy hid a reality that in the small was terribly hostile with the *foreigner*.

In Great Britain not a day went by when some newspapers reported the discovery of some German secret invasion plan, even German waiters were dormant secret agents. In Germany, German newspapers were hurled at French actors who were guilty of wearing German uniforms during a play, *Fritz le Uhlan*. In Berlin, on the other hand, the Valhalla theatre put on scene *The Terror of the Foreign Legion, or the Hellof Sidi-bel-Abbes*. In the first weeks of 1914 a newspaper denounced the growing anti-Germanic hostility in St. Petersburg. In Russia, newspapers denounced Germany, accusing it of planning a pre-emptive attack. A few weeks before the conflict General Aleksej Brusilov was being treated at the German spa town of Bad Kissingen and one evening he was shocked by a city performance in which at some point at the sound of the *1812 Overture* a model of the Kremlin was set on fire.

From 1912 until the outbreak of the war, Britain was more interested in its own backyard. Ireland. The Irish question was really putting the country in a very bad position on the political scene and above all it had split society in half. Since the 1910 elections, the liberal Government has been based on the votes of the Irish Nationalist Party. In 1912 the Government proposed a law to grant self-Government to Ireland by creating a de facto federation of states in Great Britain. The problem behind everything, however, was the religious question, much of the country was Catholic whilst a small part of Protestants were confined to Ulster. This would have

---

[455] K. Rose, *King George V*, London 1983. pp. 166 - 167.

resulted in excessive Catholic power and was unacceptable to Protestants. Most of the Liberal Party winked at the independentists whilst the Conservative Party was on the union side, the same Bonar Law, leader of the Tories, was the son of an Irish Protestant couple from Ulster. As early as 1911, when there were rumours of a law for self-Government, the Protestants, through the *Ulster Unionist* had given voice to their dissent threatening the creation of a real Protestant Government for six counties in the region. In the early months of 1912 volunteers from that region began to arm and train in the event of a civil conflict. In September of the same year, a petition against the approval of the law was signed by 300,000 Ulster citizens. The Conservatives rode the wave, fully supporting the instances of the Protestants. In July, Bonar Law had for the first-time feared a civil war. In London, the situation was anything but calm, the head of the war Office, Northern Irish Sir Henry Wilson invited his compatriots to take up arms in case of approval of the law. Wilson was a sworn enemy of Asquith and all the liberals and secretly passed information to the Tories on military operations prepared in case of riots. In March 1914, a few months after the conflict, the *House of Commons* had twice approved the law and both times the *House of Lords* had rejected it. The battle between Asquith and the Peers of the Kingdom went on since 1910 when he had repeatedly tried to reform the powers of the Lords by removing several of them, the previous year the *People's Budget* of Lloyd George had been rejected by the Upper House, this had been a snag to the tradition that see the Peers never using the veto on tax bills. To resolve the impasse, the King had called for new elections. By 1910 the budget had passed but the institutional crisis was far from over. In November 1910 Asquith and the leader of the liberals amongst the Lords had met with the King and asked the Sovereign to dissolve the chambers again and create new Equals of liberal tendencies and thus allow the reform plan to be approved. For the King, this was a very complicated situation, because refusing to do so meant taking a stand and effectively losing the impartiality of his office, not to mention the fact that the entire Government would resign in masse. The King had previously consulted with his collaborators, Lord

441

Knollys who supported the Liberals and Lord Stamfordham convinced unionist. The King, despite not liking the impositions, was forced to call new elections that were held in November of the same year. The Peers, for fear of being surrounded by new liberals, voted the reform of Asquith, with the *Parliament Act* of 1911 virtually all veto rights of the *House of Lords* were removed. Asquith, to overcome the blockade of the law, proposed to exclude the six counties of Ulster from self-Government. The Lords did not even consider such a proposal and even threatened not to vote for the annual law on the existence of the Army, a law that was passed every year since 1688. In the same period in Ireland the Curragh mutiny developed, it is not clear from who came the order but at a certain point the British officers in the base in South Ireland were informed that shortly afterwards could come the order to arm themselves against the armed Protestant volunteers of the North. Soldiers were given permission to resign or absent. Almost everyone resigned. The Secretary of State for War, Sir John Seely, supported it and left Asquith no other option but to remove him from his post. The Prime Minister thus also assumed the role of commander of the war Office. In July 1914, the King, to resolve the issue and above all to keep the idea of a civil war at home as far away as possible, summoned the leaders of all the factions to Buckingham Palace. The country was so caught up in the Irish question that the newspapers had not talked about anything else for months. The conference was followed so carefully and meticulously that hardly anyone noticed what was happening on the continent, the news of an attack in Sarajevo had laboriously found the front page, but not as the main news.

The 28th of June 1914 was a Sunday. Throughout the continent, the European population was now immense in the joys of summer. French President Poincarè was intent on following the horse races at Longchamp accompanied by his wife. In his diary he noted the joyful atmosphere in the stands, the lush grassy mantle and the complicated clothes of the ladies. Austro-Hungarian Chancellor Berchtold was busy hunting ducks in Moravia, Kaiser Wilhelm was competing, as every year, on board of *Meteor V* in the Baltic Sea, Chief of Staff Moltke had retired to a spa town, King

George V was in Windsor and Prime Minister Asquith had retired to his country house to prepare for the party conference convened at Buckingham Palace. The Tsar was at mass and Emperor Franz Joseph as well.

The heir to the throne of the Austro-Hungarian Empire, Franz Ferdinand, planned to visit Sarajevo, the capital of Bosnia, recently annexed to the Empire, that morning. It was no ordinary day, on the 28th of June 1349 the Turks had defeated the Serbs in the Battle of Kosovo. Certainly not an ideal day to visit a city inhabited by many Serbs, for them it was a tragic day certainly not suitable to celebrate the visit of the representative of their new oppressor.

Franz Ferdinand was a corpulent fifty-year-old Austrian. He was practically only loved by his wife, who was also hated by the whole court. Not having been educated since he was a child as heir to the throne, he had a very special character compared to the court label. He became heir to the throne in 1889 after the Emperor's son had been found dead in Mayerling, a hunting lodge in Lower Austria. Even today, the events that took place there are still covered with mystery and we will probably never know if Rudolf committed suicide or if he was killed with his lover. The fact is, after the death of the direct heir in the line of succession, there was him. He was not loved by his uncle and Emperor, Franz Joseph considered him arrogant and presumptuous. His main interest was hunting. In 1900 he began a relationship with a Bohemian noblewoman, Sophie Chotek. Despite the negative opinion of the court the two married but the Emperor demanded that the marriage was a morganatic marriage. The couple had to fight all their lives against the contempt and arrogance of the Viennese court. Even during the funeral service, the court officials did not spare her one last humiliation, the catafalque on which the coffin had been placed was lower than the one next to the consort.

Despite the bad environment at court being the heir to the throne, Franz Ferdinand could not be denied contact with politicians and generals of the Empire. He never hid his dislike for the Hungarians, considered the Slavs to be subhuman and considered the Serbs to be pigs. He considered the Tsarist regime a model to imitate and wanted at all costs to take back Lombardy and Venice. The couple were very religious, intransigent Catholics. They hated Jews, liberals and Masons. He did not, however, get out of balance with comments on Russia, he understood how risky it was to break the fragile balance between the two countries.

The Heir insisted a lot on a state visit to Bosnia[456] officially territory of the Empire for six years but unofficially since 1878. Unlike the other powers, the Austro-Hungarian Empire had all its colonies annexed to the motherland. And for a Catholic Empire to control a region where a large part of the population was divided between Serbs and Muslims was not easy. Since March, all the newspapers have been publishing plans for the visit, including the route of the procession. This was probably one of the reasons why some young Bosnian students joined the group of Young Bosnians and planned his assassination. Their intention was to put an end to the tyranny of the Habsburgs by bringing Bosnia and Serbia together. Serbia had become independent from the Ottoman Empire in 1903, Belgrade was its capital where the governing bodies of the new constitutional Monarchy resided. The city was the most active hearth of the Pan-Slavic movement. In the city, the organisation known as *Ujedinjenje ili Smrt,* The Black Hand, supplied the bombers with four Browning model automatic guns and six bombs. At the head of the young students was Colonel Dragutin Dimitrijevic, who together with Prince Regent and Prime Minister Pasic formed the triad of powerful people who tried to control the country. The three of them hated each other. Dimitrijevic had a strong influence on the Army. Almost all the state's civilian bodies accused the Black Hand of posing a threat to the country, but no one was strong enough to bypass the power of the Army and thus remove Dimitrijevic from his role as Head of the Secret Service. The Black Hand

---

[456] M. Hastings, *Catastrophe,* Paperback, London 2014. pp. 25 - 26.

had provided for one or more attacks against the Austrians, but we do not know if it was also the instigator of the murder of the heir to the throne. It seems very strange because, for example, after a few days in Belgrade, the best-known bomber, Gavril Princip, who had experience shooting in a city park, had to commit his coat in order to pay for his eight-day trip to Sarajevo. The three bombers travelled together, Princip, Nedeljko Cabrinovic and Trifko Grabez. It is curious, however, to note how poorly protected Franz Ferdinanad was. The farmer who helped Princip and Grabez to enter Bosnian territory was an informant of the Serbian Government and reported to the Minister of the Interior of Belgrade their destination and load, the minister had handwritten a summary to the Prime Minister that he did not spend much to communicate to Vienna the risk of an attack, however he never made the name of Franz Ferdinand as a possible target. Given the events that took place after the attack we tend to consider it a striking fact but, that was a time, and a region, where the attack was now fashionable, even the *Punch* had joked a couple of times. On the 23rd the imperial couple departed by train from the Chlumetz estate to Sarajevo. The security of the visit to the city fell on Oskar Potiorek, Governor of Bosnia, more interested on the menu to serve than to the security of the Archduke so much so that throughout the procession only 36 policemen were deployed. On the evening of the 27th, the couple arrived in town half a day earlier. Then they came back to Ilidze for a reception. The next morning, they went back to Sarajevo for their official visit. The Archduke in high cavalry general gala uniform, the wife in a white dress with white and red roses. In the late morning the procession departed from the station. The seven assassins had arranged themselves along the path read in the newspapers, the cars would have to cross three bridges. It was later named the murderers boulevard. Shortly after the start a bomb dropped by Cabrinovic bounced off the roof of the car on which the couple was travelling and exploded under the next car injuring two officers. The attacker tried to swallow cyanide and then threw himself into the river, but the water was too shallow and the poison too old, he was fished out by the police and arrested. The procession continued towards the town hall where the Archduke was very angry about the attack and expressed his desire to visit the wounded during by the explosion of the bomb. The famous photography of the couple depicts the moment they leave the Town Hall. At a certain point the procession took Franz Joseph Strasse and Potiorek protested with the driver for having taken the wrong road. The driver had to turn off the car and have it pushed by hand because it did not have reverse gear. As soon as the car, at a walking pace, arrived on the Appel Riverside for a curious chance Gavril Princip, who wandered disconsolate after the failure of the attack, passed by there, saw the couple and interpreting it as a signal extracted the revolver and exploded two shots in the direction of the couple. The first shot went through the side of the car and hit Sophie in the abdomen, the second shot hit the Archduke on the neck, his last words were addressed to his wife:

"Sophie, Sophie, don't die, live for our children."

Gavril Princip and the other attackers were all arrested in the hours immediately following the attack. An absurd attack for the incredible percentage of improvisation, both by the organisers of the visit, by the security service and especially by the attackers. Princip fired twice, could have missed them, or only hurt them instead both shots went off and killed on the stroke Sophie and Franz Ferdinand. During the interrogation Princip admitted to Leo Pfefer, the prosecutor in charge of the investigation, that it was not his intention to kill Sophie, he aimed at the Archduke.

In short, the news went around Europe. The Emperor was in Ischl and learnt the news from Count Paar. Apparently, he said, "What a relief". Poincarè was in Longchamp when he received the telegram from the press agency Havas, it was him who communicated the news to the Austrian Ambassador in France, who was also present at the racecourse. The Kaiser watched the regatta when he saw a spear approaching his yacht, first drove her away with one hand but then waited, on board there was his head of the naval cabinet, Georg von Muller, he put a note inside his cigar holder and threw it on the deck of the ship where a sailor picked it up and handed it to the Emperor. The Kaiser was very saddened by the death of his friend, he was one of the few Europeans to estimate the Archduke.

The funeral lasted just 15 minutes, the suffocating heat of the Hofburg-Pfarrkirch was unbearable, immediately after the Emperor returned to the spa. Vienna did not cry Franz Ferdinand at all. Nowhere in town you could see any form of mourning. The royal family showed almost complete indifference to the issue and this is curious when we think of the fact that the murder was used as a pretext for a war against Serbia and Russia.

After the news arrived in every European capital, the waltz of diplomacy began. 37 days passed between the murder and the outbreak of war.[457] In those 37 days all the agreements, treaties, friendships, misunderstandings and problems presented. Almost everyone agreed on an Austrian reaction against Serbia, the newspapers said almost immediately that it was the fault of the Serbs, but no one seemed really worried about a widening of the conflict.

On the 30th of June the Kaiser returned to Berlin and in a telegram to the German Ambassador in Vienna he expressed all his desire for revenge against the Serbs. On the same day the British ships that had attended the Kiel regatta sent a greeting to the German fleet before returning home:

"Friends in the past, friends forever"

On the same day Sir Arthur Nicolson, the highest official in office in the Foreign Office wrote to the Ambassador in St. Petersburg

---

[457] As part of the huge First World War production set up by the British BBC broadcaster for the Centenary of the War, a three-episode script was created that recreates the July crisis from a British and German perspective, called *37 days*.

"The tragedy which has just taken place in Sarajevo will not, I trust, lead to further complications"

On the 3rd of July the Germans announced that the Berlin-Baghdad railway would be extended to Basra, so Germany secured an outlet to the Persian Gulf and access by land to the Indian Ocean, the British did not care so much about the issue because despite having withdrawn from the deal they had made an agreement with Germany.

What was unsure of anyone, not even in Vienna, was what the role of Germany would be in a possible conflict. Vienna never seriously considered the idea of solving everything by diplomatic means, experience during the Balkan wars had shown that mobilising the Army only to put pressure on the other side only worsened the mood of men. The Austrian Chief of Staff, Conrad, learnt of the attack on Zagreb station. He was one of those who, since 1908, had been clamouring for military action against the young Serbian state[458].

The German ambassador in Vienna, the pompous warmonger Heinrich von Tschirschky, even before the Viennese Government decided what to do, had spent his time letting everyone know that Germany would side with Austria in any situation. The Germans were pushing for a punitive war against Serbia by basing their rhetoric on the honour to be defended and, above all, they were placing too much hope that France and Russia would not enter a conflict in defence of a state like Serbia. In Vienna many feared a Russian mobilisation, to help their cousins in Panslavi, and there were even those who trusted that Nikolaj and Franz Joseph would not go to war against each other because they both shared the burden of an authoritarian Monarchy and a conflict would question everything. The Germans were pushing for the conflict even making some not so veiled threats in Vienna, in

---

[458] M. MacMillan, *The war...*, p. 616.

case of further delay would have looked elsewhere for other allies. For Austria-Hungary it would have been a terrible blow, his Empire after the Ottoman Empire was the sickest in Europe, a union of 11 nations with an old and weak Emperor who had already buried four heirs to the throne and had to look for a great-grandson to have a fifth.

Inside the Double Monarchy, if on one hand the Austrian branch was now intent on sharpening the knives on the other hand, the Hungarian one, they tried in every way not to jump into a conflict by abandoning a priori the diplomatic track. The Hungarian Prime Minister, Tiska, pointed out in Vienna that they did not have clear evidence of the Serbian Government's involvement in the attack and pointed out that the Empire's weak diplomatic position on the world stage would be further damaged if they tried to convince public opinion that the causes of the conflict depended on a young and small state. Not to mention that Romania would almost certainly have escaped the clash and even if Bulgarian support had arrived, their forces would not have been enough to compensate for Romanian neutrality. As the crisis escalated, Tiska was put under strong pressure to move to more belligerent positions because without the go-ahead of the Hungarian Government, Vienna had its hands tied.

Austria sent Count Hoyos to Berlin, his sister had married Bismarck's son, and this represented a good investiture, not to mention that he was one of the most active on the front for the war. As soon as Conrad heard about the mission in Berlin, he asked Franz Joseph in a conversation:

"If the answer is on our side, do we then go to war against Serbia?"

The answer was simple but full of meaning:

"In that case, yes"[459]

Hoyos left for Berlin on the 4th of July. He gave Wilhelm a memorandum on the Balkan situation and a letter written by Franz Joseph. Neither of the two documents explicitly mentioned an inevitable conflict, but the words let it be understood without a shadow of a doubt, the letter closed with these lapidary words:

"You must also have been convinced after the recent terrible events in Bosnia, that the reconciliation of the antagonism, which divides us from Serbia, can no longer be considered and that the long-term policy of peace of the European Monarchs is threatened so long as this furnace of criminal agitation in Belgrade continues to burn unpunished"[460]

Hoyos had been instructed by Berchtold to report in person to the Austro-Hungarian Ambassador in Berlin the news that the Double Monarchy had decided that the time had come to close the matter with Serbia, but Hoyos reported another message that Vienna had decided to occupy and dismember Serbia. The Ambassador, Count Ladislaus Szogyeny-Marich, spoke with the Kaiser on the 5th of July. The Kaiser read the document carefully and listened to the information from Vienna. At the beginning he wanted to consult his Chancellor before expressing himself on the matter, but the skilful Ambassador managed to touch the right ropes and, in the end, snatched a promise of intervention alongside Austria-Hungary in case of war against Serbia and Russia. The German Government learnt the day after the decision of its Emperor and welcomed the choice made. Hoyos returned home and reported the outcome of the interview. Austria cashed a "blank cheque" from Germany and the

---

[459] L. C. F. Turner, *The role of the General Staffs in July 1914,* "Australian Journal of Politics and History" Vol 11. N° 3. Sydney 1965. p. 305-323.

[460] *Bittner and Ubersberger, Austria - Hungary's Foreign Policy,* p. 252.

last feeble attempts at diplomatic negotiation disappeared from the table. What about the British?

London realised that in Sarajevo there had not been one of the many attacks in that period only 11 days later, the consultations between Berlin and Vienna began to alarm the Government. On the 9th of July Edward Grey invited the German Ambassador, Prince Lichnowsky, to the Foreign Office. He tried to calm him down and at the same time persuade the Germans of the moves of the Russians.

In fact, the conversation was useless because Grey was unable to reassure Vienna if the Russians found themselves having to help the Slavs in any way. His diplomatic adviser, Sir Arthur Nicholson, was convinced that the whole situation would be resolved with nothing. On the same day, a report on the investigations arrived in Vienna from Sarajevo, no direct connection had been found between the attackers and the Government in Belgrade, but by now the choice to punish Serbia was a fact, it was simply a matter of deciding how. The Austro-Hungarian General Staff, after the support of Berlin, was convinced that no other power would take sides.

After the blank support of Berlin, Berchtold wanted to attack Serbia without even an ultimatum. Premier Tiska proposed to send a list of acceptable requests and in the case of an ultimatum, the power of veto of the Hungarian Premier produced a stalemate then for fear of losing German support accepted Berchtold's intermediate proposal of an ultimatum. Everything seemed to be ready, but Conrad blocked it. On the 14th of July he announced that before the 25th of July the conflict would not take place because of a long licence granted to soldiers for the harvest period, recalling all in advance would reveal the Austrian plans. The surprise attack had now vanished, whilst German diplomacy was trying to limit the conflict to a local matter. On the 19th of July, a brief communiqué requested by the German Foreign Minister was issued on the *Norddeutsche Allgemeine Zeitung*:

"The composition of the disparity of views that may arise between Austria-Hungary and Serbia must remain a matter of a local nature."

451

This communiqué was also sent to Great Britain, France and Russia.

On the 19th of July in Vienna during a council the requests of the ultimatum were drawn up, all those present knew that Serbia would never accept the conditions and that the next step would be the war. The ultimatum had to be delivered immediately but Conrad decided to postpone it to the 23rd, he had learnt that the French President had just left for a state visit to Russia, on the 21st him and the Tsar would meet together and Conrad did not want in any way for the two to be in the same room when the conflict broke out, the ultimatum was then delivered on the 23rd of July with a deadline settled of the 25th.

On the 21st Frank Joseph gave his assent to the document. Russia immediately began to put pressure on Austria. In the meantime, in London, Lloyd George reported on the situation in parliament, deceived by the recent good relations between his country and Germany, and tried to convince the parliament on the resolution of all problems at the diplomatic level.

The afternoon of July 23rd was a day full of tension, the Austrian Ambassador in Belgrade gave the Government the ultimatum. By six o'clock on the evening of the 25th it would have expired. In Vienna, the only question was whether the answer would come before the deadline or after it. Grey naively proposed to this one a kind of international conference to resolve the issue. He was convinced that Germany could help them arbitrate a peaceful solution in the Balkan region.

The Serbian Government met to discuss the points of the ultimatum, almost all would be accepted. What received the greatest rejection, however, was point 6, namely the consent of Austro-Hungarian officials to participate in the investigations in Serbia. At 5.58 p.m. on the 25th of July the Government handed over its answers to the Austro-Hungarian Ambassador, three hours before it had ordered the mobilisation of its Army, he consulted the document and then signed the note already prepared earlier announcing the breakdown of all diplomatic relations between the two countries and his departure from Belgrade that same evening with his entire

452

delegation. The two countries, however, were officially not yet in a state of war. As soon as the news reached St. Petersburg, the Russian General Staff ordered the pre-mobilisation of the troops and in Paris, in great secrecy, all the generals were called back on duty. London was the only capital to show little scaremongering over the news. Both Grey and Asquith still had high hopes for a diplomatic resolution. The proposal for an international conference was again advanced but was dropped by every European chancellery. Initially, the Tsar also proposed opening negotiations with Vienna, but the Austrians immediately rejected the proposal. The only purpose of Grey's proposal was to alarm Germany, a British interest, however diplomatic, was a dangerous wake-up call for Berlin.

After the break-up of relations between the two states the Germans became more active on the front of the war, feared that Austria could resolve the issue with an agreement and did not want to lose the face and above all aimed to finally conclude the Slavic question, the invasion of the Slavs was one of the many psychosis of the Kaiser.

Once again blocking the war plans was Conrad, he had expressed his plans on the conflict: the Army needed more weeks to prepare, not before August. Berchtold did not welcome the news.

Despite Conrad's opinion, on the 28th of July the Viennese Government ordered the mobilisation of the Army against Serbia. In Berlin, with one of his usual sudden moves, the Kaiser announced that after Belgrade's response to the ultimatum, there was no longer any need for a war because the humiliation of the response was already a de facto surrender. However, the Kaiser proposed to occupy Belgrade in order to force the Serbs to respect the pacts. On the 27th of July, Berchtold went to the Emperor and illustrated the latest events to him and formally asked him to sign the declaration of war. At 12 noon on the 28th of July 1914, the Viennese Government sent a telegram to Belgrade with the declaration of war. The First World War had begun on telegraph cables.

As soon as the news came out, on the evening of the 28th, Russia ordered the mobilisation of troops along the border with Austria. Officially, however, there had not yet been a declaration of war.

In Berlin, the Kaiser had convened a council of officers and officials. There was talk of concessions to be made to Britain in exchange for its neutrality. The Russian mobilisation had not yet reached their ears. The Kaiser refused to grant restrictions to the German fleet. Bethmann, who had put forward such a proposal, was in the minority as soon as he returned to his office, he learnt both news of the mobilisation and of Lord Grey's communication: in the event of a conflict with France, Great Britain would not remain neutral.

The Tsar tried, in the hours immediately following the Austrian mobilisation, to persuade the Germans not to enter the conflict and for his part the Kaiser tried to do the same with the Russians. The two Kings and cousins exchanged heated telegrams of supplication to stop the war machine that had been activated. The Tsar did not want to activate the total mobilisation and at first it even seemed that he and his cousin had reached an agreement, but all ended up in smoke shortly afterwards. With the news of the German pre-mobilisation, Nicolaj had no choice but to give the order to start the national mobilisations. They started on the 31st of July. Russian public opinion agreed to run in support of the Slav brothers, but the generals still had a lot of hope that they could use the mobilisation as a mere instrument of pressure.

The Kaiser was very resentful of his Russian cousin's decision. In a short time, his positions shifted to the interventionist front and this was enough for Helmuth Johann Ludwig von Moltke, German Chief of Staff, to send a request for Austrian mobilisation against the Russians. Since the position of Berlin had been definitively clarified, or at least the Austrians thought so because Moltke had overtaken Chancellor and Kaiser, the Austrians began to prepare for the clash with Russia and on the 31st of July the Emperor signed the order of mobilisation also on the Russian border.

The three men who had to decide for war or peace in Germany, the Kaiser, Chancellor Bethmann-Hollweg and Moltke, disagreed but after the news from Russia Moltke found himself in the lead because the insecurities of the first two were easily overtaken. Having taken note of the situation, they had only to activate the pre-established sequence of moves in case of conflict. First the Kaiser would declare the state of "War Danger" then would send an ultimatum to Russia and in case of refusal mobilisation and declaration of war.[461]

Bethmann-Hollweg informed Paris, London, Rome and St. Petersburg on the 31st of July that his country was in "War Danger State" and that German mobilisation would only take place if the Russians did not revoke theirs. On the same day, a written complaint by industrialist Walter Rathenau appeared on the *Berliner Tageblatt*:

"Without the shield of such loyalty, Austria would not have dared to take the steps it has taken"

Yet another proof of the absurdity of the Marxist thesis on the outbreak of conflict.

However, the Germans also had to take in consideration of France, an iron ally of the Russians. In 1904 the Schlieffen Plan was planned, which provided for a fast raid against France, passing through Belgium, in order to arrive in Paris within six weeks and then move the troops on the Russian front avoiding a war on two fronts.

Germany sent a telegram, written by the Chancellor, to the German Ambassador in St. Petersburg in which he clarified the German position on the Russian mobilisation

---

[461] L. Albertini, *Le origini della guerra del 1914. The Origins of the War of 1914 (3 volumes - vol. I: "European relations from the Berlin Congress to the Sarajevo bombing", vol. II: "The crisis of July 1914. From the Sarajevo bombing to the general mobilization of Austria-Hungary", vol. III: "The epilogue of the crisis of July 1914. Le dichiarazioni di guerra e di neutralità.")*, Fratelli Bocca, Milan 1942-1943.

and gave 12 hours to Russia to recall its mobilisation otherwise the Germans would also mobilise.

"Despite the ongoing negotiations and although [...] we had not taken any measure of mobilisation, Russia has mobilised all its Army and its fleet; it has therefore also mobilised against us. These Russian measures have forced us, to ensure the security of the [German] Empire, to declare the "dangerous state of war", which does not yet mean mobilisation. But the mobilisation must follow if within twelve hours Russia does not suspend all war measures against us and Austria-Hungary and does not make us a clear statement to that effect. Please communicate this immediately to Sazonof and telegraph the time of communication. I know that Sverbejef telegraphed yesterday to [Saint] Petersburg that we had already mobilised, but that's not true, not even at the current time".[462]

The telegram did not make explicit reference to the fact that in the event of failure to return the automatic mobilisation there would be a state of war, on this false hope the Foreign Minister Sazonov built the false hope of a possibility of peaceful resolution of the issue. However, all German plans provided for a conflict in the event of mobilisation.

On the same day, a telegram arrived in Paris. To the French, Bethmann had been explicit:

"Mobilisation inevitably means war. Please ask the French Government whether it will remain neutral in a war between Germany and Russia. The answer to this last question must be known to us here tomorrow at 4 p.m."[463]

---

[462] L. Albertini, *The Origins...,* Vol III. p. 39. (translated from Italian)

[463] L. Albertini, *The Origins...,* Vol III. p. 39. (translated from Italian)

The German ultimatum to France arrived at the desk of the French Premier, René Viviani, on the evening of the 31st of July and he assured the Ambassador that the answer would arrive by 1 pm. the following day.

On the 1st of August at 12:52 pm., almost an hour before the expiration of the ultimatum to Russia, Berlin telegraphed his Ambassador to Russia. In the text of the declaration of war, in the event of an unsatisfactory response from the Russian Government he should have handed it over to the Russian Foreign Minister at 5:00 pm. on the same day. The Chancellor and the Minister of War, Erich von Falkenhayn, went to the Kaiser at 4 pm. to have him sign the declaration of war against the Russian Empire. At 5 pm. the document was signed. Meanwhile in St. Petersburg at 7 pm. the telegram from Berlin had arrived late, Pourtalès, the German Ambassador, went to Sazonov with the declaration of war in his pocket. The Ambassador was very nervous, he asked the Russian minister three times whether the Tsar's Government had a satisfactory response for Berlin. Three times the minister said no to the fact that he was forced to make the declaration of war, then he approached a window and burst into tears. Sazonov reported in his memoirs that although they had officially been at war with each other for about two hours, they both embraced each other and understood the gravity of the moment.

In Paris that same day Schoen, the German Ambassador, went to Viviani for an answer but all he got was a statement that meant everything and nothing:

"France will be guided by its own interests"

At 3:55 pm., Chief of Staff Joseph Joffre and the Council of Ministers had sent the same telegram to the whole of France:

"The first day of mobilisation is Sunday, 2nd of August."

For a few moments Berlin rejoiced very much at news from London[464], Karl Max von Lichnowsky had suggested that in the event of non-aggression to France it would not side with Russia and consequently Britain would not intervene. Kaiser and Chancellor were euphoric whilst Moltke was out of his mind, the German war plans did not provide for this possibility. Fortunately, for him, King George himself took the trouble to let it be known that British neutrality depended solely on the British. As soon as he heard the news, the Kaiser gave the order to invade Luxembourg.

On the 2nd of August the Royal Navy was mobilised, and the British assured the French that if German ships were present in the North Sea against French ships, the British would offer all possible help. But the Germans did not care about the North Sea or the English Channel. On the 2nd of August they sent an ultimatum to Belgium, within 12 hours they should have answered yes or no to the request for transit of German troops on Belgian territory. Brussels replied no by pointing out in Berlin the existence of a treaty signed at the time also by Prussia, and still valid, which guaranteed the perpetual neutrality of the small Kingdom.

The declaration of war against France was, because, according to German French soldiers had entered German territory killing some people and some French aviators had even bombed the railway lines and Nuremberg. The German Ambassador had gone to Viviani and had delivered in the form of a letter the declaration of war, at the end of the reading the Ambassador was accompanied to his car where the two greeted each other. It was 7:00 pm. on the 3rd of July.

---

[464] S. J. Valone, *"There must be some misunderstanding": Sir Edward Grey's Diplomacy of August 1, 1914,* Journal of British Studies 27.4, p. 405 – 424; H. F. Young, *The misunderstanding of August 1, 1914.* Journal of Modern History. 48. December 1976. pp. 644 – 665.

The British had been kept as far apart as possible in this whole situation. Grey could not yet accept that the war that he had tried for years to avert had occurred. On the 1st of August he met with Lichnowsky and told him that it would be difficult for Britain to remain neutral in the event of a breach of Belgian Sovereignty. Berlin was still convinced that he was dealing with a bluff and sent the ultimatum to Belgium on the 2nd of August. As soon as he heard of the news of the ultimatum in Brussels Grey telegraphed his Ambassador to Berlin, Goschen, the British ultimatum to Germany. The answer should have been received by midnight on the 4th of August, at 11 pm. in London. It called for respect for the Belgian neutrality enshrined in the Treaty of 1839. If not, Great Britain would have defended Belgian territory at any cost. At 7 pm. on the 4th of August Goschen went to Berlin to see the German Foreign Minister, Jagow. After the ultimatum had been handed over, the minister replied that the German answer was the same as the day before, i.e. no, in fact the German troops had already been on Belgian territory for about an hour. The Ambassador then had his passports handed over and then went to the Chancellor to take his final leave. The two of them had a heated discussion. Bethmann-Hollweg accuses the British of sparking off a conflict with a country related to blood only for a "scrap of paper" and blamed Great Britain for the conflict. Goschen defended his country but then burst into tears, as his German counterpart had already done in St. Petersburg.

An hour before the ultimatum expires, the entire Cabinet had met at number 10 Downing Street, a graveyard kind of silence had fallen for several minutes, the room was poorly lit. The eyes were constantly going from the door to the clock on the fireplace shelf. A single Marconist was waiting for a message from Berlin. Everyone was looking forward to that telegram and then suddenly:

"Boom!" The deep notes of Big Ben rang out into the night, the first strokes in Britain's most fateful hour since she arose out of the deep. A shuddering silence fell upon the room. Every face was suddenly contracted in a painful intensity. "Doom!" "Doom!" "Doom!" to the last stroke. The big clock echoed in our ears like the hammer of destiny. What destiny? Who could tell? We had challenged the most

459

powerful military Empire the world has yet brought forth. France was too weak alone to challenge its might and Russia was ill-organised, ill-equipped, corrupt. We knew what brunt Britain would have to bear. Could she stand it? There was no doubt or hesitation in any breast. But let it be admitted without shame that a thrill of horror quickened every pulse. Did we know that before peace would be restored to Europe, we should have to wade through four years of the most concentrated slaughter, mutilation, suffering, devastation and savagery which mankind has ever witnessed?[465]

Twenty minutes later, the British military received a simple telegram

War. Germany. Act.

Grey's war had begun, and he never expected to be the one who would declare it. It is funny to note that the Austro-Hungarian Empire declared war on Russia on the 6th of August, in fact after a series of countries that had nothing to do with Serbia.

2. The Great War for Civilisation

The war that began on the 4th of August was a conflict completely different from anything ever experienced by a British soldier before[466]. Since Britain did not have a real Army when the war broke out, it was actually a different experience for the whole country.

---

[465] D. Lloyd George, *The War Memoirs*, Nicholson & Watson, London 1933-38. p. 456

[466] J. Paxman, *Great Britain's Great war,* Penguin, London 2013.

460

Great Britain has sprinkled its history of traditions and events linked to the past, it is a nation that has forever two feet forward, but its hands never let the past go altogether. The First World War is perhaps the greatest, most painful and most heartfelt *memory*. It is probably the country that remembers it fallen most. If for the rest of the world the Second World War somewhat obscured the memory of the First in Britain, it never happened, not even during the Second World War. Just think, for example, of the fact that until today every year everyone wears for a month the *Poppy*, the red poppy that has become the symbol of the fallen soldier. Tradition dates to 1921. And it is based on John McCrae's poem *In Flanders Fields*. A Canadian doctor. He wrote the poem on the 3rd of May 1915 after attending the funeral of his best friend who died during the Second Battle of Ypres. The poem was published on the *Punch* on the 8th of December of the same year and became, we will say today, viral. So much so that it can be used on posters for enrolment, purchase requests for war bonds. The image of red poppies growing on the graves of dead soldiers became the symbol of the fallen soldier.

In Flanders fields the poppies blow
Between the crosses, row on row,
That mark our place; and in the sky
The larks, still bravely singing, fly
Scarce heard amid the guns below.

We are the Dead. Short days ago
We lived, felt dawn, saw sunset glow,
Loved and were loved, and now we lie
In Flanders fields.

Take up our quarrel with the foe:
To you from failing hands we throw
The torch; be yours to hold it high.

461

If ye break faith with us who die
We shall not sleep, though poppies grow
In Flanders fields.

From mid-October to the 11th of November, the nation pinned the very symbol of a memory on its lapel. On the 11th of October at 11 am., to commemorate the end of the conflict, the whole country literally stops for two minutes, not only in London, where wreaths of poppies are deposited at the base of the *Cenotaph* by the Monarch, but in the smallest village from Scotland to Wales and in the colonies everything stops. The greatest gift that the nation can give to the memory of its dead men at the front it is its time.

Commemorating is the best way to forget. Only in this way was the country able to move on after that trauma, remembering the fallen but forgetting the faults in the conflict. The task of keeping the guilt spy on is a matter for history. But the people remember, commemorate, forgive but not forget. That is why the 1915 elections were the last won by the Liberals, never again was there a Government led by them in the UK. The words of Lloyd George at the end of the cabinet that prepared the ultimatum were true:

"None of us will survive this war. Politically, I mean"

England was not ready for a war, compared to other nations it had always kept away from militarism. it had always relied on two important factors, the navy and the soldiers from the colonies. But this time neither of them could play a decisive role. Or not right away. As the conflict continued, both the ships and the men of the Empire proved useful. But in a European battlefield several factors were in the field and it was unthinkable not to send their own men. First, the honour.

At the outbreak of the conflict no compulsory conscription was approved, it was widespread belief that the conflict would last for few weeks only, before Christmas most people said. The first fighters were all volunteers or part of the Army. But the

Government needed a person who could attract crowds of young people ready to die for their country, who better than Lord Kitchener? The national hero.

Kitchener was one of the few in England who understood that the conflict would last more than a few weeks. Deep in the rooms of power many thought of that perspective, in this regard Grey as he watched an attendant turn off one by one the gas-lamps under his office said:

"The lamps are going out all over Europe, we shall not see them lit again in our life-time"

After the Battle of Mons, where the small British Army was destroyed in the *Times* of the 30th of August 1914, a simple request appeared:

"To sum up, the great German effort has succeeded. We have to face the fact that the British Expeditionary Force, which bore the great weight of the blow, has suffered terrible losses and requires immediate and immense reinforcement. The British Expeditionary Force had won indeed imperishable glory, but it needs men, men, and yet more men"

The article was a despatch from France written by Arthur Moore, an envoy of the *Times*. He was working with a journalist from the *Daily Mail* Hamilton Fyfe. It was the *Times*, however, that was the first to publish the news because it was the only one to have a Sunday edition at that time. The London publishers of the newspaper were concerned that military censorship would not allow publication of the article, which also contained information on the British retreat in front of the enemy, but when the text returned from the desk of Chief Censor, F. E. Smith, they found several additions and corrections. Smith had no intention of censoring the text but of improving it, for example by adding the last sentence mentioned. The intention was clear: the Army needed new soldiers as soon as possible.

Kitchener, in his new role as *War Secretary,* was an undisputed master in the art of enlisting men. 12 million recruitment posters were printed in one year. He understood that the only way to win was to turn a *political* conflict into a *national* conflict. There was no longer a fight because Serbia had killed the heir to the Habsburg throne, and the whole chain of events until the invasion of Belgium. They fought to defend civilisation against the barbarians: *The Great War for Civilisation.* And no man could have escaped the challenge. The villages were covered with posters inviting enlistment. Not only addressed to men, but also to wives and mothers, who should have pushed them to defend their country. Virility, guilt, fear. The most famous poster is undoubtedly the one depicting Kitchener himself, with his famous moustache, pointing his finger at the observer and urging him to enlist. In their own small way, the local newspapers also worked hard to contribute to the war effort, for example in September a newspaper in Leicestershire published a photo of a woman, Martha Ainsworth, who proudly smiles and holds a sign with a writing in her hand:

"Down with the Germans I've Got six sons Fighting 'em"

In the first weeks of the war, enlisting was almost like celebrating your birthday twice. Veteran soldiers were sent around the country to give speeches and encourage the population to join the Army, or to finance it with bonds. In front of the recruitment offices long queues of festive young men formed whilst the gang played patriotic hymns. The numbers touched the 20,000 volunteers a day. The 3rd of September 1914 was the day with the most volunteers throughout the war, 33 thousand new soldiers in one day.

By Christmas, a million Britons had already signed up. Women and children were greeting their loved ones at every station in the Kingdom, a woman in Scotland died under the train that took her husband to France because she could not separate from him.

Kitchener wanted an Army of men, in the true sense of the word, and it did not matter if he spent his free time knitting clothes or discussing wallpaper with his sister. The white male who had built a huge Empire was called to arms, and to do so he had to do two things:

"Refrain the woman and wine"

That was his main teaching. A morally educated Army. To counter the barbarians Germans. From that moment on the image of the German people became caricatured. The Kaiser, always recognisable with his handlebar moustache pointing upwards, was represented like a madman aiming to conquer the world. The Belgians, who had to undergo the German invasion, were in practice sanctified. Their small Army was defeated in a few days of combat and from that moment on a popular information campaign about the citizens of that country began. In Great Britain, newspapers told of children whose hands were cut off, women raped, nurses killed, families exterminated.

In all that hustle and bustle, there was also who, taking advantage of the war, made available to the country not life but the voice: it was the case of Horatio Bottomley[467] who began to travel the country and through the theatre urged everyone to enlist. It was a huge success. At each of his shows, there were men from the Army ready to enlist new entries. In a single show he managed to enlist a thousand men.

"You cannot naturalise an unnatural beast, a human abortion. But you can exterminate it. Germany should be wiped from the face of the map"

The population contributed as best as it could and the Government did its best to keep the morale of the population high, so appeared postcards and caricatures of the

---

[467] G. S. Messinger, *British Propaganda and the State in the First World War*, Manchester University Press, Manchester 1992; D. Monger, *Patriotism and Propaganda in First World War Britain*: Liverpool University Press, Liverpool 2012; Symons, Julian, *Horatio Bottomley*, Cresset Press, London 1955.

German rulers. The Kaiser was the favourite, never really loved by the people despite his relationship with the royal family, had been spared precisely because of the relationship, but now that the two countries were at war no newspaper had any problem mocking him anymore. There were also alarmist voices, according to some the Russians had sneaked into the country to help the British to get rid of a German Army in Charing Cross. The Russians were said to still have Siberian snow in their beards. No one had seen them personally, but they knew someone who knew someone who had seen them.

However, enlisting so many men had its disadvantages, the Army was not ready to welcome all those people. During the six weeks of training before leaving for the front, the men prepared themselves by wearing their clothes and hats. Most of the training was spent on parades and marches.

"We were play-acting, it required a lot of confidence to remember we were training to face the gigantic German war machine"

Said a volunteer in the fall of 1914.

Kitchener continued with his work. It was the Army that had to adapt to new needs and not the other way around. His new and perhaps the most dramatic idea helped to further increase the number of volunteers. Join forces with friends. The *Pals Battalion* were just that, battalions of men who came from the same city, or did the same job or were part of the same club. There were battalions of City brokers, artists, professors, railwaymen, miners, low and high Society members. Even sportsmen. And it was precisely with sportspeople that we had one of the most exciting stories about recruitment. It happened in Edinburgh. There a small Scottish team brought honour to the game of football, a game that had not yet had a strong hold in society as it is today, was called the sport of cowards. The *Heart of Midlothian Football Club* stadium is in Tynecastle. The team was about to become Scotland's champion but in November 1914 all the players enlisted. They had been persuaded after listening to the speech of their local MP, Sir George McCrae, who had also enlisted at the age of 54. He wanted the players to contribute to the war by enlisting their fans:

"In the presence of the god of battles ask your conscience – Dare I stand aside?"

That is what he wrote in the local paper.

On the 5th of December, shortly before the city's Derby against the *Hibernian,* he entered the playing field accompanied by a band and 800 volunteers. Including players. That day others joined the cause, the *16th Royal Scots,* also called *McCrae's Men,* was composed by 1100 volunteers. Almost no one came back. Death touched so deeply that small town in Scotland that the postman and the boy in the newspapers changed jobs because they were tired of the bad news that came every day.

As soon as the war broke out, the Germans who had moved to Great Britain immediately became the enemy from which to escape. The German governess might have been hiding bombs under her clothes, the German barber might have been cutting English throats and the German butcher might have been poisoning the meat he was selling. Every German was accused of the worst things and the fact that on the 14th of October a German named Karl Hans Lody was arrested when it was discovered that he was pretending to be an American tourist whilst drawing warships and docks in London. The story had a huge impact on public opinion. The first real German spy. He was sentenced to death in the Tower of London, after a trial, on the 6th of November. Throughout the war, 10 more spies were shot in British soil.

British public opinion did not know the impact of the war from the descriptions of the front, however, the first impact with the conflict occurred on the 16th of December 1914. On a cold, misty morning in Hartlepool. The Germans had begun to bomb Britain from their ships. Many houses were hit and destroyed. The terror spread everywhere, many escaped because they were convinced that the Germans were landing on the beach. It was the first foreign attack on British soil after the Battle of Hastings in 1066. Two other locations were bombed that day: Scarborough and Whitby. In all, 152 dead and 592 injured. 13 children of whom the youngest was only six months old. In Scarborough, the citizens barricaded the streets in the event of an invasion. *Remember Scarborough* became a known motto every time you had to do conscription propaganda.

Unfortunately, those were not the only attacks on British soil. In 1915 the English also had to worry about a new weapon from the sky: The Zeppelins. In all the attacks from the sky more than 500 people died from the bombs dropped.

The fear of an invasion was so high as soon as the war broke out that the first to defend themselves were the inhabitants of the southern coasts. The first trenches were not built in France or Belgium but in England. People began to dig into the white cliffs of Dover to defend themselves from an enemy they thought was at the gates.

"The enemy is almost in sight of our shores. There is a possibility of disaster"[468]

The largest Empire in history had turned into an island terrified of invasion.

The first British soldier to die was John Parr, a 17-year-old London caddy. He was in Le Mans and during a bicycle reconnaissance where he ended up in an ambush on the 21st of August.

3. Indian Numbers

From the very beginning the British understood that this one would be a completely different war from all those fought up to that moment. And this idea was confirmed after the stalemate that was created after the first days of rapid battles and German

---

[468] Sir Arthur Conan Doyle

victories. Like other times Britain looked to its own Empire to buy up men, especially towards what in the past had been called the Empire's barracks, India.

During the July crisis in India no one would have expected to leave to fight, it was widespread belief that in case of war only the few lucky Indian soldiers stationed in Britain could take part in the conflict, the system of alliances and modern weapons would last no longer than a few weeks, the war would be making obsolete the use of imperial troops.

During the opening of the *Legislative Council* session on 8th of August 1914 the Viceroy, Lord Hardinge read a long telegram from the Re-Emperor, George V:

"During the past few weeks the people of my whole Empire at home and overseas have moved with one mind and purpose to confront and overthrow an unparalleled assault upon the continuity, civilisation and peace of mankind.

The calamitous conflict is not of my seeking. My voice has been cast throughout on the side of peace. My Ministers earnestly strove to allay the causes of strife and to appease differences with which my Empire was not concerned. Had I stood aside when, in defiance of pledges to which my Kingdom was a party, the soil of Belgium was violated and her cities laid desolate, when the very life of the French nation was threatened with extinction, I should have sacrificed my honour and given to destruction the liberties of my Empire and of mankind. I rejoice that every part of Empire is with me in this decision.

Paramount regard for treaty faith and pledged word of Rulers and peoples is the common heritage of England and India.

Amongst the many incidents that have marked the unanimous uprising of the populations of my Empire in defence of its unity and integrity, nothing has moved me more than the passionate devotion to my Throne expressed both by my Indian subjects and by Feudatory Princes and Ruling Chiefs of India and their prodigal offers of their lives and their resources in the cause of the realm. Their one-voiced

469

demand to be foremost in conflict has touched my heart and has inspired to highest issues the love and devotion which, as I well know, have ever linked my Indian subjects and myself. I recall to mind India's gracious message to the British nation of good-will and fellowship which greeted my return in February 1912, after the solemn ceremony of my Coronation Durbar at Delhi, and I find in this hour of trial a full harvest and a noble fulfilment of the assurance given by you that the destinies of Great Britain and India are indissolubly linked.

On the same day, Mr Sir Gangadhara Chtnavis proposed a resolution, which was voted on unanimously:

"That in view of the great war involving most momentous issues now in progress in Europe, into which our August Sovereign has been forced to enter by obligations of honour and duty to preserve the neutrality guaranteed by treaty and the liberties of a friendly State, the Members of this Council as voicing the feeling that animates the whole of people of India, desire to give expression to their feelings of unswerving loyalty and enthusiastic devotion to their King-Emperor, and an assurance of their unflinching support to the British Government.

They desire at the same time to express the opinion that the people of India, in addition to the military assistance now being afforded by India to the Empire, would wish to share in the heavy financial burden now imposed by the War on the United Kingdom, and request the Government of India to take this view into consideration and thus to demonstrate the unity of India with the Empire.

They request His Excellency the President to be so good as to convey the substance of this Resolution to His Majesty the King-Emperor and His Majesty's Government."

Compared to all the Empires involved in the conflict, only three had overseas colonies from which to get soldiers: Britain, Germany and France. India was amongst the colonies that sent the highest number of soldiers to the front. Precise numbers are difficult to calculate, according to the *Statistics of the Military Effort of the British Empire during the Great War, 1914-1920* published by *His Majesty's Stationary Office* in March 1922 by the 31st of December 1919 the total number was 1,440,337 soldiers. Of which 877,068 thousand fighters, 563,369 thousand non-combatants and 239,561 thousand already enrolled at the time of the declaration of war. Numbers that differ from the official report produced by the Government of India in 1923. According to *The India's contribution to the Great War,* there were 826,855,000 fighters and 445,582,000 non-combatants. It must be said, however, that the Indian calculation stops in November 1918. In the Indian volume we find a very interesting fact, India has never imposed the compulsory conscription because it could count on many volunteers every year. In the table in Appendix C we find that year after year the number grew instead of decreasing as in Great Britain, where from 1916 it was introduced the compulsory conscription due to the shortage of men. By the 31st of July 1915 the men recruited were 78,232 thousand. By the 31st off July 1916, the figure had risen to 110,315. In 1917 128,509. By the 31st of July 1918 the number of units reached 292,174 and in the last 4 months of the war there were more men than in the whole year from July 1916 to July 1917 or 130,708. In all, 739,938 thousand men recruited for the war. The table is divided by castes and this allows us to understand the castes that offered more men. At the top we find the Muslims of Punjab with 136,126 thousand men, followed by the Sikhs with 88,925 thousand. In another table we find the number of recruits divided by province. 683,149 thousand fighters and 414,493 thousand non-combatants. All the men of Punjab exceeded the total number of non-combatants of all India, 446,976 thousand. In addition to this number, 1,097,642, there were 58,904 men from Nepal and 115,891,000 men recruited from amongst the Indian states under direct control of the Government of India. Divided between 88,958 fighters and 26,933 non-combatants. A total of 1,272,437 men sent to war.

According to London's calculation, the total number was 1,440,437 men enlisted. Almost all of them were sent to different battlefields around the globe. In defence of India remained 344,424 thousand soldiers. Contrary to popular belief, the largest number of Indian troops were not sent to Europe but to Mesopotamia. The number of soldiers who fought in the Flanders was 138,608 thousand and that in the Middle East 675,391 thousand. 143,993 thousand sent to Egypt, 49,198 thousand to the Persian Gulf, 47,704 thousand to Africa, 26,205 thousand to Aden, 9,931 thousand to Salonica, 4,950 thousand to Gallipoli, and 33 to Palestine. A total of 1,096,013 thousand units. A total of 242,607,000 British soldiers recruited from India were also sent to the same locations. A total of 1,338,620 men.

Also, according to the British Bureau of Statistics the number of Indian soldiers who died in battle or because of wounds is 53.486 thousand. Those injured were 64,350. The missing 3,037. Those taken prisoner 302 and the alleged prisoner 523. In total 121,698 thousand. In fact, given the large numbers of the conflict, the percentage of Indians killed or injured is much lower than the average, but it is also true that their stay in the battlefields that caused more deaths on both sides, i.e. Flanders. However, nothing detracts from their usefulness for the final victory.

At the outbreak of the war the Indian population answered, as we have seen from the numbers of volunteers enrolled, with great enthusiasm. The newspapers spent their time describing the feeling of patriotism that had spread throughout the subcontinent. For *the Bengal:*

"Behind the serried ranks of one of the finest armies in the world, there stand the multitudinous people of India, ready to cooperate with the Government in the defence of the Empire, which for them means, in its ultimate evolution, the complete recognition of their right as citizens of the freest state in the world. We may have our differences with the Government – and what people have not? – but in the presence of the common enemy, be it Germany of any other power, we sink our differences, we forget our little quarrels and close our ranks and offer all that we possess in defence of the Great Empire, to which we are all so proud to belong and with which the future prosperity and advancement of our people are bound up"

The *Indian Patrol:*

"A united people three hundred millions mere standing behind the Government, imparts a moral stimulus and sense of strength which no enemy, however powerful can disregard"

For the *Beharee:*

"India's fortunes are indissolubly linked up with those of England. As Lord Curzon rightly said, India cannot do without England and England would be impotent without India. It is not implied that mother country has not enough men to fight the battles of that it cannot un-aided crush Germany. But the Indians and the Europeans in this country owe it to themselves to don the armour in defence of the Empire, to defend India and if need be, to go to any other part of the world at the call of the Motherland"

For *the Advocate:*

"Now that England is at war with foreign enemy she may absolutely depend upon the loyalty of the people of this country. They may have their grievances, they have their differences with the Government, but they are firmly attached to the British rule, they are fully prepared at the crisis to place their resources at the disposal of the authorities in the defence of their country"

The Gujrati reported that all the great religions of the country were praying for victory.

The Herald reiterated that the British would never be alone in the war against their enemies.

For the *Jam-e-Jamshad:*

"This is the time when India should feel it to be her duty to show to the world to England's foes and allies alike – how greatly she is attached to her, how staunch and resolute in her devotion to her interests, how ready and willing she is to make any sacrifice she can in men and treasure, for the defence of her possessions and the assertion of her honour and dignity"

473

Public opinion was very impressed by the declaration of war of Great Britain, the gesture was a defence of the honour of the Empire. In a letter to the Indian public dated 12th of August 1914, Dadabhai Naoroji, first Asian to sit in the *House of Commons* wrote:

"Fighting as the British people are at present in a righteous cause, to the good and glory of human dignity and civilisation, and moreover, being the beneficent instrument of our own progress and civilisation, our duty is clear – to do everyone our best to support the British fight with our life and property"

The list could continue in pages and pages, it seems that the only thing that united the country in those days was the support for the war.

At the time of the declaration of war India was able to immediately provide two infantry divisions and one cavalry division that were sent to Europe. The Viceroy also ordered the mobilisation of three divisions at the Afghan border. In September a mixed division was sent to Africa. In October the Indian Government sent two infantry divisions and a cavalry brigade and a regiment to Egypt to help whilst the Japanese, with Indians, fought against the Germans in Asia. In November a division was sent to Turkey to fight against the Ottomans.

4. Les Hindoues[469]

Khudadad Khan was born in the village of Dab in the District of Jhelum, in the Province of Punjab, today in Pakistan, on the 20th of October 1888. We know practically nothing about him and the pre-war period. We only know that his family had moved from the Afghan Frontier to Punjab.

When the war broke out, he was almost 26 years old. He enlisted in the 129th Duke of Connaught's Own Baluchi's. He was part of the *I Indian Corps*, i.e. the Army corps formed immediately after the outbreak of the war and sent to France to help the *British Expeditionary Force* also called BEF. During the conflict, India sent a total of seven expeditionary corps to the British for help. The first, *Indian Expeditionary Force A*, under the command of Sir James Willcocks consisted of four divisions organised into an infantry corps and a cavalry corp. The infantry corps consisted of the 3rd Lahore Division and the 7th Meerut Division. In France they were simply called Lahore and Meerut to distinguish them from the 3rd and 7th English divisions.

---

[469] G. Corrigan, *Sepoy in the trenches, The Indian corps on the western front 1914 – 1915*, Spellmount, Stonehouse 2006; Das, Santanu, *Race, Empire and first world war*, Cambridge university press, Cambridge 2013; Anand, Mulk Raj, *Across the black waters*, orient paperbacks, Delhi, 2008; Omissi, David, *Indian voices of the great War*, Palgrave MacMillan, London 1999; Pati, Budheswar, *India and the First World War*, Atlantic publishers and distributors, Delhi 1996.

The first Indian expeditionary corps arrived on the continent on the 26th of September from Bombay, in the port of Marseille, after a journey full of vicissitudes. The transport ships were very slow and in addition they had to avoid the two German battle ships, the *Emder* on patrol in the Indian Ocean and the *Konigsberg* on the Red Sea.

From Marseille they went to Orleans, where a sorting centre had been set up and where they were armed with modern Lee Enfield rifles and from there, still by train or on trucks bought locally, they moved to St. Omes. A small town on the outskirts of a Belgian city that from total anonymity became sadly known Ypres.

On the night of the 18th of October 1914, French trams and machinists saw for the first-time non-European soldiers on French territory. At first glance they looked like the many infantrymen of the French colonies who were soon to invade the continent, perhaps Moroccans or Berbers, but a closer look would have revealed their nationality. Some wore a turban on their heads, however, different from those used in the Arab world, almost all had a thick and well-tended beard, but others were shaved, had almond-shaped eyes and strange floppy headgear in the head and especially no one spoke French but rather soldiers and officers spoke a fluent English that would have put in trouble even the most scholar citizen of Calais, Rouen or Paris. "*Les Hindoues*" were the Indians from the eastern colonies of the British Empire.

Khan was a *Sepoy* to the British. The word comes from the Persian *sipahi* meaning soldier. It is an anglicisation of the term and indicates the Indian infantryman in the service of the British Army. *Sepoy* for the Indians, *Tommy* for the British.

The figure of the *Sepoy* is very complex and, in some ways, difficult to investigate. It was not an *Indian* category, but a term created to identify soldiers. For a long time, these fighters of the Great War have been forgotten by historiography, only in recent years has the analysis of letters and diaries allowed to insert them in the place that history has reserved for them.

The *Sepoy* was the Indian soldier, but it is difficult even to define what it means and meant by Indian. If for the British every citizen living in the Raj was Indian, it was not so for those directly involved. Most of the soldiers came from the North, especially from Punjab. The others were divided between the North-West Frontier Provinces, the United Provinces and Nepal. Compared to some *races,* the population of Punjab did not divide by ethnic base but by religious base, especially Muslims and Hindus. This led to a complex fragmentation underneath the *Sepoy*'s label.

The British and Indians had already fought side by side, the imperial history was full of military campaigns. But for the high number of men who fought and for the long duration of the war this was the first-time ever that the European population came into contact, at home, with the lower class from India. Those few Indians who lived in Europe at that time were either rich heirs at universities or servants or workers of the British Merchant Navy.

For the modern historian to reconstruct the life of some of those soldiers or to recreate the structure in which they found themselves living during the war period is quite complicated, the Indian soldiers for the most part were semi-illiterate or illiterate and this from a literary point of view is a tragedy. European citizens have filled pages and pages with memories of their experiences in war, Indians did not, or rather not so widely. Moreover, despite the existence of a corpus of letters, most of them were written by scribes who zigzagged between the poles of censorship and for that time hidden meanings metaphors were easy to understand today can make the text difficult to understand, preventing those who read them from really understanding their meaning.

However, the figure of the *Sepoy* remained etched in the memory of the conflict. The first period of war was tragic, the soldiers were trained to defend the borders and not to attack the well-equipped German troops, since it was the British who had declared war the burden of the attack lay with them. Moreover, the climate did not contribute to the soldiers' mood. They were badly dressed and badly equipped. The Indians, however, were able to adapt easily and showed great courage. Some racist ideas also went around, the Indian soldier, especially the Sikh, were a bloodthirsty warrior ready for anything and that was an advantage but there was always a certain streak of fear. Almost always the representation that was given was as far away from reality as you could think. This is the case, for example, with the illustrations and captions that appeared on *The War Illustrated*. In the number of the 7th November 1914. We find the image of a Gurkha intent on catching the surprise of a German soldier, recognisable by the *Pickelhaube*, the characteristic Prussian nailed helmet:

"The fighting qualities of the Gurkhas, the little hillmen from Northern India who form one of the most efficient sections of the Indian Army, are well-known. In addition to a rifle, the Gurkha carries a keen knife with a broad fish shaped blade. The knife he can throw for some distance with deadly accuracy, or he can use it at close quarters with terrible effect. With a cat-like noiselessness the Gurkha, knife in hand of in teeth, can glide through the grass until he is close to isolated outpost, as seen in the picture, and then comes the fatal throw or the fatal spring and slash that invariably adds one to the enemy's mortality list"

The Indian soldiers originally had to go to Egypt in this way the British troops in that country would be moved to France. Almost at the last minute they were transferred to the Flanders. Their time in Europe is also marked by the fact that they fought some of the bloodiest battles of the conflict. As soon as they arrived, they took part in the clash at La Bassée between October and November 1914. Immediately after the Division Meerut was used as an assault troop during the battle of Neuve Chapelle.

Often Indian soldiers were sent to the riskiest areas, and this is also reflected in the letters of the survivors. One of the cases, for example, is the defence of two ports, Boulogne in France and Nieuwpoort in Belgium. The Germans wanted to win them over to cut off the BEF's supply lines.

On 31st of October, during a heated attack by the Germans at the village of Hollenbeck, near Ypres, Khudadad Khan, despite his wounds, was able to stand up to the German advance in the front line. The English trenches were very bad built, too low, full of water and mud and without the defence of barbed wire. Moreover, the German artillery was superior and not only the English were outnumbered, for each imperial soldier there were five Germans. Khan's Division had not been equipped with grenades and hand grenades and he improvised using explosives and jars of jam. Together with six other machine guns he continued to shoot covering the retreat of their comrades. All night long, he never stopped shooting. The next morning, he was the only one left alive. The Germans took the trench and he ended up pretending to be dead, he then later dragged on to the second line where he reunited with his companions.

Thanks to this incredible test of courage Khudadad Khan allowed the British to regain their position and defend the two ports. He was the first non-British to be awarded the *Victoria Cross*, the highest military recognition of the Empire. He was awarded the medals by the King himself three months later at Buckingham Palace.

"His Majesty the KING-EMPEROR has been graciously pleased to approve of the grant of the Victoria Cross to the undermentioned soldier of the Indian Army for conspicuous bravery whilst serving with the Indian Army Corps, British Expeditionary Force: —

4050, Sepoy Khudadad, 129th Duke of Connaught's Own Baluchis.

On 31st October 1914, at Hollebeke, Belgium, the British Officer in charge of the detachment having been wounded, and the other gun put out of action by a shell,

Sepoy Khudadad, though himself wounded, remained working his gun until all the other five men of the gun detachment had been killed."[470]

Khan died in Pakistan in 1972 and still today, in his birthplace, is on display the medal he won in that battlefield.

5. Doctor Brighton

As in any Army during the conflict, the number of deaths and injuries was very high. But there is a separate speech to be made about the Indians. Although some thought that it was not appropriate to use imperial troops in France shortly after their arrival, the thousands and thousands of *Sepoys* had proved more than useful to the cause of war. For this reason, and in a sense to thank them, the wounded Indians were sent to England and received in a very special hospital.

The *Royal Pavilion* is a building in the centre of Brighton. The palace was built in 1787 for the future George IV. He found the city quiet and informal and had a first building built, called *Marine Pavilion* for his visits. In 1802 he wanted the whole building to be rebuilt in an oriental style. He was fascinated by the Orient and had recreated his idea of the Orient in Brighton, a cornucopia of styles and an abundance of decorations that had little to do with Asia. The interiors are mainly in Chinese style whilst the exterior has a characteristic shape that recalls Indian architecture. The villa underwent expansion work until in 1850 Queen Victoria decided to sell the building to the city of Brighton, she found the city too noisy and because his large family she had no space inside the building that despite the pomp and circumstance has a small size.

---

[470] London Gazette, 7th of December 1914

From December 1914 to January 1916 the building was used as a hospital for the wounded Indians. The basic idea was to make them feel at home, the city of Brighton and the Army were convinced that staying in a building that tried to recreate the architecture of their country could help to improve not only their physical condition but also psychological. The fact that that style was purely invented and that it had nothing oriental was never considered. The *Dome,* a gigantic dome adjacent to the palace, was converted into a dormitory and equipped with an operating room. As well as the fine rooms of the royal family. Many patients also found accommodation at the city's *workhouse* known as *Kitchener Indian Hospital* and at two schools, *York Place* and *Pelham Street.*

In December, the first patients arrived in Brighton from Belgium on a hospital train. On the *Brighton Gazette* they talked about the event with these curious words:

"It is one thing to contemplate the strangeness of it, and wonder at the greatest of British pleasure towns being made the centre of the greatest hospital system in the Kingdom"

Much attention has been being paid to the issue of castes and religions. From food to bathrooms, everything was separated and regulated according to the needs of each patient. Nine different kitchens prepare meals according to the rules of the various religions. The killing and storage of meat also followed rules divided by caste. Newspapers and hospital news were printed in Urdu, Hindi and Gurmukhi. Separate areas were used for various religious cults and, as far as possible, doctors and nurses were medical students in England who were also Indian and were also divided by castes.

For the seriously injured who died during their stay in Brighton, a special site on the hills outside Brighton near Patcham, called *Chattri,* was prepared. There was built a *ghat*, an altar for cremations. The dead soldiers Hindu and Sikh were cremated there, and the ashes were dispersed into the sea. After the war, a building was built on the exact spot where the soldiers had been cremated. The building was designed and

481

built by E. C. Henriques, a young Hindu who studied architecture in London. In Hindi *Chattri* means umbrella, the building has this name because it has the shape of a stone umbrella supported by six columns. In 1921 the Prince of Wales visited the site and dedicated it to all the dead Indians in Brighton:

"To the memory of all the Indian soldiers who gave their lives in the service of their King-Emperor this monument erected on the site where the Hindu and Sikhs who died in hospital in Brighton passed through the fire is in grateful and brotherly affection dedicated"

The Muslims who died there were taken to the nearby Shah Jehan Mosque in Woking and were buried according to the traditions of their religion and with military honours in the new cemetery prepared for the occasion at Horsell Common near the Mosque. The ancient Brookwood Cemetery was also used. The Horsell Common cemetery was later decorated by the India Office with Islamic-style walls and entrance.

In 1921 the Maharaja of Patiala donated to the city a building outside the *Pavilion* a stone door designed by Thomas Tyrwhitt with a style that recalls the buildings of the sixteenth century in Ahmadabad the main city of Gujarat. In his inauguration speech on the 26th of October he said:

"Brighton's fame as a healer was talked of in many hundreds of remote Indian villages"

There is a dedication on either side of the gate:

"This gateway is the gift of India in commemoration of her sons who, stricken in the Great War, were tended in the Pavilion in 1914 and 195. Dedicated to the use of the inhabitants of Brighton. B. N. Southall, Mayor.

In 1915, both Lord Kitchener and George V visited Brighton Hospital. In a vintage film we can see the King who awards the soldiers with some medals, including a *Victoria Cross* to Jemadar Mir Dast.

482

Not only was everything done for respect for the Indians, but the hospital also became an excellent way of doing propaganda. The British never denied the Indians' belief that the King had allowed them to stay in his palace, the building, the only case in the United Kingdom, had belonged to the city for more than 60 years. A typical paradox of that period is represented by two facts: if on one hand there was the case in which it was the whites who looked after and treated the Indians, on the other hand patients were forbidden to come into contact with the citizens of the city so much so that the entire building was surrounded by barbed wire, main explanation of course was that in this way the civilians could avoid diseases and infections and the sight of injured soldiers.

At the end of 1915 the infantry divisions arrived from India were sent to Mesopotamia, in France only the cavalry remained. The hospital closed its doors to reopen shortly after, but this time for British soldiers.

The Indian soldiers who were treated in Brighton kept forever a good memory of the city, so that from that moment the city was called *Doctor Brighton*[471].

6. Mud and Sand

The *Indian Expeditionary Force B* was formed after requests from Egypt for help in connection with an attack on German territories, in East Africa. The new forces were sent to Tanganyika. In the Battle of Tanga, the Anglo-Indian forces suffered heavy losses despite outnumbering the Germans.

---

[471] J. Collins, *Dr. Brighton's Indian Patients December 1914-January 1916*, Paperback, Brighton 2006.

The *Indian Expeditionary Force* C was established to defend the lines of communication in Africa, especially the Ugandan railway. The only real clash with the Germans was during the Battle of Kilimanjaro. The Germans, even though they were in clear numerical inferiority, were able to stand up to the Indian soldiers.

Towards the end of 1915 the British High Command decided to move the Indian infantry divisions to Mesopotamia. The climate, more like the Indian one, could have contributed to a better performance. Not to mention that even that front was becoming quite complicated, the Ottoman Empire was an ally of Germany and Britain could not risk losing the precious oil wells of the Persian Gulf and the connections with the Suez Canal. In France only the divisions of cavalry remained. The latter find themselves fighting the bloodiest battle of the whole conflict: The Battle of the Somme. The offensive of the Somme began on the 1st of July 1916, according to Anglo-French plans it should have produced a breakthrough in the German lines, and, after an infantry attack, it would have allowed the advance of the cavalry. The front was about 60 kilometres long, from Lassigny to Hebuterne. The Somme River cut these territories in two. The Battle of the Somme was for the British Army of the First World War what Dunkirk was for the Second, a defeat without justification. The offensive was strongly desired by the French who aimed to lighten the German pressure on Verdun, the British wanted to plan everything and in so doing did nothing but demonstrate their complete inability.

For a week, the British bombed German positions day and night, convinced that they would annihilate them. Tens of thousands of men were piled up in the backlines. At 7 am. on the 1st of July the attack began. 250,000 grenades were launched in an hour. About 3500 a minute. At 7:28 am. the English detonated the mine called Lochnagar under the ridge of Hawthorn. The crater, still existing today, has become a symbol of the carnage of those days. At 7:30, nine more mines were detonated. The miners, almost all Welsh, of the 179th Tunnelling companies of the Royal Engineers had been digging for days under enemy lines. The blast was so strong that the glass trembled in Downing Street. It was the most powerful explosion in history until the advent of the atomic bomb.

British officers said for days that the men could walk quietly, smoking cigars up to the German trenches, in fact when the infantry began to advance along the 40 kilometres of frontline, they exposed themselves in a ridiculous way to German machine guns, their shelters were well built and very deep and in reality, all the bombing had done nothing but raise a fuss. For days they had been taking refuge underground waiting for it to be over. In a single day of battle the British lost 19,240 soldiers, there were 35,493 wounded, 2,152 missing and 585 prisoners for a total of 57,470 losses in a single day. The offensive lasted until November and in fact resolved nothing. The German troops went back a few kilometres but as often happens all the land gained was lost and regained continuously.

During the Battle of the Somme a film was shot, *The Battle of Somme*[472], which was screened for the first-time on the 21st of August 1916 when in fact the battle was still going on. Many of the parts of what we can call the first documentary film are real footage of the conflict. Which makes it an excellent historical source. In 1914 in Great Britain there were 4500 cinemas, a law of 1909 had ordered that real buildings be built to replace the tents provisionally set up almost everywhere. The country was not new to the shooting of war, the film on the Somme, however, was a watershed because never the cameramen ran the risk of being killed during the shooting, Geoffrey Malins, who described his adventure in *How I filmed the War*, was even awarded a medal of value for his behaviour in the trenches. The film mixes real and

_____

[472] Beckett, Ian F.W., World War I, 12 points of view. Einaudi, Turin, 2013. p. 82 - 101.

reconstructed scenes to satisfy the taste of the viewer at home. Most probably the most famous image of the First World War, recorded in every documentary, the one in which you see soldiers coming out of a trench and running towards the enemy, two of them fall and one slips at the bottom of the trench. It is a typical representation of what a trench attack could be, but it happens to be a whole staging. The reality according to the shooting point would have been impossible for an operator to stand still with his tripod and film the scene without being killed, but that was what people wanted to see, the value of the British soldier against the enemy. The impact of the film on the population was enormous. The propaganda purpose was fully achieved, the nation understood how they were fighting, and this was a great way to make them stop asking why they did it.

The *Indian Expeditionary Force D* was the largest armed force to fight outside of India. It was made up of soldiers who came from India and belonged to the 6th Poona Division. Their main task, since November 1914 when they arrived, was to defend oil wells outside Basra. The Indian forces were part of the wider Mesopotamian Campaign. Until November 1915 the Army corps obtained several victories against the Ottoman troops, the first defeat was with the Battle of Ctesiphon. After the battle, General Townshend decided to retire to Kut. Shortly after their arrival the Ottomans laid siege to the city. After 147 days of siege, the British surrendered to the Ottomans. Seventy per cent of the British forces and 50 per cent of the Indian forces died of illness or treatment during their imprisonment. At that time, the British held secret negotiations with the Ottomans, for a long time, to free the besieged garrison. These agreements were also held amongst other things by T. E. Lawrence better known as Lawrence of Arabia, the spy archaeologist, that led the revolt of the Arab tribes against the Ottoman Empire, giving the Middle East to Britain. Lawrence, and his colleague Gertrude Bell were the architects of the division into states of the region. A division that still today is the cause of bloody conflicts. The figures of Lawrence and Bell are very complex and would require a separate in-depth study. Since this is not the best place to discuss their personalities and the future implications of their political and diplomatic choices, I refer the reader to the vast literature produced on the two.

The *Indian Expeditionary Force E* was entirely composed of cavalry. The 4th and 5th Division of Cavalry, which was transferred from France to Palestine in early 1918. They joined the three regiments of lancers from Mysore, Hyderabad and Jodhpur, which made up the 15th (Imperial Service) Cavalry Brigade. After the battle of Megiddo, the remaining two divisions, Lahore and Meerut, of infantry that had fought in France and Mesopotamia, joined in.

The *Indian Expeditionary Force F* was an Army corps formed in 1914 with the main purpose of defending the Suez Canal in Egypt. It consisted of the 10th and 11th Indian divisions. The Expeditionary Force also gathered other pieces from divisions such as the 22nd Infantry Brigade of the 8th Lucknow Division and a brigade service of knights. In 1916 the 10th Division was dissolved, and its brigades were scattered inside others, especially they went to supply men to those Army corps who suffered heavy losses, especially the IEF A. The year before the 11th Division had suffered the same fate, most of the brigades ended up in Persia.

The last Indian Army corps was the *Indian Expeditionary Force G.* which was sent to Gallipoli in April 1915. It was also composed of a brigade that was previously part of the 10th Division based in Suez. It was also composed of three Gurkha battalions and one Sikh battalion. After the failed British attempts to take Gallipoli, which cost Churchill the Admiralty's Lord's seat the men were sent to Egypt.

Here it is useful to remember three other battlefields that have seen the use of Indian troops. The first is the 1915 Singapore Mutiny. The garrison in defence of the city was to be transferred to Hong Kong but amongst the *Sepoys* rumours were spread that they would go to the Middle East to fight against *their* Muslim *brothers*. For five days the mutineers wandered around the city killing Europeans and releasing prisoners. Only after an attack, from troops disembarked from ships in port, did the city come under control again.

The other moment is the Siege of Tsingtao, a German port in China. The allies in Europe were concerned about Japanese interests in that region of China and sent a small contingent of 1500 men to help but above all to control the Japanese.

In 1918 a small group of soldiers was used during the Mallesons Mission. It was an aid to the socialist Mensheviks fighting against the Soviet Bolsheviks.

As we could see, even without going into the truce details of the battles, the use of imperial troops was virtually essential to the final victory. Not only the Indians but practically every *Dominion* sent troops in support of the Motherland, especially the white settlers even if, especially for a numerical issue, the largest contingent, as already seen, came from India.

Canada had sent 458,000 soldiers, 60,000 found death and 170,000 returned home injured. The independent *Dominion* of Newfoundland alone prepared a regiment of 790 men that was destroyed during the first day of the Somme. New Zealand could send as many as 112,000 soldiers, a tenth of its population. 40% of men between the ages of 25 and 40. In 1914 Australia had a population of 4 million citizens and when the war broke out it sent 332,000 men to Europe. Almost half the men who can be recruited. 167,000 returned wounded and 60,000 never returned. Australia had the highest mortality rate of all countries in the Empire, 65%. South Africa provided 136,000 men who were used mainly in Africa against the German colonies. The black South Africans could not enlist but 40 thousand of them were exploited as a workforce. The White *Dominions* put over a million men on the ground. Almost the same amount as India. They went to swell the ranks of the six million enlisted in Great Britain and Ireland. *Dominion* and Motherland used the same percentages of enlisted and fallen, respectively 53% and 12%.

In both cases, Governments initially turned to volunteers. Temporarily set aside the mandatory conscription. However, when the first reports began to arrive, and the first wounded and dead, the number of volunteers fell, causing concern to all Governments. In Canada, for example, there was an ethnic problem because the

French part of the country was not very keen on fighting for Britain. Compulsory military service in Canada was only promulgated in August 1917 after several false steps. The same goes for Australia. After the first moment of enthusiasm the number of volunteers collapsed after the disasters of the Somme and Gallipoli. William Morris Hughes, the Prime Minister, wanted the compulsory conscription but trade unions and his Labour Party were against it. The Irish in Australia were also against it because of the English treatment of Ireland. In 1916, a referendum was held against the military. In 1917 another referendum wanted by Hughes failed, as the previous one. Australia, therefore, together with India, which was not a *Dominion*, were the only countries in the Empire that did not impose the conscription. New Zealand had introduced compulsory conscription in 1916, but Maori were also accepted.

At first, the armies did not *work* independently but were placed within the British Army and were commanded by British officers. During the war, however, things changed, allowing the Army to assume an image of a national representative point, creating a kind of myth on which to base itself.

Having given so many men to a war unleashed by Great Britain gave rise in every *Dominion* to a desire for more autonomy, many imperialists had already foreseen the *danger* and were opposed to the use of imperial troops. Others saw the use of those soldiers as the only way to keep the British status quo alive. Amongst them was Lloyd George, Chancellor of the Exchequer, then Minister of Supply and then since 1916 Prime Minister. After his arrival in Downing Street, in the middle of the war, he prepared several commissions between Prime Ministers of the colonies to discuss the conditions of war and the needs of each *Dominion*. The *Dominions* then asked to transform the Empire into a sort of federation of autonomous states: *"Autonomous nations of an Imperial Commonwealth",* which meant above all autonomy in foreign policy, until then managed by London. As the war went on, the parliament could no longer ignore the issue and in 1917 an *"adequate voice in foreign policy"* was recognised, which allowed the various *Dominions to* sit at the table of the winners in Paris, each with its own delegation.

The matter for India is more complex, even though the Great War is not as heartfelt as in other countries it represented an important step towards autonomy. If for the other countries the autonomy of the *Dominions* was the starting point for greater freedom for India at that stage was the main aim. The Hindus of the National Congress and the Muslim League asked for a *Home Rule* for their country. On the 29th December 1916 they signed what was later called the Lucknow Pact. The pact provided for a series of demands to be made together with the British Government, first self-Government and, amongst other things, the majority within the representative bodies had to become Indian. With the revolution in Russia and the complicated situation during the conflict, the London Government had to move to more open positions. On the 20th of August 1917, Edwin Montagu, Minister for India, during a session at the *House of Commons,* made a vague opening towards the Indian demands: an autonomous Government and administration. In 1919, part of the administration passed under Indian control. However, India could not enjoy the privilege granted to the other countries of the Empire to have its own delegation in Paris.

7. The Kaiser conspiracies[473]

At this point, before heading towards conclusion, it is right to dwell a moment on two events that if they were not inside the period in which they happened it would certainly have a comic aspect, not so much for the basic idea but for how it was set in motion. These are two plots designed to overthrow the British Government in India.

The first of these conspiracies was the one later named *Hindu-German Conspiracy*.

This plan provided for the overthrow of the British Government in India through a mutiny of troops.

Nationalism was a growing phenomenon in India. The National Congress was founded to control this phenomenon but soon became a place that spread those ideas. Around 1890 the first clandestine and violents began to appear, especially in Bengal and Punjab. In 1905 Lord Curzon's decision to split Bengal in two, with a Muslim majority and a Hindu majority, caused an earthquake in Indian politics. It was interpreted yet another case of British *divide and rule* policy. This gave the impetus to the two movements to start working together towards a common goal. When the two regions were reunited in 1911, trying to appease those anti-imperial feelings, the damage was already done. During those years there had been several subversive acts such as the murder or attempted murder of prominent figures of the administration

---

[473] Stewart, Jules, The Kaiser's mission to Kabul, I.B. Tauris, London 2014; D. K. Dignan, *The Hindu Conspiracy in Anglo-American relations during the World War I*, University of Queensland; J. M. Jensen, *Hindu Conspiracy: A reassessment*, Pacific Historical Review, Vol 48. N° 1. 1979. p. 65-83; G. T. Brown, *The Hindu Conspiracy, 1914 – 1917*, University of California.

including the Viceroy Hardinge in 1912. The first mention of an armed plot appeared in the *Report on Revolutionary Organisation*. In which there was talk of support from the German Crown Prince visiting Calcutta in 1912. Support to be translated into weapons and ammunition.

The *India House* founded in London by Shyamji Krishna Varma on paper was only a meeting place for students but, it was a place to exchange revolutionary ideas. The organisation was involved in the murder of Secretary of State for India's aide, Sir WH Curzon Wyllie. Scotland Yard immediately shut down the place, revolutionaries fled to Germany or America.

In America the movement grew and made strong friendships with the Irish. America was an easier place for anti-British sentiment to proliferate.

In 1913 the Pacific Coast Hindustan Association was founded under the leadership of Har Dayal. It later became the Ghadar movement. His stated objective was to overthrow the British Government in India with an armed revolution. To achieve this goal, they wanted to bring the Indian soldiers to their cause, so they began to print a newspaper: *Hindustan Ghadar* of nationalist and revolutionary imprint. After the discovery of contacts in India and the distribution of copies of the newspaper, the British put pressure on the American State Department to suppress the headquarters of the movement in San Francisco. At the beginning of 1914 Har Dayal was arrested and expelled from the country. He took refuge in Switzerland. When the war broke out, he saw the conflict as a perfect time to start the revolution. At the same time, an Indian Independence Committee was established in Berlin under the control of Alfred Zimmermann, the German Secretary for Foreign Affairs. The committee gathered evidences from everywhere, especially former frequenters of the *India House*. The building that housed the committee was granted the status of an embassy. After the war the German Chancellor was convinced of the usefulness of an uprising in India. According to German plans an uprising in the subcontinent would have forced the British to move their few available men to India to quell the uprising thus allowing Germany to annihilate France and Russia. Har Dayal had left his role as leader of Ghadar to Ram Chandra, who was contacted by officials of the German Embassy in the United States whilst Zimmermann's envoys reached Dayal in Switzerland and convinced him that an armed revolt in India was feasible at that time.

In October 1914 several members of the Ghadar party began to return to India ready to organise a revolt. The fact that a large part of the Army was at the front was an advantage because the country was defended by very few men and if the plan was successful, within the armed forces, expelling the British would have been much easier. Even though the British had intercepted some revolutionaries in the various steamships bound for the ports of India, many managed to arrive and began to forge relations with members of the Army. This is the case of *Korea*, for example, a ship that sailed from San Francisco with a large part of the American part of the party. The Germans even assured that the military ships would not open fire on the steamship. When they arrived in Calcutta, however, they were immediately arrested.

The movement managed to make proselytes easily, difficult was getting weapons, ammunition and money.

First, they tried to deal with the Chinese for the purchase of a million rifles but then they blew up the deal because they discovered that the weapons were old and unusable. They also tried to mediate with Japan and explicitly asked for support for independence, but the Japanese were allies of Great Britain and failed to capture and hand over to the British the mediators.

Meanwhile in Europe a group composed of English and Indians was moving to England with the intent to assassinate Lord Kitchener and Edward Grey. The targets were also the French President and Prime Minister and the King of Italy and the Prime Minister. The cell collaborated with some Italian anarchists who were supposed to get the explosives through the German embassy in Zurich, but the

British managed to infiltrate the commandos and asked the Swiss to expel the employees.

In the U.S., the party had prepared a complex plan for sending ammunition to India via Shanghai. The Germans in the meantime decided that the only way to really implement the plan was to do it on a large-scale. Agents of Krupp companies bought $200,000 in ammunition with the help of Franz von Papen, a German military attaché in America. The ships that were to carry the weapons to India were masked under a series of fictitious names and companies and the British were persuaded to believe that they were weapons for the Mexican rebels.

The revolt was to have taken place in February 1915 but only in June of that year did the ships leave the United States with the cargo of arms and ammunition, but in India by then the British had managed to infiltrate the network of conspirators and had arrested or made almost all the members of the party flee. The two ships turned around and were immediately seized as soon as they entered the American ports and the goods were sold at auction, even though the Germans had tried to take back everything in order to supply the troops in Africa.

In 1917 the trial of the conspirators started, since everything had departed from the U.S. were tried there. It was one of the longest and most expensive trials in American history.

Some historians believe that the aforementioned Singapore Mutiny is part of this plot. If so, it would be the only successful case, albeit for a few days. Until the end of the war, with the defeat of the German Empire, the Ghadar movement did not give up completely. There were several other attempts, all of which ended in thin air. The movement suffered from disorganisation, the lack of secure lines of communication and, above all, from the easy infiltration of British agents.

The other great German plot was the one in Afghanistan. The Kaiser was convinced that by destabilising the country, perhaps persuading it to ally with the central powers, the British would find themselves in great trouble especially in the territories of northern India from where most of the soldiers were recruited.

The Niedermayer-Hentig expedition took place between 1915 and 1916. It was organised by Germany and the Ottoman Empire. The group was led by exiled Indian prince Raja Mahendra Pratap. Members of the Berlin Committee for the Independence of India also took part. The plan was part of the more complex Hindu-German plot.

The expeditionary corps reached Afghanistan by land via Persia. The English, and their Russian allies, tried to intercept, unsuccessfully, group in the summer of 1915. They saw that expedition as a serious threat. A deployed Afghanistan would have been a serious problem for the whole of Asia.

The Kaiser's trip to the Middle East in 1898 allowed the two countries to come closer together, even more. Germany was not new to the plans to weaken Britain indirectly, i.e. by creating chaos in the colonies. During his trip Wilhelm met twice in Jerusalem the father of Zionism, Theodor Herzl. Herzl had made sure to coincide his journey with that of the Kaiser, supported by the Reverend William Hechler[474] he aimed to convince the German Emperor to take to heart the Jewish question and to build some form of German protectorate for the Jewish community in Palestine, the friendship of the Kaiser with the Sultan of Constantinople was the best channel for Herzl's goals. The Kaiser immediately understood what the political potential would be for supporting the Zionist cause, not only would he become an idol for the world Jewish community, but he would also allow his Empire to forcefully wedge itself between

---

[474] He was an expert on Jewish matters, in his capacity as Chaplain at the British Embassy in Vienna he was able to meet Herzl and worked a lot in order to bring proselytes to his cause.

the interests of Britain and France in that region. Not to mention it would have attracted a lot of investment. However, the obstacles came from Constantinople, the Ottomans were not inclined towards the birth of an embryonic form of Jewish state within their borders. Wilhelm did not force his hand because he risked blowing up all the economic agreements made up to that moment.

When the war broke out, the Ottoman Empire sided with the Germans. For the British, this was an immense danger because in the event of a victory, India and Egypt were in grave danger.

As we have seen, it has been years since Germany publicly supported the Indian independence cause. With the arrival of the conflict this support became more evident, for months German newspapers talk about the social hardship in India, the treatment of Indians and the British exploitation from the country. As we have seen, the Chancellor supported this system and made sure that he encouraged and financed it. Max Von Oppenheim, German archaeologist and secret agent, was placed head of the Department for Eastern Affairs. He had travelled far and wide in the Middle East and during his pre-war journeys he had mapped all of Persia and Turkey.

The department led by Oppenheim encouraged pro-German propaganda in the region, even if there were talks of a secret conversion of the Kaiser to Islam during his trip to Mecca[475].

The Ottomans fought to destabilise Muslim subjects in the British Empire. Despite the massive spread of propaganda material, the desired effect was not achieved, Germans and Turks therefore decided to try another approach.

---

[475] T. L. Hughes, "*The German Mission to Afghanistan, 1915–1916*", *German Studies Review*, German Studies Association 25, 3, Berlin 2002. p. 447–476.

Afghanistan had declared itself neutral at the outbreak of the war, since 1907 it had been placed under the British sphere of influence and the British controlled its foreign policy. London's control over the state was null and void, the Afghan threat was always felt throughout the period of the Raj because for the British, especially after the agreement with the Russians, it was the only country able to invade India. When the Jihad launched by Constantinople against the British, the Emir of Kabul did not join for fear of creating chaos amongst his subjects.

Enver Pasha, who after the coup d'état in Turkey in 1913 was one of the three Pasha who led the Empire, had imagined an expedition to Afghanistan with Turks and Germans. The group would cross Persia escorted by about a thousand soldiers and led by German experts and explorers.[476]

The German group, which included Oskar Niedermayer and Wilhelm Wassmuss, reached Turkey in disguise pretending to be a travelling circus, but were discovered in Romania. When they finally reached Constantinople, without all the equipment they had to wait for others. The lack of co-operation between Germans and Turks disturbed the operation, which was definitively abandoned. After leaving the company Wassmuss decided to go to Persia and try to destabilise the portion of the country under British control. As he attempted to escape the British, he left behind his own vocabulary capable of deciphering German encrypted messages. For the Allies it was a precious conquest, amongst the many things thanks to that vocabulary they managed to decipher the famous Telegram Zimmermann.

---

[476] P. Hopkirk, *On Secret Service East of Constantinople*, Oxford, Oxford Paperbacks 2002. p. 85.

A new expedition, this time organised by Germany, was prepared in 1915. The Germans would have liked Har Dayal as their leader, but he refused, so Prince Pratap was given the job.

Niedermayer was again involved and with him also the former diplomatic attaché in Beijing and Constantinople, Hentig. He spoke fluent Persian. In the group also travelled some Indian members of the Berlin Committee, some doctors, interpreters and some servants taken from the prison camp of Zossen. 10,000 pounds in gold were deposited at the Deutsche Bank in Constantinople and the caravan brought a series of gifts to the Emir[477]

To avoid being intercepted the group from Berlin travelled separately, meeting in Constantinople[478].

At the beginning of May 1915, the group left Constantinople. They travelled on the not yet completed Berlin-Baghdad line, crossed the Euphrates and then arrived in Baghdad in May. Because of an extensive network of British agents in the region the group split again, one group moving to Iran and the other to the free zone in the middle of Persia. The British were aware of the sympathies of the tribes in the region towards the Germans and kept the situation under control. The imperial spies, had informed the Viceroy of the arrival of the caravan, both the Russians and the English set up a system to try to intercept them.[479]

---

[477] P. Hopkirk, *On Secret Service...*, p. 99.

[478] T. Hughes, *The German...*, p. 459.

[479] T. Hughes, *The German...*, p. 462.

They gathered again in Tebbes halfway to the Afghan border. After a difficult crossing of the desert they arrived in the city on the 3rd of July, unfortunately for them their arrival was known to the city administration, they were warmly welcomed but this meant that the British knew that they were in town.

Niedermayer had three patrols prepared to hide the tracks, one to the south to attract the British, one to the north to attract the Russians and one was sent forward to control the territory[480].

On the 19th of August the caravan finally arrived in Afghan territory. They had managed to get away from all the British and Russian agents. On the 24th the group entered Herat where it was welcomed with all the honours by the city. Hentig showed the Afghan authorities the call of the Sultan's Jihad and announced that in the event of an alliance with Germany, the Kaiser would recognise Afghanistan's independence and would donate some territories to be added to the country[481].

The Viceroy had already warned the Emir of the arrival of the Germans, he had assured that he would have the group arrested. In fact, the trip from Herat to Kabul was prepared with great care. On the 2nd of October they arrived in the capital.

Despite the warm welcome and hospitality at the Emir's palace, the members of the group were immediately aware that they were held prisoner. The Emir stayed away for a long time, he had retired to his summer residence. The foreigners continually asked for an interview, but he always answered with polite but negative answers, he was kept on the side-lines because he maintained contact with the English and in the meantime collected information about his prisoners. The Emir was a pro-British and

---

[480] T. Hughes, *The German...*, p. 463; P. Hopkirk, *On Secret Service...*, p. 136.

[481] T. Hughes, *The German...*, p. 464.

pro-European, whilst the Prime Minister, his brother was a more German pro-European.

On the 26th of October the Emir finally granted a meeting. The two German emissaries had to convince him that they were not just merchants but Kaiser's special envoys. They gave Wilhelm's and the Sultan's greetings and expressly asked the Emir to join the Holy War against the infidels in the Middle East and to declare its independence and side with Germany in the war. They also asked for Turkish troops to be allowed to transit through his country in order to be able to attack the border with India[482]. The Emir's answers, and his questions, revealed the gaps in the group. The Emir wanted guarantees and they were not allowed to promise anything; all their request was based on the call for Holy War that would lead to war. The two sides continued to meet without ever reaching a position[483]. The meeting with the Prime Minister, brother of the Emir, was more fruitful. He was more inclined to an alliance with Germany. The Prime Minister managed to change the editorial line of the only newspaper in the country, *Siraj al Akhbar*. The tone of the articles took a decidedly anti-British turn, so much to force the Raj to intercept the copies destined to India[484].

In November, after weeks of poor results, the group decided to take the situation into its own hands and after some negotiations, the Provisional Government of India was declared provisional on the 1st of December. This Government should have taken power as soon as the British Government was overthrown. Mahendra Pratap was chosen as President, Barkatullah the Prime Minister, Maulana Ubaidullah Sindhi,

---

[482] T. Hughes, *The German...*, p. 467.

[483] T. Hughes, *The German...*, p. 464

[484] T. Hughes, *The German...*, p. 468

Minister for India, Maulavi Bashir Minister for War, and Champakaran Pillai Minister for Foreign Affairs[485]. Immediately the new Government worked hard to try to receive official recognition from the Chinese Republic, Japan and later post-revolutionary Russia. Turkey and Germany obviously recognised it[486].

In the same month the Emir proposed the drafting of a treaty for a declaration of Afghan-German friendship. But he did ask for time to research. On the 24th of January 1916 a draft agreement was presented, which amongst other things provided support for a declaration of independence, support against the British and Russians in the event of war alongside Turkey and Germany, the modernisation of the Army by sending new rifles and artillery pieces and with diplomatic recognition from both sides[487]. The Emir, however, asked for a million pounds, 20 thousand soldiers in defence of the border before starting any operation against India.

The Emir continued to ask more things, knowing that he could not openly take sides against the British, rumours came from India of a British plot to kill him if he supported the German cause. The clause that caused the whole weak paper castle to collapse, however, was the Emir's request to bring his troops into the battlefield only after the revolt in India. He also demanded the signature of the Kaiser on the document and the immediate permission to the requests made. To avoid conspiracies at court, he had all the pro-German officials removed. The more time passed and the more complicated the situation for the central forces became, in 1916 with the Arab

---

[485] K. H. Ansari, *"Pan-Islam and the Making of the Early Indian Muslim Socialist"*, *Modern Asian Studies*, 20, 3, Cambridge University Press, Cambridge 1986. p. 509 – 537.

[486] T. Hughes, *The German...*, p. 474.

[487] T. Hughes, *The German...*, p. 470.

Revolt and the offensive on the Western Front the possibility of sending troops, weapons and money to Afghanistan for an offensive against India became virtually nil. On the 21st of May 1916, the group left Kabul for good. Their survival in Kabul depended simply on the ancient rules of hospitality amongst diplomats, just outside the city they knew that they risk the danger of being killed by British agents and Afghan tribes. The caravan broke up definitively and each one reached Germany or the allied countries with its own means. The Indian members remained in Afghanistan and tried in every way to make the Provisional Government work, continuing to foment the country against the British and seeking official recognition outside the circle of allies of Turkey and Germany[488].

Both plans, if properly implemented, could have represented a serious problem for Great Britain, especially the one in Afghanistan, the idea of a revolution in India was less original, it was enough to see the number of volunteers who left for the conflict to understand how deep-rooted the belonging to the Empire was. This does not mean that the Indians were deprived of any idea of self-Government, but neither does it mean that they were a priori opposed to any form of foreign domination.

The Germans also failed in their attempt to drive the British out of the Middle East, causing an Arab uprising. Germany had its own *Lawrence,* but they all failed in their intent. The *Great Game,* no longer between Russia and Great Britain but between Great Britain and Germany lasted very little and with an easy outcome, even if more for a bad German design rather than for a complex British defence.

---

[488] T. Hughes, *The German...,* p. 470; P. Hopkirk, *On Secret Service...,* p. 217.

8. *'No more parades'*

The hell of the Great War left an open wound in the heart of Britain. Wound that still hurts and bleeds today. The number of deaths, the price of conflict, the wounded, the physical and mental destruction of a world lost forever. The Big Ben chimes of that 4th of August played a sad imperial requiem. England has not been able to avoid a global conflict despite its position of dominance on the world scene and has not been able to win it immediately despite its economy, superior to any other. Not to mention the entire generation of young men swept away, men educated in a system that had evolved over the years and was now tested for the creation of a ruling class.

The First World War ended definitively at 11 am. Of the 11th of November 1918. A conflict started because of two shots fired in the Balkans is closed with some signatures inside a wagon in a French forest. Those signatures have in fact caused another world war, as they say: The pen is mightier than a sword

The stalemate of the conflict had found a turning point with the exit of Russia, the Tsarist Empire no longer existed. The German offensive, however, was resolved with nothing and with the arrival of the U.S. to Germany remained little hope. Hopes destroyed with the disappearance of the Austro-Hungarian Empire. The negotiations were held by junior officers. None of the protagonists showed up at Compiegne. During the negotiations the German Empire also disappeared, the republic was declared, and the Kaiser had to flee to Holland. The winners wanted not only to win but also to humiliate. The humiliation began in that small French wagon and ended in Versailles the following year.

Great Britain of Grey, Lloyd George, Asquith and Churchill came out winning but at a terrible price. Was it worth it? Did a war in defence of the Empire really save it?

The decline of the British system is perfectly described in the masterful tetralogy of Ford Madox Ford *Parade's End.*

Christopher Tietjens is called *the last tory*. His values, his rigour, his morals and his gait make him the last great man of Great Britain. He is a statesman in Government, the son of a wealthy family in Yorkshire. Despite being stuck in an unwanted marriage with a woman who betrays him and despite not being sure to be the father of the son he raised, he refuses both to divorce and to start a relationship with the young suffragette with whom he fell in love because both things would go against his values. The whole world of Tietjens can be summed up in a sentence he utters to a friend of his:

"For a gentleman, there is such a thing as, call it "parade". I stand for monogamy and chastity and for not talking about it."

Then, faced with a request to falsify numbers in a report and with the spread of a false gossip about him and the young Valentine Wannop, he decides to enlist and fight for his country. For Christopher Tietjens, war is not a bad thing but a way to cleanse his conscience.

In a discussion at the front he describes the British Army with a single telegram:

"Well, I'm sure that will come in useful fire-extinguishers.

We indented the Royal Engineers.

Sir.

The Royal Engineers said, as per Army directive 1BDR 3417, for fire-extinguishers, we should apply to Ordnance.

Ordnance said there's no provision for them for Canadian units passing through an Infantry Base Depot, and that the proper course would be to obtain them from a civilian firm and charge them against barrack damages.

Yes, sir.

I have here a letter from the leading British manufacturer of fire-extinguishers, telling me that they have been forbidden by the War Office to sell fire-extinguishers to anyone but to the War Office direct.

Thank God we have a navy.

Yes, sir"

The war has undermined every founding value of the world of Tietjens. When at the end of the war each regiment is demobilised the choice of the term also describes the new situation in which Christopher finds himself, but also the whole nation, and Empire:

"No more parades"

Conclusion

The First World War was the biggest mistake in British history. The means by which Britain wasted its Empire. The social structure, politics and diplomacy have never recovered. The conflict has not only produced an immense number of deaths and injuries but has also undermined certainties and created insurmountable doubts. The world changed beyond recognition, and the impact that the First World War had caused the Second World War. The dominions began to demand more rights in exchange for the blood tribute and London was unable to satisfy them. Not to mention that the conflict allowed the citizens of the Empire to leave their country and see realities unthinkable until then. The neutrality of a small country like Belgium was certainly not worth the size and political weight of the greatest Empire in modern history. The alliance with France did not impose war and England could, and in my opinion, should have remained neutral. London could have persuaded Belgium to let the German troops through and this would have spared a bloodbath and almost certainly the Empire.

The work I illustrated above also had the task of trying in some way to take away that negative label that covers the entire period of colonialism. Modern history has in a way washed its guilt by branding imperialism and colonialism of Western nations as a barbaric, racist and damaging practice for the colonies. In my opinion, this is first wrong from a methodological and, above all, historical point of view. There is a clear difference between the Spanish and Portuguese Empires, nations that saw the colonies as a mere territory to be plundered, and England first and Britain then. Just look at a map of the British Empire and a list of the richest and most industrialised countries today and you can understand how important it was for London to organise each colony in a practical and advantageous way. Mine is in no way intended to be a speech of absolute apology of imperialism, but just as it cannot have been all positive, it cannot have been all negative.

The simplest mistake you can make when studying and telling history is to see and judge the facts of the past with *the moral eye* of the present. We cannot consider all British leaders as racist imperialists because that is a concept that did not belong to that time. The contours of the concept of racism were very jagged and difficult to identify. There was already the idea, even a very widespread one, amongst the public opinion that the role of the white man was not so authoritarian and there were already reports of cases of mistreatment and harassment of the local populations, but we cannot in any way, in my opinion, reduce everything to a well-defined racist plan. When it comes to Great Britain nothing is well-defined, the Empire has always lived in a kind of limbo where there were no rules and laws but traditions and customs who dictate orders. The historian can afford, where there is evidence, to judge a character but should not judge his way of thinking. For a citizen of the nineteenth century the superiority of the white race was not a theory professed by some preacher but was simply the common *mindset*. Was it wrong? yes, but that is not why it is judged negatively. Racism is a concept like smoking, we can see it, hear but it is difficult to contain it within certain schemes. It is today and it was then.

One cannot reduce the history of a country and an Empire to the mere fact that they were more concerned with whites than with blacks. Britain wanted a strong Empire and helped its colonies, helped untapped. There was no humanitarian purpose but an economic one, but in fact that aid has served. In fact, it is the only Empire that still exists. The change was practically peaceful, the Empire ceased to exist when it turned out to be more of a cost than a gain. In fact, the British Empire has shrunk and changed its name, but it is still there, the Queen is still head of state not only in Britain but also in Antigua and Barbuda, Australia, Bahamas, Barbados, Belize, Canada, Grenada, Jamaica, New Zealand, Papua New Guinea, Saint Kitts and Nevis, Saint Vincent and the Grenadines, Solomon Islands, Saint Lucia and Tuvalu and the Isle of Man. The sun has not yet set on the British Empire. The *Commonwealth of Nations* brings together almost all the former colonies and other states that were not part of the Empire. Even today, London politics can influence several states. In terms

508

of numbers, the Empire has lost its primary role on the global chessboard, but it still maintains an economic role within itself that allows Great Britain.

We took India as an example because it was the main and most famous colony of the British Empire, a real Empire within the Empire. First England and then Great Britain struggled and not little to succeed in putting under the Crown the Indian territory. For decades India was the personal heritage of a private company, *unique* in history. With the official arrival of the British power the problems did not disappear but rather it was always a silent clash against any form of protest. We saw how hard it was to strike a balance between indigenous peoples and colonists. Throughout the Raj period, the defence of the subcontinent was a constant problem. A British problem, though. India has been a melting pot of ideas, representations, points of view and perspectives for the British. It has had an indelible influence on the Empire and society and still today represents a strong appeal to the country. A series of wrong choices and a multitude of people unable to make the right decisions led not only Britain but the whole Empire into a conflict whose end could not be seen. The country fought that war without fully realising how different it was from each previous war. Heroism and honour have produced mountains of deaths, the treaties have worked badly, the kinship has created a period of tension rather than a wake-up call at every conflict. In the summer of 1914 probably no one in Britain would have expected to lose soon after all that they had built in three centuries of history.

The Empire was stabbed in Ypres, Somme, Passchendaele, Gallipoli, Palestine, Jutland and dozens of other places. Those wounds bleed for years and years until the end of World War II. The fury of victory led the rulers to demand more than they deserved. The Treaty of Versailles was an act of bullying rather than a peace agreement. France had a lot to take revenge on and the British were not going to hold them back. The mistakes of the First paid off in the Second. When the Germans told the British that they were only going to war for a scrap of paper they were not wrong, a piece of paper signed decades earlier had condemned everyone to an uncertain future. England was not able to sustain the vast changes that took place after the end of the conflict, all the years spent in isolation had deprived it of the ability to dominate, in the true sense of the word, the world. To answer the question, we asked ourselves in the introduction was a disadvantage, the victory in the Great War did nothing but bringing the Empire to collapse by transforming Britain, India in two new entities, uncertain and in some ways contrary to everything experienced so far. The neutrality of Belgium was in no way worth either the life or the role of the English in the world. The Empire was not perfect, but the positive aspects far outweighed the negative ones, a mentality that today we will consider racist dominated the predominant but at the base of the system there was a form of tranquillity, an innocence that never appeared again.

"Never such innocence,

Never before or since,

As changed itself to past

Without a word—the men

Leaving the gardens tidy,

The thousands of marriages

Lasting a little while longer:

Never such innocence again."

Even Kipling, the prophet of British Imperialism, after the death of his only son in 1916, rethought the power and necessity of entering the war. Kipling is the question and answer to our main questions.

"If any question why we died,

Tell them, because our fathers lied"

510

Bibliography

"*The Famine in India*", Missionary Review of the World, April 1897.

Adams, R., *Tiaras and Tantrums: Twenty-Five Years in Service at Kedleston Hall*. DB Publishing, London 2010.

Adams, W. W. S., *Edwardian Heritage: A Study in British History, 1901-06,* Frederick Muller, London 1949.

Adelman, P., *Gladstone, Disraeli and Later Victorian Politics,* Longman, London 2010.

Alano, N., *Disraeli,* De Vecchi Editore, Milan 1967.

Albertini, L., *Le Origini Della Guerra Del 1914 (3 Volumes - Vol. I: "European Relations from the Berlin Congress to the Sarajevo bombing", Vol. II: "La Crisi Del Luglio 1914. From the Sarajevo attack on the general mobilization of Austria-Hungary", Vol. III: "The epilogue of the crisis of July 1914. The Declarations of War and Neutrality")*, Fratelli Bocca, Milan 1942-1943.

Aldous, R., *The Lion and the Unicorn: Gladstone Vs Disraeli,* Pimlico, London 2007.

Allen, C., *Kipling Sahib. India and the Making of Rudyard Kipling,* Abacus, London 2007.

Al-Sayyid, A. L., *Egypt and Cromer: A Study of Anglo Egyptian Relations,* Frederick A. Praeger, New York 1969. p. 3.

Altick, R., *Writers, Readers and Occasions: Selected Essays on Victorian Literature And Life,* Ohio State Uni Press, Columbus 1988.

Amendola, G., *La Grande Illusione*, In '*La Voce*', March 2, 1910.

Anand, Mulk Raj, *Across the Black Waters*, Orient Paperbacks, Delhi, 2008.

Andrew, C., *Secret Service: The Making of British Intelligence Community*, London, Guild Publishing, 1985.

Ansari, K. H., *"Pan-Islam and the Making of the Early Indian Muslim Socialist"*, *Modern Asian Studies*, 20, 3, Cambridge University Press, Cambridge 1986.

Arnold, T., *The Life and Correspondence of Thomas Arnold*, John Murray, London 1845.

Aronson, T., *Prince Eddy and the Homosexual Underworld,* John Murray, London 1994.

Bailey, H. C., *The Great Game,* Sun Dial Press, New York 1940.

Balzac, H., *Le Cousin Pons,* Calmann-Lévy, Paris 1847.

Bandyopadhyay, P., *Indian Famine and Agrarian Problems,* Star Publications, Calcutta 1987.

Barber, N., *The Black Hole of Calcutta*, Colimns, London 1968.

Barnett, C., *The Collapse of British Power,* London 1973.

Barrie, M., Peter *Pan. The Child Who Didn't Want to Grow*, Mondadori, Trad It. By P. Farese, Milan 2007.

Barth, B., *The German High Finance and The Imperialisms: Banks And Foreign Policy Before 1914*. Stuttgart 1995.

Barthorp, M., *Afghan Wars and the North-West Frontier 1839–1947*, Cassell, London 2002.

Bebbington, D. W., *The Mind of Gladstone: Religion, Homer and Politics,* Oxford University Press, Oxford 2004.

Beckett, I. F. W., *La Prima Guerra Mondiale. Dodici punti di vista* . Einaudi, Turin, 2013.

Beckett, J., *Glorious Revolution, Parliament, And the Making Of The First Industrial Nation* In *Parliament History Parliament, Politics And Policy In Britain And Ireland, C. 1680-1832 Vol XXXIII,* Clive Jones And James Kelly, Oxford 2014.

Beidelman, T. O., *A Comparitive Analysis Of The Jajmani System,* Monographs Of The Association For Asian Studies, VIII, New York 1959.

Bell, C., *Portrait of a Dalai Lama: The Life and Times of the Great Thirteenth,* Collins, London 1946.

Bennett, A., *The History Boys*, Faber & Faber, London 2006. pp. 55. Trad It. *The Students of History,* Adelphi, Milan 2012.

Bennett, Alan, *Gli Studenti Di Storia*, Adelphi, Milan 2012.

Bernstein, G. L.., *Liberalism and Liberal Policies in Edwardian England,* London 1986.

Bhargava, M. B. L., *India's Services in the War*, Allahabad: Standard Press, 1919.

Blackstock, P., *Agents of Deceit,* Quadrangle Books, Chicago 1966.

Blake, R., *Disraeli*, St. Martin's Press, New York 1966.

White, S., *History of A Phobia: The Will Of Peter the Great,* Russian and Soviet World Papers 9, Paris 1968. Pe 265-293.

Bloch, I. S., *Is War Now Impossible? Being an Abridgment Of 'The War of the Future and Its Technical, Economic and Political Relations'* London, 1899.

Borsa, Giorgio, *La Nascita Del Mondo Moderno In Asia Orientale*, Rizzoli, Milan 1977.

Bosworth, C. E., *"The Intrepid Victorian Lady in Persia: Mrs. Isabella Bishop's Travels in Luristan and Kurdistan, 1890" Iran XXVII 1989.*

513

Boulger, D. C., *Gordon: The Career of Gordon of Khartoum,* Leonaur, London 2009.

Bowen, H. V., *400 Years of the East India Company* in *History Today* Vol: L, Andy Patterson, London 2000.

Boxer, C. R., *The Dutch India Company and the China Trade, In History Today*, Vol 29. London 1979.

Brendon, Piers, *The Decline and fall of the British Empire 1781 – 1997*, Vintage Books, London 2008.

Brook-Sheperd, G., *Uncle of Europe,* William Collins Sons & Co Ltd, Glasgow 1975.

Brook-Sheperd, Gordon, *Lo Zio d'Europa*, Rizzoli, Milan 1977.

Brook-Sheperd, Gordon, *Royal Sunset*, Weindenfeld and Nicolson, London 1987.

Brook-Sheperd, Gordon, *Uncle of Europe,* Collins, London 1975.

Brown, G. T., *The Hindu Conspiracy, 1914 – 1917,* University of California.

Buchan, J., A *Prince of Captivity,* House of Stratus, Looe 1996.

Buchan, J., *Greenmantle,* G. H. Doran Company, New York 1916.

Burleigh, B., *Khartoum Campaign, 1898 or the Re-Conquest of the Soudan,* Chapman and Hall, London 1899.

Bushkovitch, P., *Peter the Great: The Struggle for Power, 1671–1725*, Cambridge University Press, Cambridge 2001.

Cain, P. J., Hopkins, A. G., British *Imperialism,* Vol. I *Innovation and Expansion 1688 - 914.* London 1993.

Caminitis, A., *La guerra Anglo-Boera. Anche l'Impero ebbe il suo Vietnam,* Frilli, Genoa. 2008.

514

Candler, E., *The Unveiling of Lhasa,* Edward Arnold, London 1905.

Canfora, Luciano, *1914*, Sellerio, Palermo 2006.

Caplan L., *Warrior Gentlemen, 'Gurkhas' in the Western Imagination* Oxford University Press, Oxford, 1995.

Caracchi, P., *Racconti Hindi Del Novecento*, Edizioni Dell'orso, Alessandria 2004.

Carrington, C., *Rudyard Kipling: His Life and Work,* Doubleday, Doran And Company, Garden City. 2001.

Carroll, L., *Through the Looking Glass, "It's A Great Game of Chess That's Being Played All over the World..."* Macmillan And Co., London 1872.

Caterino, Aldo, *La Prima Guerra Mondiale*, Il Portolano, Genova 2014.

Cawthorne, N., *The Beastly Battles of Old England: The Misguided Manoeuvres of the British at War*, Hachette, London 2011.

Chand, T., *History of the Freedom Movement in India* Publications Divisions, Ministry of Information and Broadcasting, Delhi, 1961. Vol I. p. 391.

Chesney, G., *The Battle of Dorking.*

Childers, E., *The Riddle of the Sands,* Smith, Elder & Co, London 1903. Trade It.: *L'enigma Delle Sabbie*, Bariletti, Rome, 1989.

Chomet, S., *Helena: A Princess Reclaimed*, Begell House, New York 1999.

Churchill, W., *A Roving Commissione: My Early Life,* Charles Scribner's Sons, New York 1930.

Churchill, W., *My Earl Life: 1874 – 1904,* Touchstone, New York 1996.

Churchill, W., *the Boer War: London to Ladysmith via Pretoria and Ian Hamilton's March,* A&C Black, London 2013.

Churchill, W., *The River War, an Account of the Reconquest of the Sudan,* Courier Corporation, Cambridge 2006.

Clarke I. F., *The Great War With Germany, 1890-1914* A Cura Di, Liverpool University Press, Liverpool, 1917.

Clarke, E., *The Story of My Life, "The Great Game of Politics"* John Murray, London 1923.

Clarke, I. F., *Voices Prophesying War, 1763 - 1984*, London - New York, 1992.

Cohen, S. P., *Issue, Role, and Personality: The Kitchener – Curzon Dispute.* In *Comparatives Studies in Society and History.* Vol. 10, No. 3. Cambridge University Press, Cambridge April 1968.

Cohn, B., "Representing Authority in Victorian India" In E. Hobsbawn, T. Ranger, *The Invention of Tradition,* Cambridge University Press, Cambridge 1983.

Cohn, B., *Colonialism and Its Forms of Knowledge* Oxford University Press, Oxford 1997.

Collins, J., *Dr. Brighton's Indian Patients December 1914-January 1916*, Paperback, Brighton 2006.

Conacher, J.B., *Emergence of British Parliamentary Democracy in the Nineteenth Century: Passing of the Reform Acts of 1832, 1867 and 1884-1885*, John Wiley & Sons Ltd, London 1971.

Conlin, J., *Evolution and the Victorians: Science, Culture and Politics in Darwin's Britain,* Bloomsbury Academic, London 2014.

Consolaro, A. *Madre India E La Parola*, Edizioni Dell'orso, Alessandria 2003.

Cook, M., *London and the Culture of Homosexuality, 1885 – 1914.* Cambridge University Press, Cambridge 2003.

Corrigan, G., *Sepoy in the Trenches, the Indian Corps on the Western Front 1914 – 1915*, Spellmount, Stonehouse 2006.

Corrigan, Gordon, *Sepoys in the Trenches*, Spellmount, Stonehouse 2006.

Coughlin, Con, *Churchill's First War*, Pan Books, London 2013.

Courtine, R. J., *Le Gran Jeu De La Cuisine, Larousse*, Paris 1980.

Cox, G., *War, Moral Hazard, and Ministerial Responsibility: England after the Glorious Revolution* in *the Journal of Economic History* Vol VXXI, the Economic History Association, Tucson 2011.

Cracraft. J., *The Revolution of Peter the Great*, Harvard University Press, Cambridge 2003.

Crankshaw, Edward, *Il Tramonto Di Un Impero*, Mursia, Milan 1963.

Crouchley, A. E., *Economic Development of Modern Egypt*, Hebrew University, London 1938.

Curzon, G. N., *A Viceroy's India: Leaves from Lord Curzon's Notebook*, Sidgwick E Jackson, London 1984.

Curzon, G. N., *Lord Curzon in India: Being a Selection from His Speeches as Viceroy & Governor-General of India 1898-1905*, Adamant Media Corporation, London 2002.

Curzon, G. N., *Lord Curzon's Farewell to India. Being Speeches Delivered as Viceroy & Governor-General of India. During Sept.-Nouv. 1905,* Thacker And Co, Bombay 1907.

Curzon, G. N., *Persia and Persian Question,* Longmans, Green & Co, London 1892.

Curzon, G. N., *Russia In Central Asia in 1889 And the Anglo-Russian Question,* Longmans, Green & Co, London 1889.

Curzon, G., N., *Travels with a Superior Person*, Sidgwick And Jackson, London 1985

Das, S., *Race, Empire and First World War*, Cambridge University Press, Cambridge 2013.

Das, S., *Race, Empire and First World War*, Cambridge University Press, Cambridge 2013.

Davis A., *The Empire at War : British and Indian Perceptions of Empire in the First World War : a Thésis*, University of Tasmania, 2008.

Davis, H. W. C. D., *the Great Game in Asia (1800 – 1844)*. Proceedings of the British Academy, Vol. 12, London 1926.

Davis, M., *Late Victorian Holocausts: El Nino Famines and the Making of the Third World*, Verso, London 2001. Trad It *Late Victorian Holocaust: El Ino, Famines and The Birth of The Third World*.

De Cecco, M., *Moneta e Impero: Il Sistema finanziario internazionale dal 1890 al 1914*. Einaudi, Turin 1979.

Defoe, D., *The Complete English Tradesman*, Dodo Press, London 2007.

Dennison, M., *The Last Princess: The Devoted Life of Queen Victoria's Youngest Daughter*, Weidenfeld & Nicolson, London 2007.

Devonshire, D., G. Rogers, *The Garden at Chatsworth*, Frances Lincoln; New Ed Edition, London 2001.

Devonshire, D., S. Upton, *Chatsworth: The House*, Frances Lincoln; 1st Frances Lincoln Ed Edition, London 2002.

Dewey, C., *Anglo-Indian Attitudes: Mind of the Indian Civil Service*, Continnuum-3PL, London 1993.

518

Dignan, D. K., *The Hindu Conspiracy in Anglo-American Relations during The World War I,* University of Queensland.

Dirienzo, Eugenio, *Afghanistan Il Grande Gioco*, Salerno Editrice, Rome, 2014.

Diver M., The *Judgement of The Sword,* G. P. Putnam's Sons, New York 1913.

Diver, M., *The Great Amulet,* John Lane Company, New York 1908.

Diver. M., *The Hero of Herat,* Constable & Company, London 1912.

Donattini, M., *From the New World to America. Geographic Discoveries and Colonialism (XV-XVI Centuries)* Carocci, Rome 2004.

Dragon, A. W., *Intellectual Whist: Conversations, Discussions and Anecdotes on The Great Game,* George Routledge & Sons Limited, London 1899.

Dreyfus, M., *Dreyfus, Mio Fratello*, Editori Riuniti, Rome 1980.

Drummond, H., *The Great Game,* St Paul, London 1918.

Du Fail, N., *Contes et Discours d'Eutrapel*, Librairie des Bibliophiles, Paris 1875.

Dubois, J. A., *Vice, Institutions And Ceremonies Of The People Of India,* By J. S. Merlin, Paris 1825.

Dugdale, B., *Arthur James Balfour, [1st] Earl of Balfour, 1906 - 1930,* Vol I. p. 258f. London 1928.

Elliott, J., *Imperi dell'Atlantico. America britannica e America spagnola, 1492-1830,* Einaudi, Turin 2010.

Elliott, J., *La Spagna Imperiale 1469-1716,* Il Mulino, Bologna 2012.

Ensor, R., *England, 1870-1914*, Oxford University Press, Oxford 1936,

Erickson, C., *Alexandra,* St. Martin's Griffin, London 2002.

Erickson, C., *Her Little Majesty,* Simon & Schuster, Cambridge 2002.

Erickson, C., *La Piccola Regina*, Mondadori, Milan 2001.

Erickson, C., *La Zarina Alessandra*, Mondadori, Milan 2006.

Fairbank, J. K., *Trade and Diplomacy on the China Coast,* Cambridge University Press, Cambridge 1953.

Falls, C., *Rudyard Kipling,* M. Kennerley, New York 1915.

Feaver J. R. H., Lane-Poole, A., *H. W. C. Davis, A Memoir And Selection Of His Historical Papers,* Constable And Company, Ltd, London 1933.

Ferguson, N., *Empire. The Rise and Demise of the British World Order*, Penguin, London 2003.

Ferguson, N., *Il Grido Dei Morti*, Mondadori, Milan, 2014.

Ferguson, N., *Empire. How Britain Made the Modern World*, Mondadori, Milan 2009.

Ferguson, N., *Money and Power*, Ponte alle Grazie, Milan 2001.

Ferguson, N., *The Cash Nexus: Money and Politics in Modern History, 1700-2000,* Penguin Books, London 2002.

Ferguson, N., The *House of Rothschild: Vol 1. Money's Prophets 1798 – 1848 – Vol 2. The World's Banker 1849 – 1999,* Penguin Books, London 1999 – 2000.

Ferguson, N. *The Pity of War*, Penguin, London 1999.

Ferguson, N., *The World's Banker: A History of the House of Rothschild*, Penguin, London 1998.

Ferguson, N., *Virtual History: Alternatives and Counterfactuals,* Basic Books, New York, 1997.

Ferguson, N. , *20th Century L'età Della Violenza*, Mondadori, Milan, 2008.

Fisher, J., *Gentleman Spies*, Sutton Publishing, Phoenix 2002.

Fleming, P., *Bayonets to Lhasa: The First Full Account of The British Invasion Of Tibet In 1904,* Rupert Hart-Davis, London 1961.

Follett, K., La Caduta Dei Giganti, Mondadori, Trad It. Milan 2010.

Forster, S., *Dreams and Nightmares: German Military Leadership and the Images of Future Warfare*, 1871-1914, Saggio presentato alla Conferenza Di Augsburg, 1994.

Francis. W. P., *Afghanistan: A Short Account of Afghanistan, Its History, and Our Dealings with It*, Griffith and Farran, London 1881.

Franklin J J., The *Lotus and the Lion: Buddhism and the British Empire.* Cornell University Press. London 2008.

Fraser, N., *The Importance of Being Eton, Inside the World's Most Important School,* Short Book Ltd, London 2006.

Frederick, T. G., *The Great Game of Business*, D. Appleton And Company, New York 1920.

French, P., *Oltre Le Porte Della Città Proibita*, Sperling And Kupfer Editori, Milan 2000.

Furber, H., *Henry Dundas, First Viscount Melville, 1724-1811, Humphrey Milford, London 1931.*

Fussel, P. *The Great War and Modern Memory*, Il Mulino, Bologna, 2000.

Garvin, J.L., *The Life of Joseph Chamberlain, Vol III. 1895 – 1900.* London 1934.

Gaylor, J., *Sons of John Company – The Indian & Pakistan Armies 1903–1991.* Parapress. Turnbridge Wells 1996.

Geiss, I., *"The German Version of Imperialism: Weltpolitik"*, In Schollgen, A Cura Di, *Escape into War? The Foreign Policy Of Imperial Germany,* Oxford 1990.

Gilbert, M., *La Grande Storia Della Prima Guerra Mondiale*, Mondadori, Milan 2012.

Gilmour, D., *Curzon*, John Murray Publishers Ltd, London, 1994.

Goldsmith, D. F., *The Devil's Paintbrush. Sir Hiram Maxim's Gun*. Collector Grade Publications, Toronto 1989.

Gooch, H. G., Temperley, *British Documents on the Origins of the War, 1898-1914*, Volume 1, London 1926.

Greenberg, M., *British Trade and the Opening of China1800-42,* Cambridge University Press, Cambridge 1951.

Greenhut J., *'Race, Sex and War : The Impact of Race and Sex on Morale and Heath Services for the Indian Corps on the Western Front, 1914'*, Military Affairs, 45, 2. London 1981.

Greenhut J., '*Shahib and Sepoy : An Inquiry into the Relationship between the British Officers and Native Soldiers of the British Indian Army'*, Military Affairs 48,1. London 1984.

Greenhut J., '*The Imperial Reserve : The Indian Corps on the Western Front, 1914-1915* New Delhi 1983.

Grehan, J., Mace, M., *The Boer War 1899-1902: Ladysmith, Magersfontein, Spion Kop, Kimberley and Mafeking (Despatches from the Front)*, Pen & Sword Military, London 2014.

Guha, A., *Parsi Seth as Entrepreneurs P.I.* In *Economic and Political Weekly, Bombay 29 Agosto 1970.*

Gurwood, J., *The Despatches of Field-Marshal the Duke Of Wellington,* Oxford University Press, Oxford 1837.

Gutha, V. A., *The Comprador Role of Parsi Seths 1750-1850*, P. II, In *Economic and Political Weekly* Bombay, 28 November 1970.

Habid, I., *The Agrarian System of Mughal India,* New York 1963.

Hakluyt, R., *Divers Voyages Touching the Discoverie Of America And The Ilands Adjacent Unto The Same, Made First By Our Englishmen And Afterwards By The Frenchmen And Britons: With Two Mappes Annexed Hereunto,* Woodcocke, London 1582.

Hall, C., *Defining the Victorian Nation: Class, Race, Gender and the British Reform Act of 1867*, Cambridge University Press, Cambridge 2000.

Hamilton, C. J., *The Trade Relations between England and India 1600-. 1896,* Thacker, Spinker And Co, Calcutta 1919.

Hansard, H., Parliamentary Debates, 3d Series Vol. 147, H. C. 27 July 1857.

Hanson, N., *The Confident Hope Of A Miracle: The True History Of The Spanish Armada: The Real History of the Spanish Armada,* Doubleday, New York City 2003

Hardiman, D., *The Crisis of Lesser Patidars: Peasant Agitations in Kheda District, Gujarat, 1917-34,* In D. Low (A Cura Di), *Congress and the Raj,* Heinemann Educational, London 1977.

Hargrave P., C., *A History of Playing Cards*, Literary Licensing, LLC, New York 1966.

Harris, R., *L'ufficiale E La Spia*, Mondadori, Milan 2014.

Harris, R., *The Conservatives — A History*. Bantam, London 2011.

Harrison, D., *The White Tribe of Africa,* University of California Press, Oakland 1983.

Harvey R., J., *Reading in European History, Vol II from the Opening of the Protestant Revolt to the Present Day,* Ginn And Co, Boston 1904-1906.

Hastings, M., *Catastrophe,* Paperback, London 2014.

Hattersley, R., *David Lloyd George: The Great Outsider,* Hachette, London 2010.

Hattersley, Roy, *The Edwardians*, Abacus, London 2004.

Heathcote, T. A., *The Indian Army – The Garrison of British Imperial India, 1822–1922*. David & Charles, Newton Abbot 1974.

Heber, R., *Narrative of a Journey through the Upper Provinces of India,* Carey, Lee & Carey, Philadelphia 1829.

Hentschel, V., *Wirtschaft Und Wirtschaftpolitik Imwilhelminischen Deutschland: Organised Capitalism and Intervention State?* Stuttgart 1978.

Herre, F., *Bismarck*, Mondadori, Milan, 1994.

Hershlas, Z. Y., *Introduction to the Modern Economic History of the Middle East*, Brill Academic Pub, Leiden 1964.

Hibbert, C., Disraeli*: A Personal History*. Harper Collins, London 2004.

Hibbert, C., *Queen Victoria: A Personal History*, HarperCollins, London 2000.

Hiley, N., *Introduction*, In Le Queux, *Spies of The Kaiser*, Frank Cass, London 1909.

Hobson, J. A., *Imperialism,* Cambridge University Press, Cambridge 2011.

Holmes, R. *Sahib: The British Soldier in India,* Harper Perennial, London 2006.

Hopkirk, P.*, On Secret Service East of Constantinople,* John Murray, London 2006.

Hopkirk, P., *Quest for Kim*, London 2006.

Hopkirk, P., *Setting the East Ablaze*, Oxford University Press, Oxford 1986.

Hopkirk, P., *Trespassers on the Roof of the World*, Penguin, London 2006.

Horler, S., The *Great Game,* John Crowther, Huddersfield 1935.

Horne, John, *A Companion to World War* I, Wiley E Blackwell, Chichester 2010.

524

Hughes, L., *Peter the Great and the West: New Perspectives* Palgrave Macmillan, Basingstoke 2001.

Hughes, T. L., "*The German Mission to Afghanistan, 1915–1916*", *German Studies Review*, German Studies Association 25, 3, Berlin 2002.

Hughes. L., *Peter the Great: A Biography*, Yale University Press, New Haven 2002; M. R. Massie, *Peter the Great: His Life And World,* Ballantine Books, New York City 1981.

Hughes. L., *Russia in the Age of Peter the Great*, Yale University Press, New Haven 1998.

Hyam, R., *Britain's Imperial Century, 1815-1914, "The Great Game between Ourselves and the Transvaal for the Mastery of South Africa"* Palgrave Macmillan, Basingstoke 1976.

Hyam, R., *Empire and Sexuality,* Manchester University Press, Manchester 1990.

Hyde Montgomery, H., *the Cleveland Street Scandal,* Coward, McCann & Geoghegan, New York. 1987.

Hynes, S., *A War Imaginated: The First World War and English Culture*, Random House, London 1990.

Innis, H.A., The Press: A Neglected Factor in the Economic History of the Twentieth Century, Oxford, 1949.

Issawi, C., *Economic History of The Middle East 1800-1914*, University of Chicago Press, Chicago 1966.

Jackson, D., *India's Army*, Sampson Low, London 1940.

Jarboe, A.T., *"Soldiers of Empire: Indian Sepoys in and Beyond the Imperial Metropole during the First World War, 1914-1919."* PhD, Northeastern University, 2013.

Jasanoff, M., *Edge of Empire: Lives, Culture, and Conquest in the East, 1750-1850,* Vintage, London 2006.

Jay, R., *Joseph Chamberlain: A Political Study,* Oxford University Press, Oxford 1981.

Jenkins, R., *Gladstone: A Biography*. Random House Trade Paperbacks, New York 1995.

Jensen, J. M., *Hindu Conspiracy: A Reassessment,* Pacific Historical Review, Vol 48. N° 1. 1979.

Jokic. O., *Commanding Correspondence: Letters and The Evidence of Experience In The Letter Book Of John Bruce, The East-India Company Historiographer*, In *The Eighteenth Century*, Volume LII, University Of Pennsylvania Press, Baltimore 2011.

Kaeppelin, P., *La Compagnie Des Indes Orientales and François Martin: Study on the History of Commerce and French Establishments in India under Louis XIV*, Nabu Press, Paris 2014.

Kaye, J. W., *History of the War in Afghanistan*, W. H. Allen & Co, London 1857.

Kaye, J. W., *Lives of Indian Officers,* W. H. Allen & Co, London 1867.

Kennedy, P., *Ascesa E Declino Della Potenza Navale Britannica*, Garzanti, Milan 2010.

Kennedy, P., *L'antagonismo Anglo Tedesco*, Rizzoli, Milan, 1980.

Kennedy, P., *Rise of the Anglo-German Antagonism,* London 1980.

Kent, F. R., *The Great Game of Politics,* Ayer Company Publishers, Manchester 1923.

Khan, S. A., *The Causes of the Indian Revolt,* Oxford University Press, Oxford 1873.

Kian, K. H., *How Strangers Became Kings, Javanese-Dutch Relations in Java 1600–1800, In Indonesia And the Malay World*, Vol XXXVI, Taylor & Francis, London 2008.

King, P., *The Viceroy's Fall: How Kitchener Destroyed Curzon.* Sidgwick and Jackson, London 1986.

Kipling, R., *Kim,* Norton Critical Edition, New York 2002.

Kipling, R., *Something of Unknown, Doubleday, Doran And Company, Garden City and Myself for My Friends Known.* Doubleday, Doran & Company, Garden City 1937.

Kirk-Green, A., *On Crown Service: A History of HM Colonial and Overseas Civil Services 1837-1997*, I.B. Tauris, London 1999.

Kissinger, H., *Diplomacy.* Simon & Schuster, New York 1994.

Klein I., *"Plague, Policy and Popular Unrest in British India" In "Modern Asian Studies" 22.* 4. Cambridge University Press, Cambridge 1998.

Klein, I., *"The Anglo-Russian Convention and The Problem of Central Asia, 1907-1914," Journal Of British Studies* 1971.

Knight, I., *Colenso 1899, the Boer War in Natal*, Osprey, London 1995.

Kuhn, W., *The Politics of Pleasure —A Portrait of Benjamin Disraeli.* The Free Press, London 2006.

Kulke, H., Rothermund, D., *Storia dell'India*, Garzanti, Milan 1991.

Kynaston, D., *The City of London,* Vol. I. A World of Its Own, 1815-1890. London 1994.

Landon, P., *Opening the Tibet,* J. J. Jetley. New York 1905.

Landon, P., *The Mysterious City,* J. J. Jetley. New York 1905.

Landon, P., *The Opening of Tibet,* J. Jetley, New Delhi 1996.

Lane, C., *The Ruling Passion: British Colonial Allegory and the Paradox of Homosexual Desire,* Duke University Press, London 1995.

Larson, E., *Thunderstruck,* Broadway Books, New York 2007.

Lasswell, H.D., *Propaganda Technique in the World War*, London, 1927.

Law, E., Lord Ellenborough, *A Political Diary, "If We Play the Great Game, Striking at The Mass, We Must Succeed",* Cambridge Scholars Publishing, Cambridge 1881.

Lawrence, T. E., *Secret Despatches from Arabia,* Bellew Publishing, London 1918.

Lawson, P., *The East-India Company: A History,* Longman, London 1993.

Lazare B., *The Dreyfus Affair. Un errore giudiziario* A Cura Di Paolo Fontana, Mobydick, Milan 2001.

Le Queux, W., *Spies of Kaiser*, Frank Cass, London 1909.

Lees-Milne, J., *Harold Nicolson: A Biography. Volume 2: 1930-1968*, Chatto & Windus, London 1965.

Leonhard, J., Von Hirschhausen, U., *Empires and National States In the 19th century.* Il Mulino, Bologna 2014.

Lindemann, A. S., *The Jew Accused. Three Anti-Semitic Affairs: Dreyfus, Beilis, Frank. 1894-1915*, Cambridge University Press, Cambridge 1993.

Lippmann, W., *Public Opinion*, Greenbook Publications, New York 1922.

Lloyd G., D., *The War Memoirs*, Nicholson & Watson, London 1933-38.

Longford, E., Victoria *RI*, Weidenfeld & Nicolson, London 1964.

Lord Curzon in India: Being a Selection from His Speeches as Viceroy & Governor-General of India 1898-1905. Macmillan and Co. Limited, London 1906.

Lord Curzon's Farewell to India. Being Speeches Delivered as Viceroy & Governor-General of India. During Sept.-Nouv. 1905, Nabu Press, Charleston 2013.

Lo-Shu F., *A Documentary Chronicle of Sino Western Relations 1644-1820*, 2 Vol, Association for Asian Studies, Tucson 1966.

Lotti, P., *India*, English Translation by George Inman, T. Werner Laurie, London 1995.

Louis, W. R., Brown J. M, *The Oxford History of the British Empire. Vol. 4. 5 vols.* Oxford; New York: Oxford University Press, 1998.

Luttikhus, A., Moses, A. D., *Mass Violence and the End of the Dutch Colonial Empire* in *Indonesia, Journal of Genocide Research*, Vol XIV Routledge, Sidney 2012.

Lycett, A., *Rudyard Kipling*, Weidenfeld And Nicolson, London 1999.

Mac Nair, H. F., *Modern Chinese History Selected of the Nemesis*, Commercial Press, Shanghai 1923.

Macmillan, M., *1914*, Rizzoli, Milan 2013.

Macmillan, M., *The War That Ended Peace*, Paperback, London 2013.

Maharatna, A., *The Demography of Famines: An Indian Historical Perspective*, Oxford University Press India, Delhi 1996.

Mahomet, D., *The Travels of Dean Mahomet, A Native of Patna In Bengal, Through Several Parts Of India, While In The Service Of The Honourable The East-India Company written By Himself, In A Series Of Letters To A Friend*, University Of California Press, Barkeley 1997.

Majumdar, R. C., Raychaudhuri H.C., E Datta, K., *An Advanced History of India*, Macmillan, London 1956.

Manchester, W., *The Last Lion: Winston Churchill: Visions of Glory, 1874 – 1914*, Bantam Books Trade Paperbacks, New York 2013.

Mangan, J. A., *The Games Ethic and Imperialism: Aspects of the Diffusion of an Ideal*, Frank Cass Publishers, London 2003.

Mann, C., *1493. Pomodori, Tabacco e Batteri. Come Colombo ha creato Il Mondo In Cui Viviamo*, Mondadori, Milan 2013,

Martelli, A., *La Disfatta Dell'invincibile Armada*, Il Mulino, Bologna 2008.

Martin, L. C., *Tea: The Drink That Changed the World*, Tuttle Publishing, London 2007.

Marx, K., Kapital, D., *The Discovery Of India*, Oxford University Press, Oxford 1994.

May, A. J., *La Monarchia Asburgica 1867-1914*, Il Mulino, Bologna, 1991.

McCants, A., *Poor Consumers as Global Consumers: The Diffusion of Tea and Coffee Drinking in the Eighteenth Century*, In *the Economic History Review*, Vol VXI, Wiley-Blackwell, London 2008.

McElwee, W. L., *The Art of War: Waterloo to Mons*, Weidenfeld and Nicolson, London 1974.

McKinlay, B., *The First Royal Tour, 1867–1868*, Robert Hale & Company, London 1970.

McLane, J., Indian *Nationalism and the Early Congress*, Princeton University Press, Princeton 1977.

Mead, G., *The Good Soldier, a Biography of Douglas Haig*, Atlantic Books, London 2007.

Memorandum on India's contribution to the war in men, material and money, August 1914 to November 1918. Delhi 1919.

Messinger, G. S., *British Propaganda and the State in the First World War*, Manchester University Press, Manchester1992.

Metcalf, T. R., *Ideologies of the Raj*. The New Cambridge History of India III, 4. Cambridge; New York: Cambridge University Press, 1994.

Metcalf, T. R., *The Aftermath of Revolt, India 1857-1870,* Princeton University Press, Princeton. 1964.

Meyer, Karl, *La Polvere Dell'Impero*, Corbaccio, Milan 2003.

Mezin, S. A., Zaveshchanie *Petra Pervogo: Evropeiskie Mify I Rossiiskaia Realnost,* Rossiiskaia Istoriia 5, Moscow 2010.

Milford, L. S., *Haileybury College, Past and Present*, BiblioBazaar, Charleston 2009.

Millman, R., *Britain and the Eastern Question, 1875–78,* Oxford University Press, Oxford 1979.

Monger, D., *Patriotism and Propaganda in First World War Britain*: Liverpool University Press, Liverpool 2012; Symons, Julian, *Horatio Bottomley*, Cresset Press, London 1955.

Monger, G. W., *The End of Isolation: British Foreign Policy 1900 – 1907*. London 1963.

Monnypenny, W. F., Buclke, G. E., *The Life of Benjamin Disraeli, Earl of Beaconsfield*. Volume I, 1804–1859. London 1929.

Morelli, F., *il Mondo Atlantico. Una storia senza confini (Centuries XV-XIX)* Carocci, Rome 2013.

Morris, J., *Farewell the Trumpets: An Imperial Retreat,* Faber & Faber, London 2012.

Morrow, A., *Cousins Divided George V and Nicholas II,* Sutton Publishing, Phoenix 2006.

Morse, H. B., *East-India Company Trading to China,* 5 Vol. Oxford University Press, Oxford 1926.

Morton J., G., *The Indian Army on the Western Front: India's Expeditionary Force to France and Belgium in the First World War*. Cambridge: Cambridge University Press, 2014.

Morton, F., *The Rothschilds,* Athenaeum, New York 1962.

Mosley, L., The *Glorious Fault: The Life of Lord Curzon,* Harcourt, Brace & Co, London 1960.

Mulligan, W., *Le Origini Della Prima Guerra Mondiale*, Salerno Editrice, Rome 2010.

Muratori, L., *Annali d'Italia. From the beginning of the vulgar era to the year 1749.* Vol. XV. Society of Italian Classics. Milan 1820.

Murray, H., *Historical and Descriptive Account of British India,* 3 Vol, J & J Harper, Edinburgh 1843.

Nasta S., *India in Britain: South Asian Networks and Connections, 1858-1950.*

Nath, A., *"The Indian Contribution in the First World War."* In the Indian Contribution in the First World War: A Grand Spectacle-Indian Cavalry and Infantry Regiments in the Great War, edited by R.T.S. China. India and the Great War 1. Manohar Publishers, New Delhi: 1998.

Niggemann, U., *Some Remarks on The Origins of The Term 'Glorious Revolution'* In *The Seventeenth Century*, Manchester University Press, Manchester 2013.

Noel, G., *Princess Alice: Queen Victoria's Forgotten Daughter*, Constable and Company Limited, London 1985.

Norton Medlicott, W., *Congress of Berlin and After*, Routledge, London 1963.

O' Mallei, L.S.S., The Indian Civil Service, Murray, London 1931.

O'Donnell, C. J., *The Failure of Lord Curzon,* Forgotten Books, London 1903.

Offner, A., *The First World War: An Agrarian Interpretation,* Oxford University Press. Oxford 1989.

Omissi D., Indian *Voices of the Great War: Solders' Letters, 1914-18.* Hound mills, Basingstoke, Hampshire: New York: Macmillan Press, St. Martin's Press, 1999.

Omissi D., *The Sepoy and the Raj*, Abacus, London, 1994.

Omissi, D. *"Europe through Indian Eyes: Indian Soldiers Encounter England and France, 1914-1918."* The English Historical Review CXXII, no. 496, April 1, 2007.

Omissi, D. E., *"Sikh Soldiers in Europe during the First World War, 1914-1918."* In Sikhs across Borders: Transnational Practices of European Sikhs, edited by Knut A. Jacobsen and Kristina Myrvold. Bloomsbury Religious Studies. New York: Continuum International Publishing Group, 2012.

Omissi, D., *Indian Voices of the Great War,* Palgrave Macmillan, London 1999.

Osborn, E. B., *The Muse in Arms,* "The Greatest of All Great Games", John Murray, London 1917.

Pakenham, T., *The Boer War*, Abacus, London 2006.

Pakula, H., *An Uncommon Woman: The Empress Frederick, Daughter of Queen Victoria, Wife of the Crown Prince of Prussia, Mother of Kaiser Wilhelm,* Touchstone Press, Cambridge 1995.

Panadikar, S. G., *Some aspects of economic consequences of the war for India,* Bombay 1921.

Pande, R., *The Viceroyalty of Lord Elgin II,* Janaki Prakashan, Patna 1986.

533

Parliamentary Papers Westminster Parliament Press, London 1840.

Pastori, G., *Dall'Indian Army All 'Army Of India,* Centre of Culture Italy - Asia "G. Scalise" Asian Notebooks. N° 75. Milan September 2006.

Paterson, M., *Winston Churchill,* David & Charles Book, Cincinnati 2005.

Pati, B., *India and the First World War*, Atlantic Publishers and Distributors, Delhi 1996.

Paxman, J., *Empire,* Penguin, London 2012.

Paxman, J., *Great Britain's Great War,* Penguin, London 2013.

Pett, W., *Rules and Regulations of the Great Game of Jetball,* Exeter, Exeter 1914.

Pitt, W., *The State of the Nation,* 1770.

Poidevin, R., *Les relations economiques et financières entre la France et l'Alemagne De 1898 à 1914.* Paris 1969.

Prasad, Y. D., *The Indian Muslims and World War I: A Phase of Disillusionment with British Rule, 1914-1918.* New Delhi: Janaki Prakashan, 1985.

Pritchard, H., Anglo-*Chinese Relations during the Seventeenth and Eighteenth Centuries,* University of Illinois Press, Urbana 1930.

Pritchard, H., *The Crucial Years of Anglo-Chinese Relations 1750-1800* in *Research Studies of the State College of Washington,* Vol IV. N. 3-4, Washington 1936.

Ragsdale, H., *Détente in The Napoleonic Era: Bonaparte and the Russians,* the Regents Press of Kansas. Lawrence 1980.

Ramage, C., *The Great Indian Drought Of 1899,* Boulder Cole Habour 1977.

Raugh, H. E., *The Victorians at War, 1815–1914: An Encyclopedia of British Military History* ABC-Clio Inc., Santa Barbara 2004.

Reed, John, *I dieci giorni che sconvolsero il mondo*, Bur, Milan, 1980.

Rei, C., *Careers and Wages in The Dutch East-India Company*, In *Cliometrica*, Vol VIII, Springer Berlin Heidelberg, Berlin 2014.

Reis, A., *Russophobia and the Testament of Peter the Great,* Slavic Review 44 (4), Urbana 1985.

René Lesage, A., *Gil Blax De Santillane,* Pierre Ribou, Paris 1715.

Report of The Select Committee on East-India Affair, London 1833.

Richards, E., *Britannia's Children: emigration from England, Scotland, Ireland and Wales Since 1600: Emigration from England, Scotland, Wales and Ireland since 1600,* Hambleton and London, London 2004.

Roberts, A., *Salisbury: Victorian Titan,* Orion, London 1999.

Robson, B., *The Road to Kabul.* Spellmount. Stroud 2007.

Roebuck, T., *The Annals of the College of Fort William: From the Period of Its Foundation to the Present Time,* Cambridge University Press, and Cambridge 2013.

Rogger, H., *La Russia Pre-Revolutionaria 1881-1917*, Il Mulino, Bologna 1992.

Ronaldshay, *The Life of Lord Curzon: Being the Authorised Biography of George Nathaniel Marquess Curzon of Kedleston,* Kessinger Publishing, London 2010.

Rose, K., *Curzon: A Most Superior Person,* Macmillan Papermac, London 1985.

Rose, K., *King George V,* London 1983.

Rotberg, R. I., *The Founder: Cecil Rhodes and the Pursuit of Power,* Oxford University Press, Oxford 1990.

Rowland, P., *The Last Liberal Government,* Vol II: Unfinished Business, 1911 – 1914. London 1971.

Rowse, A. L., *Homosexuals in History,* Carroll & Graf, New York 1977.

Royle, T., *Britain's Lost Regiments,* Aurum Press Ltd, London 2014.

Royle, Trevor, *The Kitchener Enigma*, Michael Joseph, London 1985.

Sangiuliano, G., *Scacco Allo Zar*, Mondadori, Milan, 2012.

Scardigli, M., *Viaggio Nella Terra Dei Morti*, Utet, Torino 2014.

Seccia, G., *La Guerra Tra I Due Fiumi*, Nordpress Edizioni, Chiari 2007.

Seeley, J. R., *The Expansion of England*, Macmillan And Co, London 1883.

Sinclair, A., *The Other Victoria: The Princess Royal and The Great Game of Europe*, Littlehampton Book Services Ltd, Faraday Close 1981.

Singha R., *The Recruiter's Eye on 'The Primitive': To France – and Back – in the Indian Labour Corps, 1917-18* in *Other Combatants, Other Fronts: Competing Histories of the First World War*, Edited by Kitchen, James E., Alisa Miller, and Laura Rowe, eds. Cambridge Scholars Publishing, 2011.

Smith, A., *An Inquiry into the Nature and Causes of the Wealth of Nations (1776)*, Hackett Publishing, London 1930.

Smith, F.B., *Florence Nightingale,* Croom Helm, London 1982. p. 125.

Snook, C. M., *Beyond the Reach of Empire: Wolseley's Failed Campaign To Save Gordon And Khartoum*, Frontline Books, London 2011.

Solmi, A., *Nicola II e Alessandra Di Russia,* Rusconi, Milan 1989.

Speeches on India, Delivered by Lord Curzon of Kedleston, Viceroy and Governor-General of India, While In England In July-August 1904, John Murray, London 1904.

Spencer, E., *The Great Game: And How It Is Played,* Grant Richards, London 1900.

St Aubyn, G., Queen *Victoria: A Portrait*, Sinclair-Stevenson London. 1991.

St John, I., *Disraeli and the Art of Victorian Politics,* Anthem Press, London 2010.

St John, I., *Gladstone and the Logic of Victorian Politics*, Anthem Press, London 2010.

Steinbach, S. L.., *Understanding the Victorians: Politics, Culture and Society in Nineteenth Century Britain*, Routledge, London 2011.

Steinberg, J., *The Copenaghen Complex*, Journal of Contemporary History. 1966.

Stern, P.J., *Soldier and Citizen in The Seventeenth Century English East-India Company*, In *Journal Of Early Modern History* Vol XV, Brill, York 2011.

Stevenson, D., *The First World War and International Politics*, Clarendon Press, Oxford 2001.

Stewart, J., *The Kaiser's Mission to Kabul*, I.B. Tauris, London 2014.

Stice, E., *"Empire between the Lines: Constructions of Empire in British and French Trench Newspapers of the Great War."* PhD thesis, Emory University, 2012.

Stone, N., *La Prima Guerra Mondiale*, Feltrinelli, Milan 2014.

Surkhang Wangchen, G., *"Tibet: The Critical Years: The Thirteenth Dalai Lama"*. *The Tibet Journal*. Vol. VII, No. 4. Winter 1982.

Tamm, E. E., *"The Horse That Leaps Through Clouds: A Tale of Espionage, The Silk Road and The Rise Of Modern China."* Douglas & McIntyre, Vancouver 2010.

Taylor, A. J., *The Struggle for Mastery in Europe 1914-1918*, Oxford University Press, Oxford 1963.

Taylor, A. J. P., *The Struggle for Mastery in Europe, 1848 – 1918*. Oxford University Press, Oxford 1954.

Temperley, H., England *and the Near East: The Crimea*, "The Great Game of Improvement Is Altogether Up for the Present", Green Longmans, London 1936.

The Lancet, May 16, 1901.

The London Gazette: No. 24992. Pp. 3300-3301. 1 July 1881.

The National Trust, Kedleston Hall, the National Trust Press, London 1999.

The Tablet, 5 Maggio 1928, Tablet Publishing Company, London.

The Times, 9 January 1877; A. Harlan, *Owen Meredith,* New York 1946.

Thomas, P. F., *Can the Great Game Really Be Deconstructed? A Geopolitical Challenge for Philosophers and Warriors,* Kashtan Press, Kingston 1996.

Trevelyan, G.M., *Grey of Falloden,* London 1937.

Troyat, H., *Peter the Great*, E.P. Dutton, New York 1987.

Tucker, A. V., *"Army and Society in England 1870-1900: A Reassessment of the Cardwell Reforms,"* In *Journal of British Studies*, Cambridge University Press, Cambridge 1963.

Turner, L. C. F., *The Role of the General Staffs in July 1914,* "Australian Journal of Politics and History" Vol 11. N° 3. Sydney 1965.

V. Lehvich, D., *The Testament of Peter the Great, American Slavic and East European Review, Association for Slavic*, East European, And Eurasian Studies, *Pittsburgh* April 1948.

Valone, S. J., *"There Must Be Some Misunderstanding": Sir Edward Grey's Diplomacy of August 1, 1914,* Journal of British Studies 27.4.

VanKoski S., *"Letters Home, 1915–16: Punjabi Soldiers Reflect on War and Life in Europe and their Meanings for Home and Self,"* International Journal of Punjab Studies 2, 1995, 43–63.

Verrier, A., *Francis Younghusband and the Great Game,* Jonathan Cape, London 1991.

Weber, E., *France: Fin De Siècle,* Harvard University Press, 1988.

538

Wilcox, J., *I Soldati che cambiarono la Guerra Mondiale*, Newton E Compton Editori, Milan, 2014.

Willcox J. *With the Indians in France,* London 1920.

Williamson, J. A., *The Evolution of England,* Clarendon Press, Oxford 1931.

Wilson, K. M., *The Policy of the Entente: Essays on the Determinants of British Foreign Policy,* Cambridge University Press, Cambridge 1985.

Winegard, T. C., *Indigenous Peoples of the British Dominions and the First World War.* Cambridge: Cambridge University Press, 2012.

Winterberg, Y., E S., *I Diari Segreti Dei Bambini Sopravissuti alla Grande Guerra,* Newton E Compton, Milan, 2014.

Wocker, K.H., *La Regina Vittoria*, Garzanti, Milan 1981.

Woodard, N., *A Plea for the Middle Classes,* Joseph Masters, London 1848.

Woodward, E. L., *The Age of Reform 1815-1870,* Oxford University Press, Oxford 1963.

Wyman, H., *The Great Game: The Life and Times of a Welsh Poacher,* Fieldfare Publications, Cambridge 1993.

Yapp, M., *The Legend of the Great Game,* In *Proceedings of British Academy,* the British Academy, London 2001.

Yong, L., *The Dutch East-India Company's Tea Trade with China*, 1757–1781. *In History of the Asian-European Interaction* Vol VI. Leiden, Brill, 2008.

Young, H. F., *The Misunderstanding of August 1, 1914.* Journal of Modern History. 48. December 1976.

Younghusband, F., *India and Tibet,* Gautam Jetley, New Delhi 2005.

Zahedieh, N., *Regulation, Rent-Seeking, and the Glorious Revolution in the English Atlantic Economy* in *Economic Historic Review* 63, 4, Steve Hindle, Steven Broadberry, Hoboken 2010.

Acronyms

CV: Companion biography Winston Churchill, volume 1, 2, 3...

WSC: Winston Spencer Churchill biography V volumes

PRO: Public Record Office

WO: War Office

KV: Personal Files

CAB: Cabinet Papers

FO: Foreign Office

IWM: Imperial War Museum

Printed in Great Britain
by Amazon

35463525R00322

The Uses of Social Investment

The Uses of Social Investment provides the first study of the new post-crisis austerity context and associated crisis management politics, to take stock of the limits and potential of social investment. It surveys the emergence, diffusion, limits, merits, and politics of social investment as the welfare policy paradigm for the twenty-first century, seen through the lens of the life-course contingencies of the competitive knowledge economy and modern family-hood.

Featuring contributions from leading scholars in the field, the volume revisits the intellectual roots and normative foundations of social investment, surveys the criticisms that have been levelled against the social investment perspective in theory and policy practice, and presents empirical evidence of social investment progress together with novel research methodologies for assessing socioeconomic 'rates of return' on social investment. Given the progressive, admittedly uneven, diffusion of the social investment policy priorities across the globe, the volume seeks to address the pressing political question of whether the social investment turn is able to withstand the fiscal austerity backlash that has re-emerged in the aftermath of the global financial crisis.